D0215723

✓

Witchcraft Today

Witchcraft Today

An Encyclopedia of Wiccan and Neopagan Traditions

James R. Lewis

ABC-CLIO

Santa Barbara, California
Denver, Colorado
Oxford, England

Library of Congress Cataloging-in-Publication Data
Lewis, James R.
    Witchcraft today : an encyclopedia of Wiccan and neopagan
traditions / James R. Lewis.
        p.   cm.
    Includes bibliographical references and index.
    ISBN 1-57607-134-0 (alk. paper)
    1. Witchcraft—Encyclopedias.   2. Neopaganism—Encyclopedias.
3. Magic—Encyclopedias.   I. Title.
BF1571.L49   1999
299—dc21   99-40345
                                                                         CIP

05   04   03   02   01   00   10   9   8   7   6   5   4   3   2

ABC-CLIO, Inc.
130 Cremona Drive, P.O. Box 1911
Santa Barbara, California 93116-1911

This book is printed on acid-free paper ∞.
Manufactured in the United States of America.

Contents

Preface, ix
Introduction, xi

WITCHCRAFT TODAY:
AN ENCYCLOPEDIA OF WICCAN
AND NEOPAGAN TRADITIONS

CONTENTS

Preface

To the average citizen of North America or Europe, the word *witch* brings to mind images of ugly, evil, old women dressed in black who ride around on broomsticks and eat little children. Regarded as remnants of the superstitious folklore of our ancestors, these once-feared figures rarely intrude into contemporary consciousness except in such trivialized forms as Hallowe'en costumes and characters out of horror movies.

It may thus come as a surprise to find groups of otherwise ordinary people who not only refer to themselves as Witches but who also demand that they be treated seriously as members of a religion—on a par with Jews, Methodists, Catholics, and the like. This unusual state of affairs has come about as the result of a mid-twentieth-century movement that arose with the explicit goal of reviving the ancient Pagan religions of pre-Christian Europe as serious modern religious options. Because many members of this "Neopagan" movement view the Witch hunts of Europe as efforts by the Christian Church to destroy all remnants of the old Pagan religions, they also refer to themselves as "Witches."

Witchcraft is one of the fastest-growing religions in the world. In the United States alone, it is conservatively estimated that adherents number 300,000, not including members of related movements, such as certain strands of the women's spirituality movement. Yet, with occasional exceptions, Witches are rarely in the news and do not tend to otherwise attract public attention. This low visibility is at least in part because modern Neopaganism is a decentralized movement whose organized groups do not generally possess large church buildings or temples and that therefore remains mostly invisible on the religious landscape.

This book offers a concise overview of this fascinating movement. The Introduction explains the origins and structure of Neopaganism, and the core of the book is an A-to-Z encyclopedia of Neopagan concepts, holidays, rituals, spirit beings, and so forth. Following the main text are a detailed resources section and two appendixes containing a timeline of events and some key documents.

This book grew out of a project I originally undertook with Aidan A. Kelly. I would like to acknowledge the pervasive influence of Kelly's scholarship on this volume, especially in the introductory essay and in the more historical entries. I would also like to thank Cynthia Eller for her excellent entry on the women's spirituality movement; my partner and wife, Evelyn, for her multifaceted support; the Frosts for introducing me to Neopaganism; and Todd Hallman, my editor at ABC-CLIO, who bore up well at several stressful junctures in the project. Finally, I would like to express my gratitude to the many Neopagans who have generously shared their wisdom with me over the past dozen years and who contributed to my understanding of modern Witchcraft.

Introduction

James R. Lewis and Aidan A. Kelly

High Priest: Listen to the words of the Great Mother, who was of old also called among men Artemis, Astarte, Dione, Melusine, Aphrodite, Cerridwen, Diana, Arianrhod, Bride, and by many other names.

High Priestess: Whenever ye have need of anything, once in the month, and better it be when the moon is full, then ye shall assemble in some secret place and adore the spirit of Me who am Queen of all Witcheries. There ye shall assemble, ye who are fain to learn all sorcery, yet who have not won its deepest secrets. To these will I teach things that are yet unknown.

And ye shall be free from slavery, and as a sign that ye be really free, ye shall be naked in your rites, and ye shall dance, sing, feast, make music, and love, all in my praise.

For mine is the ecstasy of the Spirit, and mine is also joy on earth, For my Law is Love unto all beings.

Keep pure your highest ideals. Strive ever towards it. Let naught stop you or turn you aside.

For mine is the secret which opens upon the door of youth; and mine is the cup of the Wine of Life: and the Cauldron of Cerridwen; which is the Holy Grail of Immortality.

I am the Gracious Goddess who gives the gift of Joy unto the heart of Man.

Upon Earth I give the knowledge of the Spirit Eternal; and beyond death I give peace and freedom; and reunion with those who have gone before; nor do I demand aught in sacrifice; for behold, I am the Mother of all things; and my love is poured out upon earth.

High Priest: Hear ye the words of the Star Goddess, She in the dust of whose feet are the hosts of Heaven; whose body encircleth the Universe.

High Priestess: I who am the beauty of the green earth; and the White Moon amongst the Stars; and the mystery of the Waters; and the desire of the heart of man; I call unto thy soul; arise and come unto me.

For I am the Soul of nature who giveth life to the Universe; "From me all things proceed; and unto me, all things must return"; Beloved of the Gods and men; thine inmost divine self shall be enfolded in the raptures of the infinite.

Let my worship be within the heart that rejoiceth; for behold, all acts of Love and Pleasure are my rituals; and therefore let there be Beauty and

Strength; Power and Compassion; Honour and Humility; Mirth and Reverence within you.

And thou who thinkest to seek me; Know that thy seeking and yearning shall avail thee not unless thou know the mystery, that if that which thou seekest thou findest not within thee, thou wilt never find it without thee. For behold: I have been with thee from the beginning, and I am that which is attained at the end of desire.

This short text, "Charge of the Goddess," is a central theological document for the contemporary Neopagan movement. Originally composed by Gerald Gardner, the founder of modern Witchcraft, the speech was revised and rewritten into the above form by Doreen Valiente, one of Gardner's close associates. Like the roughly comparable Masonic charges, it was intended to be read at initiations.

The "Charge of the Goddess" is broadly emblematic of modern Neopagan Witchcraft—also referred to as "Wicca" or "the Craft"—in a number of ways. In terms of theological (or, more properly, "thealogical") ideas, this text reflects the dominant tendency of this movement to view the Divine as female—specifically, as a goddess whose primary embodiment is the natural world. In the Wiccan subculture, theological refers to the male god, whereas thealogical refers to the female goddess. As a fertility religion, Neopagan Witchcraft also takes seriously the notion that "all acts of Love and Pleasure are my rituals," in sharp contrast to the world-denying tendencies of more "mainstream" religious traditions.

Beyond such explicit *content*, however, there are other characteristics of the movement reflected in the *form* of the speech: Although a contemporary (mid-twentieth-century) piece, the "Charge of the Goddess" was written in King James–style English to convey a sense that it is very old (as well as, apparently, the sense of authority associated with the language of traditional scriptures). In point of fact, much of the appeal of the modern Neopagan Witchcraft movement has been its claim that it embodies an ancient lineage dating back to the pre-Christian religions of Europe. However, as a number of recent investigations have decisively demonstrated, Wicca was founded in the twentieth century by Gerald Gardner, a retired British civil servant.

The word *wicca* was originally the Saxon name for a male Witch and was pronounced "witch-ah"; the female *wicce* was pronounced "witch-ay." However, the term *Wicca* was adopted by Gardner as a general name for the Witchcraft religion he founded—or, from another perspective, helped to found—in the 1930s, and it is now used mainly in that sense, pronounced "wick-ah." A member of the religion is therefore a Wiccan, pronounced "wick-un." The religion is also referred to as "the Craft"; Gardner began using this term, originally a Masonic term for Freemasonry, as a name for the Neopagan Witchcraft movement in the late 1950s.

There have been a great many descriptions of this religion published by now, and there is no need to repeat all of those descriptions here. However, as an initial brief description, we can assert that Wicca has the following characteristics:

- Worship is polytheistic and almost always includes an exalted concept of a goddess as being close to the ultimate level of divinity.
- Worship occurs in the small group known as a coven (which may consist of anywhere from 3 to around 20 members) according to the phases of the moon. These monthly meetings for worship (and the working of practical magic) are referred to as "Esbats." Worship also occurs in larger groups. Several hundred people, some coming from long distances, may meet, as when two covens converge for Sabbats, of which there are eight each year.
- In addition to worship, coven activity focuses on the working of magic, including practical folk magic and a much more abstract magical system, based essentially on the system of the Hermetic Order of the Golden Dawn (HOGD), which is highly psychologized, eclectic, and variegated. The magical training procedures used in any one coven depend on what training in magic, psychic abilities, psychology, or other disciplines the coven's leaders have had in academic, metaphysical, or other groups in the larger Western occult tradition.
- Despite the anarchism of Neopagan Witches and their freedom to innovate within their covens and their lives, they are just as clear as members of other religions about which individuals and groups belong to their religion and which do not. The distinguishing criteria might be hard for an outsider to perceive, but a Wiccan coven always knows whether another group is, in fact, also Wiccan or whether it is instead a Ceremonial Magic lodge, a New Age group, or a group practicing some other sort of Western occult tradition. This clear intuitive awareness of membership boundaries is one of the distinguishing characteristics of a religious movement.

Neopagan Witchcraft is a growing phenomenon, but how large a movement are we really talking about? By a variety of independent methods, scholarly insiders have been able to estimate the size of the movement at around 300,000 serious adherents. To give some perspective on that number, note that there are only 40,000 Quakers and about 180,000 Unitarians in the United States. Hence, the Neopagan Witchcraft movement is no longer a tiny "cult." Still, one may ask why, if the Craft is that large, is it not more obvious on the American scene?

First, the emphasis on secrecy in the Craft has prevented blatant publicity-seeking, unlike most other religious groups. The secrecy of the Craft has been attributed to its history—believing that they have survived from "the Burning Times" (the Witch hunts of the sixteenth and seventeenth centuries) and on into the twentieth century. The Craft movement is, however, one of the best-documented new religious movements ever to arise in the United States, largely because the movement's penchant for producing newsletters and other periodicals (there have been over 500 to date) has preserved data that usually remained unrecorded for other movements.

Second, news media normally report only bad news. Except for minor stories about harassment, congressional bills, and the like, the Craft has remained relatively anonymous, doing nothing except growing quietly and creatively.

Third, the Neopagan movement does not produce the kind of flashy leaders who attract the attention of reporters. Even relatively famous and politically active Craft Priestesses tend to be quiet, modest people. As a result, the Craft is not particularly visible until one goes looking for it; then its existence becomes quite obvious.

Finally, believing themselves to be in league with greater spiritual forces striving to restore natural balance to the Earth, most Neopagans feel little need to promote their views in public arenas. Instead, they meet together in a variety of informal settings—forests, fields, and suburban living rooms—to quietly craft their world. And, rarely building such visible institutions as organized churches, they tend to go unnoticed by the outside world.

Precursors to Modern Witchcraft

Modern Witchcraft had several different starting places. Because of its dependence on earlier movements and organizations, it might best be viewed as the most recent manifestation of the Western occult tradition. This tradition is a religious movement in its own right, since it serves the same functions for occultists that religions generally serve for their followers: It provides a way for them to interpret history and their own life experiences as meaningful. However, it is hard for most people to perceive the Western occult tradition as religious precisely because it lacks many of the characteristics that we normally associate with religion—especially because it is not organized into large, formal "churches" that have existed for generations or centuries.

Most of the strands of information and belief that make up the Western occult tradition took root in Hellenistic times, especially in Alexandria, Egypt, which was the closest thing to a "college town" in the classical world. From Franz Cumont's description in *Pagan Religions in the Roman World* we know that all the religions of the then-known world were preached on the street corners of Alexandria and we can imagine that, in some ways, it must have been much like Berkeley, California, or Greenwich Village around New York University, or the Harvard Square area in Boston, Massachusetts, and so on.

Given this sort of beginning, the Western occult tradition continued to be a religion of and for intellectuals, learned from and passed on largely by means of books, down to the beginnings of our modern era in the sixteenth century. That is, the tradition continued to be a system of belief preserved by college professors, students, and other intellectuals—a system that, although not exactly secret, was not often discussed in public. In fact, before the modern era, dissemination of the sort of information that makes up the tradition was almost always considered heretical or subversive and was swiftly punished by the authorities.

Viewed in terms of intellectual history, our modern era begins, in fact, with a fight over whether "ordinary" people have a right to access to key documents, the first one in question being, of course, the Bible. With the spread of printed books and the beginnings of what we now call "public" education (that is, education of the nonclerical classes), the medieval clerical monopoly on information, and hence on religious authority, was broken. The relatively monolithic Catholic Church of the fifteenth century shattered into dozens of state churches by the end of the sixteenth century. At this point in history, as knowledge of the Western occult tradition began to spread down through the social classes of Europe, the tradition began to be transformed into increasingly more popular (in the sense of "of the people") religious movements. The first wave of movements was the founding of Rosicrucian and Masonic organizations during the Reformation and Enlightenment periods. These were organizations open only to wealthy, upper-middle-class white males— precisely the people at that time who were given the sort of education previously available only to clerics. Rosicrucian and Masonic organizations began to form in England as soon as Henry VIII's expropriation of church property turned the libraries of religious orders over to the universities where the new English capitalists were being educated. Thus, knowledge of the Western occult tradition grew rapidly.

Widespread acceptance of the occult tapered off sharply among the educated by about 1750, but it did not cease altogether and may have remained more or less constant among peasants. During the next century, a number of social and intellectual changes in society marked the beginnings of the modern recrudescence of the occult. The Romantic revival of Neoplatonism, Medieval German Mysticism, astrology, the introduction of Asian (and especially Indian) esotericism, a sudden enthusiasm for secret societies, Mesmerism, and Swedenborgianism all created an atmosphere conducive to the renewed interest in the Western occult tradition. With varying degrees of popularity, faddishness, and intellectual respectability, this tradition has remained a nearly ubiquitous factor in Western cultural life ever since.

In 1801 Francis Barrett, who had gathered a working magical group around himself, published *The Magus*, the first modern book that attempted to make the arcane practice of magic accessible to the middle class. At mid-century, Alphonse-Louis Constant, who wrote under the name Eliphas Levi, published his *Dogma and Ritual of High Magic*, *History of Magic*, and *Key to the Great Mysteries*. These works pulled together the disparate strands of Western occultism into the beginnings of a unified system and so became the textbooks for all later magical groups.

The late nineteenth century saw the rise of "spiritual occultism," whose practitioners—as represented by Theosophy, Rudolf Steiner, Gurdjieff, and Ouspensky and a ritual-magical wing (various Rosicrucian organizations, the Hermetic Order of the Golden Dawn, and its offshoots)—determined that occultism was not a religion. Though the mind-set of spiritual occultism leads most modern occult organizations to deny that they are religions as well, they exhibit the same ambiguous relation between their foundational myths and their ordinary history as religions in general. For example, the *Chemical Wedding*, a major Rosicrucian document, claims that the movement has survived since ancient times, but in fact it appears to have begun as a secret organization among Lutherans, since Luther's family crest was a rose on a cross.

Modern occult organizations typically claim great antiquity for themselves but, in fact, are all quite recent, and almost all highly interrelated. The scholar T. M. Luhrmann has documented the overlapping memberships in magical organizations in the London area in the 1980s; this interwoven relationship between the organizations has been typical for the past two centuries. The pattern we see is that of a charismatic leader who begins an organization that flourishes during his or her lifetime and usually attracts as its most prominent members people who have been or still are members of most other extant occult organizations. Upon the leader's demise, the organization usually fractures into two or many factions as the members struggle to decide who will assume the mantle of the founder. These factions generally become independent occult organizations, which repeat the cycle.

Richard Cavendish's *A History of Magic* does an excellent job of detailing the complex interrelationships between teachers and students and founders and followers among occult organizations, especially in France, in the late nineteenth century. James Webb does the same for European occultism in general. Relatively few of the organizations these authors discuss are direct ancestors of the modern religion of Wicca, but among these few are the Hermetic Order of the Golden Dawn (HOGD), the Stella Matutina, the Fraternity of the Inner Light, and the Ordo Templi Orientis.

The magical system used by Neopagan Witchcraft is not anything inherited from a secret tradition but instead finds its roots in the HOGD, an offshoot of a Masonic-Rosicrucian organization, the Societas Rosicruciana in Anglia (SRIA). Founded by Robert Wentworth Little in 1865, the SRIA's system supposedly was based on old manuscripts. The London Lodge of the Theosophical Society opened in 1883, and members of both of these lodges were among the early members of the HOGD, founded in 1888 by W. R. Woodman, A. F. A. Woodford, W. Wynn Westcott, and Samuel Liddell Mathers (1854–1918). Interestingly, Liddell Mathers was a relative of Alice Liddell, whose father coauthored the most important Greek dictionary of the nineteenth century and whose adventures in Wonderland were chronicled by the Reverend Charles Lutwidge Dodgson (otherwise known as Lewis Carroll). All but Woodford had been members of the SRIA, but it was Woodford who, in 1885, inherited the magical manuscripts that had been owned by Fred Hockley, a nineteenth-century psychic. Westcott proceeded to "decode" them, and then Mathers built a new magical system upon them. These papers also included the address of one Anna Sprenger in Nuremberg, who was a Rosicrucian Adept in touch with the Masters in the East. Mathers claimed to have written to her and to have received a great mass of information and rituals from her, along with a charter for the Isis-Urania Temple.

After the other two founders died, Westcott resigned in 1887 from the HOGD to concentrate on the SRIA, of which he was Supreme Magus, leaving Mathers in complete control of the HOGD. In 1892, Mathers moved to

Paris and married Moira, the daughter of the philosopher Henri Bergson, and proceeded to direct the affairs of the HOGD.

The four HOGD founders claimed to have a charter and a set of rituals from the "secret chiefs" of the Rosicrucian order in Germany, but, in fact, all of the documents were written by Mathers, who was one of the most brilliant amateur scholars of his generation. He translated *The Greater Key of Solomon* and several major Cabalistic treatises and wrote an important book on the Tarot. The HOGD attracted a stellar cast of members from among Britain's middle-class intellectuals. These members (as revealed in the appendixes of Ithel Colquhoun's *Sword of Wisdom: MacGregor Mathers and the "Golden Dawn"*) included Arthur Machen, Arthur Edward Waite, James M. Barrie, Sir E. A. Wallis Budge, Hugh Schonfield, Florence Farr (at one time a lover of George Bernard Shaw), and Maud Gonne (mother of Sean McBride, the founder of Amnesty International).

The most famous member of the HOGD was William Butler Yeats (Maud Gonne was his lover), who joined in 1890 and remained a devout member (according to Virginia Moore's biography) until 1900 when the organization splintered into several factions due to a fight over whether Mathers could bring Aleister Crowley rapidly up into the leadership of the organization. Most of the members left with Yeats to form the Stella Matutina ("Morning Star"), where Yeats served from 1901 to 1917 as Grand Master.

Mathers and Crowley kept the original name for the HOGD, but their organization, consisting only of a small faction of the original group, soon foundered. Crowley, after "channeling" the *Book of the Law* in 1904, founded his own organization, the Astrum Argentinum ("Silver Star"), or AA. In 1907, Crowley began publishing *The Equinox* in 1909 to spread his ideas. He had become a member of the Ordo Templi Orientis (Order of the Eastern Temple), or OTO, by 1912. The OTO, founded around the turn of the century by a German named Karl Keller, taught a form of sex magic. Its system was based largely on the secret sex-magic teachings of P. B. Randolph, founder of the Fraternitas Rosae Crucis, a major Rosicrucian society in America. Crowley succeeded Theodor Reuss as Outer Head (or "public leader") of the OTO in 1922 and was recognized as head of the OTO by a majority of its members in 1924–1925, when the organization divided in two over whether to accept Crowley's *Book of the Law* as authoritative.

In March 1945 he moved to a decrepit boardinghouse in Hastings, England, which is not far from Southampton or, for that matter, from the New Forest area where the New Forest Coven originated. Since the OTO had always taken pride in its Rosicrucian affinities, it is very likely that Crowley would have gravitated to the Rosicrucian Theatre and to its members. Crowley could easily have known Dorothy Clutterbuck, Gerald Gardner, and other members of the New Forest Coven during this period. Hence, Crowley's colorful life may have led to his possible connection with Gardnerian Witchcraft (named for Gerald Gardner).

What was the nature of the relationship, if any, between Gardner and Crowley? It is clear that they did know one another. Gardner was only 10 or so years younger than Crowley, being about 60 in 1945. The files of the Wiccan Church of Canada, which bought the relevant contents of Gardner's Castletown museum from Ripley's International, contain handwritten notes from Crowley to Gardner informing Gardner of OTO events—apparently there were some such activities in the years 1946 and 1947. Also among the museum's holdings is a warrant issued by Crowley that awarded Gardner the magical name "Scire" and the grade 4 = 7 in the OTO; the document was on display in the Ripley's Museum of Witchcraft at Fisherman's Wharf in San Francisco in 1974. Designating Gardner an Exempt Adept in the Astrum Argentinum is not something Crowley would have done without substantial firsthand knowledge about the other man. The designation implies that, in Crowley's view, Gardner had attained a dialogue with his higher self. In addition, the Exempt Adept Degree (higher than that of the Degree of Adeptus Major) implies that Gardner possessed a broad range of magical powers. The warrant, therefore, in Crowley's mind at least, would have given Gardner an official warrant to establish a new religion of an unspecified type. This may cast new light on the motives for Gardner's actions during the 1940s.

Another important occult influence on modern Witchcraft was the activities of Dion Fortune (Violet Firth). Firth was initiated in 1919 into the Alpha et Omega (AEO), the HOGD offshoot presided over by Mathers's widow, Moira Bergson Mathers. In 1922, Firth organized the Fraternity of the Inner Light as an "outer court" for the AEO. She and Mathers clashed more and more as Firth matured as a leader; when Mathers expelled her in 1927, Firth, now using the name Dion Fortune, took the Fraternity of the Inner Light with her and it became the ancestor of many other important magical organizations now functioning in England.

The Fraternity of the Inner Light was divided into at least two autonomous inner sections, one of which was avowedly "Pagan"—that is, non-Christian. From the mid-1930s into the 1940s, the acting heads of the Pagan section of the group were Charles R. F. Seymour and Christine Hartley. Seymour wrote an essay, "The Old Religion—A Study in the Symbolism of the Moon Mysteries," in 1937, but it was not published until 1968, when it appeared in *The New Dimensions Red Book*, edited by Basil Wiltby. In another essay, "The Ancient Nature Worship," also written in 1937, Seymour said, "The witch-hunting of the fourteenth to eighteenth centuries was an effort to stamp out an old religion surviving from pre-Christian days. Its sin was that it celebrated with joy and laughter the great nature festivals." In his diary on June 21 (summer solstice), 1938, he wrote, "I got the idea of linking the old symbolism of indigenous women's mysteries with the pagan mysteries of England right down to the present day and through the witchcraft period." He had obviously been reading Margaret Murray's *The Witch-Cult in Western Europe*.

Christine Hartley, who worked as Seymour's High Priestess, recorded in her diary on June 28, 1938, "Started when I walked over the threshold of the house and felt witchcraft all around me. Went upstairs extremely desirous of being a witch. When we had settled down I kept getting little pictures of Ishtar worship through the ages, the most constant being one of silhouetted witches in pointed hats and ragged skirts dancing round a fire. Then . . . I was aware of the goddess standing before us mistily veiled." Seymour and Hartley were certainly in the occult network connected with the people who began the New Forest Coven in the late 1930s, and their own ideas obviously pointed in the same direction.

Yet another line of organizational succession connecting earlier occultism with the Craft movement is Co-Masonry, an offshoot of the Freemasonry movement that admitted both women and men into membership; women are still excluded by the United Grand Lodge of England, a traditional Freemason lodge. Co-Masonry originated in France and spread to England when its first British Lodge was formed in London in 1902. Annie Besant was initiated in this lodge and became the national delegate for Britain. When H. P. Blavatsky died and Besant lost to Bishop Leadbeater in her struggle to succeed Blavatsky as head of the Theosophical Society, she shifted her efforts to organizing Co-Masonry in Britain, and in 1922 Co-Masonry was affiliated to the Grand Orient in France. When Besant died, the leadership of Co-Masonry in Britain devolved upon her daughter, Mabel Besant-Scott, who was Gerald Gardner's neighbor in Highcliffe, England, and a leading member of the Rosicrucian Fellowship of Crotona.

Origin and History of Modern Neopagan Witchcraft

All religions seem to have both foundation stories (or foundation "myths")—which almost always claim to be historical in order to propose a meaning for the religion—and actual histories. Modern Gardnerian Witchcraft is no exception to this general rule. The foundation story of Wicca has grown up around Gardner's claim that in the late 1930s he was initiated into one of the very last of the English covens, and that he later built upon its system of worship and magic to create the Gardnerian system that has formed the basis for almost all of modern Witchcraft.

The story, based in part on the speculative scholarship found in Margaret Murray's *The Witch-Cult in Western Europe* (1921), proposes that modern Witchcraft can claim continuity with the Witches who were persecuted during the "Burning Times" as well as with pre-Christian Pagan religions going back to the Stone Age. One of the best-known forms of this story is woven into the second and third editions of Robert Graves's *The White Goddess: A Historical Grammar of Poetic Myth.*

Whether or not the Witches persecuted by the Inquisition were actually practicing Pagans, relatively recent publications, such as Doreen Valiente's *The Rebirth of Witchcraft* and Aidan A. Kelly's *Crafting the Art of Magic*, have decisively demonstrated that modern Witchcraft was the creation of Gerald Gardner. Specifically, Gardnerian Witchcraft began as a new religion in England in the late 1930s.

Gerald Brosseau Gardner was born at Great Crosby, near Blundell Sands in Lancashire, England, on June 13, 1884. His father was a timber merchant and a justice of the peace. His education for the most part was managed by a governess to whom he was devoted. He did not obtain a university education but instead went to work for the commercial branch of the British Civil Service in the Far East. In 1927, at age 43, he married Donna Rosedale, a clergyman's daughter. In 1936 he retired from the civil service—he had served as overseer of a rubber plantation in Malaysia, among other posts—and settled in the south of England, in the area of Hampshire known as the New Forest. He had been fascinated with the occult for his entire life and had accumulated a collection of magical implements and pamphlets issued by a great variety of new religious movements, which he brought home with him. He also had been initiated into dozens of occult organizations.

Before the outbreak of World War II, Gardner wrote a letter to the *London Times* suggesting the formation of civilian defense units in the event of war, a letter for which he was denounced in the Nazi press as a warmonger. The Home Guard was formed—whether or not in part because of his letter—and he served as a unit commander during the course of the war. Gardner's experience during the war, worrying about a possible German invasion, seems to have set the mood for much of his writing about the "Burning Times" in his books and documents.

In 1939, Gardner joined the Folklore Society, through which he became friends with Margaret Murray and other prominent British scholars. He served many times on the society's board of directors and did not resign from membership until after the publication of *Witchcraft Today* in 1954, which had begun to make him notorious because of his claim that real Witches still existed.

More directly important for the history of modern Witchcraft is the fact that, in the New Forest area, Gardner became friends with the local occultists, including Theosophists, Co-Masons, and others. In particular, he met a woman named Dorothy Clutterbuck Fordham, who seems to have been as enthusiastic about Witchcraft as Gardner was. Apparently, she was the dominant personality in their relationship for as long as she lived. Another acquaintance of Gardner's, whose Craft name was Dafo, helped found the Rosicrucian Theatre in Christchurch (it opened on June 15, 1938) and took part in the plays presented there.

It may be that the circle of occultists around Clutterbuck Fordham had begun to reify Murray's vision of Witchcraft as a surviving form of Paganism sometime between 1935 and 1939, and that Gardner was, in fact, initiated into an existing coven in September 1939, as he claimed. Or it may be that, in 1939, probably on September 28, the evening of the full moon, Gardner, Fordham Clutterbuck, Dafo, and other friends sat in Fordham Clutterbuck's living room, discussing England's perilous state now that it was at war with Germany. Was England in danger of perishing spiritually for want of a truly native British religion in which they could all believe? Gardner, at least, had been thinking for years about how to go about creating one. Encouraged by the tension of that moment, perhaps they decided to re-create the "witch cult of Western Europe" as described by Margaret Murray in her writing. If the creation of their coven occurred at that moment, each of the participants would later feel that his or her own initiation into the coven started that night; this could be why Gardner claimed to have been initiated in September 1939 and why that particular date appears in his writings. For those who assert that Gardner was Wicca's founder, this is the date of origin for Gardnerian Witchcraft.

The New Forest Coven, as it came to be called, worked until the end of World War II to reconstruct the religion envisioned by Murray. In *The Rebirth of Witchcraft*, Doreen Valiente provided the names of people who were in Gardner and Fordham Clutterbuck's circle of occult friends and who therefore *could* have been members of the coven in late 1939 or the early 1940s. These are the people who were most likely to influence the activities that were undertaken by the coven.

In addition to Dafo and "Old Dorothy" (Fordham Clutterbuck's nickname), there was Dolores North, who was almost certainly a member of the coven from the very beginning. Another likely member of the first coven was Louis Wilkinson, who wrote novels under the name of Louis Marlow. Wilkinson contributed to Crowley's *Equinox,* and was one of Crowley's literary executors. In 1947 Wilkinson achieved brief notoriety by reading Crowley's non-Christian funeral service at the municipal crematorium. Later, his report about the coven written to Francis King and recorded in King's *Ritual Magic in England* included details that Wilkinson could only have known if he had been in the circles he describes; that is, if he were acting as a member of the coven.

Another influence on the coven was George Watson McGregor Reid, Chosen Chief of the Druid Order, the group that held sunrise services at Stonehenge on Midsummer's Day, and his son, Robert McGregor Reid, who succeeded his father as Chosen Chief of the Druid Order in 1946. Fordham Clutterbuck owned the sword that these Druids used for their rituals at Stonehenge and in Valiente's initiation. Gardner also served on the Druids' board of directors.

Another possible influence on the coven was J. S. M. Ward, a close friend of Gardner's, a leading Freemason, author of several learned books on Freemasonry, and a pioneer in the rescue and conservation of ancient buildings. Ward had been the owner of the "witch's cottage" that Gardner bought and had rebuilt near St. Albans. He probably was not actually a member of the coven because he was a very devout, though unorthodox, Christian bishop, but he was part of the coven's larger surrounding support group. Ward was probably the source of Gardner's own consecration as a bishop, the certificate for which is among the papers in Toronto.

Charles Richard Foster Seymour and Christine Hartley, the heads of the Pagan Section of the Fraternity of the Inner Light, were also possible influences on the coven. They are discussed in great detail in Alan Richardson's *Dancers to the Gods*. Both were active as Co-Masons from 1941 on and may have met Gardner and Dafo in that context, if they were not already acquainted.

The Creation of Rituals

It is likely that most of the people discussed thus far were actually active members of the New Forest Coven (however, there also may have been some less notorious members) and their influence helped the rituals take shape. At first the New Forest group probably met weekly, much like a committee working on a project, and those who showed up regularly for these working sessions would have considered themselves to be the members of the coven. (Murray does not mention meeting at the full moon, a concept that came instead from Godfrey Leland's *Aradia*.) If the coven began working in September 1939, as surmised previously, they probably would have gathered for a party on Hallowe'en in that year, but they could hardly have had more than the outline of a ritual ready by then. Even aside from Murray's descriptions, May Day and Hallowe'en are the two dates European custom universally associates with Witches. Their first ritual was perhaps worked for Brigid at the beginning of February 1940 and certainly would have been worked by May Day in 1940. It is widely assumed among English occultists that a "real Witch coven" was meeting during 1940 and there is no documentation of this rumor during earlier years—therefore there were probably no such meetings. Given the concept that the Sabbats were for all members of the religion, the New Forest Coven would have quietly invited sympathetic friends and acquaintances from the local occult circle, and the Rosicrucian Theatre would have been a logical place to hold them.

As this New Forest Coven began to reconstruct the religion described by Murray, what would its first model have looked like? If the New Forest group was indeed based on the concepts Murray proposed, then the first coven would have focused its rituals on the god and on the male High Priest, *not* on a Priestess. We know from her writing that Murray focused almost entirely on the god of the Witches and on the man whom the Witches believed to be the living incarnation of that god. He often wore an animal skin or costume and would dress entirely in black—and hence was called the Black Man. Although Murray said that a woman sometimes served as the incarnation of the god, for the most part women took a secondary role in the rituals. Murray did not mention the concept of a goddess as the *chief* deity of witches except to dismiss it. (In fact, the Craft concept of the goddess comes primarily from Charles Godfrey Leland's 1899 book, *Aradia: The Gospel of the Witches,* and then from the classical sources to which Leland refers.) In addition to the Black Man, there were officers who took care of business in the absence of the Grand Master, and who were heads of their own covens. Contrary to the practice of the present-day Craft, this male orientation seems to have been the emphasis in Gardner's rituals until about 1957.

What might this New Forest Coven have done at a Sabbat? The litany of a "Witches' Sabbath" as given by Murray included the following:

1. worship of the incarnate deity by (a) renewing vows, (b) kissing, and (c) turning withershins (counterclockwise) several times

2. a business portion of the ceremony, consisting of (a) reports of and instructions on magic, (b) admissions of new members into the society, and (c) marriages of members
3. the religious service, consisting of (a) a ceremony that varied with the seasons, (b) fertility rites, (c) feasting, and (d) dancing until dawn

In records of Witch trials, the feast at a Sabbat often appeared to be a confused version of the Christian Eucharist, was thought to be a parody of the Eucharist, or was represented as a simple meal. None of these possibilities suggests much in the way of a Pagan ritual.

Aside from mentioning several kinds of dances, folk-magic procedures, and some customs generally associated with Witchcraft, such as riding a broomstick, lighting candles, boiling a cauldron, and so on, Murray gave no other specific details of what Witches might have done. Clearly, then, the New Forest group needed to exercise much creativity and ingenuity in attempting to "reconstruct" this religion. They were, in fact, faced by a dilemma: The Old Religion described by Murray focused on the practice of magic, but none of the systems for working magic that they knew about were practical for their purposes. For example, the "ceremonial," or "high," magic of the grimoires and secret societies was inherently Judeo-Christian in concept and in vocabulary. Not only was the theory behind these systems derived from certain special branches of Judeo-Christian theology, but the systems were so complex that the resulting practical details were almost impossible to carry out. In the so-called Abramelin system, for example, any given working would require great expense and months of preparation to carry out, as would the procedures detailed in Mathers's *Greater Key of Solomon*. The magical system of the Hermetic Order of the Golden Dawn was somewhat more sophisticated, and its rituals were easier to carry out—*if* the lodge's members could each subscribe 100 pounds sterling a year to support it (that is, more than the annual income of the average English home at that time). Obviously these rituals would not be suitable for a coven of Witches.

The New Forest group was interested in folk magic, which is always nondenominational, and they made as much use of it as they could. But the problem with folk magic was that it was all practice, no theory: To cure a wart, use this herb; to win a girl, recite this charm. This sort of "low magic" did not offer the sort of theological structure the New Forest people needed in order to give their new religion meaning. To ensure the success of their revival of the Old Religion, they needed to have what would be, in fact, a new system for working magic. To create it, they needed to use some sort of ritual other than that of Cabalistic magic as a framework. Since the coven members were Rosicrucians, Masons, Co-Masons, and so on (and also liked theater), they already knew of existing rituals that they could, and almost certainly did, adapt for their own purposes. For instance, much in the Gardnerian Book of Shadows (liturgical manual) is Masonic in underlying structure. As can be seen, it seems logical that much of what seemed odd about the New Forest rituals can be explained by considering that the data from Murray's writings were the template, within which everything else had to fit.

However, one identifying characteristic of the entire Gardnerian Neopagan Witchcraft movement is the basic structure of its ritual:

- casting the circle
- calling the quarters (north, east, south, and west)
- invoking the deities
- raising and using the magical energy
- partaking in a small symbolic feast of "cakes and ale"
- dismissing the deities and quarters
- closing down the circle

It is still not clear where the group came up with this particular sequence of actions. What was its origin? *This* sequence cannot be derived logically from any sort of Masonic, Golden Dawn, Ceremonial Magic, or other published procedure at that time. Were these actions genuinely peculiar to the Craft?

The answer may lie in the group's knowledge of the practices employed by the major school of the Order of Woodcraft Chivalry (OWC), a British alternative to the American Boy Scouts, which was located in the New Forest area. The OWC was based on the American Woodcraft movement, begun in 1917 by Ernest Thompson Seton, which made great use of what was then generally "known" about Native American spiritual practices. Its practitioners met in a circle, invoked the spirits of the four directions, danced around the circle as they were accompanied by drumming (as, of course, the "Indians" were thought to do), shared a small feast, thanked and dismissed the spirits, and opened up the circle. The leaders of the OWC even referred to their ritual as Witancraft, the "Craft of the Wise." Furthermore, it seems that Fordham Clutterbuck and her Rosicrucian Theatre group came as guests to the OWC circle, thus providing yet another source in the evolution of the Craft's rituals.

In addition to its basic ritual, the New Forest Coven must have begun creating *initiation* rituals for its own use. Whether or not its members performed some sort of initiation at the Sabbats, they certainly must have begun creating initiation rituals for use *within* the coven almost immediately. No identified copy of those rituals survives, but the rituals described in Rhiannon Ryall's *West Country Wicca* probably are very similar to the New Forest Coven's original ones.

Murray stated that there were apparently three different "admission ceremonies": one performed in public, one for consecration as a Priestess, and one for inducting an officer of the coven. These ceremonies could take place at either a Sabbat or an Esbat (ritual gatherings) and were the same for either sex. They could involve being rebaptized, being renamed, being marked or tattooed, or being asked to sign one's name in a book.

Ryall's book, plus stray remarks from others familiar with stories about the New Forest Coven, indicate that the coven's members had become widely scattered all over England by the end of World War II. Reduced to working with a small core group by that time, Gardner began to rewrite the rituals and create new ones. Some members continued to practice the Craft, like those in Ryall's home area, and, from her descriptions, we can see what the rituals were like prior to Gardner's revisions.

Of course, the rituals on which Gardner focused were those created by the New Forest Coven, and these went back not to any surviving Pagan traditions but to the obvious sources in the Western magical tradition: Aleister Crowley's developments of the HOGD system; Mathers's *The Greater Key of Solomon*; Masonic and other fraternal rituals; the scholarship of Margaret Murray and James Frazer, author of the influential *Golden Bough*; and the Cambridge classicists, scholars who romanticized the classical world.

Gardner began his rewriting of the New Forest ideas and rituals in a leatherbound manuscript book labeled *Ye Bok of ye Art Magical*. In Gardner's system there were three initiations, and they incorporated elements like those described by Murray within a framework taken from the three-Degree initiation system of the Masonic Blue Lodges. He incorporated a great deal of "binding and scourging," all of which were Gardner's own additions to the earlier raw materials. The initiation rituals in *Ye Bok of ye Art Magical* were designed to be worked by one person for one other person at a time. Although this arrangement indicates that his coven was very small, Gardner was not working in isolation as he created the rituals in the *Ye Bok of ye Art Magical* manuscript, which is clearly intended for liturgical use in the circle. Rather, like all liturgy, the rituals resulted from a lengthy group process.

Gardner did not alone create the vision of a medieval Pagan religion in the novel *High Magic's Aid*, which he wrote around 1946 and which was published in 1949; rather, that book seems to be the product of a group process. In fact, Gardner was working on the novel and rewriting the rituals simultaneously around 1946. *High Magic's Aid* is a fanciful and rather detailed description of the beliefs and practices of an English Witch cult in about the fifteenth century. It reveals that Gardner and his friends gave much thought to what a medieval, magical, Pagan religion might have been like and to how such a religion might now be "reconstructed." It also reveals how thoroughly familiar Gardner and his people were with Murray—dozens of elements from Murray's *The Witch-Cult in Western Europe* were incorporated in *High Magic's Aid*. The latter book included step-by-step descriptions of the First- and Second-Degree initiation rituals, following the text of *Ye Bok of ye Art Magical* rather closely, and explained that these "witch" initiations had to be worked within a magical circle cast by a ceremonial magician. This description is antithetical to current Craft practice—but it is how the Gardnerian circles had been worked, and would apparently continue to be worked, until perhaps as late as 1957.

The *Sunday Pictorial* for July 29, 1951, carried an article by Allen Andrews titled "Calling All Covens." It announced the forthcoming opening of the Folklore Centre of Superstition and Witchcraft, founded by Cecil H. Williamson at The Witches Mill, Castletown, Isle of Man. The opening ceremony was to be performed by the "resident Witch, Dr. Gerald B. Gardner." Williamson had erected a memorial to the estimated nine million people killed during the Witch persecutions in Europe. In 1952, Gardner bought the museum from Williamson and used it to display the magical and occult curiosities he accumulated all his life.

In 1951, the very last British anti-Witchcraft law—enacted in 1736—was repealed because of lobbying by Spiritualist churches. This change, Gardner implied later, made it possible for him to admit the existence of the religion. However, the members of the original New Forest Coven probably never intended to claim that their group had survived from the Middle Ages. Gardner's statements that the coven members insisted on secrecy and would allow him to publish a description of their beliefs only in the form of a novel may reflect more than a desire for privacy. Dorothy Clutterbuck Fordham may not have allowed Gardner to claim a continuity with the past that she knew was not true. In any event, it was only after she died in 1951 that Gardner, freed of her guidance and concerns, began thinking about how to write *Witchcraft Today* in such a way that it would present a plausible claim to such continuity.

After Clutterbuck Fordham's death, the coven continued. Dafo, who had been the coven's Maiden, became the new High Priestess. Gardner remained in touch with Dafo, Dolores North, and probably others all along, and they worked together when they had a reason to—for example, Dafo helped initiate Doreen Valiente in 1953. There were probably never more than half a dozen people active in the coven at any one time from 1946 to 1953, although there probably continued to be an informal "Outer Court" consisting of people in occult circles who were privileged to know of the coven's existence, and who were invited to the larger Sabbat rituals. By 1953, Gardner had started a new coven in London, and the new religion that he and his friends had founded had evolved far beyond Murray's concepts. However, their system for working magic had not progressed much beyond the situation described in *High Magic's Aid*; there was still the uneasy amalgam of the male ceremonial magician and the female folk-magic witch.

In the September 27, 1952, issue of the English popular magazine *Illustrated* appeared an article titled "Witchcraft in Britain" by Allen Andrews. The article quoted at length remarks by Cecil Williamson on the "Old Religion of the witches." Doreen Valiente, upon seeing this article, wrote to Williamson and was referred by him to Gardner, who, after an exchange of letters, invited her to meet him and Dafo at Dafo's house near Christchurch. This she did late in 1952, and in the summer of 1953 she was initiated into the New Forest Coven by Gardner and Dafo.

Gardner came to Dafo's house from his home on the Isle of Man in order to attend the Druids' midsummer ritual at Stonehenge, bringing with him the sword that the Druid Order used in its ceremony, which had belonged to Dorothy Clutterbuck Fordham. In his brochure about the Witches' Mill, Gardner said, "She had a very fine ritual sword, which for many years was lent to the Druid Order which holds the annual Midsummer ceremony at Stonehenge, because it fitted exactly into the cleft in the Hele Stone." Gardner had been a friend of both the current Chosen Chief of the Druid Order, Robert McGregor Reid, and his father, George Watson McGregor Reid, whom Robert had succeeded as Chosen Chief in 1946; and certainly Clutterbuck Fordham must have been a friend of George. Furthermore, Gardner was a member of the board of directors of the order, according to Ronald Hutton.

At her initiation, Valiente reported, the ritual was virtually identical to that in *High Magic's Aid*, except that it also contained a section called "The Charge" that Gardner read to her. She recognized passages as being from Leland's *Aradia* and from Crowley's *Book of the Law* and "Gnostic Mass" in *Magick in Theory and Practice*. Later that year Gardner invited her to his London flat to meet the rest of his coven. There were about eight or ten of them, most being members also of the nudist society Gardner belonged to, some claiming to have been Witches even before joining the coven. Valiente promptly threw herself into work on the new religion, rewriting the existing rituals and creating new ones, and some of this work was reflected in the final draft of *Witchcraft Today*.

About the time that Valiente was initiated, Gardner was using two different Books of Shadows (liturgical manuals). He led her to believe that the first, and shorter, one had been copied out of a Book of Shadows owned by Dorothy Clutterbuck Fordham, but there is no evidence that any such book ever existed. Instead, Gardner had copied its contents out of *Ye Bok of ye Art Magical*, the existence of which he kept secret from Valiente. He kept the manuscript at the museum and used it as a notebook for drafts of passages that would later appear in *Witchcraft Today*, as well as for drafts of new rituals that he copied into the longer Book of Shadows, the one used during Valiente's initiation. Once *Ye Bok of ye Art Magical* was full and no longer useful even as a notebook, Gardner hid it in the back of a cabinet in the museum, where it was found in 1971 by the team from Ripley's Believe It or Not, Inc., which had purchased the contents of the museum from the Wilsons, a couple who assisted Gardner with housekeeping and management of the museum after the death of Gardner's wife; the Wilsons, who arrived after the manuscript had been retired, probably didn't even know it existed.

In 1954, *Witchcraft Today* was published. In it Gardner claimed that Margaret Murray had been right: that the "Witchcraft" of the Middle Ages had been a surviving Pagan religion. He knew, he said, because that religion had survived in secret into the twentieth century. Having stumbled upon one of the last surviving covens in England, he had been initiated into it and was now free to write a description of its actual beliefs and practices, which went back to Elizabethan times and ultimately to the Stone Age religions of Europe. Gardner may have actually told Margaret Murray that his group had begun by trying to reconstruct the religion she described. This may be why she failed to notice, in her enthusiastic "Introduction" to *Witchcraft Today*, what Elliot Rose pointed out: The religion Gardner described in *Witchcraft Today* was utterly unlike what Murray had described 20 and 30 years earlier. Many current members of the Craft movement fail to see that the "Great

Goddess" is not one of the concepts in *Witchcraft Today*, which instead presents a domesticated sort of classical polytheism.

As time went on, Valiente became, in practice, Gardner's High Priestess and was more vocal about her dissatisfaction with the Book of Shadows as it stood when she was initiated. Many of the rituals asserted to exist in *Witchcraft Today* were only in the planning stages then. If a "Gardnerian" coven is defined as one that works the basic Gardnerian rituals—and this is one of the basic rules by which Gardnerians judge the authenticity of any coven that claims to be Gardnerian—then no Gardnerian coven could have existed before 1955, because the basic Gardnerian rituals had not been written yet. In fact, none of the circle rituals in use in 1953 were based on a "Pagan" theology; instead, they all were adapted from the Cabalistic procedures of the *Greater Key of Solomon* and contained great amounts of Christian terminology, as well as lengthy quotations from Crowley.

After Gardner got over the discomfiture of his realization that Valiente had spotted all the Crowley quotations in his rituals, he defended their presence by telling her that the rituals he had received from the old coven were fragmentary and that, in order to make them workable, he had supplemented them with other material. Gardner invited her to try rewriting the rituals, and she proceeded to do so. After creating a poetic version of the "Charge of the Goddess," she wrote the prose version that is now recognized as one of the basic theological statements of the Craft movement. She, or she and Gardner jointly, continued to rewrite the rituals and delete the Christian terminology in his Book of Shadows until 1957.

Meanwhile, in 1956, two factions developed in the coven: a propublicity faction consisting of Gardner and mostly newcomers and an antipublicity faction consisting of Valiente and most of the other "old-timers." Gardner's inability to be cautious when speaking to news reporters had been a longstanding problem. These two subgroups also differed about how to run a coven, so, in February 1957, the New Forest Coven divided in half. Valiente took about six others with her as well as all the correspondence and the operative Books of Shadows.

The remaining members of the original coven decided to use a circle-dance-and-drop technique as the best way to raise power, rather than the bound scourging that had always been Gardner's favorite technique. As a result, Gardner soon "wandered off" to initiate new Priestesses and found new covens. The original coven continued to exist and was studied by Tanya Luhrmann in her scholarly study of British magical groups, *Persuasions of the Witches' Craft*.

At first, splitting the new coven was a peaceful process and the two new covens cooperated with one another and met jointly on occasion. However, because Gardner sought publicity, tensions rose. As a last resort, Ned, Valiente's High Priest, drew up a set of proposals titled "Proposed Rules for the Craft" in the hopes that Gardner would agree to abide by them. These rules inspired Gardner to write the document now known as the "Old Laws" or the "Craft Laws."

Eventually the two groups went separate ways. Gardner rewrote the Book of Shadows rituals, and it was these revised rituals, rather than Valiente's versions, that became the authoritative text of the Book of Shadows passed on to the Gardnerian covens in the United States. Gardner also initiated a great many new High Priestesses during the last seven years of his life, including Patricia Crowther; Eleanor "Ray" Bone; Lois Hemmings; and Monique Wilson, or "Lady Olwen." Some of these new members were well accepted by his previous initiates; others were not.

Gardner's wife, Donna, died in 1960. Her health had been failing for some time, so at some point in the late 1950s two of Gardner's initiates, Monique and Campbell Wilson, took over the full-time tasks of housekeeping for him and running the museum. When Gardner died in 1964, they inherited his museum and his library of books and manuscripts, which they sold to Ripley's Believe It or Not, Inc., in 1971.

Gardner died while on a sea voyage in February 1964 and was buried in Tunis, Africa. Some years later, Eleanor Bone discovered that the cemetery in which he was buried was to be redeveloped; so she raised a collection among Britain's Witches and succeeded in having him reburied in a different cemetery, where he could rest in peace.

Gardnerian Witchcraft in America

Gardnerian history in the United States begins with Raymond and Rosemary Buckland. Raymond Buckland recognized the importance of the Gardnerian movement and traveled to Britain to be initiated and bring the Craft to America.

Buckland was born in London on August 31, 1934. He was educated at King's College School in London and served in the Royal Air Force from 1957 to 1959. He married his first wife, Rosemary, in 1955. Ray had been studying the occult for many years when he first read Gardner's *Witchcraft Today* in the late 1950s and felt that Witchcraft was the religion for which he had been searching. He wrote to Gardner, who was living on the Isle of Man, and struck up a relationship. When he and Rosemary emigrated to the United States in 1962 and settled in Long Island, he became Gardner's spokesperson in the United States.

After several years of correspondence, Buckland finally met Gardner in 1963, when he and his wife journeyed to Perth, Scotland, where, as Gardner had arranged, they underwent a brief, intense training by Lady Olwen (Monique Wilson) and were initiated. The Bucklands then brought the Gardnerian Book of Shadows back to New York. They founded the New York Coven in Bay Shore, Long Island, which became the center of the Gardnerian movement and the Neopagan movement in America for the next 20 years. Almost all "official" Gardnerians in America are descendants of that coven.

The Bucklands did their best to screen people carefully and train them thoroughly according to the principles and procedures in the Gardnerian

Book of Shadows. Over the years, however, more and more people came banging on the door, demanding to learn the Craft and threatening to start covens of their own based on the horror movie *Rosemary's Baby* if they weren't admitted to the coven. In order to prevent the creation of inferior covens, the Bucklands gradually relented—they admitted members more frequently, trained them less rigorously, and elevated them to higher Degrees sooner. Still, according to Raymond Buckland, there were fewer than 20 women raised to the Third Degree during the nine years of their "administration" of the New York Coven.

In 1972, Lady Rowen (Monique Wilson) tired of her duties as High Priestess and retired. She appointed Theos as High Priestess of the New York Coven on November 17, 1972, and the members of the coven swore and signed an oath of fealty to Theos. It read, "We the undersigned, present members of the New York Coven, do swear allegiance to our new High Priestess, the Lady Theos." It was signed by the Third-Degree members Robat (Raymond Buckland), Phoenix (Theos's husband), Ea (Ed Fitch), and Sea, as well as the First-Degree members Gillis, Retep, Puck, and Tanith.

Theos and Phoenix took over responsibility for the New York Coven with great enthusiasm, moved the covenstead to their home in Commack, New York, and quickly rebuilt the group. It is a great distance from Manhattan to Commack in Suffolk County, Long Island, but the coven's members seem to have made that trek happily at least once a month—many made it about once a week.

At first, the Bucklands remained as Elders in the coven, but they became less active in the group when their marriage crumbled and they became separated. When Theos and Phoenix realized that Lady Rowen would soon be unavailable to answer questions because of her retirement, they debriefed her on everything she knew about oral traditions and about how the coven actually operated. From this information they created the longest single document in the current Gardnerian Book of Shadows, the "Notes and Guidelines," apparently intended to be just that, mere guidelines. However, over the years the notes and guidelines hardened into rules and regulations. In 1973, Lady Rowen, Robat, Lady Theos, Phoenix, Ea, and Sea, as the actual Elders of the Gardnerian movement in America, signed the new materials they added to the First-Degree Book of Shadows, thus certifying it as authentic and authoritative.

At this juncture, having been forced to retire as High Priest of his original coven and needing a High Priestess to form a new coven, Raymond Buckland raised Deirdre to Third Degree by himself, as was allowed under the procedural rules in effect at the time. However, for some years Theos and Phoenix refused to recognize Deirdre's elevation or any of her initiations because one of the new "guidelines" (Theos learned from Rowen) stated that valid initiations could be carried out only in a circle cast by a Third-Degree High Priestess. This rejection of his Priestess led Buckland to found Seax-Wica—a form of the Craft that did not suffer from the drawbacks he perceived in the Gardnerian model.

When Deirdre moved to Louisville, Kentucky, to teach at a university, she and her consort, Modred, began the Coven of the Silver Trine; covens descended from the Silver Trine are known collectively as the "Kentucky Lineage." At first, the Kentucky Lineage covens were treated by the New York Coven as heretical and schismatic. However, Theos later persuaded Deirdre to accept a "re-initiation" by the procedures of the New York Coven, thus grafting the two lineages together and healing the schism. The number of Gardnerian covens in North America in 1973 was not more than two or three dozen.

Although no list of members is likely to be available in the near future, it can be estimated that Lady Theos and Phoenix elevated many people to Third Degree during their tenure as heads of the Gardnerian movement in America. (In fact, Raymond Buckland expressed some criticism of the freedom with which they elevated people in the second edition of his *Witchcraft from the Inside*.) One of the most important of these initiations was the elevation of Athena and Dagda to Third Degree in 1974; their California Coven (later named Our Lady of the Hills) thus became the first officially Gardnerian coven in California, and several California lineages sprang from it.

Deirdre and Modred in Louisville were training initiates too, and the Craft expanded rapidly from that base of operations. In 1977, they began *The Hidden Path* as a journal for Gardnerians only, and it continues to be the in-house Gardnerian newsletter. In 1985, Deirdre resigned as Queen of the Kentucky Line, bestowing her Queenship equally on her three daughters (Priestesses), who continue to oversee the Kentucky Lineage jointly.

Lady Morda and her consort in Chicago, Illinois, also were training initiates in their Gardnerian line, the source of which could be traced back to England (via a route different from that of Lady Rowen). Morda worked in England in 1969 with Madge Worthington and Arthur Edmonds, two of Eleanor Bone's initiates, and was raised to Second Degree by them. Morda was also close friends with Lois Bourne, who succeeded Doreen Valiente as High Priestess of the original London coven. Morda then brought the Gardnerian Craft to Chicago, teamed up with Herman Enderle and Ginnie Brubaker, adapted Ed Fitch's new Pagan Way materials as an Outer Court, and thus helped create the Temple of the Pagan Way as an eclectic tradition with a Gardnerian core. Theos again solved an institutional problem by paying Morda's expenses to come to Long Island to be initiated and elevated according to New York Coven procedures, again grafting two lines together. Covens that descend from the Temple of the Pagan Way are Gardnerian by several different definitions.

Other non–Long Island lineages descend from Frederick Folter's Coven of Artemis Orthia, active in British Columbia in the early 1970s; from Carol Bulzone's Enchantments covens, which were imported from England by a route independent of Long Island; and from a coven in Nova Scotia that apparently predates Lady Olwen.

During the last two decades of the twentieth century, some large fraction of these Third-Degree Witches turned out initiates and, in turn, these third-generation, Third-Degree Witches turn out yet more initiates, resulting in extremely rapid growth of the Craft. It would be difficult indeed to document the historical details of every Gardnerian coven in America today.

Almost all "official" Gardnerians in America are descendants of the New York Coven, and they maintain their identity by ensuring a strict apostolic succession of High Priestesses who trace their initiation back to Lady Theos, Lady Rowen (Rosemary Buckland), and Lady Olwen (Monique Wilson). However, these "official" Gardnerians are now only a small fraction of Gardnerian Witchcraft and of the Neopagan Witchcraft movement in general. This is largely because they adhere to a fairly strict interpretation of the rules gradually established by the New York Coven in its steadily expanding text of the Book of Shadows. Therefore they tend to elevate new High Priestesses and found new covens fairly slowly and cautiously. Most American Witches, being spiritually akin to anarchists, libertarians, and other proponents of radical theories, practice the Craft much more flexibly, using whatever they like from the Gardnerian repertoire and creating what they need from elements of past or present religions. These "non-Gardnerian" Witches, free to train Priestesses and found covens more rapidly than Gardnerian Witches, have become the majority of the population in the Craft movement.

Almost all traditions of Neopagan Witchcraft in America began as an imitation of the Gardnerians. Some of the imitators admitted their dependence on the Gardnerians openly from the start. Other imitators claimed an ancestry of European Witchcraft independent of the Gardnerians—these claims almost always proved to lack substance. The very few Witches in America whose traditions seem to predate Gardner (and which differ radically from Gardnerian theology) enthusiastically adopted Gardnerian "reforms" because of their popularity and usefulness. Despite the overwhelming influence of Gardnerian Witchcraft, "Gardnerianism" is but one component—albeit the most influential—of the larger Neopagan movement.

The Neopagan Movement

Neopaganism as a religious concept is based on a desire to re-create the Pagan religions of antiquity, usually not as they actually were, but as they have been idealized by romantics since the Renaissance. The gap between ancient reality and modern reconstruction is exhibited most clearly by the fact that all classical Paganism—like first-temple Judaism—was based on animal sacrifice, which is avoided by all modern Neopagans. (Animal sacrifice is still central to several African-American religions, such as Vodun, Santeria, or Macumba, but they constitute an entirely different religious movement.)

The idea of re-creating lost ancient Pagan religions is not a new one. Early in the Renaissance, such Italian scholars as Pico della Mirandola and Marsilio Ficino became Neopagans (as well as occultists and magicians) out of their desire to re-create lost religions of the past. This desire has remained a common theme in Western Occultism ever since. While fascination with the classics was a major theme of Romanticism, the revival of classical religion gained momentum during the late nineteenth century as well, at which time attention was divided between Greco-Roman and Norse Paganism. The nineteenth-century revival was further strengthened as the new discipline of classical archaeology revealed the existence of civilizations in the Middle East that predated the Greeks by millennia, turning up Pagan religious texts that had been baked in clay as palaces burned down around them.

Later, in the late nineteenth and early twentieth centuries, there were many attempts to re-create Pagan religions, most of which left only literary remains, as in the poetry of Swinburne and the magnificent paintings of the "Pre-Raphaelite Brotherhood" and their colleagues. Other types of Paganism emerged during this period also, as Celtic and Near Eastern studies revealed more and more about the cultures that existed before biblical, Roman, or Christian times.

Attempts to re-create Paganism began to succeed only in the 1960s, apparently because the new magical and theological technology of Wicca lent these Neopagan experiments a crucial ingredient. Typically, a Neopagan group would be founded—usually by college students—and would remain very small in size. Then in the late 1960s or early 1970s, group leaders began to learn the religion of Wicca from their interactions with Gardnerian-style Witches, adapting various aspects of Wicca to the needs of their own Neopagan group. At this stage the enthusiastic synergism of this eclectic enterprise inspired the groups to expand rapidly, both by recruiting new members and by multiplying the frequency and variety of its activities.

Until the mid-1970s, Wicca appeared to be just one among many equally important Neopagan religions because these other Neopagans had coopted the best traits of Wicca for their own. During the next decade, this situation changed remarkably. In the mid-1980s, Margot Adler, in her *Drawing down the Moon,* observed, "Wiccan organizations have come to the foreground as the primary form of Neopaganism in America, and these organizations now dominate the discussion." Well over 50 percent of all Neopagans in the United States had become Neopagan Witches not simply because Witchcraft groups were growing in numbers (and continue to grow faster than any of the other Neopagan religions), but because many Neopagans realized that Wicca provided everything they had been hoping to gain from other Neopagan religions, and so shifted their focus more exclusively onto Wicca.

Wicca, therefore, is the most important of the Neopagan religions, and Witches always form the backbone of Neopagan voluntary associations. However, there are other Neopagan religions with substantial followings, as well as with theologies quite distinct from that of Wicca. Following are descriptions of the largest of these.

The Church of All Worlds

Inspired by Robert Heinlein's *Stranger in a Strange Land,* the Church of All Worlds was begun by Tim Zell, Lance Christie, and their wives, in St. Louis in 1962. During the initial years, when it was based strictly on a science-fictional theology, it hovered on the edge of extinction, until 1968, when Zell and other members of the St. Louis Nest met Bobbie Kennedy, Carolyn Clark, and perhaps a few other Gardnerian-style Witches. They learned the Craft system, were initiated as Witches, and combined the theology of Wicca with Heinlein's libertarian philosophy. The resulting synergism catapulted the Nest's newsletter, *Green Egg,* into national prominence as the major communication channel for the Neopagan movement between about 1971 and 1976.

The Druid Groups

The Neopagan Druids of the United States have no historical connection with either British Druidic groups (such as the Ancient Order of Druids or the Order of Bards, Druids, and Ovates) or with the American Druids' lodge, which is a form of Freemasonry. Rather, the American Neopagan Druids are almost entirely a new movement, created from scratch by their founders.

The earliest of these groups to form was the Reformed Druids of North America (RDNA), founded at Carleton College in 1962 as a not especially serious protest against the college's anachronistic requirement of weekly attendance at chapel services. Much to the founder's surprise—but not to that of anyone who has looked dispassionately at how religions actually begin—the RDNA quickly took on a life of its own and began to serve its members as a religion. By the mid-1970s, the RDNA had proliferated into such varieties as the New Reformed Druids of North America, the Hasidic Druids of North America, and others. Its history to this point was ably documented by Isaac Bonewits in *The Druid Chronicles*.

Bonewits, who joined the RDNA in the late 1960s, became dissatisfied with his role in the group by the late 1970s, and founded a rival organization, Ar nDraiocht Fein (ADF), "our own Druidism." The ADF subsequently has become the largest and most active of the Neopagan Druid organizations, with Groves and Proto-Groves scattered by the dozens across North America.

As Ronald Hutton explained in *The Pagan Religions of the Ancient British Isles,* we actually know nothing whatsoever about the beliefs of the ancient Druids, and we know very little about their religious activities in general. All descriptions of "Druid beliefs" have been modern inventions (some based on medieval inventions), and are of interest only as artistic creations. The greatest creator of a "Druid" group was Edward Williams, who wrote as Iolo Morganwg (Iolo of Glamorgan) in the late eighteenth and early nineteenth centuries; he was a contemporary of William Blake and was almost as great a creative genius as well. Unfortunately, where Blake never claimed his writings were anything but his own creations, Williams took a different route.

Williams combed the libraries of the Welsh upper classes and found many unique manuscripts of medieval Welsh writings and music (in a notation system seemingly indiscernible today). However, none of these documents provided the kind of coherent Pagan religion that Williams hoped to find. To repair this deficit, he proceeded to "create" the missing documents himself—his work so skillful that it took Welsh scholars a century after Williams's death to distinguish his contributions from authentic documents. Williams's work affected modern Neopaganism in two ways:

1. Especially through the codifications by the Reverend Williams in *Barddas*, it was made the theological basis for several Druidic organizations and, in part, for the Church and School of Wicca
2. Through Robert Graves's use of it in *The White Goddess*, it has been incorporated into the background mythology of Wicca and Neopaganism in general

Other types of Celtic and especially Irish Neopaganism are highly important within the Neopagan movement overall. Not enough is known about Irish Pagan religion to allow even a wild guess at how worship was conducted. Only when Wicca provided an a priori framework to determine what Irish Paganism must have been like did (now called) "Celtic Tradition" arise. In practice, many Wiccan covens and Pagan associations focus largely or exclusively on the Irish pantheon, or on other Celtic divinities, for celebrating the Sabbats—not, of course, on how these deities were conceived centuries ago, but on how they were described and idealized in such speculative writings as Graves's *The White Goddess*.

Norse Paganism

There have been several attempts to re-create a practical form of Norse Paganism during recent decades, the two largest being the Odinist movement and the Asatru Free Assembly. As with the other forms of Neopaganism, these attempts succeeded only because they actually became a sort of Norse-flavored "Outer Court" with an essentially Gardnerian-style, Wiccan core. For example, a leader of the Odinist movement and a writer of excellent popular books on the subject, Ed Fitch, was one of the first Gardnerian High Priests in the United States and was one of the cofounders of the Pagan Way movement that flourished during the 1970s.

Neopagans tend, for the most part, to operate well within the political mainstream, though with the "liberal tendencies" most associated with the defense of citizens' right to religious freedom. Hence, it is a cause of acute embarrassment to Neopagans that there exists another sort of Norse Paganism in the United States: one associated with Neo-Nazis, Survivalists, Skinheads, and other types of radical, right-wing politics and religion. Furthermore, there is no easy distinction between the practices of these two types of Norse Paganism, especially since subgroups have formed that fall into a grey area that endorses theories of both types of Norse Paganism. Initiates are cautioned to engage their group's leaders in a frank discussion regarding their beliefs about Jews, Catholics, African-Americans, and Socialists. This should quickly reveal whether the group is essentially Wiccan or essentially Neo-Nazi in its underlying beliefs.

Covenant of Unitarian Universalist Pagans

Another form of Neopaganism in the United States is that created by the Covenant of Unitarian Universalist Pagans. This national organization does not yet constitute a separate form of Neopaganism by and of itself. Rather, it represents the overlap between Unitarians and Neopagans in the United States. In 1990, the Covenant of Unitarian Universalist Pagans had 60 chapters scattered across the country, almost all associated with a local Unitarian Universalist church.

Egyptian Neopaganism

Egyptian Neopaganism is exemplified by the Church of the Eternal Source, one of the few Neopagan organizations to have successfully resisted the pressure to transform into a sort of Egyptian-flavored Wicca. On the other hand, there are Wiccan covens that focus on worship of the Egyptian deities. One of the most prominent of these is Ellen Cannon Reed's Sothistar Coven, the practices of which she details in her *Evocation of the Gods*. Sothistar is one of half a dozen covens of the Western Isian Tradition, which originated in Texas in 1975. The Goddess Isis is, by herself, one of the most popular goddesses in coven worship and evocation; however, it is usually the Isis of the Mysteries who is worshipped rather than the pre-Hellenistic Isis.

Greco-Roman Paganism

This movement is almost entirely a subsidiary of modern Neopaganism. There have been a few attempts to replicate an authentic classical temple's litany, as done by the Temple of Pomona in Kansas City. Again, these movements have not involved animal sacrifice in their worship. For the most part, the Greek and Roman deities are worshipped and aspected only within the standard liturgical structure of a Wiccan circle.

Since the late 1960s, enough information on the theory and practice of Gardnerian-style Witchcraft has been available in books that any small group who wanted to do so could train themselves as a coven. Those who did have been recognized as members of the Wiccan Tradition; more and more covens began this way as a number of "how-to" Witchcraft books became available in the 1970s and 1980s.

Women's Spirituality Movement

The Women's Spirituality Movement overlaps the Neopagan movement; in 1971, many women at a women's rights conference in Los Angeles attended the World Science Fiction Convention there and heard an address by Julia Carter Zell on the Craft. This event led to the foundation of "Dianic" covens, which were for women only, whereas all other Neopagan covens had been mixed in gender. Soon afterward, covens for men only—some gay, some "straight"—were also founded.

Structure of the Neopagan Movement

To understand the overall structure of the Neopagan movement, we will need to acknowledge that there is a complex relationship between various types of magical groups. All of these groups make up a single religious community, even though, within this community, there are differences in how the groups relate to one another.

This relationship can be illustrated by a series of concentric rings: At the center are the traditionalist Gardnerians, who sparked the growth of Neopaganism when Ray Buckland brought Gardnerian Neopagan Witchcraft to the United States in 1963. The next ring is composed of "Reform" Gardnerians, who attempt to adapt Gardnerian rules to life in the United States.

As we move outward from the first two rings of the circle, the groups become progressively less secretive and generally are more willing to work freely with other Neopagans and magical groups. The third ring is composed of Eclectic Gardnerians, who wish to maintain their connection with the Gardnerian community, but whose adaptations of rituals go farther afield than the reform Gardnerians. Within these first three rings there are lineages: family trees of related covens that all trace back to the same High Priestess who serves as the active Queen of the Lineage; these lineages continue to exist within the Gardnerian Tradition.

The fourth ring from the center is composed of Gardnerian offshoots that do not attempt to formally comply with any orthodox Gardnerians' rules and regulations. These offshoot groups are even more eclectic.

The fifth ring from the center of the circle is composed of other, supposedly "non-Gardnerian" Witches. Within the last two rings (sometimes overlapping slightly with the Eclectic Gardnerians and with other Neopagan religions) there are traditions: family trees of covens that go back to some founder other than Gardner. Traditions that openly admit to their recent foundation present no problem. Others, who may claim to have descended, independently of Gardner, to a Witchcraft religion surviving from antiquity, are historically fraudulent (whether well intended or not), with a very few exceptions.

Wicca, thus, is organized into traditions: Gardnerian, Alexandrian, British Traditional, Celtic Traditional, NROOGD (the New Reformed Orthodox Order of the Golden Dawn), Isian, and others. The tradition consists of all the detailed ways in which each coven carries out its liturgy and works its initiation rituals; of what rules it follows internally and in relating to other Witches and pagans; of what materials are in its Book of Shadows, which only its initiates are allowed to see; and so on. One might expect a structural description or family tree of the Craft to display the importance of these traditions—but in fact it does not. Why? Because the High Priestess of any coven will proceed to run her coven as she sees fit, rewriting rituals or adding to the Book of Shadows. Once fully empowered to run her own coven when she receives the Third Degree of initiation, a High Priestess does not have to seek permission from her initiator for anything she chooses to do; there is no hierarchic authority. As a result, traditions, in practice, are not important at all. Many covens are self-founded, many have no records of their own ancestry, and few have any practical reason to care about such historical matters. Instead, the actual structure within the Neopagan and Western occult tradition movements in general is that of regional and national networking associations, which function at several different levels of integration.

The most tightly integrated networking associations are those of covens whose traditions are so closely related that they can participate in each other's monthly Esbats, and sometimes even in each other's initiations. The practical reason for such an association is to allow the covens to handle training classes for newcomers and buy needed business or legal services more easily. Usually these associations are strictly local. There have been such networking associations for Gardnerians only or for Alexandrians only, but they have not been prominent since they tend to disappear into the social structure already provided by the tradition. Probably the most successful such organization has been the New Wiccan Church, which is made up of British Traditional covens—strictly Gardnerian in all but name.

The next level of integration of covens is networking associations that are for Witches only. Again these provide an economy of scale and, on the local level (covens that are within a day's drive from each other), allow coven leaders to maintain their autonomy but communicate with one another regularly. Coven leaders use this opportunity to create a climate of opinion within their overall religious community that serves as peer pressure and thus some analog of government. Often such a networking association will also serve to coordinate local Sabbats. An example of this sort of association is the Covenant of the Goddess, which functions at both national and local levels.

Returning to the concentric ring model, the sixth ring from the center is for other Neopagan religions. These religions are all essentially the same as Wicca, but their members refer to themselves as Pagans rather than Witches. To some extent, Gardnerian Wicca is self-defined as an Anglo-Celtic religion native to the British Isles; those interested in reconstructing Pagan religions of other times and places (ancient Egypt, classical Greece, India, or Africa, for example) sometimes hesitate to call themselves Witches. Also, groups that began as a very different sort of religion (such as the Church of All Worlds) and blossomed only when they discovered and began to assimilate the theology and practices of Neopagan Wicca still hesitate to define themselves strictly as Witches and not as Pagans.

For the most part, training of clergy in all the active Neopagan religions is the same sort of training that a Neopagan Witch would receive in a coven—but is very often carried out in a manner considered more rigorous and professional. The Neopagan organizations that have survived during the last several decades are precisely those in which a central decision-making body functions as a Craft coven. In 1893, the secret Inner Court within the Hermetic Order of the Golden Dawn was a Rosicrucian chapter; in 1993, the secret Inner Court within one Golden Dawn offshoot in Southern California was a Witchcraft coven.

The sixth ring also contains an even looser level of integration between covens in the current incarnation of the Western magical tradition: regional associations of covens of diverse traditions and Neopagans of other sorts.

These groups get together for the semiquarterly Sabbats or for festivals, which are sometimes tied to the Sabbat dates. They regard each other as members of the same general sort of Neopagan religion and so can participate in public worship together. The association usually provides the framework for a working committee that can handle the organization of these semipublic events. There are several dozen examples of such associations in this encyclopedia.

And this brings us to ring seven—Ceremonial Magical Lodges, which historically predate the Neopagan movement by almost a century and were one source for Gardner's (and others') creation of modern Witchcraft in the 1930s. But the truth is that many Magical Lodges now are very different from Magical Lodges then—different in membership, in purposes, in structure, and in interests. It might even be possible to sort Magical Lodges into two categories: those more aligned with Neopaganism and those more aligned with the older sort of Judeo-Christian magic. In the former category there is much overlapping of membership with Neopagan organizations.

Here we might logically expect to find a level of networking associations: of Neopagans, of Ceremonial Magicians, and perhaps of members of other magical religions. But, in practice, these various people do not regard their religions as similar enough to comfortably allow common worship services (it took Witches and Ceremonialists quite a while to grasp this). However, these people do attend each other's semipublic gatherings as individuals if they choose.

In the eighth ring we find other sorts of magical religions, of Rosicrucian, Masonic, Theosophical, or even Mormon provenance, but they are not so plentiful now compared to the Neopagans. And in the ninth ring we find all the sorts of "third-world" religions that Neopagans find similar enough to be of some use or interest, such as Hinduism, or the African-American religions. (Of course, this is not how the situation looks to a Hindu or a Vodun Priestess, but the purpose here is to explain only the structure around the Neopagan movement.)

There seem to be no specifically religious associations that include both Neopagan Witches and members of magical religions in general, largely because Neopagan Witches cannot understand or tolerate the apparently "Christian" vocabulary of the older Magical groups. Instead, at this level the common concerns are more political. That is, although Witches, occultists, and New Agers, for example, do not agree on theology, they do agree that they all have a right to their own theology and so form associations to defend those rights. (This willingness to form associations with other followers of the Western occult tradition appears to have originated with the Neopagans, since other Western occult tradition groups did not form such associations.) Some of the more important such groups include The Aquarian Anti-Defamation League and AMER, among others.

At this level the associations often function nationally, at least in their use of local chapters, groves, nests, or contact persons scattered across the country. In addition, these associations are generally concerned with outreach, that is, they can simultaneously perform the functions of contacting potential members and then of screening those potential members in order to connect them with suitable groups nearby. If one scans the lists of local contacts for such organizations during the last few decades, one finds that the same names tend to turn up in all the lists. It is precisely the people who have done such necessary local work who have served as national leaders for the Neopagan movement. There are many folk sayings regarding the fact that those who do the dirty work are also the ones who reap its benefits.

Sometimes leaders of covens, or of other kinds of small Western occult tradition groups, will form "leaders' groups" that provide peer counseling, discussion of leadership problems, and professional networking opportunities. These groups may exist separately or within the structure of an association.

A key to understanding all this is that there are never any enforceable rules. All membership at any level is voluntary; anyone is free to leave any meeting at any time. If a group decides that it does not approve of a person's or group's behavior, they can ask that person or group not to attend further meetings. Followers of the Western occult tradition like it this way: They do not believe that any group, let alone a "church," ought to have the authority to punish any individual. Hence, the network of relationships—to one's teachers, to other members of a group, to one's peers in other groups, to one's students—is continually shifting as individuals grow and change, learn, and move on.

Despite all the apparent differences in theology, practices, and organization, Neopagans have a great deal of common ground in their worship practices and have developed a national system of public worship services that are extremely popular and attract hundreds of participants. These festivals are based on the Sabbats, developed as part of Wiccan belief and practice, and lead to the establishment of permanent sanctuaries and temples analogous to the temples of classical Paganism.

Neopagans and the New Age

The Neopagan and New Age movements, two recent manifestations of the Western occult tradition, share so many characteristics that one might expect their respective members to feel a certain amount of kinship; but such feelings do not exist. Both movements, for example, are extremely interested in psychic phenomena and in developing personal psychic abilities to the extent possible. However, New Agers eschew the terms *magic* and *witchcraft*, especially the latter, perhaps because it is equated with Satanism by the uninformed. New Age bookstores (like the East/West Foundation bookstore in Menlo Park, California) almost never have sections labeled "Magic" or "Witchcraft." Instead, books on magic are shelved with works on spiritual disciplines, such as Yoga; and books on Neopagan Witchcraft are shelved with books on Women's Studies.

Second, many typical New Age assumptions about religion are generally rejected by Neopagans. Many New Agers assume, for example, that all religions are ultimately the same; that spirituality is best learned at the feet of a master teacher or guru, preferably from one of the Eastern religions. The New Agers also feel that a new-world teacher or messiah will appear to usher in the New Age. Neopagans, in contrast, like the Craft specifically because it is so different from the puritanical, otherworldly Christianity in which almost all of them were raised. Most Neopagans believe in karma and reincarnation, but they reject the dualism of the Eastern traditions and consider the guarantee of rebirth to be the goal of their spiritual practices. They believe that they practice an ancient folk religion, whether as a survival or a revival of the "Old Religion," and, focused on the Pagan religions of the past, they are not particularly interested in a New Age in the future. Neopagans also believe that many religions are radically and irreconcilably different from each other; that the "reformed" religions (especially the monotheistic ones) established by Moses, Jesus, Mohammed, the Buddha, and similar figures were *not* an improvement on the folk religions they replaced. They feel that if there were a single worldwide religion in the future, it might very well be even more repressive of human freedom than the Roman Catholic Church was in Europe during the "Burning Times." Hence, Neopagans are not at all receptive to teachers and teachings from monotheistic religions nor to any from the East, with the possible exception of Hinduism, which is seen (accurately so or not) as an "unreformed" polytheism similar to that of the Greco-Roman world. Neopagans tend to be especially interested in Tantric traditions, since these can easily be seen as a type of magic parallel to that developed in the Western occult tradition.

Neopagans can be extremely antiauthoritarian and so are not at all inclined to accept the personal authority of any guru. The only people in the Neopagan movement who function as a type of guru are women (such as Starhawk, Zsusanna Budapest, Margot Adler), and the followers who relate to them as gurus are members of the women's rights/women's spirituality movements, rather than Neopagan Witches as such. The authoritarian structure of the official Gardnerian Witches in America might seem to be anomalous, but it does not in fact work that way—although the appearance of authority is a reason why there are at least ten times as many Gardnerian-imitating Witches as official Gardnerians in the Neopagan movement.

Neopagan Witches also operate with an ethic that forbids them to accept money for initiating or training anyone in the essential practices of the Craft as a religion. Neopagan festivals have grown into national gatherings during the last decade, often of several thousand people, but they remain quite inexpensive, since no one attempts to make a profit from them. As a result of this ethic, Neopagans look critically upon the relatively expensive "Psychic Fairs" and "New Age Expos."

Nonetheless, there is a minority of Neopagan Witches who consider themselves to be members of the New Age movement. This minority tends to consist of Witches who postulate that not only is the Gardnerian Witchcraft movement a new religion, but that age does not matter. Every religion is created at some time and place; certainly for the major "world" religions, this date can be specified quite precisely by current scholarship. This minority believes that the Craft may be a new religion, but it contributes to the spiritual growth in the modern world as much as any other ancient religion.

Probably the most prominent of the New Age Witches is Selena Fox, who carries out her ministry not only in the Neopagan community, but she also acts as an ecumenical and interfaith ministry, hoping to improve communication and mutual respect among followers of all religions. Her approach emphasizes that all persons have the right to differ and to follow their own spiritual paths, so long as others' paths are respected as well. Her successful fight to enable her Circle Sanctuary to exercise the same rights as any other church has gained her some deserved national notice, and her *Circle Network News,* with a circulation of some 15,000, is a major communication channel for both the Neopagan and New Age movements. The Neopagan movement as a whole is addicted to small periodicals: There have been hundreds of them, of varying degrees of viability, since the early 1960s. Several of the current periodicals that have a national circulation speak to the New Age movement: *Green Egg, Magical Blend,* and *Shaman's Drum* are certainly worth mentioning.

Other Magical Groups

We have considered contemporary Neopaganism in the context of its links with the Western occult tradition. Whatever one believes about the origins of modern Wicca, it is clear that the larger Neopagan movement has been decisively influenced by ceremonial magic (as embodied in such organizations as the Golden Dawn, the Ordo Templi Orientis), occult esotericism (the Theosophical Society, Freemasonry, or Rosicrucianism), and spiritualism or spiritism.

There are, however, other magical groups that have a more problematic relationship with contemporary Witchcraft. Chief among these is organized Satanism. With few exceptions, contemporary Witches view themselves as endorsing a totally different religion: Satanists worship the Christian devil, whereas Neopagan Witches follow a nature religion. From the Wiccan perspective, the only association between Neopagans and Satanists is that they have been mistakenly grouped together by conservative Christians, who tend to view all non-Christian organizations as inspired by the devil.

While Satanism is distinct—and should be clearly distinguished—from Neopaganism, it is nevertheless true that contemporary Witchcraft and organized Satanism have been influenced by the same tradition of ceremonial magic. As a consequence, both movements utilize roughly comparable magic rituals. Further, they express similar interests in divination, psychic phenomena, and other topics.

Another group of magical religions are African-heritage syncretisms, such as Santeria and Vodun ("Voodoo"), currently active in the Americas. While these traditions developed independently of the Western occult tradition, there are certain parallels between modern Neopaganism and these syncretistic movements, such as the invocation of spiritual powers and the working of magic.

There is also a recent trend for Neopagans to draw information, if not actually seek initiation, in African-heritage groups. Thus white Americans as well as black Americans have found their way to Santeria, Vodun, and related religions. While there are still relatively few white initiates in these religions, it is likely that there will be more as the religion becomes better known and spreads further beyond its immigrant roots.

Neopagan interest in African-heritage traditions is reflected in a relatively recent issue (July/August 1996) of *The Green Egg*, widely acknowledged as the premier Neopagan magazine in North America, that was devoted to "African Diaspora Religion." Thus it seems likely that we will soon see elements of such traditions incorporated into modern Neopaganism. In terms of a presence in the United States, the largest of these traditions are Vodun and Santeria.

Vodun ("Voodoo") is a magical religion that originated in Haiti in the late 1700s. The precursor of Vodun was the religion of the Fon people of West Africa who were brought as slaves to Haiti. *Vodun* (or *vodou*) means "spirit" in the Fon language. In Haiti, the Fon system of veneration of the spirits came in contact with other African religious traditions and French Catholicism, to produce what we call Vodun. It has spread via emigration to New Orleans and major cities in the United States, most notably New York City.

Santeria is a magical religion that originated among the Yoruba people of West Africa. In the early nineteenth century, the Yoruba were enslaved in great numbers and taken to Cuba and Brazil, where they were able to form Yoruba-speaking communities. Yoruba Priests and Priestesses created new lineages of initiates dedicated to the Yoruba spirits, called *orishas*. Translated into Spanish, *orishas* are *santos* (literally, "saints"). This led the people to call the Yoruba traditions in Cuba *santeria*, "the way of the saints." Since the Cuban revolution of 1959, over one million Cubans have come to the United States, many of them Priests and Priestesses of Santeria.

Yet other traditional magical systems are represented by the umbrella term *Shamanism*. Shamans are the religious specialists of hunting and gathering cultures. They are particularly associated with the aboriginal peoples of Central Asia and the Americas and are perhaps most familiar to us as the "medicine men" of traditional Native American cultures. Contemporary Neopagan Witches often associate themselves with shamanism, identifying contemporary Witchcraft as the lineal descendant of pre-Christian European Shamans.

Within the past decade or so, Shamanism has become somewhat of a fad in the West's occult-metaphysical subculture due to the recent development of interest in American Indian religions. While there is a long tradition romanticizing Native Americans and their spiritual traditions, Euroamericans had rarely been prompted to engage in actual Indian religious practices. This changed in the 1960s, when certain groups of counterculturists made an effort to adopt what they conceived of as "tribal" lifestyles. In the late 1980s, the occult-metaphysical subculture began to focus attention on the Native American religion when Shamanism—and, more particularly, the phenomenon that has come to be known as "Neoshamanism"—became popular.

Witchcraft Today

A

Abramelin

Abramelin was a fifteenth-century German Jew who created a body of magical works that influenced magicians for centuries. Abramelin claimed to have obtained his knowledge of magic from angels. He was an expert on the Cabala, which served as the basis for his system of magic.

The central principle of Abramelin magic is that the material world is the creation of evil spirits who work under the direction of angels. Abramelin claimed that every human has an angel and a demon that attends him or her. Abramelin magic dispensed with much of the complicated paraphernalia and ceremonies of European ritual magic and concentrated on the practitioner, who would acquaint himself with his Guardian Angel after which the magician would use spirits and demons as his private servants.

Abramelin's magic was contained in his three-volume work, *The Sacred Magic of Abramelin the Mage,* which was originally written in Hebrew in 1458. The book contains a large number of magic squares that are used to accomplish invisibility, the power of flight, command of spirits, necromancy (conjuring up the spirits of the dead), and shapeshifting. *The Sacred Magic of Abramelin the Mage* was translated into French in the eighteenth century and was translated into English at the turn of the twentieth century by S. L. MacGregor Mathers, one of the original members of the Hermetic Order of the Golden Dawn. The English translation strongly influenced Aleister Crowley, who, through Crowley's influence on Gerald Gardner, in turn influenced contemporary Neopagan Witchcraft.

See Also: Cabala; Mathers, Samuel Liddell
Further Reading
Mathers, S. L. MacGregor. *The Book of the Sacred Magic of Abra-Melin the Mage.* Wellingborough, Northamptonshire, U.K.: Aquarian Press, 1976.

Adept

In everyday language, to be adept means "to be skilled at—and knowledgeable of—one's craft." By extension, an *adept* is a person who is a master of her or his craft. In the specialized terminology of esotericism, an Adept is an individual who is considered highly proficient in a particular body of occult knowledge and, especially, certain occult practices. Among Neopagan Witches, an Adept is someone who, by virtue of her or his accomplishments and study, has mastered a particular magical system. It should be noted that someone can be adept at one magical system but a novice in other systems.

Further Reading

Matthews, Caitlín, and John Matthews. *The Western Way: A Practical Guide to the Western Mystery Tradition*. London: Arkana, 1994.

African Religions

Africa is one of the few remaining large-scale regions where, despite a colonial history and the growing presence of such "world-historical" religions as Islam and Christianity, indigenous pagan religious beliefs and practices have maintained their place in the lives of a substantial portion of the population. One estimate has placed the number of Christian converts in tropical and southern Africa at 160 million and the number of Muslim converts at 130 million. This leaves approximately one-third of the sub-Saharan population in the indigenous religions category, with a small percentage relegated to "other religions." It must be emphasized that conversion to either Islam or Christianity does not necessarily mean a sudden expunging of all former traditions and beliefs. A large percentage of Christian converts in Africa have assimilated indigenous beliefs and practices with Christian beliefs and practices, often with little practical change in orientation.

Traditional societies such as those in Africa do not depend on written accounts or sacred texts for the transmittal of rituals and beliefs, but rely on elders, or particular authoritative persons, to pass on the worldviews from one generation to the next. The communities of belief so formed are small-scale, usually related to particular ethnic populations. Thus within any one political region there may be represented dozens or even hundreds of different religious traditions, along with different linguistic and cultural histories. Traditional societies are oriented around either hunting and gathering or agriculture, and these two pursuits in turn influence the shape of the societies' cultures, including religious beliefs. Anthropologists have noted that agricultural societies tend to have ancestor cults with a fairly developed conception of an afterlife, and hunting-and-gathering societies tend not to have ancestor cults, nor do they give much recognition to afterlife beliefs. Although the beliefs and practices of traditional societies are seldom acknowledged in contemporary (and relatively recent) industrial/technological societies, it is instructive to remember that over 99 percent of human cultural history has been lived within the context of such small-scale, traditional groupings.

The indigenous religions of Africa, though modified by colonial and postcolonial experience, continue to exist alongside Christianity and Islam.

A Baoule Priestess covers herself in kaolin for the Festival of the Yam. (Corbis/Marc Garanger)

These indigenous religions are closely tied to ethnic groups, although there are many similarities among the religious beliefs of groups that share major cultural and linguistic areas. A number of characteristics are common to almost all African religions and constitute a distinct African pattern of religious belief and practice.

The notion of the imperfect nature of the human condition is common to almost all African religions, which usually have a creation myth about the origin of human life and the origin of death. This myth generally will claim that the ancestors of the religious group were once immortal. However, because of an accident or an act of disobedience—usually committed by a woman (as for the Dinka of southern Sudan, and the Nuer, who live near the Dinka, as well as the Ganda of central Uganda) or an animal—this situation ended, and humanity passed into a state of mortality. However, the myths assert, human problems may be alleviated through ritual action, although there is no promise of personal salvation in the afterlife. African religions are characterized by their promise of a form of salvation in *this* world (as opposed to salvation that is granted in an afterlife), and are given to the assumption that human beings are generally responsible for their misfortunes and that they possess the means to overcome those misfortunes.

The sources of human suffering, as well as of social illness, lie in humanity's misdeeds and in social conflicts and tensions that can be cured through the consultation of a Priest who can identify the problem and prescribe a solution. Traditional moral and social values represent the guidelines for the good life and are emphasized in ritual religious performances in order to renew commitment to them.

Both monotheistic and polytheistic principles are contained in African religions, which, in turn, combine principles of unity and multiplicity, as well as transcendence (beyond the world as we ordinarily experience it) and immanence (within the everyday world), into a single system.

The concept of an impersonal power by which all things are created is typical of certain African traditions, as among the Yoruba. However, many traditions believe in supreme gods who are like kings who reign but do not rule, and who are rarely seen or heard. As their ultimate underlying principle, supreme gods usually have no cult, images, temples, or priesthood. Supreme gods usually belong to the dimension of myth, although the real world would cease to exist without them. Supreme gods have tended to be viewed as corresponding to the concept of God in Christianity and Islam since the time when African societies first came into contact with Muslims and Christians. These gods are often associated with elements of nature, though, and the most common form of encounter with them is said to be spirit possession— the temporary presence of a deity or spirit in the consciousness of a person. "Possession" behavior is culturally stylized and highly symbolic.

On the other hand, the lesser gods and ancestor spirits are constantly involved in the daily affairs of the society and are highly visible through shrines, images, and priesthood. Their powers are immanent, and their relation to human beings is reciprocal and interdependent. Believers usually make offerings to them in the form of animal sacrifice, which is especially powerful as it is believed that the life of the victim and its blood are potent spiritual forces.

A number of African deities are believed to have been heroes who died and returned in spiritual form to serve as guardians and protectors of people. While ordinary people become ghosts after death, only those who led families and communities in the past as founders, elders, chiefs, or kings may become "ancestors" and serve in the afterlife as social and political guides of the future. Almost every African family and village has its ancestor shrines. The ancestors are believed to have helped create and protect the world, and their deeds represent the foundations of African myth, history, and culture. They are regarded as immortal spirits who transcend historical time.

In African religions, the individual is seen as a composite of social, moral, and physical elements, and a person's life is seen to pass through several stages—birth, puberty, marriage, elderhood, death, and ancestorhood—each stage having its own particular duties. Rites of passage ensure that people know their responsibilities and maintain important traditional offices, such as kingship, chieftaincy, and priesthood.

Rites of passage generally consist of rites of separation, transition, and reincorporation, with the purpose of creating or maintaining fixed and meaningful transformations in the life cycle, in the ecological and temporal cycle, and in the accession of persons to high office. During these ceremonies people are "remade" into new social beings—seasonal transitions are also marked and celebrated in this way—when the old is symbolically destroyed and the new is created. The most important rite of passage is the initiation of the young into adulthood, in which a youth is moved into new social roles, and his or her moral and mental dispositions are molded toward the world, a process formally known as socialization. Some form of bodily marking is usually involved, such as circumcision. The marks' significance may vary, although they usually mean that the transition to adulthood is permanent and painful and that society has successfully imprinted itself upon the individual.

Diviners, prophets, priests, and sacred kings serve as communication links between the human world and the sacred world. Diviners and mediums are usually spiritual consultants, whereas prophets are leaders of the people who may go directly to the community with programs of action and can organize religious and political movements. Sometimes priestly mediums may develop prophetic powers, as during colonial times when traditional prophets became leaders of political resistance in parts of Sudan, Uganda, Tanzania, Zimbabwe, and Kenya.

In these African belief systems, another form of communication with the spirit world involves the use of divination tools, which are manipulated and interrogated by the diviner to reach a diagnosis of human problems. The most complex system of divination, Ifa, consists of a large number of poems that are related to a set of 256 divination patterns. When one of the patterns is cast, the diviner recites the appropriate poem. This is practiced by the Yoruba of southern Nigeria; by the Igbo, Igala, and Nupe of Nigeria; and by the Ewe of Togo and the Fon of Benin.

A number of illnesses, including cases of infertility, stomach disorders, and a variety of psychological disorders, are viewed as uniquely African in nature, and therefore as untreatable by Western methods. The methods of treatment for these maladies employed by diviners and mediums usually involve a mixture of psychological, social, medical, and ritual means. Although Western medicine is used for the treatment of infectious diseases, ritual techniques continue to be used in both rural and urban areas of Africa as methods of treatment today.

The forms of Christianity found in African societies generally are characterized by rituals that aim to address the physical and spiritual ills of society. Islamic tradition has been adapted in Africa along similar lines. Africa has given birth to innumerable new religions, most of which represent syncretisms (combinations) of Christianity or Islam and indigenous beliefs. Few of these have been imported directly into the United States in ways that make them visible on the religious landscape. There is, however, a marked African component in such Caribbean traditions as Santeria, a significant religious tradition in certain areas of the country.

See Also: Candomblé; Ifa; Macumba; Orishas; Santeria; Vodun
Further Reading
Adefunmi, Baba Oseijeman. *Ancestors of the Afro-Americans*. Long Island City, NY: Aims of Modzawe, 1973.

Adefunmi I, Oba Efuntola Oseijeman Adelabu. *Olorisha, A Guidebook into Yoruba Religion*. Sheldon, SC: n.p., 1982.

Keizer, Lewis S. *Initiation: Ancient and Modern*. San Francisco, CA: St. Thomas Press, 1981.

Murphy, Joseph M. "Santeria and Vodou in the United States." In *America's Alternative Religions*. Ed. Timothy Miller. Albany, NY: State University of New York Press, 1995.

Odunfonda I, Adaramila. *Obatala, The Yoruba God of Creation*. Sheldon, SC: Great Benin Books, n.d.

Air

Air is one of the four classical elements of nature that form the basis for all life. Along with fire, it is considered to be a male element. In antiquity air was thought to be the essence of the soul. Ghosts were felt to be of the same substance as air. Thus they were invisible, but their presence could be felt like the wind. It also was believed that in death the soul departed the living body with the body's last breath and entered the surrounding air. Some items associated with air are the cardinal direction east, intellect, energy, endeavor, sociability, squandering, frivolity, the color yellow, the metal silver, the wand (the Witches' tool), and the wand that represents one of the Tarot card suits.

See Also: Earth; Fire; Sylphs; Wand; Water
Further Reading
Cirlot, J. E. *A Dictionary of Symbols*. New York: Dorset Press, 1991.
Heisler, Roger. *Path to Power*. York Beach, ME: Weiser, 1990.

Alexandrian Tradition

The Alexandrian Tradition is, in terms of ritual, a minor variant on Gardnerian Witchcraft, although its adherents now far outnumber orthodox Gardnerians. The tradition began in 1963 in England, when Alexander Sanders, who was initiated into Gardnerian Wicca by Pat Kopanski, an initiate of Patricia Crowther, was allowed to copy her Book of Shadows (a manual defining rituals to be performed). As soon as Gerald Gardner died, Sanders claimed that he had been initiated as a Witch at age nine by his grandmother and had received the Book of Shadows from her. Sanders attracted a substantial following, and Alexandrian Witches make up one of the largest subgroups in the Neopagan Witchcraft movement.

One of the first Americans to travel to England to become initiated as an Alexandrian Witch was Jim B. of Boston, who founded the coven Du Bandia Grasail and began teaching the Craft there in 1970. Jim B., a trained historian, also studied some of the issues associated with Craft history in the early 1970s, and soon arrived at the conclusion that the Craft had been constructed entirely from literary and social materials available in the 1940s and 1950s—which, of course, was not commonly thought. Feeling betrayed and uncomfortable at having passed on false information about the origins of the Craft to his coveners, he closed the coven in 1974. He lectured publicly on the subject in the 1970s, causing much controversy. The members of Du Bandia Grasail then dispersed into several successor organizations.

Another early Alexandrian in America was Mary Nesnick, who began her Craft career in Lady Theos's Gardnerian Long Island coven, until she grew dissatisfied with their approach. She wrote to Sanders in England and asked if she could transfer her allegiance from the Gardnerian Tradition of Witchcraft to the Alexandrian Tradition. He agreed and conferred on her the title of "Grand High Priestess of the Americas." She received her Alexandrian training from Patrick Sumner, who traveled to America on occasion. An energetic woman, Nesnick immediately set about to expand and regularize the Alexandrian groups in America. Nesnick created what she called the "Algard Tradition," blending Alexandrian and Gardnerian practices. One of her more prominent initiates was Roy Dymond of Toronto, whose High Priestess, Lady Arianrhod, in turn initiated Charles Arnold, who was responsible for the official recognition of Wicca as a religion from the Canadian government.

Another important Alexandrian initiation arranged by Nesnick was that of Lady Ayeisha (Carolyn K.) of Baltimore, worked by Jim B., Roy Dymond, Lady Morgana (Ayeisha's mother), and several others in Boston on September 18, 1971. Lady Ayeisha went on to become the first High Priestess of KAM, Keepers of the Ancient Mysteries, created by the Elders of several Witchcraft traditions in Maryland. Nesnick fell into obscurity in the late 1970s.

See Also: Introduction

Further Reading

Farrar, Stewart. *What Witches Do: The Modern Coven Revealed.* New York: Coward McCann, 1971.

Johns, June. *King of the Witches: The World of Alex Sanders.* New York: Coward McCann, 1969.

American Tradition

The American Tradition was created in about 1971 by the founders of the Pagan Way to serve as a form of Wicca that was not as restricted by oaths of secrecy as the Gardnerian covens had become. They hoped that this new tradition would allow more people to become Witches than could possibly be accommodated by the extant Gardnerian covens, with their strict rules on how long candidates for admission had to remain in training. The major founders—Ed Fitch, Thomas Giles, and Joe Wilson—combined knowledge from their various traditions and created new rituals to replace those that had been previously bound by oath. A major influence on the work was the *Grimoire of the Shadows* that Fitch had written while stationed by the military in Thailand in the 1960s.

American Tradition covens are scattered about the United States, although they have never been numerous. A continual process of creation takes place as groups splinter off the American Tradition covens to create their own covens. One of these is called the Moseyin' Tradition.

One notable Witch of the American Tradition is Lady Dana Corby, who was originally initiated in 1975 and trained by Bran and Moria at Corax Covenstead in La Verne, California. Corby was a coeditor of *The Crystal Well*, a member of the working committee that created the Covenant of the Goddess (a networking group), and a member of the group who helped record Gwydion Pendderwen's first album, *Songs for the Old Religion,* on which she wrote and sang the *Hymn to the Sun God.*

After living in Boise, Idaho, for some years, Corby moved to the Seattle area, where she founded a small publishing company, Rantin' Raven Pamphleteers. Her American Tradition students are scattered across the United States, from California to Wisconsin.

See Also: Pagan Way
Further Reading
Corby, Dana. *What Is Wicca: An Overview.* Seattle, WA: Rantin' Raven
    Pamphleteers, 1998 [1992].

Amulet

The word *amulet* is derived from the Latin *amuletum,* the name for the cyclamen plant, which was planted near homes in ancient Italy in the belief that its magical influence prevented any poisonous drug from having the power to harm. Amber was called *amuletum* also, because it was believed to avert evil influence and infection. Some sources state that the word *amulet* is derived from the Latin *amolior,* meaning "to repel or drive away."

An amulet is something typically worn, often around the neck, as protection from injury or evil. They may also appear on homes, tombs, and buildings. The use of amulets dates back to the earliest cave dwellers, who kept natural objects with unusual shapes or colors to protect themselves. Amulets were crafted into animal shapes and, later, into symbolic shapes. Ancient Pagans wore figurines of their gods as amulets. This practice continues today in the Catholic Church and other religious traditions.

The ancient Egyptians used amulets everywhere. The frog was a symbol of genesis and reproduction because of its metamorphosis from egg to tadpole to four-legged creature. Therefore, amulets in the shape of frogs protected fertility. The looped cross known as the Ankh was the symbol of everlasting life and generation for Egyptians and is often worn as jewelry by contemporary Neopagans, Witches, and occultists.

This amulet is traditionally used for success in business matters. (Dover Pictorial Archive Series)

Amulets in the shape of an eye protected good health and comfort and warded off evil. The Udjat-eye, the characteristic stylization of the eye of the youthful Egyptian Sun God Horus, was used on pottery, rings, and other amulets to ward off the forces of darkness. Eyes protect against evil spirits and are found on tombs, walls, utensils, and jewelry. The scarab beetle symbolized resurrection after death and protection against evil magic and so was placed on the breasts of mummies, known as "heart scarabs." Scarab amulets also appeared as seals and jeweled charms to protect wearers against evil.

The Assyrians (2500–612 B.C.) used cylindrical seals embedded with semiprecious and precious stones, each with its own magical power. Other common Assyrian amulets were made in the form of the ram to protect virility and the bull to guard virility and strength. As early as 2200 B.C., Hebrews wore crescent moons to ward off the "evil eye" and attached bells to their clothing to ward off evil spirits. An ancient form of the modern-day charm bracelet originated in Greece between 1600 and 323 B.C.

Phoenicians (1200–332 B.C.) imitated the Egyptian scarabs and fashioned them out of hard semiprecious stones like jasper and quartz. From 800 to 400 B.C. the Etruscans also crafted scarabs and traded them in all Mediterranean markets and as far away as the Crimean Peninsula.

In ancient Rome (753 B.C.–A.D. 476) bronze figures of hands stood in houses to ward off evil, placed as though the hand was instinctively raised in front of a face to ward off approaching evil. Interestingly, the position of the fingers on these pre-Christian amulets is the same as that used today for a Christian blessing, with the thumb and first two fingers upright and the other two fingers closed. A popular amulet of Islamic peoples beginning

The Udjat Eye, also called the Eye of Horus, is worn as an amulet of health and protection against evil. (Dover Pictorial Archive Series)

in the sixth century A.D. was the "Hand of Fatima," frequently made of silver and set with semiprecious stones. This amulet was named after the daughter of the prophet Mohammed. Hands were also used as amulets on gates of Islamic buildings.

Arabians gathered dust from tombs and carried it in little sacks as protection against evil. They would wear pieces of paper on which prayers, spells, magical names, or the attributes of God—"the compassionate" or "the forgiver"—had been written. Indeed, pieces of parchment with scripture quotes, carried in boxes or pouches, are amulets in various religions and holy books of every culture (the Koran, Torah, and Bible) and are generally considered to have protective powers.

Peoples of the west coast of Africa carried amulets that were sometimes referred to as fetishes or gris-gris. Some were wooden dolls that were supposed to represent and be possessed by spirits. Others consisted of a pouch or box of herbs, teeth, hair, bones, or stones that had medicinal properties. They were often worn as ornaments or were carried on the body. Wearers believed that these fetishes contained a spirit that would help them obtain their desires or protect them from injury. Fetishes and gris-gris were brought to the New World by slaves. Possession of a fetish by a slave was punishable by torture or death because it was regarded by slave-owners as a graven image of a foreign god and represented tribal ways that were feared by Europeans. Gris-gris are ritually made at an altar and are consecrated with the four elements: earth, air, water, and fire. The number of ingredients used in the creation of gris-gris even has meaning—always one, three, five, seven, nine, or thirteen. Fetishes and gris-gris are still made today for such purposes as attracting money or love, stopping gossip, protecting the home, or maintaining good health.

Amulets with inscriptions are sometimes called charms, a term that also applies to spoken incantations. "YHWH," the Hebrew name for God, appeared on many amulets and talismans in different spellings to help magicians conjure demons and protect them from attack by the spirits. The "Sator square" consists of magical words arranged in the pattern of a square:

S	A	T	O	R
A	R	E	P	O
T	E	N	E	T
O	P	E	R	A
R	O	T	A	S

This square was inscribed on walls and vessels in Rome from as early as 753 B.C. until A.D. 476 and was considered to be protection from sorcery, poisonous air, colic, and pestilence and was even used to protect cow's milk from Witchcraft. Similarly, circles inscribed with the names of God were used in England as recently as 1860 to repel demons. The phallic symbol, often represented by a horn, was supposed to protect against evil just as wearing an amulet shaped as an eye would.

The hand as an amulet is an idea that has carried forward to the present day. Hand gestures have long been used to ward off the evil eye. Two of the best-known gestures for doing this are "making horns" (*mano cornuta*), in which the index and little finger are extended with the other two fingers and the thumb folded into the palm; and the *mano in fica* or "the fig," a symbol of female genitals, in which the hand is in a fist with the thumb protruding between the first and second fingers. Crystal amulets set in gold of a hand in the sign of the fig were made in southern Germany circa 1680.

Knots are another symbol traditionally believed to repel the evil eye. Knots have long been tied in garments to ward off evil, and such knots are also found in carvings and metalwork. In Europe nurses wore elaborately patterned silver buckles on their belts because unexplainable illnesses were typically blamed on the "evil eye." The elaborate rope-like interlacings and patterns of Celtic and Saxon decorative art probably arose from their ancient use in warding off the spirits.

"Witch balls" are bright, reflective balls of glass that can be found today hanging in antique shops. Their purpose was to ward off spirits by reflecting the evil back to its own source. It was believed that the glass ball would attract and hold all the influences of ill luck that would otherwise have fallen upon the household.

Early Christians continued to use many of the amulets of their ancestors. The eye surrounded by sunbeams or inside a triangle with its apex pointing upward was a symbol of divine omnipresence or of the trinity. The scarab found favor among early Christians as a symbol for the resurrection. The medieval Catholic Church promoted the use of numerous holy charms, including rosaries and holy relics. The most common charm was the Agnus Dei, a small cake of wax originally made out of Passover candles, bearing images of a lamb and a flag. When blessed by the Pope, the Agnus Dei protected the wearer against attacks by the devil, thunder, lightning, fire, drowning, death in childbirth, and other dangers. In the seventeenth century, rosaries were blessed as amulets against fire, tempest, fever, and evil spirits.

The idea that a charm needed to be consecrated in order to be effective stemmed from the belief that a charm given as a gift was more potent than if it was kept for oneself. The goodwill behind the gift, in a sense, consecrated the charm. Bells have long been used as amulets to protect children, horses, camels, cows, asses, and other important animals. Shopkeepers hung bells over their thresholds to keep evil spirits from entering the premises.

Plants can also act as amulets. Garlic, of course, is used by some to ward off vampires. But garlands of garlic worn around the neck or hung in a house are also said to ward off evil spirits, creatures, and spells. In Mexico, the *ajo macho* is a huge garlic bulb, sometimes as big as a baseball, used exclusively as an amulet against evil in general, but not against specific curses. According to custom, the *ajo macho* will work only if it is given as a gift, not if it is purchased. Ancient Roman soldiers wore garlic into battle for extra courage. In ancient Greece and Rome, garlic was placed at crossroads as an offering to

Hecate, the Goddess of Witchcraft and the night. Odysseus used garlic as protection against the Witchcraft of Circe, who turned his men into swine.

In Neopagan Witchcraft, the most powerful amulet, sometimes seen on rings, is the silver pentacle, a five-pointed star with a single point upright. Silver itself is considered to have the properties of an amulet and is used in jewelry along with various crystals and gems.

A Witch who wishes to give someone an amulet will choose some small object that is unusual and will make a strong impression on the recipient. The Witch then "charms" the object with some ceremony or formula of words and, when the gift is given, will ask the recipient to keep it a secret. The belief in amulets can be explained with practical psychology. People often develop negative mind-sets that doom them to failure. Acquiring an amulet can restore their self-confidence and change their "luck."

Amulets differ from talismans in that they passively protect their wearer from evil and harm. They are *protection* devices. Talismans, on the other hand, possess magical, or supernatural, powers of their own and transmit them to the owner. A talisman will attract some benefit to its possessor, whereas the amulet only acts as a shield to repel harm. Many ancient magical symbols are regarded today as both amulets and talismans, able to attract good fortune as well as repel bad luck. Examples of these are the swastika, the Ankh, the five-pointed star or pentagram, and the six-pointed star or Solomon's seal.

See Also: Charms; Fetish; Gris-gris; Horseshoe; Pentagram; Rings; Seal of Solomon; Talismans

Further Reading

Lockhart, J. G. *Curses, Lucks, and Talismans*. Detroit, MI: Single Tree Press, 1971 [1938].

RavenWolf, Silver. *To Ride a Silver Broomstick: New Generation Witchcraft*. St. Paul, MN: Llewellyn, 1996.

Ancient and Mystical Order of the Rosae Crucis (AMORC)

The Ancient and Mystical Order of the Rosae Crucis is an esoteric fraternal movement founded in 1915 in New York by young occultist H. Spencer Lewis (1883–1939). Lewis, who had been affiliated with a number of British occult orders, such as the Ordo Templi Orientis, and had met Aleister Crowley, attempted to establish the Rosicrucian Order in 1909, when he met French members of the International Rosicrucian Council in Toulouse. After being initiated into the Rosicrucian Council, he went back to the United States, where he began to hold meetings with people interested in occult teachings. After a few years of massive publicity efforts, the Order was firmly established.

Soon a number of conflicts emerged between the AMORC and other Rosicrucian bodies. In 1928, the older Fraternitas Rosae Crucis criticized the

AMORC's right to the designation "Rosicrucian." At the same time, Lewis accused alternative healer R. Swinburne Clymer of fraudulent behavior. An intense polemic between the groups has continued to the present day.

Rosicrucians focus their teachings on God's purpose for life and believe that God created the universe according to immutable laws. Mastership, which is the ability to transform into material expression one's mental images, can lead one to success. Various techniques are taught to students to help them achieve such mastery. Students visualize health, wealth, and happiness, and then draw these characteristics to themselves. After completing a first series of lessons, students may strive for more advanced mastery over their own lives. Particular lodges, chapters, or pronaoi (groups) are designated for Rosicrucian group activities.

The AMORC presents itself as a continuation of the ancient mystery schools of Amenhotep and Solomon. Isaac Newton, René Descartes, Benjamin Franklin, and Francis Bacon are listed in AMORC literature as famous Rosicrucians. According to AMORC literature the cycles of the fraternity's work last 180 years. After a period of silence and secrecy, members generally emerge and do their work in public. It is said that a new public cycle began in 1909.

The organization of the AMORC includes the Grand Lodge, which has jurisdiction over America, the British Commonwealth, France, Germany, Switzerland, Sweden, and Africa. The head of the Order is represented by the Grand Imperator. Ralph M. Lewis (1904–1987) succeeded his father, Spencer, in this post from 1939 to 1987. At his death, Gary L. Stewart became Grand Imperator, but he was removed from office three years later, accused of fraudulent behavior. He was succeeded by Christian Bernard, who is currently Grand Imperator. Members of the Order may be found in 85 countries around the world. The *Rosicrucian Digest*, published in San Jose, California, is the periodical of the movement.

Further Reading

Lewis, James R. *The Encyclopedia of Cults, Sects, and New Religions*. Amherst, NY: Prometheus Books, 1998.

Melton, J. Gordon. *Encyclopedia of American Religions*, 5th ed. Detroit, MI: Gale Research Inc., 1996.

Ankh

The ancient Egyptians used many different amulets, including the looped cross known as the Ankh. The Ankh was the symbol of everlasting life and regeneration. It represented the union of the male principle (the staff) and the female principle (the loop). In ancient Egyptian art, the Ankh was carried like a scepter in the right hand of deities and was held up to the nostrils of the dead in order to bring them back to life. Ankh amulets also graced tombstones to guard the eternal life of the deceased. Ankh amulets were made of faience, semiprecious and precious stones, wax, metal, and wood. Today the Ankh is worn as jewelry by many Neopagans, Witches, and occultists.

See Also: Amulet; Jewelry and Degrees of Initiation
Further Reading
Barrett, Clive. *Egyptian Gods and Goddesses: The Mythology and Beliefs of Ancient Egypt.* Wellingborough, Northampshire, U.K.: Aquarian Press, 1991.

Anointing Oil

Oils have long been an important element in religious and magical rituals. Magicians in ancient Egypt rubbed oils on their bodies and various oils were used in the mummification process. Catholic ministers use oil in the Ointment of the Sick sacrament. And oils are common in Vodun and Santeria ceremonies.

Pure or aroma-infused oils have a variety of functions in Neopagan rituals. Herbs and essences are added to olive or other vegetable oils and Witches rub oil on parts of their bodies, on effigies, on candles, and on tools, and use them to perfume the air during rituals. The preparation of oils is a ritual in itself and is done for a variety of purposes. After the preparation, several days are required for the mixture to acquire the desired power. Olive oil preparations containing either lemon, rose, or gardenia are said to favor good health. Mixtures also exist that fight sickness and negative influences in general.

See Also: Flying; Ointments
Further Reading
Chevalier, Jean, and Alain Gheerbrant. *The Penguin Dictionary of Symbols.* London: Penguin, 1996.
Shepard, Leslie A., ed. *Encyclopedia of Occultism and Parapsychology.* Detroit, MI: Gale Research Inc., 1991.

Aradia

Aradia is the heroine of "Witches Gospel" given to Charles Godfrey Leland by a Witch named Maddelena and published by him (actually, by Charles Scribner and Sons) as *Aradia: The Gospel of the Witches of Tuscany* in 1897. The text of the actual gospel, which is quite brief, begins with a creation myth in which Diana and Apollo are the female and male polarities by which all things—including human beings—are created. Aradia is the daughter engendered by their passion. The central passage of the gospel begins when Diana sends Aradia to Earth to liberate humanity from oppression by teaching them Witchcraft. Aradia's activities and teachings bear a certain resemblance to those of Jesus, but, because of archetypical patterns, this would be so whether they were historical or mythical. She ends her ministry on Earth

The title page of the original edition of Charles Leland's Aradia, *a source document for modern witchcraft. (Leland Charles,* Aradia, *1899)*

with a sermon, or Charge, to her followers about how to practice Witchcraft, and then she returns to her mother in Heaven, from where she grants powers to Witches who pray to her. The gospel concludes with a collection of folk-magic techniques.

There has been some controversy about the authenticity of the gospel. Many have suggested that Maddelena manufactured the whole thing, and some feel that Leland forged the document. In addition, although most scholars assume that the character Aradia is a version of the biblical Herodias, Carlo Ginzburg has reported the discovery of Celtic inscriptions in Italy dedicated to a Goddess Hera Dea. Hence, although it still seems improbable, the raw materials used by Leland or Maddelena, or whomever else, may have preserved some extant traditions.

The specific relevance of the *Aradia* to current Neopagan Witchcraft is, first, that it appears to present a Witchcraft tradition that predates Gerald Gardner—although the situation is confused by the fact that Aradia's longest sermon became a source for the "Charge of the Goddess" composed by Gardner and then was rewritten by Doreen Valiente into its current form. Second, the Aradian Tradition asserts that Aradia was, in fact, an actual person who preached in Italy in the fourteenth century and whose teachings were preserved and brought to America after World War II.

See Also: "Charge of the Goddess"; Diana
Further Reading
Grimassi, Raven. *The Teachings of the Holy Strega*, 2d ed. Escondido, CA: Moon Dragon Publications, 1991.
———. *Whispers: Teachings of the Old Religion of Italy; An Introduction to the Aradian Tradition*, 2d ed. Escondido, CA: Moon Dragon Publications, 1991.
Leland, Charles Godfrey. *Aradia: The Gospel of the Witches of Tuscany*. Buckland Museum, 1964 [New York: Scribner's, 1897].

Asatru

The Icelandic term *Asatru* means "belief in the Aesir," one of two branches of Norse deities—the race of sky gods, including Odin and his wife, Frigga; Thor; Loki; Balder; and others. The other branch of Norse deities is called the Vanir, the elemental gods concerned with earth, agriculture, fertility, and the cycle of death and rebirth. Unlike Odinism (which recognizes only Aesir), Asatruers, who reportedly existed long before the appearance of an organized Asatru community, embrace belief in both Odin and the Vanir, and in a host of lesser *wights*—"beings."

The American Asatru community, the precise size of which is difficult if not impossible to ascertain, is generally divided into four primary categories: 1) members of the Asatru Alliance, 2) members of the Ring of Troth, 3) members of independent groups, and 4) unaffiliated individual adherents. Asatru is overwhelmingly white, male, and relatively young. The occupations pursued by Asatruers tend to reflect a mix of blue- and white-collar professions. Most hold at least a B.A. degree, and many return to school in order to obtain training in other languages or knowledge relevant to Asatru.

Asatru groups sprang up in at least three countries in about the same period. The Viking Brotherhood, the first American Asatru organization, was founded in 1972 by Stephen A. McNallen, then a student at Midwestern University in Wichita Falls, Texas. McNallen, who had been a follower of the Norse deities for several years, began to publish *The Runestone,* a quarterly periodical, and, shortly after forming the Viking Brotherhood, he went into the army, serving as an officer with NATO in Europe. After returning to civilian life in 1976, he began to perfect the ritual and doctrine of the brotherhood that was renamed Asatru Free Assembly (AFA).

The organization, whose purpose was to promote and practice the Norse religion as it was epitomized during the Viking Age, lauded the primary values of freedom and individuality, sacrifice, pride, family, and individual and collective heroism. It rejected Christianity as well as all collective ideologies, including fascism. While worship was regarded as a contradiction of the spirit of the Viking religion, AFA basic rituals were designed to celebrate particular events, such as initiations, name-givings, and burials, and to recognize the gods.

Among AFA celebrations were Yule (December 22); Ragnar's Day (March 28) in commemoration of Viking Ragnar Lodbrok, who sailed up the Seine River in A.D. 845 and sacked Paris, France; Lindisfarne Day (June 8); and Midsummer Day (summer solstice). One of the major gatherings for this group was the Althing, a national assembly of kindreds gathered for religious ceremony, competitive games, and discussion of organizational policies. In November 1987, the assembly was disbanded due to a failure to reorganize, and publication of its periodical was discontinued. Among the factors that destabilized the AFA was the presence of racist and National Socialist adherents at the Althings, who could not be ignored. Two very different organizations succeeded the Asatru Free Assembly: the Asatru Alliance and the Ring of Troth.

The Asatru Alliance emerged quickly thanks largely to the energy of Mike Murray and to the resources of the Arizona Kindred, centered in Payson, Arizona, who control the organization. The Alliance is generally described as a free association of kindreds and individuals organized along tribal and/or democratic lines. It has no established priesthood and is composed of a majority of racial kindreds, although members are determined to keep the Alliance nonpolitical.

The Ring of Troth, on the other hand, was formed by Edred Thorsson on December 20, 1987, almost contemporaneously with the Asatru Alliance. Thorsson had previously developed a specialized organization, the Rune Gild, which today functions primarily through the mails with the purpose of spreading knowledge of the religious, magical, and divinatory aspects of the Futhark, or runic alphabets. However, the Ring of Troth is not primarily magical in nature and it aims to function as a religious institution within which reconstruction of the Norse/Germanic religious heritage can be accomplished in a relatively short time and as a fully "modern" religion. Thorsson's *A Book of Troth* (1992) is the official basic document of the Ring of Troth organization.

See Also: Norse Neopagans; Odinists; Runes

Further Reading

Hundingsbani, Heigi. *The Religion of Odin: A Handbook*. Red Wing, MN: Viking House, 1978.

Lewis, James R., ed. *Magical Religion and Modern Witchcraft*. Albany, NY: State University of New York Press, 1996.

McNallen, Stephen A. *Rituals of Asatru*. Breckenridge, TX: Asatru Free Assembly, 1985.

Aspecting

Aspecting means taking on the personality of a deity and speaking or acting as that deity when a person or group calls upon that deity. Aspecting is somewhat similar to the spirit possession phenomenon found in many African-American religions, but is almost always presented in a much milder form. It can be considered a form of self-hypnosis, yet it differs from auto-induced psychological states in some significant ways. Those who do aspecting say that they do not lose consciousness or a sense of self and can remember clearly afterward exactly what happened—although, as with dreams, the details are soon forgotten. In aspecting, the ordinary personality "steps back," as if into a corner of a room, and another personality, from somewhere else, "steps forward" and takes control of the voice and body of the aspecter. Aspecters say that what is essential at this stage is for the ordinary personality to will the other personality to assume control—the ordinary personality may resume control at any time. In a coven, when a Priest or Priestess is aspecting, the members feel that they are in the physical presence of a deity, receiving healing, blessing, and counsel from a source not available to most persons.

See Also: Drawing Down the Moon; Possession
Further Reading
Adler, Margot. *Drawing Down the Moon: Witches, Pagans, Druids, and Other Goddess-Worshippers in America Today*, 2d ed. Boston, MA: Beacon Press, 1986 [1979].
Valiente, Doreen. *The Rebirth of Witchcraft*. London: Robert Hale, 1989.

Aspergillum

The aspergillum is a magical tool apparently derived from the Christian liturgy, although it may have other sources as well. It is simply a "sprinkler" that is dipped into water and used to sprinkle a congregation. The aspergillum can be used in a Craft circle as part of a "four-element casting"— the creation of a sacred space by carrying symbols of the four elements around it. The *Greater Key of Solomon*, a traditional manual of ceremonial magic, goes into detail about how the aspergillum should be constructed, and some Craft traditions have adopted these instructions into their own practice. In other traditions, an aspergillum might never be used at all.

See Also: Cast; Circle, Magic
Further Reading
Shepard, Leslie A., ed. *Encyclopedia of Occultism and Parapsychology*. Detroit, MI: Gale Research Inc., 1991.

Astral Plane

The astral plane is the concept that there exists one or more "otherworlds" alongside our world of ordinary, everyday experience. This different "dimension" is taken for granted in almost every religious and cultural tradition. One of the more significant points on which many religions agree is that some essential part of the human being survives death and goes on to reside in this other realm. Many religions also agree that communication between this world and the otherworld—between the living and the dead—is possible. Dreams, which often seem to be experiences of a confused parallel world to our own, are frequently thought to be the medium of communication between our world and that parallel world. Yet another shared theme is the idea that living human beings—or their spiritual essences—can journey to the otherworld without having to die.

Modern Neopaganism's understanding of the nature of reality is a variation on this traditional worldview. Neopagan thinking about other realms is rooted in the Western occult tradition, which postulates that there are many levels of reality. The most familiar of these, the so-called astral level or astral plane, is very close to the tangible, physical realm, and is intermediate between the physical and other, more spiritual planes. According to some writers, magic works when astral forces are set in motion. The astral plane is also sometimes identified with Summerland, the Neopagan afterlife realm in which souls of the departed reside while awaiting reincarnation.

See Also: Astral Projection; Aura; Inner Planes; Summerland
Further Reading

Lewis, James R. *Encyclopedia of Afterlife Beliefs and Phenomena*. Detroit, MI: Gale Research Inc., 1994.

Shepard, Leslie A., ed. *Encyclopedia of Occultism and Parapsychology*. Detroit, MI: Gale Research Inc., 1991.

Astral Projection

The term *astral projection*, also known as etheric projection or out-of-the-body traveling, refers to the ability to travel outside the physical body. The astral body is said to be an exact replica of the physical body but more subtle. An astral body is able to detach itself from the physical body at will (or under special circumstances) and is inhabited after death. The astral body remains attached to the physical body via a stream of energy commonly called the *silver cord*. The astral body is able to spontaneously leave the physical body during sleep, trance, or coma, under the influence of anesthetics or drugs, or as the result of accidents.

The astral body of a dying person is often projected into the presence of loved ones a few moments before the physical body dies, and this phenomenon is said to arise from the strong desire of the dying person to see and be seen. There are many reports of this phenomenon, and it has been found possible to project the astral body at will during subjective experiments, though the existence of such a body has not been proven to the satisfaction of mainstream science.

The astral body is said to be composed of subtle elements, ethereal in nature, which correspond to what the Yogis consider the vital centers of the physical body, more connected with the life force than with matter. The concept of bilocation is associated with the concept of astral projection. Bilocation is the ability to be in two places at the same time, but since a person cannot be in both places at once, one can postulate that the physical body could be in one place, while the astral body could be in another.

Many experiences of astral projection have been reported. Among the researchers who have studied this phenomenon is the British scientist Robert Crookall, who compared hundreds of cases in which people claimed to have left the physical body and reentered it after traveling, unseen, in the astral body. Sylvan Muldoon and Hereward Carrington, in their famous books *The Phenomena of Astral Projection* and *The Projection of the Astral Body*, maintain that there are three kinds of projection: conscious projection, in which the subject is awake; partially conscious projection; and unconscious projection. Unconscious projection has two distinct forms, the first of which is immotive astral projection—unconscious astral catalepsy (a state of suspended animation in which there can be no voluntary motion) in a perpendicular or standing position. The second type of unconscious projection is motive astral projection, in which the subject is lying down. Besides describing the phenomenon, Muldoon and Carrington also report some techniques for experiencing the astral projection at will. These methods are based on a simple, strong desire to project one's own astral body.

In contemporary Witchcraft, conscious astral projection is practiced in association with certain kinds of magical workings. For example, contemporary Witches sometimes utilize astral projection to communicate with spirit entities, to examine the future, and for distant healing.

See Also: Astral Plane
Further Reading
Muldoon, Sylvan J., and Hereward Carrington. *The Phenomena of Astral Projection*. London: Rider and Company, 1969.
———. *The Projection of the Astral Body*. York Beach, ME: Weiser, 1970.
Shepard, Leslie A., ed. *Encyclopedia of Occultism and Parapsychology*. Detroit: Gale Research Inc., 1991.

Astrology

Astrology is the science (or study, Greek: *logos*) of the stars *(astron)*. The general public is familiar with only a tiny portion of this subject, namely the 12 signs of the Zodiac as they relate to the personality of individuals and the use of astrology for divinatory purposes. The Zodiac (literally the "circle of animals") is a belt constituted by the 12 signs—Aries, Taurus, Gemini, Cancer, Leo, Virgo, Libra, Scorpio, Sagittarius, Capricorn, Aquarius, and Pisces.

The notion of the Zodiac is ancient, with roots in the early cultures of Mesopotamia. The first 12-sign Zodiacs were named after the gods of these cultures. The Greeks adopted astrology from the Babylonians, and the Romans, in turn, adopted astrology from the Greeks. These peoples renamed the signs of the Mesopotamian Zodiac in terms of their own mythologies, which is why the familiar Zodiac of the contemporary West bears names out of Mediterranean mythology.

From a broad historical perspective, Zodiacal symbolism can be found everywhere, and zodiacal expressions are still in use in modern English—e.g., "bull-headed" (an allusion to Taurus) or "crabby" (an allusion to Cancer). The popularity of sun sign astrology (the kind found in the daily newspaper) has kept these ancient symbols alive in modern society, so that even such prominent artifacts as automobiles have been named after them (e.g., the *Taurus* and the *Scorpio*).

Approaches to astrology differ widely. One approach stresses the study of the stars as a natural science (and consequently attempts to distance itself from occultism). Other approaches emphasize the spiritual or occult dimension of the study of planetary influences. The former perspective, using the

An astrologer works on a star chart at the Tibetan Medical Astrological Institute in Dharamsala, India. (Corbis/Alison Wright)

natural science model, tends to conceive of astrological influences in terms of forces, analogous to the forces of gravity and magnetism, that are actually "radiated" by the planets.

While often speaking in terms of "occult forces," the more spiritual perspective usually emphasizes correlations between celestial and mundane spheres that result from a kind of "pre-arranged harmony" built into the very structure of the cosmos. In other words, this harmony is a result of "synchronicity" (to use Carl Jung's term) rather than cause and effect. A large number of astrologers attempt to adhere simultaneously to both a natural science and a spiritual approach in the study of astrology.

Magic, the art of influencing events by occult means, is clearly related to the science of the stars. While astrology is not, in the proper sense of the term, "magical," techniques such as electional astrology—determining the best times to perform certain actions—border on magic. Traditional Western magic views astrology as providing insight into the occult forces that are playing on the Earth at any given time, and a specialized form of electional astrology is utilized by magicians to determine the best times for performing particular rituals.

Much of the astrological lore traditionally associated with magic is focused on the days of the week, the planetary hours, and the gems and metals connected with the planets. Each of the traditional seven "planets"—the Sun, Moon, Mars, Mercury, Jupiter, Venus, and Saturn—are said to *rule* (meaning "to have a special connection with") the seven days of the week. Thus, Saturn rules Saturday, the Sun rules Sunday, and so forth.

A similar relationship exists between the planets and the hours of the day. Magicians utilize these relationships and other traditional associations with the planets in various ways. For example, rituals to gain love would be performed on Friday ("Fri-" comes from "Frigga," the Norse Venus) during an hour ruled by Venus (the planet of love), rituals to gain money would be performed on Thursday ("Thur-" comes from "Thor," the Norse Jupiter) during an hour ruled by Jupiter (the planet of wealth), and so forth.

Amulets, which are fabricated objects used as charms, are also constructed during days and hours in symbolic harmony with the task the amulet is intended to perform. Additionally, such objects are constructed from materials ruled by the relevant planet. In the above examples, for instance, an amulet designed to attract love might be constructed from copper (the metal traditionally associated with Venus), and an amulet intended to attract prosperity might be made from tin (associated with Jupiter).

Magicians who are competent astrologers also pay attention to the sign in which the relevant planet is located, as well as the aspects (angular relationships with the other planets) the planet is making at the time of the ceremony. Thus, once again taking Venus as an example, a magician would wait until Venus was located in a favorable sign (which, for Venus, would be Libra, Taurus, or Pisces) and favorably aspected (making harmonious aspects with other planets) before performing a love ritual or constructing a love amulet.

See Also: Amulet; Divination; Magic

Further Reading

Daniels, Estelle. *Astrologickal Magick*. York Beach, ME: Weiser, 1995.

Denning, Melita, and Osborne Phillips. *Planetary Magick: The Heart of Western Magick*. St. Paul, MN: Llewellyn, 1989.

Lewis, James R. *The Astrology Encyclopedia*. Detroit, MI: Gale Research Inc., 1994.

Athame

The athame is a black-handled ritual knife—one of the most common distinguishing marks of the Neopagan Witch. Gerald Gardner, in *Witchcraft Today*, called the athame one of the three most essential tools of the Witch. It is clear that this tool is derived from the black-handled knife of ceremonial magic, as described, for example, in Mathers's translation of *The Greater Key of Solomon*, but it is not at all clear where Gardner got the term *athame*. Despite much scholarly speculation, the source and etymology of the word remain unclear.

There is nothing unclear about the athame's current functions, however. The athame is the main tool used to cast a circle during a coven Esbat (regular meeting of a coven during a full moon); the sword, being an enlarged and grandiose magical athame, is used more often at Sabbats and for rituals during festivals. The athame is often associated with the element of fire; but differ-ent covens may have different systems of association for the athame. Cere-monial magical traditions require that it never be used to actually cut any-thing, because it will lose its accumulated "magical charge" and will have to be cleansed, reconsecrated, and slowly "recharged" by use. These traditions state that if something *must* be cut, the white-handled knife, also derived from ceremonial magic, must be used. The white knife has no charge, posi-tive or negative, and so will not magically affect what is being cut. Other tra-ditions feel that if a Witch uses an athame to cut fruit, for example, the fruit is then consecrated, calling attention to the presence of sacredness in this everyday task.

See Also: Cast; Circle, Magic; Fire; Knife, White
Further Reading

Buckland, Raymond. *Witchcraft from the Inside*, 3d ed. St. Paul, MN: Llewellyn, 1996 [1971].

Farrar, Stewart. *What Witches Do: The Modern Coven Revealed*. New York: Coward McCann, 1971.

Aura

An aura is a field or body of subtle (nonphysical or quasi-physical) energy that envelops living entities, and is sometimes conceived of as emanating from nonliving minerals. Belief in the existence of an aura is widespread in the larger occult subculture, and its reality is taken for granted by most Neo-pagan Witches. Invisible and undetectable to human sight, the aura can be seen by people with the gift of clairvoyance, or "psychic sight." Individuals with such gifts describe the aura as a colorful field that can have rays, stream-ers, and other distinct phenomena associated with it. The size, brightness, and colors indicate different things about the individual's emotional and physical state, from strong desires to low vitality. Clairvoyant healers assert that illness begins as an irregularity, a disturbance in the aura, and that it takes months or sometimes even years before a physical illness manifests itself after the aura is disturbed.

Because its perception is restricted to clairvoyants, an aura is, as might be anticipated, not the subject of mainstream scientific research. Although liv-ing tissue does emit a magnetic field, termed a biofield, this magnetic field would seem to be much too weak to be the aura described in occult literature. A popular quasi-scientific theory postulates that the aura is a form of light vi-brating at frequencies that normal vision cannot perceive. The existence of the human aura is widely accepted in the occult-metaphysical subculture, in-cluding contemporary Neopaganism. Many basic magical techniques tap the energies that flow through the human aura.

The concept of an envelope of subtle, vital energy emanating from the body and from other forms of life has been widely accepted in many cultures and times. There are written records and artifacts that indicate such a belief existed in ancient India, Egypt, Rome, and Greece. The great sixteenth-century occultist Paracelsus was one of the earliest Westerners to write at length on this envelope of energy, which he referred to as a "fiery globe." In the late eighteenth century, Franz Anton Mesmer explained hypnotism via his notion of "animal magnetism," an electromagnetic energy that could emanate from one person to another in healing situations. In the mid–nineteenth century, Baron Karl von Reichenbach described a similar energy, which he termed an "odic force."

In the second decade of the twentieth century, Dr. Walter J. Kilner, an electrotherapist at St. Thomas's Hospital in London, invented an apparatus for detecting what appeared to be a human aura. This device contained dicyanin, a coal-tar dye that allowed one to see ultraviolet light. Kilner asserted that the state of the aura indicated the state of one's physical health, and, in 1919, he claimed to have developed a way to use the aura to diagnose illness. Kilner also claimed that weaker auras tended to draw off the energy from the more vigorous auras with which they came into contact. Kilner's early research was published in his 1911 book, *The Human Aura*. Despite the criticism with which the book was greeted, he continued his research until World War I interrupted it. When a revised edition of *The Human Aura* was published in 1920, his studies were greeted more sympathetically. Kilner passed away soon afterward, on June 23, 1920. A more recent procedure for sensing the aura, developed in 1939 by a Russian electrician, Semyon Davidovich Kirlian, produces photographs of the energy field.

Many religious traditions, as well as traditional occultism, view the aura as emanating from a subtle, nonphysical "body." This subtle body can be one of several secondary "bodies" in which the soul is "clothed" and which constitute intermediary levels between the physical body and the soul proper. Because auras are nonphysical, they survive the death of the physical body. Some traditional cultures have gone so far as to map out the anatomy of some of the subtle bodies. The best known map of auras is used in Chinese acupuncture. Another tradition with a complex understanding of the subtle body is the Hindu yoga tradition, in which the subtle body is referred to as the *linga sharira*. Different strands of the Western occult tradition postulate about the different set of bodies. The most common are said to be:

1. Ethereal, or vital, energy body
2. Astral, or emotional, body
3. Mental body
4. Causal body (containing the seeds of all of one's karma)
5. Spiritual body

See Also: Astral Plane; Chakras
Further Reading
Bagnall, Oscar. *The Properties of the Human Aura.* New York: University Books, 1970 [1937].

Becker, Robert O., M.D., and Gary Selden. *The Body Electric: Electromagnetism and the Foundation of Life*. New York: William Morrow, 1985.

Kilner, Walter J. *The Human Aura*. New Hyde Park, NY: University Books, 1964 [1920].

Ostrander, Sheila, and Lynn Schroeder. *Psychic Discoveries behind the Iron Curtain*. Englewood Cliffs, NJ: Prentice-Hall, 1970.

Aurum Solis

Aurum Solis was founded in 1897 in England by Charles Kingold and George Stanton. It was originally opened as a school of high Cabalistic magic; its philosophies centered around the magician who chose to follow a path of sacrifice, and who was reborn and passed into the light of glory. The Aurum Solis system is explained in *The Magical Philosophy* by Vivian and Leonard Barcynski under the pen names of Melita Denning and Osborne Phillips, Grand Master and Administrator General (respectively) of the order Aurum Solis. They came upon the Aurum Solis order while in England and helped to revive it in 1971 and brought it to the United States in 1978. Membership in the order is by invitation only. The teachings of the order still rely heavily on the writings of the Barcynskis.

Further Reading

Denning, Melita, and Osborne Phillips. *The Magical Philosophy*. 5 vols. St. Paul, MN: Llewellyn, 1974–1981.

B

Bale-Fire

The bale-fire is a large fire lit on Beltane, or May Day, in British folk custom. The word *Beltane*, which is now the common Irish name for the month of May, can be interpreted as "bright fire," and refers to these customary fires. Some think the fires were dedicated to the Celtic god Bel, but this is improbable. More likely the name indicates that the fire was thought to ward off evil influences.

See Also: Beltane

Further Reading

Campanelli, Pauline. *Wheel of the Year: Living the Magical Life.* St. Paul, MN: Llewellyn, 1989.

Kelly, Aidan A. *Religious Holidays and Calendars: An Encyclopedic Handbook.* Detroit, MI: Omnigraphics, 1991.

Baltic Tradition

The Baltic Tradition in America is derived from the native Pagan religion of the Baltic area, which, its proponents claim, never entirely died out despite the vicissitudes of history. Some of the principal deities of the Latvian tribes were:

- Dievs, more or less parallel to Zeus
- Perkons, similar both to Zeus and to Hephaestus, the Smith God
- Usins, or Jurgins, who protects horses and bees, oversees the moving of herds to pasture, and the moving of households; festival on May 10
- Janis, who seems to personify the midsummer sun, and may be derived from St. John the Baptist; festival on June 23
- Jumis, a God of Prosperity and Plenty associated with the harvest; festival at autumn equinox
- Martins, somewhat parallel to Mars, protector of horses and warriors; festival on November 10
- Meness, the Moon, friend of warriors and bringer of death

- Saule, the Sun Goddess, who travels across the heavens in a chariot drawn by her steeds
- Mara, who rules Earth, rivers, seas, and air, and all living things; said to be present at birth and at death; festival on August 10
- Laima, a Goddess of Fate
- Austra, the Goddess of Dawn; her name may be a variant of the word *Ostara*, from which the word *Easter* is derived

There were other goddesses, called the Mothers, of the winds, forests, roads, the sea, and souls.

It seems clear that this pantheon and its festivals have been adjusted to accord with the usual Neopagan Wheel of the Year (festival cycle).

Further Reading

The quarterly journal of the Baltic Tradition is *Sacred Serpent*, available by subscription at Box 232, Station "D," Etobicoke, ON M9A 4X2.

Baphomet

Frequently misinterpreted as a symbol of Witchcraft, the Baphomet—also known as Goat of Mendes, the Black Goat, and the Judas Goat—is the symbol of Satan, and is generally depicted as a half-human and half-goat figure, or as a goat head. It does not play a role in mainstream Neopagan worship. Its name has unclear origins, although it is believed to derive from a combination of the Greek words *baphe* and *metis*, meaning "absorption of knowledge."

During the Middle Ages, the Baphomet was an idol supposedly worshipped by the Order of the Knights Templar as the source of fertility and wealth. The order was later accused of anointing the idol with the fat of murdered children. In 1818, various idols, called "heads of Baphomet," were discovered in the Imperial Museum of Vienna among forgotten antiquities.

Baphomet, the half-goat, half-human figure worshiped by Satanists. (Dover Pictorial Archive Series)

The Baphomet appears also in a drawing by the nineteenth-century French magician Eliphas Levi, who combined elements of the Tarot devil card and the he-goat worshipped in antiquity in Mendes, Egypt. According to Levi, the attributes of his Baphomet symbolized the sum total of the universe and included intelligence, the four elements, divine revelation, sex and motherhood, sin and redemption.

See Also: Levi, Eliphas; Satanism
Further Reading
Gordon, Stuart. *The Encyclopedia of Myths and Legends*. London: Headline, 1993.
Sykes, Egerton. *Who's Who: Non-Classical Mythology*. New York: Oxford University Press, 1993.

Bells

The use of bells in religious rites is evidenced in civilizations as ancient as the Assyrians and the Babylonians. Throughout the history of humanity the ringing of bells has been believed to have a variety of magical, ritual, and symbolic roles. Folk magic, Neopagan Witchcraft, Vodun (Voodoo), and most major religions of the world use bells during their rites and ceremonies both to create harmony and to follow rhythmic dances and chants. The sound of bells is widely believed to drive away evil spirits. Small bells worn on hats or clothing, placed around the necks of domestic animals, and displayed at the entrance of shops represent modern traces of this belief.

During the Middle Ages, church bells were rung especially to fight Witches and evil spirits. The sound of church bells was believed to make Witches fall to the ground when they were flying in the night sky. When a villager passed away, church bells were rung to assist the journey of the soul to Heaven. Also, the sound of bells of any kind was thought to keep villages safe from storms and other natural calamities; bells could also enhance fertility, purify the air, and cure illnesses if potions were drunk from them.

See Also: Amulet; Exorcism
Further Reading
Chevalier, Jean, and Alain Gheerbrant. *The Penguin Dictionary of Symbols*. London: Penguin, 1996.
Cooper, J. C. *An Illustrated Encyclopedia of Traditional Symbols*. London: Thames and Hudson, 1978.

Beltane

Beltane is the Irish Gaelic name for the month of May, pronounced "bee-yawl-cheen." As a holiday, it is celebrated on May 1 (beginning at the preceding sunset), as one of the Greater Sabbats, which, with the Lesser Sabbats,

Modern Witches have revived the ancient custom of the May pole as part of annual Beltane celebrations. (Circle Sanctuary archives)

make up the eight Sabbats of the "Wheel of the Year." The Greater Sabbats of Brigid (February 1), Beltane (May 1, better known as May Day), Lughnasad (August 1), and Samhain (better known as Hallowe'en—November 1) are the traditional holidays peculiar to Celtic culture.

Beltane, or May Day, appears to have been a festival that always took place at the beginning of the dependable period of good weather in northern Europe, when herdsmen could safely take their herds up to high summer pastures and when wild fruits and berries began to grow and ripen. European folklore is full of May Day customs, a great many of them methods for young women to divine who their future husbands would be. It was a day for May pole dances, preceded by all-night outings when people would look for flowering branches and other prizes, for young women to work folk-magic rituals to divine who (and if) they would marry, and to make gifts of flowers for friends and lovers. Its dedication as a festival of the Blessed Virgin Mary—marked by an annual ritual that crowns the statue of Mary in the parish church with a wreath—was intended by the Christian Church to co-opt its traditional importance as a folk festival, since it has never been a feast of Mary in the official Christian Church calendar of saints' days and other observances. May Day, or Labor Day, on the first Monday in May, is observed as a holiday throughout Great Britain and Northern Ireland.

The night of April 30 through the night of May 1, called *Walpurgisnacht*, was traditionally a night on which the Witches met on the Blockula in Sweden and on other mountain peaks in Europe for a Grand Sabbat. It is still observed as a folk festival in the Harz Mountain region of Germany and in Scandinavia as a night on which to scare away evil spirits by lighting bonfires and making various kinds of loud noises—some musical, some not. The only apparent source for the name *Walpurgisnacht* is St. Walburga, but the festival to celebrate her falls on February 25. It also is obviously a relic of the Celtic festival of Beltane.

The legends about *Walpurgisnacht* do, of course, inspire Neopagan Witches to hold a Sabbat on this night if they possibly can, or at least on the closest weekend. There are many long-standing traditional festivals held near the date of Beltane.

See Also: Bale-Fire; Sabbats; Wheel of the Year
Further Reading
Campanelli, Pauline. *Wheel of the Year: Living the Magical Life*. St. Paul, MN: Llewellyn, 1989.
Kelly, Aidan A. *Religious Holidays and Calendars: An Encyclopedic Handbook*. Detroit, MI: Omnigraphics, 1991.

Bibliomancy

This word refers to the use of the Bible as a means of finding answers, making decisions, or bringing fortune. Through the time of the Reformation, a common medieval belief in England and other European countries was that the reading of randomly chosen pages of the Bible could reveal future events or favor a safe delivery for pregnant women. The simple laying of the Bible on children's heads could make them fall asleep. Decisions about the guilt of persons charged with the crime of Witchcraft were sometimes made by weighing the accused against the great Bible present in every church—weighing more than the book would result in a guilty verdict.

See Also: Divination; Fortune-Telling
Further Reading
Shepard, Leslie A., ed. *Encyclopedia of Occultism and Parapsychology*. Detroit: Gale Research Inc., 1991.

Binah

The third sephira of the Cabala. *Binah* means "understanding" in Hebrew. It is the first feminine principle, the womb of the divine mother, which receives the divine energy of Chokmah. Along with Kether and Binah, it makes up the upper, or supernal, triangle of the ten sephiroth, which is also the head of the divine body. Binah is also symbolic of the palace.

See Also: Cabala

Further Reading
Fortune, Dion. *The Mystical Qabalah*. York Beach, ME: Weiser, 1994 [1935].
Myers, Stuart. *Between the Worlds: Witchcraft and the Tree of Life—A Program of Spiritual Development*. St. Paul, MN: Llewellyn, 1995.

Binding

Contemporary Witches regard casting negative spells as both dangerous and unethical. Nevertheless, cases of people affected by negative spells, or by unhealthy energy at large, have been reported. Such unpleasant situations can be countered by binding spells, which annul the undesired effects of negative influxes.

A binding spell is typically not directed toward the author of the negative spell, but simply toward the negative effects per se. However, in some cases a so-called boomerang or mirror spell can be performed. The result is that the effects of the original negative spell return to their originator. The performer of the binding spell is, however, advised to specify that the effect on the person who cast the original negative spell will cease as soon as the negative influx ceases.

During a binding spell, an image made from wax or other materials representing the originator is instructed on the effects that have followed the negative spell, and that henceforth such effects are annulled. In the case of a boomerang spell, the representative image is also informed that until the negative spell is voided, its effects will be mirrored on him or her. The binding of the image in black tape or cloth and, in certain rituals, the temporary burial of the image conclude the binding spell.

See Also: Hex; Knot Magic; Spells

Further Reading
RavenWolf, Silver. *To Ride a Silver Broomstick: New Generation Witchcraft*. St. Paul, MN: Llewellyn, 1996.
Starhawk [Miriam Simos]. *The Spiral Dance: A Rebirth of the Ancient Religion of the Great Goddess*, 2d ed. San Francisco, CA: HarperSan Francisco, 1989 [1979].

Blessed Be

This is the standard greeting among Neopagan Witches, derived from Gardnerian practice, as discussed by Gardner in his book *Witchcraft Today*. It is not clear from where it originated, and it could in fact be a Christian liturgical phrase in some contexts; but "Blessed be" has served Witches as a recognition code for the last several decades. This greeting is not very useful today as the Neopagan movement, and especially the festival phenomenon, have grown so explosively that the phrase is known to many people other than initiated Witches.

See Also: Introduction
Further Reading
Gardner, Gerald B. *Witchcraft Today*. London: Jarrolds, 1954.
Guiley, Rosemary. *The Encyclopedia of Witches and Witchcraft*. New York: Facts on File, 1989.

Blue Star Tradition

The Blue Star Tradition combines the English Family Tradition in which Tzipora Katz was originally trained with generic Gardnerian-style Wicca. Blue Star was started in the early 1970s by Katz and Frank Dufner. Initially based in Pennsylvania, Blue Star moved to New York City, where Katz had an occult bookshop for several years. Like Dufner, Katz had had a traditional Wiccan training.

At the time Kenny Klein entered Blue Star, the group was working in an Alexandrian framework (Katz had Alexandrian lineage from Ron P. of Lunastra Coven in Massachusetts) combined with a good deal of pre-Gardnerian tradition. Klein became Priest of Blue Star in 1983. At that time Katz and Klein began a career in music as a duo. They broke farther away from the Alexandrian model and restored more of their various traditional trainings to the way Blue Star practiced Wicca. Several teachers and colleagues aided them in this, including Tamara James of the Wiccan Church of Canada. Some of the ways in which practitioners of the Blue Star Tradition differ from Gardnerian models include:

- The use of a round altar in the center of the Circle, on which each elemental tool and symbol is placed in its respective element (that is, the athame and incense in the east, wand and candle in the south, and so on). At the center of the Blue Star altar are symbols of the particular goddess and god being honored in the ritual.
- Circles are cast through a series of songs and dances that have been used ritually in Britain for, the group believes, many generations (these are not "power-raising" free-form dances, but precise dances performed in a specific ritual manner).
- Theologically, the Blue Star Tradition reveres each goddess and god as separate and unique: They do not adhere to the notion that "all Gods are one God, all Goddesses one Goddess, and there is but one initiator," as Dion Fortune wrote. They believe that each Wiccan is drawn into a relationship by and with a particular goddess or god, and that a student might be drawn to Blue Star because the group teaches the worship of that student's particular patron or patroness (like English Wicca, which a British god or goddess would want his or her devotees to learn).
- The Blue Star Tradition reveres the four elements as powerful partners in the worship of the gods, and they guide students through a four-year process in which pacts are created with each element, a process that

begins after initiation. Initiation is perceived as a lifelong commitment—a beginning, not a goal in one's training. They practice aspecting of gods whom they perceive to be real gods speaking through them in a literal sense.

Until 1986, Blue Star followed the standard coven model that includes a Priest, Priestess, and eight or ten students, with a focus on ritual and teaching. In 1986, Katz and Klein began extensive touring to promote their musical career. As they traveled to any part of the United States and Canada that would have them, they met literally thousands of Pagans, many of whom desperately sought teachers and fellowship. Katz and Klein attempted to teach the Blue Star Tradition through the use of tapes, personal visits, and mail. This was not a mail-order course, however—they did not charge money and they considered each student they taught to be a member of Blue Star. In time, the Blue Star Tradition grew to encompass about 200 people living in every area of the country. At that point they stopped referring to Blue Star as a coven and adopted the name Blue Star Family.

In 1992, Katz and Klein parted ways and there was a good deal of reorganization in Blue Star. Klein moved to the Kansas City area, where he and Kimberly H. have organized the Rose and Antler Coven. There are presently three or four separate hubs of Blue Star activity: one in the East, involving covens in New Jersey, New York, and Boston; one in the Midwest, from Minnesota through Missouri and down to Tennessee; and several small groups scattered around the United States. These groups keep in constant contact through a council of initiates originally organized by Katz and Klein.

Further Reading
Fortune, Dion. *Sane Occultism*. London: Aquarian Press, 1967.
Guiley, Rosemary. *The Encyclopedia of Witches and Witchcraft*. New York: Facts on File, 1989.

Bolline

Traditionally, a bolline is a curved, white-handled knife. It is utilized for such practical tasks as cutting herbs, slicing a branch from a tree for a wand, and other such magical or ceremonial purposes as may require a sharp instrument. The white-handled knife stands in sharp contrast to the athame, or black-handled knife, which is a specially consecrated ceremonial instrument reserved for ritual work in ceremonial magical traditions. In most traditions the athame is never used for practical purposes, and particularly never used for any form of bloodletting.

Further Reading
Farrar, Stewart. *What Witches Do: The Modern Coven Revealed*. New York: Coward McCann, 1971.
K., Amber. *True Magick: A Beginner's Guide*. St. Paul, MN: Llewellyn, 1991.

Book of Shadows

The Book of Shadows contains rituals for a Neopagan coven's Esbats (regular meetings during full moons); for the eight Sabbats at the solstices, equinoxes, and cross-quarter days; and for various rites of passage. The book can outline some basic magical techniques—whatever topics the coven records in it. Gerald Gardner probably saw the term *Book of Shadows* in a magazine in about 1948; before then he always referred to the Witch's book as a "black book" or as a "book of the art magical."

The Gardnerian Book of Shadows as such is, at least in America, a standardized liturgical manual, and membership in the traditional Gardnerian lineages is decided in terms of whether initiations have been carried out exactly as specified in this book. The fact that Gardner was still revising these rituals as late as 1960 has caused both difficulties and controversies.

Almost all of the British version of Gardner's Book of Shadows has now been published several times. The American version of the Book of Shadows is about three times the size of the British version, and almost none of this new material is publicly distributed and is not considered authoritative in any way by British Gardnerians.

See Also: Esbat; Introduction; Rite, Ritual; Sabbats

Further Reading

Bell, Jessie W. *The Grimoire of Lady Sheba*. St. Paul, MN: Llewellyn, 1972.
    Incorporates her earlier *Lady Sheba's Book of Shadows*.
Gardner, Gerald B. *High Magic's Aid*. New York: Michael Houghton, 1949.
Kelly, Aidan A. *Crafting the Art of Magic, Book I: A History of Modern Witchcraft, 1939–1964*. St. Paul, MN: Llewellyn, 1991.
Valiente, Doreen. *The Rebirth of Witchcraft*. London: Robert Hale, 1989.

Brigid

Brigid, on February 1, is the midwinter Sabbat (coven meeting) of the Neopagan Witches. The holiday is named for both the Irish Goddess Brigid, patron of poets and daughter of the Dagda, and the Catholic Saint Brigid, who was obviously named after the goddess and came to share many of her qualities and attributes. Brigid is one of the eight Sabbats of the "Wheel of the Year" celebrated by Neopagan Witches in the United States, and it is one of the four Greater Sabbats—the other three being Beltane (May 1), Lughnasad (August 1), and Samhain (better known as Hallowe'en—November 1). These are the traditional Celtic cross-quarter days and have always been said in folklore to be days on which Witches meet. The Sabbat is usually devoted to celebrations of light, poetry, and the overflowing bowl.

Another name for this holiday is Candlemas, a day on which candles were blessed in order to be used for healing and in rituals during the rest of the year. Yet another name for this holiday is Groundhog Day—folk belief has it that if a groundhog (or some other creature in other regions) wakes

An altar from a 1999 ritual at Circle Sanctuary. (Photo by Angie, Circle Sanctuary archives)

from his hibernation, comes out of his burrow, and sees his shadow, there will be six more weeks of winter. Of course, the season of winter does not officially end until March 21, and there normally *are* six more weeks of cold weather until then. Observance of this day appears to be a relic of the Celtic midwinter festival of Brigid.

See Also: Sabbat; Wheel of the Year
Further Reading
Campanelli, Pauline. *Wheel of the Year: Living the Magical Life*. St. Paul, MN: Llewellyn, 1989.
Kelly, Aidan A. *Religious Holidays and Calendars: An Encyclopedic Handbook*. Detroit, MI: Omnigraphics, 1991.

Broom

The broom is popularly known as a means of travel for Witches, who were traditionally said to have ridden them through the air. The broom has a long and ambivalent symbolic history. Brooms are both a phallic symbol and a symbol of female domesticity. In ancient Rome sacred midwives used special brooms to sweep the threshold of the house after childbirth in order to repel evil influences away from mothers and their babies. In the Middle Ages, a broomstick propped outside the door of a house or pushed up the chimney was a sign to neighbors and callers that the woman of the house was away. Witches were reported to be able to fly brooms up chimneys. As most Witches were women, brooms became associated with the female gender.

While a broom could be turned to a Witch's purpose by means of flying ointment, a broomstick placed across the threshold of a house was supposed to keep Witches out. In ancient Greece it was forbidden to step over a broom. This belief carried forward to England where Yorkshire folklore had it that it was unlucky for an unmarried girl to step over a broomstick—this meant that she would be a mother before she was a wife. The wedding couple jumped back and forth across a broom in Gypsy wedding ceremonies in the fifteenth century.

Pagans performed fertility rites to induce their crops to grow well. They mounted brooms and pitchforks and rode them like hobbyhorses in the fields, dancing and leaping. Sexual symbols represented life itself, so it was natural that the broomstick be employed in such rites. Before Witches were recorded as riding on brooms, they were said to have danced with them, sometimes holding brooms up high in the air or dancing astride them. In addition to riding brooms, sixteenth-century art portrays Witches riding fireplace pokers, benches, pitchforks, animals, and shovels through the air.

Sorcerers (those who practice magic without the religious emphasis of Witchcraft) also were said to fly on brooms, although more often they were depicted as riding on pitchforks. Even the orientation of the Witch on the broom was thought to convey meaning: Witches shown with the broom brush pointing at the Earth were said to be sweeping their tracks from the sky; Witches riding with the brush pointing at the sky often would be shown with a candle amongst the bristles to light the way. Ringing church bells supposedly had the power to "ground" brooms and make Witches fall off them. In Neopagan Witchcraft, the broom is placed at the altar with other Witches' tools. The broom is used symbolically to sweep away evil.

See Also: Flying; Sorcery; Tools, Witches'
Further Reading
Chevalier, Jean, and Alain Gheerbrant. *The Penguin Dictionary of Symbols*. London: Penguin, 1996.
Valiente, Doreen. *An ABC of Witchcraft: Past and Present*. New York: St. Martin's Press, 1973.

Burning Times

Among Neopagan Witches, the phrase "the Burning Times" commonly refers to the period in European history when "Witches" were actively pursued, prosecuted, and executed. This period is also sometimes referred to as "the Inquisition" or "the Witch hunts."

The Inquisition (that is, the Holy Office of the Inquisition of the Roman Catholic Church) was established in 1188 by Pope Lucius III, who had been

Correctly or incorrectly, contemporary Witches view themselves as the spiritual descendants of the "Witches" executed by the Church during the late Middle Ages and Early Modern Period, the so-called Burning Times. (Bibliothèque Nationale, Paris, Art Resource)

Ubaldo Allucingoli of Lucca, Italy. The office was established due to a rise in the number of religious movements the Church administration considered heretical—they feared that there had been a new outbreak of Gnosticism: The last of the Valentinian Gnostic Churches had been suppressed only a few centuries before, and the Cathars of France and Waldensians of Italy had been suppressed only about a century previously.

The Inquisition came to be administered by a new order of mendicant monks called Dominicans. For about the first 300 years of the Inquisition's existence, its activities were confined to the detection and suppression of heresy; relatively few people were executed due to its operations during this period. It was not until Pope Innocent VIII issued a Bull in 1486 that equated "Witchcraft" with heresy that the Inquisition began to increase in scope and fury.

Elsewhere in Europe Catholics and Protestants went to war against one another in the religious wars from 1520 to 1648, and Jews were commonly persecuted. Keep in mind that the Witch hunts did not take place during the Middle Ages—they took place in modern times, after the invention of printing and mercantile capitalism, after Columbus's discovery of the New World, and especially after the Reformation and Counter-Reformation. How many Witches perished during these turbulent times? Probably only a tiny fraction of the number of Christians and Jews who died.

It is commonly suggested that some nine million men, women, and children died in the Witch hunts. There is no historical evidence to support this figure and, in examining records of the Witch trials, scholars have determined that about 40,000 demonstrable executions took place. This figure may be too small, as some Catholic scholars who have had access to unpublished documents in the Vatican Library have reported that they found evidence for several hundred thousand deaths during the Burning Times.

In modern times, it is perhaps difficult to appreciate the strong religious component in the American Revolution. The overthrow of the Anglican Church, as well as of the English government, was the major goal of most Patriots. The Patriots remembered the Witch trials in Salem, Massachusetts, where some of the very last executions for the practice of "Witchcraft" in the English-speaking world took place. Supporters of the Bill of Rights argued that one of the purposes of the First Amendment was to ensure that nothing like the Salem Witch trials could ever happen again.

Further Reading

Lea, Henry Charles. *A History of the Inquisition of the Middle Ages.* 3 vols. New York: Harper and Bros., 1888. On the Cathars, see vol. I, chapters 3 and 4, especially pp. 91–107.

Midelfort, H. C. Erik. "Recent Witch Hunting Research, or Where Do We Go from Here?" *Papers of the Bibliographical Society of America,* LXII, 1968, 373–420. Lists 509 publications, almost all published since 1940, some of which are relevant to the Gardnerian Craft.

Robbins, Rossell Hope. *The Encyclopedia of Witchcraft and Demonology.* New York: Crown, 1959. Lists virtually everything published about any kind of Witchcraft up to 1958.

Cabala

The Cabala (also Qabalah, Kabala) is a system of symbols, commonly known as the Tree of Life (in Hebrew, *etz chaim*), that maps out the relative positions between humankind and divine forces of creation. Like the Chinese Book of Changes, or I Ching, the Cabala is a systems theory that charts the changes and interrelationships between Heaven, Earth, and humans. Cabala is also a way of reinterpreting myths and texts (usually the Old Testament of the Bible) based on these symbols. Finally, Cabala includes mystical techniques that allow the initiate to explore pathways between divine forces. The keystone of many systems of ceremonial magic, Cabalistic notions can be found in some Neopagan traditions.

God, in the Cabala, is known as *ain soph*, "without end," or simply, *ayin*, meaning "not" or "none"—one cannot know anything of God for he possesses no qualities. According to the Cabala, only through his different aspects, or emanations (the Ten Sephiroth, or emanations, that form the Tree of Life), can one know of God. In other words, one can ascend through various layers, spheres, or worlds, through meditations or incantations, to come face-to-face with the Divine.

Although Cabala is often used today to mean any generic mix of occultism, theosophy, and numerology, it is, in fact, a specific body of Jewish doctrine. The word *Cabala* derives from the Hebrew root *qbl*, meaning "to receive." Cabala is the received aspect of Jewish tradition, which for many centuries was never written down but was transmitted orally.

According to legend, the Cabala was taught by God to the angels. Cabala was then transmitted from Adam to Noah to Abraham to Moses, who passed it on to 70 elders and coded it into the first four books of the Pentateuch (the first five books of the Hebrew Bible). Deuteronomy, for some reason, is "Cabala-less." Cabala probably has its origin in the Jewish mystical tradition of Merkabah, called "throne mysticism" because it involved meditation upon images of God on his throne. Merkabah was an esoteric practice of rabbis in Babylon from the fourth to the tenth centuries.

The most famous book of the Cabala is the Zohar, or the Book of Splendor. Moses de Leon claims to have discovered this work, which was originally written in the second century A.D. The Zohar contains cryptic verses that serve mystical commentaries on the Pentateuch. By the middle of the thirteenth century, Cabala included practical techniques for reaching ecstasy, such as breathing meditation or recitation of the names of God.

The first center of Cabala was the Spanish region of Castile where de Leon wrote the Zohar (de Leon claimed discovery but scholars assert that he actually authored it). After Spain expelled the Jews in 1492, cities in Palestine became Cabalistic centers: first Jerusalem, followed by the Galilean mountain town of Safed (*Tzfat*). It was in the heady air of sixteenth-century Safed that Isaac Luria, the mystical saint and premier Cabalist of his time, developed a new theosophy.

In the beginning of time, according to Lurianic Cabala, God was everywhere. To allow for the existence of the cosmos, God withdrew into himself. The central act of creation is thus a withdrawal (*tsimtsun* in Hebrew). God then created the world from a series of ten emanations (*sephiroth* in Hebrew). These emanations, or rays, form the Tree of Life (*etz chaim*)—an upside-down tree whose roots are in the Godhead, descending into the infinite multitude of branches and twigs that is our world.

According to Luria, after God retracted his being, the divine essence was contained in vessels. But these vessels could not contain the Godhead and broke, spilling divine sparks into the universe, which became embedded in matter. All of creation, therefore, contains divinity. The broken vessels represent the fractured, incomplete nature of reality. The central project of the Cabalist, thus, is to repair the broken vessels, or "heal the world" (in Hebrew, *tikkun olam*), thereby restoring the Godhead. By this philosophy, God needs humankind as much as humankind needs God.

In Renaissance Europe, Cabala became the realm of alchemists and magicians. They used combinations of Cabalistic numbers and divine names in esoteric rituals. The famous Italian humanist Pico della Mirandola (1463–1494) believed Cabala to be the original divine revelation, once lost and now recovered. In the late fifteenth century, Cabala was harmonized with Christian doctrine, most notably by della Mirandola's follower, Johannes Reuchlin, and by Wittenberg associates of Martin Luther. They believed the true Cabala revealed the nature of Christ.

Cabala powerfully affected modern magic. Most members of the late-nineteenth-century occult Order of the Golden Dawn, including Aleister Crowley, were Cabalists. Dion Fortune (1891–1946), British occult author and another Golden Dawn member, wrote *The Mystical Qabalah*, one of the most lucid introductions to the subject.

In the meantime, after falling out of favor with the rational Judaism of the eighteenth and nineteenth centuries, Cabala has undergone a revival in the twentieth century. Some modern Jewish scholars have historicized the Cabala, emphasizing one strand of the development over another (the practical versus the idealist, for example) or finding Christian, neo-Platonic, and even Sufi (Muslim mysticism) influences in the Cabala. Others have endeavored to popularize Cabala for Jewish laypeople, who have found in this ancient system a way to explore mysticism while staying true to their own religious heritage. Today, Cabala has been almost fully integrated with New Age and Pagan spiritualities.

See Also: Abramelin; Binah; Chesed; Chokhmah; Hermetic Order of the Golden Dawn; Hod; Kether; Malkuth; Netzach; Tiferet; Yesod

Further Reading

Fortune, Dion. *The Mystical Qabalah*. York Beach, ME: Weiser, 1994 [1935].

Matt, Daniel C. *The Essential Cabala: The Heart of Jewish Mysticism*. San Francisco, CA: HarperCollins, 1995.

———, ed. and trans. *Zohar: The Book of Enlightenment*. New York: Paulist Press, 1983.

Myers, Stuart. *Between the Worlds: Witchcraft and the Tree of Life—A Program of Spiritual Development*. St. Paul, MN: Llewellyn, 1995.

Cakes and Wine

An invariant element of every Wiccan and Neopagan celebration is the consecration (or "charging") and consumption of some sort of food and drink. This practice, of course, parallels similar rituals in almost every other religion in the world. The phrase "cakes and wine" or "cakes and ale" is a reference to Jeremiah 44 of the Bible, where the Jewish women in exile in Egypt tell Jeremiah that they will go back to offer cakes and wine to the Queen of Heaven. The charging of the wine is almost always done by lowering the point of the athame (ceremonial dagger) into the cup of wine and speaking the appropriate words, which differ from one tradition to the next. This action is often called the "symbolic Great Rite." Done in a magically efficacious way, it can complete an initiation. The cakes are also charged, usually just with words, and then cup and platter are offered to the congregation, coven, or community.

See Also: Athame; Initiation

Further Reading

Campanelli, Pauline. *Wheel of the Year: Living the Magical Life*. St. Paul, MN: Llewellyn, 1989.

Starhawk [Miriam Simos]. *The Spiral Dance: A Rebirth of the Ancient Religion of the Great Goddess*, 2d ed. San Francisco, CA: HarperSan Francisco, 1989 [1979].

California Gardnerian (CalGard) Tradition

In 1979, a woman, who will be called "Wanda Wombat" here to hide her identity, the inventor of Wombat Wicca and author of "The Wombat Laws," became coordinator of the Mensa Witchcraft, Occult, and Paganism Special Interest Group, and founded its newsletter, *Robin Hood's Barn*. From 1981 to 1983, Jani H. of Dayton, Ohio, was initiated and trained by Wanda, who introduced Jani to her own Queen, Judy Harrow.

In 1983, having moved to the San Francisco Bay area, Jani H. changed her name to Meredydd Harper and founded the Moonsilver Outer Grove of the Circle of Our Lady of the Well in Berkeley, California. She still did not have full Gardnerian credentials but was able to receive Third-Degree elevation (witches typically go through three initiations, after which a woman can become a High Priestess) in 1984 from Harrow and her working partner, Daystar (Fred Kuhn).

Harper set out to found the first official Gardnerian coven in Northern California; it came to be called Tobhar Bhride. In this new Gardnerian coven, Brendan, Lady Marian, Morgann, and Lady Bride were trained. During this period Meredydd served as the Covenant of the Goddess's National Membership and Correspondence Officer, 1984–1985, and as National Co-Membership Officer, 1985–1986.

By 1987 Meredydd had turned Tobhar Bhride over to Lady Bride and Morgann and had moved on to other affairs. Brendan and others in the South Bay had begun Our Lady of the Wild Oak Way coven, and Marian had begun Beannacht Danaan in San Jose. From August 1987 to May 1988, Meredydd worked with Taliesin, Epona, Shlon, and several others in a coven called *He Synodos tes Basileias tou Ouranou* (Greek for "The Coven of the Queen of Heaven") in Alameda, California.

At Lughnasad (one of the four Greater Sabbats) in 1989, tired of being challenged over internal Gardnerian political issues, the California line issued its Declaration of Independence from the rest of the Gardnerian community. This document appeared in the Lammas issue of *The Hidden Path*. Meredydd has since continued to function as the reigning queen of an autonomous tradition.

Further Reading
Kelly, Aidan A., ed. *Neo-Pagan Witchcraft*. 2 vols. New York: Garland, 1990.
    Volumes 23 and 24 in the Garland series on *Cults and New Religions*, edited by J. Gordon Melton.

Candles

The earliest evidence of candles made of beeswax has been found on the island of Crete and in Egypt, where candles were used 5,000 years ago. Magic rituals involving candles are documented in Egypt and in Rome in the early centuries A.D., while Christians introduced the use of candles in their rituals in the fourth century and began consecrating and placing them on altars in the twelfth century. Along with their practical use as sources of light, candles have long been considered a means to repel unfavorable spirits and favor good ones. Besides this instinctive connotation, candles have played an important role in a multitude of rites and spells. They have been used both by Witches during Sabbats (regular coven meetings during the eight holidays of the Wheel of the Year) and by Christians in exorcism rituals.

Witches and Pagans sometimes use candles to form sacred circles. This candle labyrinth is part of the celebration of the Summer Solstice at the 1997 Pagan Spirit Gathering sponsored by Circle Sanctuary. (Photo by Jeff Koslow, Circle Sanctuary archives)

It is an ancient Jewish tradition to place candles in the room where a dying or dead person lies—candles are believed to ward off evil spirits and purify the air in the room. Subsequently, Christians adopted such a custom and folkloric traditions have even elaborated on it; in particular, the American folkloric tradition has produced interpretations concerning the places and the ways in which candles burn.

The interpretations and uses of candles are particularly rich in the magic tradition. Candles made of other substances than beeswax were used in magical rituals, often made of human or other animal tallow and fat. In recent centuries such candles appeared in Satanist black masses and were also part of treasure-hunting expeditions.

In today's Witchcraft, candles play an important role during different rituals, such as spells and, following patterns of color and sign association, in rites based on the Zodiac.

See Also: Magic; Rite, Ritual; Spells
Further Reading
Barrett, Francis. *The Magus*. London: Lackington, Allen, and Co., 1801.
Chevalier, Jean, and Alain Gheerbrant. *The Penguin Dictionary of Symbols*. London: Penguin, 1996.

Candomblé

Candomblé is the name given to an early Afro-Brazilian group, largely female in membership and centered in Bahia. It derives from the name of one of

A priestess of the Candomblé religion sits in a ritual house in Salvador, Brazil. Most important Candomblé rituals take place in such houses, and they are always conducted by a woman. (Corbis/Barnabas Bosshart)

three drums used during the group's rituals, when particular members are possessed by ancestors. Candomblé closely resembles the ancient Yoruban religions and retains the Yoruban names of the *orishas* (deities).

The first Candomblé center was established in 1830 in Salvador, the capital of the state of Bahia, by three former slaves who became High Priestesses, or "Mothers of the Saints." They trained other women, called "Daughters of the Saints"—*daga* or *sidaga*. Men were excluded from major responsibilities within the group.

Members believe that a supreme god, usually called Olorun or Zaniapombo, created the universe. He has intermediaries who look after the affairs of human beings. Rituals are performed in the *terreiro* (church center), where the gods and the dead mingle with humans, listen to their complaints, give advice, grant favors, resolve problems, and provide medicines for illnesses.

There is no ritual or material representation for Olorun, who is generally mentioned in songs and myths. Oshala, on the other hand, is a divine spirit considered to be the father of all other orishas and the grandfather of all mortals. Below these two divinities are the *orisha, Vodun* (of West African origin), *inkices*, and *encantados*. Almost all female orishas are highly esteemed in the Candomblés, and the various orishas are associated with different Catholic saints.

Candomblé ceremonies follow much the same pattern as those of Santeria and Vodun, usually starting with the sacrifice of animals, whose blood is used to wash the altar stones of the orishas in a secret propitiatory ceremony at the altar. Special dances are performed for each orisha by the "daughter," who feels vibrations in her body, becomes dizzy, loses her balance, walks as if drunk, is taken over by the orisha, acquires another physiognomy, and then recovers somewhat. She may take a sick person in her arms and cure him by lifting him into the air or blowing on his stomach or ears. Whenever the possession is too extreme, the women assistants, *ékédes*, restrain her. Meanwhile, other gods take possession of their daughters. The stronger the orisha, the more violent the possession.

Followers of Candomblé ask the *Exus*, primal forces of all nature acting as divine tricksters and messengers to the gods, to let the spirits enter their churches and their bodies. Among the major celebrations to the orisha *Yemanja*, "Goddess of the Waters," is the one held every January 1, during which a Priestess lights candles and then purifies and ordains other young Priestesses.

See Also: African Religions; Orishas
Further Reading
Hess, David J. *Samba in the Night: Spiritism in Brazil.* New York: Columbia University Press, 1994.
Hinnells, John R., ed. *A New Dictionary of Religions*, 2d ed. London: Blackwell, 1997.

Cast

The term *cast* is used in a technical sense in Neopaganism: One casts a circle by drawing it magically with the athame, consecrating it by the four elements (in some traditions), then invoking the Guardians (Lords of the Watchtowers) to guard the four cardinal directions. Sometimes the word *cast* is used to mean only the drawing with the athame (or with a sword at large rituals); sometimes it is used to mean the entire opening procedure that establishes the circle as "sacred space." This usage of the word is probably related to the phrase "to cast a spell." Most Neopagan Witches do not speak in terms of "casting spells" because this seems to refer to the working of magic that affects people without asking their permission to do so. This type of spell-casting is a violation of the current ethical standards generally observed in the Craft. Establishing the difference between "black" and "white" magic (an old philosophical dilemma) has been resolved by requiring that any persons who will be affected by a spell be asked whether they are agreeable to this. (Apparently, this resolution was first devised by the New Reformed Orthodox Order of the Golden Dawn in about 1971.)

See Also: Circle, Magic; Spells
Further Reading
Kelly, Aidan A., ed. *Neo-Pagan Witchcraft.* 2 vols. New York: Garland, 1990.
    Volumes 23 and 24 in the Garland series on *Cults and New Religions*, edited by J. Gordon Melton.

Starhawk [Miriam Simos]. *The Spiral Dance: A Rebirth of the Ancient Religion of the Great Goddess*, 2d ed. San Francisco, CA: HarperSan Francisco, 1989 [1979].

Cauldron

The cauldron, an iron pot, is one of the most popular tools of Witches and sorcerers. According to medieval lore, poisons, ointments, and philtres (love potions) were brewed in such pots. Among contemporary Witches, the cauldron is used primarily for burning fires and incense in rituals when it is placed on the Witches' altar inside the magic circle. The cauldron is also a feminine symbol associated with the womb of the Mother Goddess.

The cauldron has been a significant element in the magical lore of several cultures. During ancient Irish feasts, it was said that cauldrons never ran out of food. Celts regarded cauldrons as symbols of fertility and abundance, as well as of revival of the dead. The Cauldron of Regeneration is associated with the Celtic Goddess Cerridwen and with the Babylonian fate-Goddess Siris. According to Greek mythology, the Witch Goddess Medea used a magic cauldron to restore people to youth. Cauldrons were used by alchemists for seeking formulas to change lead into gold and silver, and mold small gems into large ones. The cauldron is even associated with legends of the Holy Grail, in which it was transformed into a chalice.

Throughout history, cauldrons have been portrayed as playing a part in human sacrifices. In medieval art, literature, and folktales, cauldrons are pictured as if they existed in every Witch's house, usually set over a blazing fire. Witches were said to use cauldrons for brewing such ingredients as bat's blood, decapitated and flayed toads, snakes, and baby fat. Flying ointments and drugs were also prepared in cauldrons before a Sabbat (the regular meeting of a coven during the eight holidays of the Wheel of the Year), during which the same pots were used for boiling small children for the feast. It was believed that if a Witch dumped the contents of her cauldron into the ocean, she could cause storms at sea.

See Also: Cerridwen; Magic
Further Reading

Chevalier, Jean, and Alain Gheerbrant. *The Penguin Dictionary of Symbols*. London: Penguin, 1996.

Cooper, J. C. *An Illustrated Encyclopedia of Traditional Symbols*. London: Thames and Hudson, 1978.

Celtic Tradition

Many covens describe themselves as being of "Celtic tradition," but in fact there is no such tradition, not in the same sense as there is an Alexandrian Tradition, a Blue Star Tradition, or a 1734 Tradition, for example. Rather, the term *Celtic tradition* is used to indicate a type of Wiccan practice that focuses more on the Celtic deities than on those of the Mediterranean areas. Aside from that, Celtic traditional covens generally seem to practice a sort of generic Wicca, derived, like almost all modern Witchcraft, originally from the Gardnerians.

On the other hand, today there has been a recurrence of interest in Pagan Celts. Careful research into Celtic (Irish, Welsh, or Breton) literature, and into European prehistory in general, has been undertaken in order to gain a better understanding of what Celtic Paganism could be as a distinct subgroup within the overall Neopagan movement. This effort has been spearheaded by several Pagan scholars, such as Dr. Alexei Kondratiev, longtime head of the Celtic Research and Folklore Society in New York City, whose *The Apple Branch*, a study of Celtic culture, has recently been published.

Further Reading

Bowman, Marion, "Cardiac Celts: Images of the Celts in Paganism." In Harvey, Graham, and Charlotte Hardman, eds., *Paganism Today: Wiccans, Druids, the Goddess, and Ancient Earth Traditions for the Twenty-first Century*. London and San Francisco: Thorsons, 1996, 242–251.

Kondratiev, Alexei, Ph.D. Interview by Ellen Evert Hopman and Lawrence Bond. In *People of the Earth: The New Pagans Speak Out*. Rochester, VT: Destiny Books, 1996.

Rees, Aylwin, and Brinsley Rees. *Celtic Heritage: Ancient Tradition in Ireland and Wales*. London: Thames and Hudson, 1961.

Censer

Censers, also known as thuribles, are magical tools used to burn incense. Incense-burning encourages and welcomes good spirits and banishes evil ones. During the Middle Ages, censers were made of bronze or silver and lamps were made of gold, silver, brass, or iron. The chalice used was made of different metals according to its use in magic rites. For instance, chalices used in "black" magic were engraved with symbols of the moon. Human skulls were said to have been used for the same purpose as chalices.

See Also: Tools, Witches'
Further Reading

Cooper, J. C. *An Illustrated Encyclopedia of Traditional Symbols*. London: Thames and Hudson, 1978.

Guiley, Rosemary. *The Encyclopedia of Witches and Witchcraft*. New York: Facts on File, 1989.

Cernunnos

This name, which means "the horned," was used by the Celts, the Gauls, and the Romans to refer to the horned God of Fertility and the Hunt. Cernunnos also ruled the underworld and was its gatekeeper. The picture of Cernunnos as a man with horns, the best known representation of the god, appears on a cauldron found in Denmark that dates to about 100 B.C.

See Also: Horned God
Further Reading
Gordon, Stuart. *The Encyclopedia of Myths and Legends*. London: Headline, 1993.
Sykes, Egerton. *Who's Who: Non-Classical Mythology*. New York: Oxford University Press, 1993.

Cerridwen

In ancient Celtic mythology the Goddess Cerridwen (also Keridwen) was endowed with the gifts of metamorphosis and prophecy and was worshipped as the Goddess of Wisdom, Divination, and Enchantment. Her symbols were the Moon, water, and the cauldron where she prepared a magical brew that could confer knowledge and inspiration after a year and a day of constant boiling. Neopagan Witchcraft, Neopaganism, and Celtic magic acknowledge her fundamental role in their initiatory and mystery rituals.

See Also: Cauldron; Divination
Further Reading
Gordon, Stuart. *The Encyclopedia of Myths and Legends*. London: Headline, 1993.
Sykes, Egerton. *Who's Who: Non-Classical Mythology*. New York: Oxford University Press, 1993.

Chakras

The human being and other living things are said to be surrounded and interpenetrated by a field or body of subtle (nonphysical or quasi-physical) energy, the chakras. Some traditional cultures have mapped out the anatomy of these subtle bodies. The best known of these is Chinese acupuncture, which maps the vessels (meridians) along which a form of subtle energy (the *chi*) flows. When the flow of energy is disturbed, bodily illness results, and the practice of acupuncture is devoted to correcting these energy imbalances.

Undoubtedly the most complex understanding of the subtle body is provided by the Hindu yoga tradition, in which the subtle body is referred to as the *linga sharira* (Sanskrit for "body of characteristics"). Similar to acupuncture, this tradition postulates an intricate map of energy channels (*nadis*) along which subtle energy (*prana*) flows. Additionally, the ancient yogis described a series of energy centers (the *chakras*) arranged along the spinal column. Unlike the Chinese acupuncturists, the Hindu yogis were less interested in healing than they were in achieving release from the cycle of death

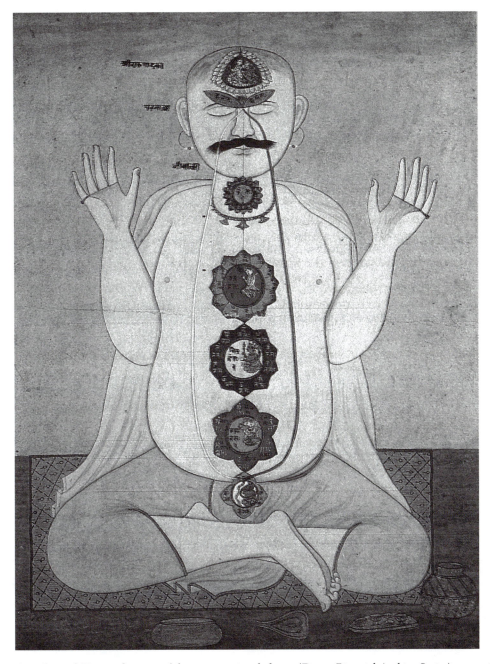

A traditional Tantric diagram of the seven major chakras. (Dover Pictorial Archive Series)

and rebirth, and traditional discussions of the *linga sharira* revolve around ways of regulating the *prana* to achieve this end.

While every juncture of *nadis* can be referred to as a chakra, in most discussions this term is restricted to the principal seven junctures arranged along the spine. Somewhat like transformers, the chakras regulate subtle energy.

The chakras are also centers of consciousness, and each center from the base of the spine to the crown of the head is said to represent a different state of consciousness, from the urge to survive (first chakra) to God consciousness (seventh chakra). The state of enlightenment takes place when the normally latent energy at the base of the spine (the *kundalini* energy) "awakens," travels up the spine, and fully activates the chakra in the crown of the head. The existence of the chakras is taken for granted in Neopaganism and within the larger spiritual subculture in which Neopaganism is rooted.

See Also: Aura; Kundalini
Further Reading
Feuerstein, Georg. *Encyclopedic Dictionary of Yoga*. New York: Paragon House, 1990.
Judith, Anodea. *Wheels of Life*. St. Paul, MN: Llewellyn, 1987.

"Charge of the Goddess"

The "Charge of the Goddess" is a central document in the Gardnerian Book of Shadows, cited at the beginning of its introduction. The term *charge* here is borrowed from Masonic vocabulary: in a Masonic initiation a "charge" is a speech or set of instructions read to a candidate standing in a Temple.

Gardner's first draft of the "Charge of the Goddess" was a hodgepodge of quotes from Crowley's *Gnostic Mass* and Leland's *Aradia*. He intended it to be a theological statement justifying the Book of Shadows' ensuing sequence of initiations. Doreen Valiente later rewrote the charge into its present, widely popular form.

See Also: Aradia; Introduction
Further Reading
Gardner, Gerald B. "Ye Book of ye Art Magical." Unpublished manuscript, written between about 1945 (or earlier) and 1953. Formerly owned by Ripley's International, Ltd., now owned by the Wiccan Church of Canada in Toronto.
Kelly, Aidan A. *Crafting the Art of Magic, Book I: A History of Modern Witchcraft, 1939–1964*. St. Paul, MN: Llewellyn, 1991.
———. *Inventing Witchcraft: A Case Study in the Creation of a New Religion*. Los Angeles, CA: Art Magickal Publications, 1996.
Valiente, Doreen. *The Rebirth of Witchcraft*. London: Robert Hale, 1989.

Charms

A charm is used to protect against or cure disease; ward off evil, disaster, and Witchcraft; secure or rid oneself of a lover; ensure chastity, fertility, or potency; gain victory, riches, or fame; exact revenge; protect crops and farm animals; or rid one's house of vermin. A charm can be a word, phrase, chant, incantation, inscription, or object and can even be an action, such as spitting.

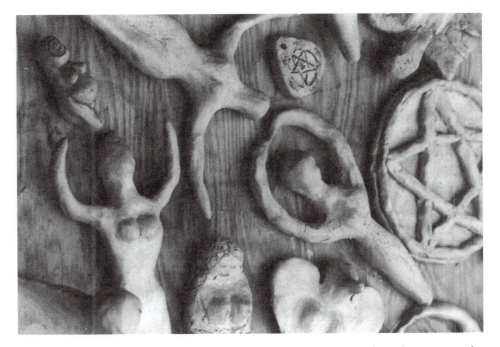

Goddess images, pentagrams, and other sacred symbols can serve as amulets, altar pieces, and ritual tools. These charms were crafted by participants in the 1997 Pagan Spirit Gathering sponsored by Circle Sanctuary. (Photo by Jeff Koslow, Circle Sanctuary archives)

Love charms include lucky roots, scented oils, and powders. John the Conqueror Root is a dried root of the herb St. John's Wort which has a prong or a spike growing out of it. It is carried in a little bag of chamois or red cloth as a lucky piece. Another amusing love charm was the use of Cockle-bread, a small loaf of bread that a woman kneaded with her bare thighs and genitals ("cockles" was an old term for the labia minora). The bread was then baked and given to the man she desired. If he ate the bread he was hers.

See Also: Spells; Talismans
Further Reading
Budge, E. A. Wallis. *Amulets and Superstitions*. New York: Dover, 1978 [1930].
Lockhart, J. G. *Curses, Lucks, and Talismans*. Detroit, MI: Single Tree Press, 1971 [1938].

Chesed

The fourth sephira of the Cabala, *Chesed*, means "love" in Hebrew. It represents mercy. It is also sometimes called *Gedullah*, "greatness." Symbolically, Chesed is the right arm of God. The energy is that of grace and free-flowing love.

See Also: Cabala
Further Reading
Fortune, Dion. *The Mystical Qabalah*. York Beach, ME: Weiser, 1994 [1935].
Myers, Stuart. *Between the Worlds: Witchcraft and the Tree of Life—A Program of Spiritual Development*. St. Paul, MN: Llewellyn, 1995.

Chokhmah

The second sephira of the Cabala. *Chokhmah* means "wisdom" in Hebrew. Chokhma is the point of creation, the point where God enters the world. By extension, Chokhmah represents a phallus. Along with Kether and Binah, Chokhmah makes up the upper, or supernal, triangle of the ten sephiroth.

See Also: Cabala
Further Reading
Fortune, Dion. *The Mystical Qabalah*. York Beach, ME: Weiser, 1994 [1935].
Myers, Stuart. *Between the Worlds: Witchcraft and the Tree of Life—A Program of Spiritual Development*. St. Paul, MN: Llewellyn, 1995.

Church and School of Wicca

The Church and School of Wicca (CSW) was founded by Gavin Frost and Yvonne Frost in 1965. Initially located near St. Louis, Missouri, it was moved to North Carolina in the late 1970s, and, in late 1996, it was moved to West Virginia. CSW practices and teaches a form of Neopagan Witchcraft but operated originally with a theology derived directly from an aristocratic British tradition into which Gavin Frost was initiated in 1948—instead of the widespread Gardnerian system based on the writings of Margaret Murray and Robert Graves. The differences between the theologies led to some unfortunate misunderstandings with other Neopagans in the early 1970s. In recent years, CSW has evolved a more eclectic theology that is more compatible with the beliefs of other Neopagan Witches and has also developed a uniquely Western form of Tantric Yoga.

Gavin Frost was born in 1930 in Staffordshire, England, to a Welsh family. In 1948 he was initiated into an aristocratic coven that apparently hailed back to the Pentangle Society, a student group at Cambridge that, in the mid-1930s, tried to reconstruct the Pagan Witchcraft religion proposed by Margaret Murray in her *The Witch-Cult in Western Europe* (1921). It is possible that this group was connected with the New Forest Coven into which Gerald Gardner was initiated in 1939. From 1949 to 1952, Frost attended London University, graduating with a B.S. in mathematics; he went on to earn a doctorate in physics and mathematics. While working for an aerospace company on the Salisbury Plain, he became curious about Stonehenge, and his investigation of it deepened his knowledge of the Craft.

Yvonne Frost was born Yvonne Wilson in 1931 in Los Angeles, California, into a Baptist family. Married in 1950, divorced in 1960, she earned an A.A. degree in secretarial skills and went to work for an aerospace firm in Anaheim. There, she met Frost, who had arrived via Canada. She was involved with the Spiritual Frontiers Fellowship and, together, they studied psychic development. Another career move took them to St. Louis, Missouri, where they pursued the Craft. Together Gavin and Yvonne Frost have authored more than 20 books that are now available in five languages. They are proud to describe themselves as "spiritual libertarians."

They founded the Church and School of Wicca and wrote *The Witch's Bible*, based on the correspondence courses they taught. The book was published in 1971 and caused much controversy among Neopagan Witches, almost none of whom recognized that the Frosts' tradition was based on eighteenth-century Druidic concepts but took a pathway different from that of Gardnerianism. Over the years, the Frosts have forged a theological interface that allows them to get along with Neopagan Witches, who, in turn, have generally accepted that there is more than one variety of Witchcraft in the world.

The Church and School of Wicca is one of the largest and most accessible of the current Witchcraft groups and sponsors some of the largest festivals. Its Samhain (Hallowe'en) Seminar has been held, usually in Atlantic Beach, North Carolina, every year since 1972 and is one of the models on which the current system of festivals in the broader Neopagan subculture is based. Over the years, the CSW has chartered 28 independent CSW Tradition churches. In 1985, a federal appeals court recognized the CSW as equal to any other church—a milestone of which the church is proud.

More than 50,000 students have enrolled in CSW correspondence courses since its inception, and roughly 250 students graduate from the program each year, so that the CSW Tradition has become one of the most widespread of its kind. Its official journal, *Survival*, is available by subscription and to students enrolled in the school.

Further Reading
Frost, Yvonne, and Gavin Frost. Interview by Ellen Evert Hopman and Lawrence Bond. In *People of the Earth: The New Pagans Speak Out*. Rochester, VT: Destiny Books, 1996.
———. *The Magic Power of Witchcraft*. West Nyack, NY: Parker, 1976.
———. *Tantric Yoga: The Royal Path to Raising Kundalini Power*. York Beach, ME: Weiser, 1989.
———. *Who Speaks for the Witch? The Wiccan Holocaust*. New Bern, NC: Godolphin House, 1991.

Church of All Worlds

The Church of All Worlds (CAW) is an organization of individuals who regard the Earth and all life on it as sacred. The CAW considers living in harmony with and understanding the natural world a religious act. While the community prescribes no particular dogma or creed, the commonality of the members lies in their reverence and connection with Nature and with Mother Earth, seeing her as a living entity. Human beings are not only her children, but evolving cells in her vast, organic body. Indeed, in 1970, it was the CAW's founder, Oberon Zell, who first formulated and published the thealogy of deep ecology that has come to be known as "The Gaia Thesis."

The CAW embraces philosophical concepts of imminent divinity and emergent evolution. The CAW is also a self-described "Neopagan" group, implying an eclectic reconstruction of ancient Nature religions and combining archetypes of many cultures with other mystic, environmental, and spiritual disciplines. The CAW mission statement describes its purpose as being "to evolve a network of information, mythology, and experience to awaken the divine within and to provide a context and stimulus for reawakening Gaia and reuniting her children through tribal community dedicated to responsible stewardship and the evolution of consciousness."

The Church of All Worlds grew out of a "water-brotherhood" called "Atl," formed by Tim (now Oberon) Zell, Lance Christie, and their wives at Westminster College in Fulton, Missouri, in 1962 and then at the University of Oklahoma in Norman, Oklahoma, in the mid-1960s. After Zell moved to St. Louis, Missouri, in 1968, the group was incorporated as the Church of All Worlds, a name derived, along with some central theological concepts, from Robert Heinlein's novel *Stranger in a Strange Land*. In that year Zell also began *Green Egg*, the church's newsletter. In 1971, the CAW became the first Neopagan religion to win federal tax-exempt status; the state decision that ruled against this status was overturned as unconstitutional.

The results of this social experiment will not be in for many years to come, of course, but its seriousness and ingenuity cannot be doubted. Still, one can observe that during the initial years, when CAW was based strictly on a science-fiction theology, it hovered on the brink of extinction. Then, in about 1970, Zell and the other members of the St. Louis Nest (local chapter) came into contact with Bobbie Kennedy, Carolyn Clark, and perhaps a few other Gardnerian-style Witches. They learned the Craft system, became initiated as Witches, and combined the theology of Wicca with Heinlein's libertarian philosophy. The resulting synergism catapulted the Nest's newsletter, *Green Egg*, into national prominence as the major communication channel for the Neopagan movement between about 1971 and 1976.

The CAW and *Green Egg* continued to be a major force in the Neopagan movement until 1976, when Zell and his new wife, Morning Glory, moved to Northern California, leaving church administration and the magazine in the hands of others. The CAW became virtually moribund within a few months. However, several subsidiary or affiliated organizations (including Nemeton, Forever Forests, and several Neopagan covens) kept the CAW going during the late 1970s and early 1980s. In 1978, the CAW merged with Nemeton, founded by Alison Harlow and Thomas DeLong, on whose land the Zells were living, and Nemeton became the publishing arm of the CAW. In 1987, five years after DeLong's death, the CAW, which had inherited his land, absorbed Forever Forests, which was overseen by several caretakers, including Anodea Judith.

In 1988, with the advent of desktop publishing, Zell decided to revive *Green Egg*, whose niche in the Neopagan scene had never been filled by any of the hundreds of periodicals that had come and gone over the intervening years. This was a timely move: The magazine grew rapidly; the CAW has reemerged as a major force in the Neopagan movement. The *Green Egg*, under the aggressive editorship of Diana Darling, has become a major national Neopagan journal. The available membership statistics confirm the existence of this growth pattern. In 1988, the CAW reported 100 members in six Nests. In 1993, membership was around 500 dues-paying members nationally in several dozen Nests.

The CAW's spiritual pathway is organized into nine Circles, which are subdivided into three Rings. The first Ring consists of laypeople; the second Ring consists of Scions (somewhat parallel to deacons in the Christian church); and the third Ring consists of ordained clergy. The church is governed by a board of directors elected by the general membership at the CAW's annual meeting. The Scions elect a special representative and the presidency is held by a member of the CAW's ordained clergy, which numbered ten persons in 1994. The office of president has been held in recent years by Anodea Judith and by Tom Williams. There is an uneasy balance between the secular aspects of the organization and the processes that lead to ordination of clergy; much effort is spent to find creative ways to resolve this tension.

Further Reading

Judith, Anodea. "CAW: Who Are We? Where Are We Going? And How Will We Get There?" *Green Egg* 81 (May 1988): 15.

Zell, Oberon, and Anodea Judith. Interview by Ellen Evert Hopman and Lawrence Bond. In *People of the Earth: The New Pagans Speak Out*. Rochester, VT: Destiny Books, 1996.

Church of Circle Wicca

The Church of Circle Wicca (Circle) was founded by Selena Fox and Jim Alan in 1974. In 1975 they moved the church to a farm, soon known as Circle Farm, near Sun Prairie, Wisconsin. Circle helped to found the Midwest Pagan Council in 1976, and so became a sponsor of the Pan Pagan Festival, one of the first major national Pagan festivals.

The Church of Circle Wicca was incorporated in 1978 and, in 1979, was one of the first midwestern groups to join the Covenant of the Goddess. Fox began publishing the *Circle Guide to Pagan Groups* in 1979 and has issued a new edition of the guide approximately every two years since then.

In November 1979 Fox was evicted from Circle Farm because of neighbors' complaints about her religion, and she began a search for a more permanent site for the church. In 1983 a parcel of land was purchased by the church near Barneveld, Wisconsin, and the corporation named the land, and renamed itself, Circle Sanctuary. After a five-year battle with neighbors and the local government, Fox won rezoning of the sanctuary as a church. Fox's successful fight to gain recognition of Circle Sanctuary as a legal church gained her deserved national notice, and her *Circle Network News,* first published in 1979, reached a circulation of some 15,000 in 1986. It continues to be a major communication channel for both the Neopagan and New Age movements. Fox defines her ministry as one of interfaith outreach designed to raise public consciousness of nature spirituality by addressing her message to an audience beyond Neopagan circles; this emphasis made her one of the most vocal spokespersons nationally for Neopaganism in general. Circle's School for Priestesses, headed by Fox, is intended to evolve into one of the first seminary training centers for Neopagan Witchcraft in North America.

After the Midwest Pagan Council split into three factions in 1980, the Pagan Spirit Alliance was founded as a larger network for Circle, which sponsored its first Pagan Spirit Gathering (PSG) in 1981. Circle has continued to sponsor many Sabbats (regular coven meetings during the eight holidays of the Wheel of the Year) and festivals in Wisconsin, beginning with the Lammas Campout, the Mother Nature Healing Festival, the PSG (which has remained one of the largest of all festivals), and the Pagan Unity Festival in 1981. The PSG always falls near the summer solstice; the Pagan Unity Festival occurs near the fall equinox. Circle began holding an annual Hallowe'en Festival in Madison, Wisconsin, in 1982.

Fox and Alan separated in 1984, and Fox married her current husband, Dennis Carpenter, in 1986. In 1994 Carpenter received his Ph.D. in psychology from the Saybrook Institute and founded the Pagan Academic Network, whose first meeting took place at the annual meeting of the American Academy of Religion in Chicago, Illinois, in November 1994.

Further Reading

Carpenter, Dennis. "Emergent Nature Spirituality: An Examination of the Major Spiritual Contours of the Contemporary Pagan World View." In Lewis, James R., ed., *Magical Religion and Modern Witchcraft.* Albany, NY: State University of New York Press, 1996, 35–72.

Fox, Selena. "Grist for the Mill: An Interview with Selena Fox." By Anodea Judith. *Green Egg* 93 (June 1991).

———, and Dennis Carpenter. Interview by Ellen Evert Hopman and Lawrence Bond. In *People of the Earth: The New Pagans Speak Out.* Rochester, VT: Destiny Books, 1996.

Circle, Magic

The Witches' working circle is a sacred space as defined by Mircea Eliade. This circle is an area and a period of time during which the rules of ordinary exis-

Blessing of the ritual circle at the start of the 1997 Pagan Spirit Gathering sponsored by Circle Sanctuary. (Photo by Jeff Koslow, Circle Sanctuary archives)

tence do not apply—at least not as strongly as usual. The procedures by which Neopagan Witches cast a circle are almost always derived from those constructed by Gerald Gardner and the other members of the New Forest Coven, and those, in turn, were largely derived from the procedures of ceremonial magic, of Freemasonry, and perhaps of the Order of Woodcraft Chivalry, a group similar to the American Boy Scouts in which Gardner was active.

In the Craft, the circle is conceived as containing positive energy raised by the ritual, whereas in ceremonial magic it was thought to keep out hostile spirits who were being evoked. Neopagans think of the circle as having protective functions also, but only in terms of keeping out negative and confusing energies that might interfere with the magical work being done.

There are many ways to create sacred space. The casting of the circle is almost always done by a Priestess who walks deosil—that is, clockwise—around the circle, tracing its circumference in the air with an athame (or a sword at large gatherings), although sometimes the casting may be done by a Priest and may be laid out with a cord. This casting may be followed by other procedures to further consecrate and strengthen the circle; this differs from one tradition to the next. The casting is always followed by an invocation of the guardians of the four cardinal directions, after which the group is ready to begin the ritual or magical work for the occasion.

Neopagan Witches also refer to a coven as a circle, though more often the term is used to mean a "training circle" in which uninitiated novices gather to work with a Priest or Priestess to be prepared for initiation. Witches also use the term *circle* as a verb: "to circle" means "to meet for a ritual" or "to work a ritual."

See Also: Cast; Coven; Rite, Ritual

Further Reading

Farrar, Stewart. *What Witches Do: The Modern Coven Revealed.* New York: Coward McCann, 1971.

K., Amber. *True Magick: A Beginner's Guide.* St. Paul, MN: Llewellyn, 1991.

Co-Masonry

Co-Masonry, a form of Freemasonry that admits females as well as males, originated in France and spread to England in 1902. Annie Besant, of Theosophical Society fame, was initiated into Co-Masonry and helped to spread the movement in Great Britain. After Besant's death, her daughter, Mabel Besant-Scott, became the head of English Co-Masonry. Besant-Scott, in turn, was Gerald Gardner's neighbor near New Forest and, apparently, through this connection Gardner became involved with the Co-Masons. It has been observed that certain phases of Gardnerian Witchcraft rituals closely resemble aspects of Masonic rites. Until very recently, this has been explained as evidence of an ancient connection between these two strands of occultism. However, the common view that the system of Witchcraft mediated to the world by Gerald Gardner is ancient, has been reexamined by such works as Doreen Valiente's *The Rebirth of Witchcraft* (1989) and Aidan Kelly's *Crafting the Art of Magic* (1991). As a consequence, it makes sense to discuss the various components of Gardner's synthesis.

In the case of Freemasonry, the influence on Gardnerian Witchcraft is reasonably straightforward: Gardner was a Co-Mason. Some of the parallels between Wicca and Masonry are described by Valiente: "[T]here are terms such as 'the Working Tools'; the reference to the candidate's being 'properly prepared' for initiation; the 'Charge' which is read to the new initiate; and the existence of three Degrees through which the initiate must advance, which are all very reminiscent of Masonic procedure when one finds them in the Witch rituals. Indeed, both Masons and Witches today refer to their cult as 'the Craft'" (pp. 55–56).

See Also: Freemasonry; Introduction

Further Reading

Adler, Margot. *Drawing Down the Moon: Witches, Pagans, Druids, and Other Goddess-Worshippers in America Today,* 2d ed. Boston, MA: Beacon Press, 1986 [1979].

Kelly, Aidan A. *Crafting the Art of Magic, Book I: A History of Modern Witchcraft, 1939–1964.* St. Paul, MN: Llewellyn, 1991.

Valiente, Doreen. *The Rebirth of Witchcraft.* Custer, WA: Phoenix, 1989.

Cone of Power

The *cone of power* is a term used in the Craft movement to describe the psychic or magical energy raised in a circle by dancing, chanting, or whatever other means employed. Sometimes the energy is visualized as cone-shaped, but not necessarily. Some Witches contend that what they experience is a ball of energy, somewhat like ball lightning.

Once the cone of power has been raised, and remains contained within the magic circle, it can be put to use. In most covens, it is used for the healing of either someone in the circle or of someone elsewhere who requested or agreed to the working. Sometimes the cone of power is raised essentially for the sake of the experience itself; we have heard this procedure described as "throwing the energy up in the air and letting it rain down on everyone." Generally, all members of the group say that they feel as if they each received more energy than they exerted.

Obviously, the uses for this magical energy are limited only by the imaginations and ethics of the group. Current books written by Witches that describe their work and experiences in a coven give many examples of the use of the cone of power.

See Also: Circle, Magic; Healing
Further Reading
Farrar, Stewart. *What Witches Do: The Modern Coven Revealed*. New York: Coward McCann, 1971.
K., Amber. *True Magick: A Beginner's Guide*. St. Paul, MN: Llewellyn, 1991.

Conjure

Conjure men, variously known as witch doctors, jujumen, obeahmen, root doctors, and leaf doctors, are Priests and physicians among African tribes as well as among believers in Vodun, Santeria, Macumba, and those who believe in the healing powers of herbs. In Africa, conjure men, who claim to know the sources of evil and how to use them, treat patients for illnesses induced by a witch, and the conjure men often control entire villages. A general practitioner is called a *nganga* and divines the source of a victim's adversity through the *hakata*, or "bones." *Ngangas* are supposed to use their power only for good.

Poisons represent powerful weapons for Witch doctors, who use them to detect witches and to perform spells. When poisons are used in spells, they can induce the desired effects promised by conjure men. When a poisonous drink, administered to someone suspected as evil by a witch doctor, is well tolerated, the suspect is proved to be an evil Witch.

African healers dispense herbal medicines, divine futures, and seek alternative methods of treatment for their patients. Among the chronic illnesses treated by witch doctors are high blood pressure, asthma, mental illness, and venereal disease. Some healers claim to have cured AIDS, for which animal sacrifices, chants, and charms are used. Conjure men also can be found in the Deep South of the United States as well as in Haiti, where herbal medicine is used to cure a variety of diseases. Such healers do not, however, treat the serious illnesses caused by spirit intervention and Witchcraft.

See Also: African Religions; Spells
Further Reading
Hess, David J. *Samba in the Night: Spiritism in Brazil*. New York: Columbia University Press, 1994.
Hinnells, John R., ed. *A New Dictionary of Religions*. London: Blackwell, 1997.
Randolph, Vance. *Ozark Magic and Folklore*. New York: Dover, 1964 [Reprint of *Ozark Superstition*. New York: Columbia University Press, 1947].

Cords

Cords have significance as amulets and in the casting of spells. In Babylon, cords were used as healing amulets because of the rebirth connected with this symbolic umbilical cord. In Egypt, magical cords with or without knots signified matriarchal law.

Witches used knotted cords to tie up the weather or anything else they wished to bind magically. They also used cords to lay out mystical figures on the ground. Austrian Witch-midwives braided red and white "cords of life" and omitted the black cord of death during baptisms.

In Neopagan Witchcraft, a nine-foot-long red cord is used in a Witch's initiation. In a First-Degree initiation the candidate is blindfolded and bound with cords. Then the candidate is ritually scourged (whipped lightly with cords) and is measured with a cord, which is tied in knots to mark the measures.

Cords are knotted by Witches while they chant a spell. The knots are tied in certain patterns and are only untied at just the right moment, which releases the magic energy and puts the spell into effect. Cords also are used to bind parts of the body to reduce blood circulation as a means of achieving an altered state of consciousness in the raising of psychic awareness.

See Also: Binding; Initiation; Spells
Further Reading
Gardner, Gerald B. *High Magic's Aid*. York Beach, ME: Weiser, 1975.
Kelly, Aidan A., ed. *Neo-Pagan Witchcraft*. 2 vols. New York: Garland, 1990.
Volumes 23 and 24 in the Garland series on *Cults and New Religions*, edited by J. Gordon Melton.

Correspondences

Correspondence between different sets of concepts has been part of Western occultism as far back as can be traced. Correspondence between accessible and inaccessible objects forms the basis of certain magical operations; for example, a certain gemstone can be magically equivalent to the (astrological) planet Venus—so all the qualities of Venus can be applied to a person, object, or situation via the gemstone.

Lists of correspondences published in Craft and other occult books are so numerous that they cannot be repeated here. It can be assumed, however, that the correspondence lists are generally concerned with sets of four things, sets of twenty-two, and sets of seven, in about that order of emphasis.

For Neopagan Witchcraft, sets of four are most important, mainly because the guardians of the four cardinal directions are evoked ritually. Every tradition and every coven, therefore, has a set of correspondences that associate items that make up various natural (and some arbitrary) sets of four. These typically include:

- the four cardinal points of direction (north, south, east, west)
- the four elements of earth, air, fire, and water
- the four working tools that correspond to the Four Jewels of Celtic mythology and to the four suits of the Tarot deck, that is, cup, pentacle, sword, and wand
- colors
- ruling deities
- astrological signs and/or planets
- other items specific to the particular coven or tradition

There is no one "true" set of correspondences in the Craft. In fact, the complicated set of correspondences a coven uses is sometimes thought to serve as a "combination lock" on its workings; the correspondences cannot be easily undone if one does not know how they have been constructed.

See Also: Astrology; Elements
Further Reading
Buckland, Raymond. *Buckland's Complete Book of Witchcraft.* St. Paul, MN: Llewellyn, 1986.

Crowley, Aleister. *Magick in Theory and Practice.* New York: Dover, 1976. Contains numerous lists of correspondences.

Reed, Ellen Cannon. *The Goddess and the Tree: The Witches' Qabala, Book I,* 2d ed. St. Paul, MN: Llewellyn, 1989 [1985].

Coven

The coven is a small working group of Witches. Generally, a coven is restricted to initiated Witches and First Degree initiation is what confers the right to be a member of, and work in, a coven. Before the First Degree initiation, the candidates work in a training circle or Outer Court of some sort. However, covens differ widely in their rules about initiation, most being absolutely and resolutely autonomous. This autonomy also means that any Witch who feels sufficiently trained to do so (usually having received Third Degree training and initiation) is free to start a coven.

The word *coven* is easily found in unabridged dictionaries: It is related to the words *convene, convent,* and *covenant,* and can be applied to any small group gathered for religious purposes. The current concept of the Witches' coven is, however, derived from Margaret Murray's theories on the subject. This is partly because it was Murray's description of what she thought a coven *had been* (used by the group that became the New Forest Coven) to reconstruct the Pagan religion that Murray thought she was perceiving behind the records of the Witch hunts.

Murray defined a coven as consisting of 13 members; some covens interpret this as a maximum number, others as an ideal number. Thirteen members per coven is a very practical number simply because of small-group dynamics—if the size of a coven is much larger than 13, say, 16 regular members, then the coven will generally find it practical to split into halves, each of which can continue growing. Gardnerians initially insisted that covens must have equal numbers of men and women, but by the mid-1970s this attitude was considered sexist. Covens made up entirely of men or entirely of women, whether gay or "straight," now are considered equal in every way to "mixed-membership" covens.

The regular meetings of a coven for full moons are called Esbats, and those for the eight holidays of the Wheel of the Year are called Sabbats. These two terms are also derived from Murray. Any meeting can also be called a circle.

Governance of covens also differs widely, from extremely hierarchic to extremely democratic. Hence, some covens are ruled absolutely by a High Priestess or sometimes a High Priest; some are ruled by a committee of Elders; and some are ruled by consensus, with "High Priestess" being only a ritual title that is rotated among all the members.

There was some controversy in the early 1970s about whether a Witch must belong to a coven, at least at some point in his or her life. The consensus in the Neopagan community now is that such membership is not necessary: Solitary Witches can get their training from whatever sources they please, and they are judged by other Witches on their own merits.

See Also: Covenstead; Initiation; Introduction; Solitary

Further Reading

Adler, Margot. *Drawing Down the Moon: Witches, Pagans, Druids, and Other Goddess-Worshippers in America Today,* 2d ed. Boston, MA: Beacon Press, 1986 [New York: Viking, 1979]. Provides an excellent survey of all the variations among covens and traditions.

Buckland, Raymond. *The Tree: The Complete Book of Saxon Witchcraft.* York Beach, ME: Weiser, 1974. A Book of Shadows for a tradition with democratic governance of covens.

Budapest, Z. [Zsusanna]. *The Holy Book of Women's Mysteries,* 2d ed. 2 vols. Oakland, CA: Thesmophoria, 1986. The Book of Shadows on Dianic Wicca and consensus governance of covens.

Murray, Margaret A. *The Witch-Cult in Western Europe.* London: Oxford University Press, 1962 [1921].

Covenant of the Goddess

The Covenant of the Goddess (CoG) was established as a California non-profit corporation on Hallowe'en 1975, to serve the Craft movement nationally as a legal church. Although only a small minority of all the covens in America (less than 100 out of probably several thousand) have yet to become members of CoG, it is the largest organization serving this purpose at present.

The Covenant of the Goddess evolved out of a series of meetings in 1974 and 1975 organized by Gwydion Pendderwen between the major Neopagan organizations in California. Many of those involved in these negotiations had previously belonged to the Council of Earth Religions, which was intended to evolve into a legal "umbrella" organization that could serve Neopagans as a church. The meetings alternated between Northern and Southern California, and, although much goodwill was evident, it became clear that the Neopagan organizations overall were too diverse, both structurally and in doctrine, to be able to agree on enough common principles to allow an umbrella organization to form.

In late 1974 Aidan Kelly suggested that an organization might be set up just for Neopagan Witches, all of whom believed themselves to practice the same religion. In March 1975, representatives of more than a dozen California covens met at the house of Gwydion Pendderwen and Alison Harlow in Oakland and ratified and signed the Covenant document prepared by Kelly. This document said that covens, rather than individuals, would be members of the CoG and that the autonomy of the member covens could never be compromised by the Covenant organization.

By the summer solstice, by means of voluminous correspondence, a set of by-laws was amended and agreed upon at the Litha Sabbat held near Ukiah, California, when the full Covenant document was signed by representatives of 20 covens. Harlow was elected to serve as the initial first officer of CoG. By the fall, local councils had been established in Northern and Southern California.

CoG remained confined essentially to California due to the CoG's rather cautious admissions policy, although a few covens outside California became members, which requires some sort of personal knowledge about potential new member groups. This situation changed in 1981, when Ginny Brubaker and Dave Norman of Chicago were brought out to California and then were elected co–first officers of CoG, thus ensuring that the next Merrymeet (annual membership meeting) would have to take place in the Midwest. This plan worked well: At the Merrymeet in 1982, covens from all over the United States were represented in the CoG, and a truly national board of directors was elected.

The local councils of CoG consist of covens within a limited geographic area; these are intended to serve as coordinating committees to run local festivals and intercoven Sabbat celebrations, but these functions have largely been taken over by other local networking organizations that include other varieties of Neopagans. To date there have been local councils in Chicago, Florida, Minnesota (Northern Dawn), New England, Northern California,

Ohio, the Pacific Northwest, Southern California, Texas, and Wisconsin. Recently Grey Cat of Northwind and the Church of the Iron Oak have organized the Dogwood Council for southern states, and Amber K., who moved to New Mexico, spurred organization of the Cimarron Council for southwestern states.

A high point in CoG's history was reached at the 1993 Second World Parliament of Religions in Chicago. There, the CoG was represented by First Officer Phyllis Curott and many other delegates. Curott had the pleasure of asking the Roman Catholic Archbishop of Chicago, Joseph Cardinal Bernardin, on live television, to support the Witches' right to circle in a park near the parliament meeting. The Archbishop graciously allowed this, and the subsequent circle, attended by representatives of most of the world's major religions, was held precisely on the spot where the riot at the 1968 Democratic Convention had broken out 25 years earlier. The event received front-page coverage in newspapers across America.

Further Reading

Harrow, Judy, Phyllis Curott, Rowan Fairgrove, and Russell Williams. Interview by Ellen Evert Hopman and Lawrence Bond. In *People of the Earth: The New Pagans Speak Out*. Rochester, VT: Destiny Books, 1996.

Kelly, Aidan A. *Hippie Commie Beatnik Witches: An Historical Memoir on Witchcraft in California, 1967–1977, with the NROOGD Book of Shadows*, 2d ed. Los Angeles, CA: Art Magickal Publications, 1996.

Covenstead

The covenstead is the meeting place of a coven. It may be a fixed, regularly used place, even a specific room dedicated to and decorated as a Pagan temple, or it may be only a concept that rotates amongst the living rooms of the coven's members. There are some passages in the Craft Laws that apply to covensteads and some covens (even non-Gardnerian ones) that use these as important rules for how a covenstead should function. However, interpretation of these passages in the Craft Laws is highly controversial.

The Witches' circle is a sacred space created for a specific occasion. A dedicated covenstead is, to some extent, a permanent circle and always feels like sacred space for precisely the same reasons that, say, a Catholic church feels sacred to its parishioners. A dedicated covenstead merely renews the continually existing circle at the beginning of a meeting or a working and does not recast the circle "from scratch."

See Also: Coven, Craft Laws
Further Reading
Farrar, Stewart. *What Witches Do: The Modern Coven Revealed*. New York: Coward McCann, 1971.

K., Amber. *True Magick: A Beginner's Guide*. St. Paul, MN: Llewellyn, 1991.

Cowan

To Neopagan Witches, a "cowan" is any non-Witch, although the term is not actually applied to Neopagans who do not call themselves Witches. In practice the term means "outsider"—anyone who is not a member of the Neopagan movement and therefore does not understand its vocabulary, concepts, or customs.

The term *cowan* is actually Masonic in origin and, perhaps, was even used in medieval times. In that context, a cowan is someone not trained in the Craft of Masonry and is therefore not competent to erect a temple—excluding both the inner and outer parts of a temple. The Pagan Craft uses many terms derived from the Masonic Craft, including the term *the Craft* itself.

Further Reading

Waite, Arthur Edward. *A New Encyclopedia of Freemasonry*. New York: Weathervane Books, 1970. On the term *cowan*, see p. 152.

Craft, The

The Craft was actually a Masonic term for Freemasonry. Stonemasonry used to be regarded as a craft in that there was a "craft" of making necklaces, etc. In Freemasonry the idea is to build (i.e., to "craft") the inner temple. Gardner borrowed this term for Freemasonry. Neither Gerald Gardner nor any other members of his covens seem to have used *the Craft* as a general term for the Wiccan religion until late in the 1970s. Before then, in his books and in the Book of Shadows, Gardner always referred to Witchcraft as "the cult" (as in Margaret Murray's writings) or "the Art" (one of the terms used in *The Greater Key of Solomon*). The term is useful because one can refer to "the Craft" within earshot of cowans (non-Witches) without alarming them, whereas the term *Witchcraft* just might.

See Also: Freemasonry; Introduction
Further Reading

Harvey, Graham. *Contemporary Paganism: Listening People, Speaking Earth*. New York: New York University Press, 1997.

Kelly, Aidan A. *Crafting the Art of Magic, Book I: A History of Modern Witchcraft, 1939–1964*. St. Paul, MN: Llewellyn, 1991.

Craft Laws

The Craft Laws are contained in an important document that some think of as ancient, but which most likely was created by Gerald Gardner, the founder of the modern Witchcraft movement. Whatever their origin, this fundamentally theological document of the Craft movement is almost as important as the "Charge of the Goddess," and is continually invoked and argued over. The Craft Laws are reproduced in full in Appendix B of this book.

Further Reading
Bell, Jessie W. *The Grimoire of Lady Sheba.* St. Paul, MN: Llewellyn, 1972. This book incorporates her earlier *Lady Sheba's Book of Shadows*, which was the second publication of the Craft Laws.
Johns, June. *King of the Witches: The World of Alex Sanders.* New York: Coward McCann, 1969. The text of the Craft Laws was first published as an appendix to this book.
Kelly, Aidan A. *Crafting the Art of Magic, Book I: A History of Modern Witchcraft, 1939–1964.* St. Paul, MN: Llewellyn, 1991.
———. *Inventing Witchcraft: A Case Study in the Creation of a New Religion.* Los Angeles, CA: Art Magickal Publications, 1996.

Craft Name

It is customary for Neopagan Witches to take a new name upon initiation into a coven. This is parallel to the custom of taking a new name given one upon his or her ordination or reception into a religious order (a custom found in many religions, including Roman Catholicism and Buddhism). In the 1960s and 1970s, the new name was kept a secret from all but the members of one's coven—the name was to serve as a device for building a new magical personality. Witches who chose to identify themselves publicly as Witches always did so under their real names or under an ordinary-sounding pseudonym.

It was apparently Starhawk (Miriam Simos) who first adopted a Craft name, which she used to create a new *public* persona for herself as author of *The Spiral Dance*, published in 1979. Since then a great many publicly known Witches have adopted such names as a way to shield their privacy, and some even use these names to hide their ordinary identities from other Witches. In addition, newcomers, even before beginning any training, tend to adopt a new name.

See Also: Initiation
Further Reading
Guiley, Rosemary. *The Encyclopedia of Witches and Witchcraft.* New York: Facts on File, 1989.

Crone

In Robert Graves's theory, set forth in his book *The White Goddess* (in many ways one of the most basic "thealogical" texts for the Neopagan movement), the goddess appears as a trinity, under the aspects of Maiden, Mother, and Crone. Graves believed that these terms referred back to ancient and/or non-

A caricature of a fortune-teller titled La bonne aventure *(Good fortune) by L. Boill shows a typical Crone image. (Corbis/Leonard de Selva)*

Western models in which the Maiden is a pre-adolescent or unmarried girl, the Mother is a married woman of childbearing age, and the Crone is a post-menopausal woman. As described here, the concept sounds quite sexist, but it is not viewed as such even by radical Dianic Witches, because other aspects of the model are extremely empowering for women.

The Crone, for example, is an archetype of the Wise Old Woman—that is, the village healer and Priestess who, in Margaret Murray's theory, was the reality behind the Christian stereotype of the toothless hag who was probably a Witch. Whether there is any historical merit to Murray's theories or not, the concept of the Crone is valuable now because it does serve to empower older women in American society. When women were thought to be useful only for bearing children, they obviously became useless when they could no longer do so—this attitude was common in the United States not very many decades ago. Now, when a woman reaches menopause, it can begin a period of liberation for her. Since a menopausal woman now has a useful life expectancy of 30 or 40 more years and probably is no longer raising children, she is able to spend more time developing mentally, physically, and spiritually. Thus, a Crone is no longer "the toothless hag" of folklore, but is considered a valuable, wise member of society.

See Also: Graves, Robert
Further Reading
Budapest, Zsusanna. *The Grandmother of Time*. San Francisco, CA: HarperSan Francisco, 1989.
Graves, Robert. *The White Goddess: A Historical Grammar of Poetic Myth*, 3d ed. London: Farrar, Straus, 1966 [1948, 1956]. None of the references to Murray's theories about Witchcraft were in the 1948 edition; they were added after Gardner and Graves linked up.

Cross-Quarter Days

Cross-quarter days are the four traditional Celtic festivals now celebrated in the United States by Neopagan Witches. The four Lesser Sabbats, on the quarter days (solstices and equinoxes), and the four Greater Sabbats (holidays that "cross" the quarter days about halfway in between) make up the "Wheel of the Year." Despite the traditional names, there is not much difference in the enthusiasm with which these holidays are celebrated. The most common names used by Witches for the Greater Sabbats are Brigid (February 1), Beltane (May 1, better known as May Day), Lughnasad (August 1), and Samhain (November 1, better known as Hallowe'en).

See Also: Beltane; Brigid; Lughnasad; Samhain; Wheel of the Year
Further Reading
Campanelli, Pauline. *Wheel of the Year: Living the Magical Life*. St. Paul, MN: Llewellyn, 1989.
Kelly, Aidan A. *Religious Holidays and Calendars: An Encyclopedic Handbook*. Detroit, MI: Omnigraphics, 1991.

Cup

The cup is one of the basic magical working tools of Neopagan Witches. It is used to hold wine used in rituals or shared among coveners. Cups are also referred to as chalices or goblets. Before they can be used in rituals, cups must be consecrated in rites that expose them to all four elements: water, fire, air (usually represented by incense smoke), and earth. Cups are often inscribed with symbols. To Witches and alchemists, the cup symbolizes the element of water. In the Tarot, the suit of cups also stands for the water element. The cup is also symbolic of the womb and therefore symbolizes birth.

See Also: Tools, Witches'; Water
Further Reading
Chevalier, Jean, and Alain Gheerbrant. *The Penguin Dictionary of Symbols*. London: Penguin, 1996.
Cooper, J. C. *An Illustrated Encyclopedia of Traditional Symbols*. London: Thames and Hudson, 1978.

Curses

Unlike blessings, curses are meant to cause harm, illness, or even death to one on whom they are laid. Curses evoke supernatural forces to cause a change in someone's fate. People have traditionally hired Witches or sorcerers to perform curses on enemies. With few exceptions, curses are not a part of contemporary Neopagan Witchcraft.

Once a Witch has laid a curse on someone, however, the victim can either ask the Witch to undo the curse or can hire another Witch to help her. Often in these cases, a magical battle takes place between the cursing Witch and the Witch who tries to undo the curse.

Curses can affect whole families and their descendants or can be laid as a protection of treasures or sacred buildings, such as in the case of the Tutankhamen tomb. A curse does not necessarily affect its victim when it is issued—it can remain dormant for long periods of time. Once it becomes effective, though, the duration of its effect can vary considerably.

A common way to lay curses, generally known all over the world, is to execute certain rituals on an effigy of the victim. Small figures of wax are very commonly used as effigies, but also clay, wood, and cloth puppets are used. Clothing, hair, nails, or other belongings of the victim are associated with the effigy, which is eventually burned or melted, thereby causing the victim to suffer or die. In other rituals the effigy is pierced with pins or knives, or parts of the effigy are substituted with animal parts, carcasses, or eggs. The decomposition of these items causes the negative effect on the victim.

It is believed that the most effective curses are laid on waning-moon nights. The power of a curse can be enhanced when it is performed by people on their deathbed, religious authorities, or poor and disregarded persons.

See Also: Hex; Spells
Further Reading
Gordon, Stuart. *The Encyclopedia of Myths and Legends*. London: Headline, 1993.
Valiente, Doreen. *An ABC of Witchcraft: Past and Present*. New York: St. Martin's Press, 1973.

D

Degrees

The initiation system most widely used in Neopagan Witchcraft is a three-Degree system derived from the three-Degree system of what were called the "Blue Lodges" of Freemasonry (which also met at the full moons). However, some traditions use a one-Degree system, in which there is only one significant initiation ritual.

There are three initiations—the First Degree of initiation, the Second Degree of initiation, and the Third Degree of initiation. The First Degree of initiation is sometimes used to begin the process of training within a coven since, at this stage, there can be some knowledge and practices that the coven wants to keep "oath-bound," that is, secret. In other covens and traditions, a full year of training in the coven will precede the First Degree initiation ritual.

The Second Degree of initiation is rather more ambiguous in meaning. As with an M.A. degree from a college or university, it is often difficult to discern what additional privileges or authority it confers. In some covens, particularly Gardnerian covens, a woman is sometimes required to be "of Second Degree" before she is allowed to serve as Assistant High Priestess or to preside over a complete ritual. In other covens, only at the Second Degree can a member be called a Priest or Priestess.

The Third Degree of initiation is universally understood in Neopagan Witchcraft to be the Degree of full empowerment. A Third Degree High Priest or Priestess is fully empowered to operate autonomously, to run her coven as she sees fit, to begin a new coven, to initiate other Witches when and how she sees fit, and so on. Among the more conservative Gardnerians, this autonomy is quite restricted in practice by the close ties that may exist between a High Priestess and her Queen, and High Priests simply are not allowed to do many things that they could do in other traditions. Traditional Gardnerian covens have always bestowed much more power on a High Priestess than on a High Priest.

There is also a five-Degree system of initiation, although its existence is not as widely recognized. This is the system of "elemental pacts" that appears to have originated with the Temple of the Pagan Way in Chicago, Illinois. In this system, the initiate spends a year each working on the elements earth, water, fire, air, and spirit before reaching full empowerment. If a coven uses a system like this, its lineage probably extends back to the Temple of the Pagan Way.

See Also: Coven; Elements; Initiation; Pagan Way
Further Reading
Matthews, Caitlín, and John Matthews. *The Western Way: A Practical Guide to the Western Mystery Tradition*. London: Arkana, 1994 [1985].
Waite, Arthur Edward. *A New Encyclopaedia of Freemasonry*. New York: Weathervane Books, 1970 [1921, 1898].

Demons

The notion of the existence of some form of conscious, demonic force has been a part of the human imagination since prehistoric times. The belief that malicious entities lie behind natural disasters and other unpleasant aspects of human life is still prevalent in certain traditional societies, particularly in such cultural areas as Africa and Oceania, in the form of natural elements (typically animals or such phenomena as floods), or as spirits of the ancestors. Especially before the development of scientific discoveries that proffered inanimate explanations for the irregularities of nature, demons were believed to be responsible for unexplainable natural disasters and diseases. While scientific explanations have gradually supplanted metaphysical explanations, demons and devils presently survive in the mythology of Jung's collective unconscious and in other schools of the study of the mind that interpret evil forces as projections of human fear and/or as hallucinations. Although associated with the traditional stereotype of Witches, demons have no place in modern, Neopagan Witchcraft.

While often the two words *devil* and *demon* are used interchangeably— *devil* from the Greek *dia-ballo*, "to throw across," in the sense of an "accuser"; and *demon* from the Greek *daemon*, "spirit" (originally "soul")—their meanings evolved through the centuries and in different religious traditions. The Greek *daemon* came to be associated with invisible spirits who occupied the ethereal spaces between God and humanity. They were beings flying between the world and the sky—the lower and the upper regions—connecting what was above with what was below. In the writings of Homer, the word *daemon* refers to a god or, in a rather vague sense, to a divine efficacy. In a famous passage of Plato's *Symposium*, Diotima described Eros as a "great spirit—daimon—and like all spirits a being intermediate between the divine and the mortal." The Greek notion of *daemon* as a personal, familiar spirit originally was derived from similar notions widespread throughout the Near East, from Greeks to Babylonians, from Egyptians to Persians. The *daemon* of Socrates is the most familiar example of this type of spirit. A later variation on this basic idea is that of a guardian spirit who mediated between the spirit world and humankind, bringing dreams and foretelling the future.

The ancient Jewish philosopher Philo said that air was the region inhabited by incorporeal souls, which the philosophers called *daemons*, but which the Scriptures more appropriately call angels. The role of *daemons* was of considerable importance in Plutarch's universe. They were regarded as a crucial intermediary link between the gods and humanity, intervening in the affairs of human life in ways that would be unworthy of more exalted beings. In the *De defectu oraculorum*, Plutarch's chief concern was the way *daemons* administered the oracles, but he also considered them in the much wider context of mythology in general. Some *daemons* are evil, and Plutarch's belief in them afforded him an explanation of Typhon and the other giants in mythology: These were, in fact, fallen *daemons*, confined in bodies as a punishment.

In the early stages of Judaism, demons did not have a big impact on the religious belief system. During the first diaspora, when the Jews were in contact with the dualist vision of Zoroastrianism, a more defined role for demons was developed within the tradition, in particular in the *aggadah* that reflected the popular rabbinical beliefs. These mythological figures drew from the indigenous Pagan beliefs (such as the *shedim*) and were believed to be either creations of God or offspring of Lilith, the first wife of Adam. In the Cabala during the Middle Ages, the evil forces of the Jewish tradition took definite forms, names, and roles, although they were never really fully accepted into Orthodox Judaism.

The Greek word *daemon* was introduced in the Roman and Hellenistic world to indicate evil forces, and thus entered early Christian writings with the negative connotation of impure spirits. The Judeo-Christian tradition elaborated on the concept of the devil as the fallen angel who tempted Adam and Eve and was forever banished from Paradise. Christian literature also drew upon the belief system of other cultures in the depiction of the Apocalypse, wherein appear demons that recall Jewish, Persian, and Mesopotamian myths.

In the transmission of the texts of the Scriptures the devil (in Hellenistic Greek, *diabolos*) came to be identified with Satan (the name used in the Hebrew Bible to mean "adversary"). The belief in evil powers as the source of sicknesses and problems for humans is found in all the early Christian literature, and Christian theology acknowledges evil as necessary for the fulfillment of free will. From very early in its history, Christianity developed the practice of exorcism to expel evil spirits who had taken control of human individuals. In medieval Europe, the belief in the existence of demons came to be associated with Witchcraft and contributed to the development of the practice of exorcism and Witch hunting, fading only after the rise of religious skepticism during the eighteenth-century Enlightenment.

Since the early drafting of the Quran, Muslims also have believed in the existence of demonic forces, known as *shaytan*, who are in constant revolt against God—*ifrit*, *marid*, and *jann* (also known as *jinn*, pre-Islamic hostile spirits associated with the desert). Sometimes these evil forces are identified with animals (such as the snake and the scorpion) or with natural elements. *Iblis*, an ambiguous figure, divine and evil at the same time, partially resembles the devil of the Judeo-Christian tradition—a fallen angel. Believed to be eternally expelled from the Garden of Heaven for refusing to bow upon God's order, in front of Adam (a being made of earth), he gradually also came to be called Satan.

The Hindu tradition is rich with mythic figures of divine, or semidivine, superhuman nature. In Hindu literature demons are ranked hierarchically in cosmic layers. Demons who belong to the lower part of hierarchy are dark beings, such as the *asuras*, who are always adversaries of humankind. *Raksasas* are demons who embody various hostile animals (snakes or vultures, for instance) and who are identified with spirits of the night that kill people and resemble vampires. Other demons of the Indian tradition that passed into Buddhism are *bhutas*, *pretas*, and *pisacas*.

Buddhism, especially at the popular level, inherited the lore of mythological Hindu images, the *asuras* and other demons. These figures belong to the category of sentient beings (like humans and gods) and, as such, are subject to the cycle of reincarnation. The Buddhist archfiend is Mara, who, in vain, tempted Gautama shortly before his enlightenment. Evil forces are encountered in the Burmese Buddhist figures *nats* and other ghosts who inflict pain on humans. In Mahayana Buddhism, demons are alternately good or evil in their effort to keep their devotees in the faith.

A number of female demonic figures also have developed to explain children's sicknesses or death. In medieval Central and Eastern Europe the *lamias*, mythic figures of Greek and Roman origin, were believed to kill children by drinking their blood; the Hindu Churalin, who embody women who died in childbirth (in Islam, *ghul*), are female demons who lie in wait and practice cannibalism. In Judaism, Lilith, considered to be the first wife of Adam, typically was believed to attack children.

Most of the traditional cultures of the world visualize the universe as a three-tiered cosmos of Heaven, Earth, and underworld. Heaven is reserved for deities, living human beings occupy the middle world, and demons often reside primarily in the underworld. The spirits of the dead are also often perceived as living underground, perhaps as a result of the custom of burial in the ground.

In Christianity, the ancient underworld that, originally, was the common fate of humanity became a realm of torture in which sinners and unbelievers were tormented for eternity. In the Christian tradition in particular, underworld devils acquired employment tormenting the souls of the damned, though the earliest Christian idea was that stern, righteous angels tormented the damned. Righteous angels were replaced in popular thought by Satan, ruler of all other devils, who became the king of the underworld.

Although, as noted, demons play no active role in modern, Neopagan Witchcraft, there *is* a place for *mischievous* spirits such as poltergeists. Poltergeist (from the German *poltern*, "to knock," and *geist*, "spirit") activity is often explained as the result of elementals (low-ranking spirits). Poltergeists are mischievous spirits who make noises, move objects around or cause them to fly across a room, and generally cause physical disturbances. Poltergeist activity has been documented all over the world, with records of such disturbances dating as far back as ancient Rome.

See Also: Exorcism; Genie; Satanism
Further Reading
Eliade, Mircea, ed. *Encyclopedia of Religion*. 16 vols. New York: Macmillan, 1987.
Turner, Alice K. *The History of Hell*. New York: Harcourt Brace and Co., 1993.
Zimmer, Heinrich. *Philosophies of India*. New York: Bollingen, 1951.

Deosil

The term *deosil*, or *deiseal*—Irish for "a turning to the right" or "the holy round"—refers to a clockwise circular movement used in magic and Witchcraft for the casting of positive spells and magic circles. The movement is associated with the rotation of the Sun around the Earth in the sky, as well as with blessing and good fortune. Deosil dances and circuits are common around magic circles and Sabbat fires, as well as around holy objects like sacred stones, crops, fields, homes, and buildings. Deosil is the opposite of withershins.

See Also: Cast; Circle, Magic; Withershins
Further Reading
Farrar, Stewart. *What Witches Do: The Modern Coven Revealed*. New York: Coward, McCann, 1971.
Starhawk [Miriam Simos]. *The Spiral Dance: A Rebirth of the Ancient Religion of the Great Goddess*, 2d ed. San Francisco: HarperSan Francisco, 1989 [1979].

Diana

Diana, also known as Artemis, is the classical Goddess of the Moon and of the Hunt. She is one of the most significant figures in modern Witchcraft. Besides independence, self-esteem, and fierce aggressiveness, she personifies the positive characteristics of the moon. Diana, like Selene and Hecate, belongs to the lunar trinity as patron Goddess of Witches and represents power over the Earth. She rules during the new and waxing moons, when magical power related to new beginnings, growth, and achievement is at its height. At the full moon, she is succeeded in power by Selene.

Mythology reports that Artemis, born of Zeus and Leto, was thrust into the role of protector and helper of women. Since she served as a midwife, women have traditionally prayed to her for an easy childbirth. She showed a taste for adventure and independence and she wanted to protect wildlife and animals, as well as women who were victimized by men. According to British myth, Diana directed Prince Brutus of Troy to flee to Britain after the fall of that city. A Dianic cult emerged among European Pagans during the fifth and

This painting, The Druidess *by Rover Lionel, shows a typical Diana image.*
(Corbis/Bettmann)

sixth centuries, and, as Europe became Christianized, Diana became associated with evil and Satan. During the Middle Ages, she also was regarded as the patroness of sorcery and as the leader of Witches' processions and rites.

Diana was associated with the wife of Herod, Herodias, who was responsible for the execution of John the Baptist. Herodias, whose name became

Aradia in Italian lore, took on the aspects of a demon and was condemned to wander the sky forever, although God allowed her to rest in trees from midnight to dawn. Aradia was believed to have been sent to Earth to teach Witches their craft. An organized Dianic cult of Witches is believed to have existed throughout the Middle Ages and the Witch-hunt centuries. Among contemporary Witches, Diana is revered as an archetype of a great goddess, particularly among feminist Witches.

See Also: Dianic Wicca/Goddess Religion; Hecate; Mythology
Further Reading
Gordon, Stuart. *The Encyclopedia of Myths and Legends.* London: Headline, 1993.
Grant, Michael, and John Hazel. *Who's Who: Classical Mythology.* New York: Oxford University Press, 1993.

Dianic Wicca/Goddess Religion

There is a strong women's religious movement in America that focuses on Goddess worship and overlaps (but is not identical to) the Neopagan movement. Although all-women's (now called "Dianic") covens came into being in the 1960s, they did not proliferate until the early 1970s, when the women's movement and the Neopagan movement began to interpenetrate. A key event was a talk given by Julia Carter Zell to a women's group at the Worldcon (the science-fiction world convention) in Los Angeles in 1971. Many all-women's covens consider themselves part of the larger Neopagan Craft movement.

Goddess religions have empowered women to fight for full equality in America and in Western societies in general, a fight that is far from over. Many women argue that a religious tradition that presents divinity as embodied only in male beings devalues women and relegates them to second-class status within the culture. In contrast, a religion that presents divinity as female potentially can give women a status in society that they have long been denied. The fundamental theology of Judaism and Christianity does not propose that God is only male, as is evidenced by, for example, passages in the Psalms that speak of God as a mother. However, the long-standing custom of thinking of God as male in mainstream Western religions makes it almost impossible—in the eyes of many feminists—for women to be considered of equal status to men in those religious communities. The ordination of women as priests in many Protestant and Anglican churches during recent decades has improved the overall situation, but many women argue that they have the right and duty to be Priestesses, not Priests—that is, to define a very different set of roles for themselves within religious communities. So far, this has been possible only within extremely liberal forms of Christianity and within the Neopagan movement.

The first Dianic coven in Venice, California, was developed by Zsusanna Emese Budapest. That original coven was known as the Susan B. Anthony

Coven No. 1. Early in the 1980s, Budapest moved to Oakland, California, and began a second coven. She left the Venice coven under the leadership of Ruth Barrett, a High Priestess that Budapest trained. Under Barrett's leadership, the Venice coven changed its name to the Circle of Aradia. Budapest's Oakland coven then took the name Susan B. Anthony Coven No. 1. In Oakland, Budapest led in the formation of the Women's Spirituality Forum, an organization dedicated to bringing Goddess consciousness into the mainstream of feminism, Earth conservation, and peace and justice work in the United States.

The first Dianic coven in Dallas, Texas, was founded by Morgan McFarland and Mark Roberts, both freelance writers and photographers. McFarland began to explore Witchcraft in her early teens and briefly published a Neopagan periodical, *The Harp*. The occult group founded by McFarland and Roberts was originally called The Seekers. In 1972, they began to publish *The New Broom*.

Individual Dianic covens may be all-female separatist groups or mixed male-female groups with a strong feminist emphasis. Within the Dianic coven, the High Priestess represents the Goddess. She is assisted by a "maiden" who represents the child and occasionally (where men are allowed) is assisted by a High Priest who represents the consort. Dianic Witches are monotheistic in that they worship the Goddess as the essential creative force and they are pantheistic in their consideration that every creation in nature is a child of the Goddess. The majority of all female Dianic covens operate in the nude. Some Dianic covens believe in parthenogenesis, or virgin birth. It is the belief of Dianic Witches that the worship of the Goddess in the primeval past coincided with a period of peace on Earth that was destroyed by the rise of men and patriarchal deities.

Dianic Witchcraft has been criticized for losing the balance implied in the acknowledgment of the God as well as the Goddess. It has withstood these attacks to become recognized as an important part of the Goddess tradition in North America.

See Also: Susan B. Anthony Coven; Women's Spirituality Movement
Further Reading
Culpepper, Emily. "The Spiritual Movement of Radical Feminist Consciousness." In Needleman, Jacob, and George Baker, eds., *Understanding the New Religions*. New York: Seabury, 1978, 220–234.
Graves, Robert. *The White Goddess: A Historical Grammar of Poetic Myth*, 3d ed. New York: Farrar, Straus, and Giroux, 1966 [1948, 1956].

Divination

In the broadest sense, the term *divination* can be applied to any means used to learn what the will of God(ess) or the god(esse)s is, on any general or specific topic. Divination is particularly associated with the religious specialists of traditional, tribal religions, such as Shamans. Contemporary Neopagans are almost invariably active in several forms of divinatory practice. Divination is often equated with foreseeing the future, although the term can also be applied to such activities as locating lost objects. Many divinatory methods can be used for character reading (determining a person's characteristics).

There are many traditional systems used for divination. The most prevalent of these are astrology, runestone reading, card reading, palmistry, dream interpretation, and scrying (gazing into a crystal ball), but, in fact, the list is endless. Any set of data that is sufficiently complex and unpredictable can be used for divination. A psychological model that modern intellectuals seem comfortable with is that the data are used to distract the ego, so that the Deep Mind (the "unconscious" mind) can send the ego information that seems to be embodied somehow in the data or symbols that are being used. How and why the Deep Mind could do this is, in fact, a subject on the cutting edge of radical psychological research. Very often some or all of an ancient divinatory or magical technique has evolved into a modern science, leaving the rest of its heritage in the hands of "occultists." This has obviously been the case with astronomy and astrology, and with chemistry and alchemy, but it is also true for some areas of psychology.

The interpretation of dreams as foretelling the future is at least as old as written history, and probably much older still, but it has always been regarded as an occult science; its popularity waxes and wanes with fashion and politics. It is hard to remember, now barely 100 years later, how radical Sigmund Freud's use of dreams to understand the deeper workings of the mind seemed when he introduced the concept. Every school of psychology derived from Freud's now uses dream analysis as a standard therapeutic tool.

Even so, there is little agreement about what dreams mean or even why we dream. Modern research has established that we dream only during periods when the eyes exhibit Rapid Eye Motion (REM), as if watching a play. If a sleeping person is awakened whenever the REM sleep phase begins, so that dreaming is never allowed to begin, he or she will rapidly develop all the symptoms of sleep deprivation, even though he or she has had more than enough hours of the other phases of sleep. Although we do not know what function dreaming actually performs, it seems to be essential for the restorative function that sleep plays for us.

It is fairly common among occultists to assume that dreams are a medium for receiving clairvoyant or spiritual information. As a result, various traditional occult systems of dream interpretation are being revived to be used for this purpose. The modern understanding of dreams is almost always along the lines used in humanistic astrology—the assumption that the dream information indicates probabilities, not certainties, and especially indicates strengths and weaknesses.

See Also: Astrology; Bibliomancy; Fortune-Telling; Oneiromancy; Pendulum; Runes; Scrying
Further Reading
Casewit, Curtis W. *Graphology Handbook*. Para Research, 1980.

Freud, Sigmund. *The Interpretation of Dreams*. New York: Modern Library, 1950.
Tart, Charles. *Altered States of Consciousness*. New York: John Wiley and Sons, 1969.

Dowsing

Dowsing was known to Chinese and Egyptians already 5,000 years ago. The search for water, metals, and other objects located under the Earth's surface led to this ancient divination method.

Dowsers traditionally used forked rods made of hazel or other kinds of wood, although metal forked rods and pendulums are employed. After exposing the tool to the desired object, almost as a dog used in a search is first given the item to be searched for to sniff, the dowser walks in the field until the tool vibrates or shakes to signal the presence of the substance being sought. Some dowsers perform their search simply by swinging a pendulum over a map of the region they want to search.

In Europe, dowsing was popular during the Middle Ages, and, even though bitterly criticized in the nineteenth century, it is practiced today. In Europe dowsing is currently practiced for searching and for medical purposes, but this latter use is forbidden in the United States. The association of dowsing (also called water witching) with Witchcraft was common throughout the Middle Ages and was a cause of persecution for many practitioners.

See Also: Divination; Pendulum
Further Reading

Bletzer, June G. *The Donning International Encyclopedic Psychic Dictionary*. Norfolk, VA: Donning, 1986.
Shepard, Leslie A., ed. *Encyclopedia of Occultism and Parapsychology*. Detroit, MI: Gale Research Inc., 1991.

Drawing Down the Moon

"Drawing down the moon" is a part of the basic Gardnerian ritual that consecrates a Priestess as the embodiment of the Goddess. The text of this procedure from published versions of the Gardnerian Book of Shadows is outlined below:

High Priestess stands in front of Altar and assumes Goddess position (arms crossed).

The Magus, kneeling in front of her, draws a pentacle on her body with a Wand and invokes, "I invoke and beseech Thee, O mighty Mother of all life and fertility. By seed and root, by stem and bud, by leaf and flower and fruit, by Life and Love, do I invoke Thee to descend into the body of thy servant and High Priestess [name]."

Once the moon, having been drawn down, that is, a link having been established, the Magus and other men give the Fivefold Kiss to the High Priestess.

Witches drawing down the moon, from a Greek vase ca. 200 B.C. *(Reprinted from Valiente, Doreen,* The Rebirth of Witchcraft, *Phoenix Publishing, 1989)*

If there be an initiation, then at this time the Magus and the High Priestess in Goddess position (Arms Crossed) say the Charge of the Goddess while the Initiate stands outside the circle.

Probably this procedure was used for some period in Gardner's original coven and by covens derived from it, but, at some point, an entirely different procedure was adopted. The sequence of drawing down the moon and reading the "Charge of the Goddess" was left unchanged in the Book of Shadows.

The High Priestess would first channel the Goddess, and then aspect her into the High Priestess's body. The Priestess was no longer merely a symbol for the Goddess, but took on the persona of, and became, the Goddess present in the flesh. The phrase "drawing down the moon" refers to this transubstantiation of the Priestess.

Some covens use a procedure called "drawing down the sun," in which a Priestess invokes the god to become embodied in a Priest. In most covens now, the Priest aspects a god—becoming, for a while, a God present in the flesh.

There has been some mild controversy over whether it is appropriate (or even possible) for a woman to aspect a god, or a man a goddess. Most Witches believe that if a person can aspect in this way, and so serves the needs of the coven, there are no realistic grounds to question the rightness of the working.

See Also: Aspecting; Possession
Further Reading

Adler, Margot. *Drawing Down the Moon: Witches, Pagans, Druids, and Other Goddess-Worshippers in America Today*, 2d ed. Boston, MA: Beacon Press, 1986 [New York: Viking, 1979].

Valiente, Doreen. *The Rebirth of Witchcraft*. London: Robert Hale, 1989.

Druids

All modern "Druidic" organizations, beliefs, and concepts date back no further than the eighteenth century, when some British antiquarians believed John Aubrey's seventeenth-century guess that Stonehenge might have been built by Druids. The existence of Druids became known through translations of Greek and Roman literature. The Druid Order claims that its foundation took place at a meeting of "British Druids" in 1717, organized by John Tolan and William Stukely. Stukely later became known as the "Arch Druid" and as the founder of modern Druidism. However, this date is probably actually that of the foundation of Freemasonry.

In 1781, the Ancient Order of Druids was founded by Henry Hurle, a carpenter. The order was a Masonic offshoot and a charitable organization (the Fraternal Lodges provided the equivalent of life and health insurance for their members throughout the eighteenth and nineteenth centuries). Another Romantic proponent of Druidism was Edward Williams, who wrote as Iolo Morganwg, a brilliant but eccentric scholar who founded modern Welsh studies, but whose forgeries of Welsh manuscripts confounded scholars for about a century—and still confound the unwary layperson. Morganwg held what is now considered the first Neopagan Sabbat on Primrose Hill in London in 1792; his Gorsedd ritual, created entirely by himself, was adopted by the Welsh as part of the annual Eisteddfod (Welsh poetry competition).

In 1833 the Ancient Order of Druids split over the issue of whether charity was its primary purpose, with the United Ancient Order of Druids continuing purely as a charitable organization and the Ancient Order of Druids retaining the "mystical" traditions. By the early twentieth century, there were at least five Druidic organizations in England, including the Druidic Hermeticists and the British Circle of the Universal Bond. In 1963, the Order of Bards, Ovates, and Druids split away from the Ancient Order of Druids, Ross Nichols becoming its Chosen Chief in 1964.

The number of Druid orders has multiplied greatly in Britain during the last decade or so. Several dozen exist, and their interrelationships have become extremely complex.

There is also a Council of British Druid Orders, of which Elizabeth Murray is secretary, in London. It was formed in 1989, initially with four Druid organizations as members. It now has 14 orders that send delegates regularly, with others who communicate with the council but do not send delegates. The council also has links with Druid groups in France, Holland, Ireland, the United States, and Australia.

Druid groups probably have a total of about 9,000 members and there may be thousands of people that work a Druid path learned from John and Caitlin Mathews and similar writers. Various Druidic groups exist in North America also, such as Ar nDraiocht Fein; the Druidic Craft of the Wise, or Mental Science Institute; and the Reformed Druids of North America.

See Also: Grove

Further Reading

Carr-Gomm, Philip. *Elements of the Druid Tradition*. Shaftesbury, England: Element Books, 1991.

Hutton, Ronald. *The Pagan Religions of the Ancient British Isles: Their Nature and Legacy*. Cambridge, MA: Blackwell, 1991.

Nichols, Ross. *The Book of Druidry: History, Sites, and Wisdom*. Edited by John Matthews and Philip Carr-Gomm. London: Aquarian/Thorsons, 1990.

Shalcrass, Philip, ed. *A Druid Directory*. St. Leonards–on–Sea, England: British Druid Order, 1995.

E

Earth (element)

Earth is one of the four classical elements of nature thought to constitute the universe. Some characteristics associated with earth are the direction north, fertility, darkness, quiet, practicality, thrift, acquisition, patience, responsibility, boredom, stagnation, the color green, the pentacle (the Witches' tool), and the Tarot suit pentacle. Earth is considered to be a female element. All known names for earth (Ertha, Terra, and Europa, for example) have been female.

See Also: Air; Fire; Gnomes; Pentagram; Water
Further Reading
Cirlot, J. E. *A Dictionary of Symbols*. New York: Dorset Press, 1991.
Heisler, Roger. *Path to Power*. York Beach, ME: Weiser, 1990.

Elders

In a Craft coven, the Elders are initiates of at least the Second Degree and sometimes only of the Third Degree. In a coven with a fairly democratic structure, Elders constitute the normal governing body with the authority (ability) to appoint or depose a High Priest or High Priestess and to do whatever else is needed to keep the coven functioning. In theory, according to the Craft Laws, in a Gardnerian coven the High Priestess's authority should be counterbalanced by that of the Elders as a group. However, when no one is elevated to the Third Degree, or when any Third-Degree initiates are required to hive off immediately and form their own covens, some Gardnerian Priestesses have managed to avoid any such sharing of power.

In a broader sense, within the overall Wiccan and Neopagan community, Elders are those who have been around for a while and have accumulated practical experience in solving the problems that tend to come up over and over again in covens or local committees. Although there is no firm rule that dictates who is and who is not considered an Elder, for the most part, people are judged in terms of how much they have really contributed to the movement. As a rule of thumb, an Elder usually is someone who has been active in the movement for 20 years or more. It is the network of friendships and relationships among Elders that persists while covens and local groups come and go that provides the real continuity and structure within the Neopagan movement.

These Elders have no tools except their moral authority and personal reputations for exerting influence on the movement, whether locally or nationally. Nevertheless, if, despite all else that might be happening, the Elders of the Neopagan movement itself reach a broad consensus about an issue, then the Neopagan movement will shift its direction, slowly but surely, toward the recommendation by the Elders.

See Also: Coven; Degrees; Initiation

Further Reading

York, Michael. "New Age and Paganism." In Harvey, Graham, and Charlotte Hardman, eds., *Paganism Today: Wiccans, Druids, the Goddess, and Ancient Earth Traditions for the Twenty-First Century.* London and San Francisco: Thorsons, 1996, 157–165.

———. *The Emerging Network: A Sociology of the New Age and Neo-Pagan Movement.* Plainfield, NJ: Rowman and Littlefield, 1995.

Elementals

The term *element* has come to be associated with the atomic elements in modern times. Prior to the modern era, dating back to at least the time of the ancient Greeks, this term referred to the four classical elements of earth, air, water, and fire. It seems that by these "elements" the ancients meant to refer to what we might call "states of matter" today: solid, gas, liquid, and (for lack of a better term) energy.

The Western occult tradition postulated that these "states" were the result of the activity of small, invisible spirits called elementals. While some branches of the occult tradition view elementals as transitory and soulless, others see them as representing a conscious life that evolves from elementals through fairies and devas (angels). The task of the elementals is to build forms in the natural world, providing an arena in which other beings, such as human souls, can evolve spiritually. Earth elementals have traditionally been designated Gnomes, water elementals Undines, air elementals Sylphs, and fire elementals Salamanders.

Poltergeist (from the German *poltern*, "to knock," and *geist*, "spirit") activity is sometimes explained as resulting from elementals. Poltergeists are mischievous spirits who make noises, move objects around or cause them to fly across a room, and generally cause physical disturbances. Poltergeist activity has been noted in all areas of the world, with records of such disturbances dating back as far as ancient Rome.

Poltergeists have been a topic of investigation since the very beginnings of parapsychology in the late nineteenth century. Theories advanced to explain these disturbances range from unconscious psychokinesis to the activities of restless spirits of the dead. In occult or metaphysical circles, one standard hypothesis is that poltergeist activity is caused by mischievous elemental spirits who entertain themselves by disrupting human lives.

Elementals are also associated with the directions. Almost every traditional society invests special significance in the four cardinal directions—north, south, east, and west. The directions are the dwelling places of specific gods or other spiritual beings, who often "rule" the energies associated with the directions. Contemporary society, for the most part, has lost all sense of the sacredness of the directions. One of the few places in which this archaic view of the world can be found is the classic movie *The Wizard of Oz*, which associates specific "Witches" with each of the directions.

The elemental energies are often invoked in Neopagan rituals, particularly in the initial invocation of the directions. The association of each element with a specific direction varies from tradition to tradition. In one popular schema, the earth element is associated with the north, air with the east, fire with the south, and water with the west.

See Also: Air; Earth; Fire; Water

Further Reading

Andrews, Ted. *Enchantment of the Faerie Realm: Communicate with Nature Spirits and Elementals.* St. Paul, MN: Llewellyn, 1993.

Shepard, Leslie A., ed. *Encyclopedia of Occultism and Parapsychology.* Detroit, MI: Gale Research Inc., 1991.

Elements

The four classical elements—earth, air, water, and fire—constitute the foundation of natural magic. They are considered to be the basis of all life. Each of the four elements is ascribed certain characteristics. Many different things, including beings, gems, minerals, metals, planets, constellations, personality traits, and geometrical shapes, have been viewed as corresponding to the different elements. Some of these associations are:

air	*water*	*earth*	*fire*
birds	fish	terrestrials	stars
east	west	north	south
wand	cup	pentacle	sword
male	female	female	male
yellow	blue	green	orange
silver	silver	gold	gold
breath	blood	flesh	vital heat
spring	autumn	winter	summer
heart	brain	spleen	liver

Earth is the heaviest element, followed by water. Air is lighter, and fire is the lightest of all. Alchemy was based on the four elements. It was believed that if all of the elements could be combined harmoniously and equally, the result would be the Philosopher's Stone, which could transmute base metals into gold. Modern Witches consecrate their working tools and ritual objects with the four elements.

Some, whose only contact with the notion of elements has been in a science class, will immediately think of the materials diagrammed by the periodic table—oxygen, iron, hydrogen, silicon, and the like—when they hear the term *element*. It thus strikes them as strange to consider earth, air, fire, and water as elements. The four elements of modern Neopaganism derive from the elements of ancient Greek philosophy. Classical philosophy and modern science share an interest in discovering the basic—the "elementary"—building blocks of the world. Prior to the advent of contemporary atomic theory, intelligent people who examined the world in which they lived observed that all tangible things could be classified as solids (earth), liquids (water), and gases (air). Sources of heat and light, such as fire and the sun, seemed to constitute a fourth factor (fire), which we might think of as "energy." When reworded as *solid, liquid, gas,* and *energy,* this ancient scheme of classification is not really so strange.

When the ancients analyzed the human being in terms of these four factors, it appeared to them that the physical body was earth-like, feeling and emotions water-like, and thoughts air-like. The fire element provided the spark of life that animated the human frame with activity. Given this way of looking at human nature, it was but a short step to regarding sensitive, emotional people as having more of the water element in their constitutions than their fellows; intelligent people as having more air; practical people as having more earth; and energetic, active people as having more fire.

See Also: Elementals; Gnomes; Salamanders; Sylphs; Undines
Further Reading
Cirlot, J. E. A *Dictionary of Symbols*. New York: Dorset Press, 1991.
Heisler, Roger. *Path to Power*. York Beach, ME: Weiser, 1990.

Enochian Magic

Enochian Magic is a system of communication with angels and spirits and with travel through different planes of consciousness. Its origins can be traced back to the sixteenth century, when English astrologer John Dee joined Edward Kelly in an attempt to communicate with the spirits through a practice known as scrying.

Communication with the spirits was possible thanks to the use of the Enochian language, a complex language of unknown origin. Its melodic sound is similar to that of Sanskrit, Greek, or Arabic. Each Enochian letter

An eighteenth-century engraving depicts the English alchemist, geographer, and mathematician Dr. John Dee (1527–1608), one of the originators of the practice known as Enochian Magic. (Corbis/Michael Nicholson)

features a numerical value, and is associated with elemental, planetary, and Tarot properties.

See Also: Correspondences; Magic
Further Reading

Schueler, Gerald J. *Enochian Magick: A Practical Manual*. St. Paul, MN: Llewellyn, 1987.
Suster, Gerald, ed. *John Dee: Essential Readings*. Wellingborough, Northamptonshire, U.K.: Crucible, 1986.

Eostar

Eostar is the spring-equinox holiday, one of the four Lesser Sabbats of the Neopagan Witches. The Lesser Sabbats comprise the English quarter days, that is, the solstices and equinoxes, and, with the four Greater Sabbats, comprised of the Celtic cross-quarter days, they make up the eight Sabbats of the "Wheel of the Year." The other Lesser Sabbats are Litha (summer solstice, about June 22), Mabon (fall equinox, about September 22), and Yule (winter solstice, about December 22). The name *Eostar* is derived from the Venerable Bede, who pointed out that the Christian festival of the Resurrection of the Lord is called Pasch (or something similar, derived from the Hebrew for "Passover") everywhere else, but in Britain the festival is named after a goddess, Eostar, to whom rabbits were apparently sacred.

See Also: Sabbats; Wheel of the Year
Further Reading
Campanelli, Pauline. *Wheel of the Year: Living the Magical Life*. St. Paul, MN: Llewellyn, 1989.
Kelly, Aidan A. *Religious Holidays and Calendars: An Encyclopedic Handbook*. Detroit, MI: Omnigraphics, 1991.

Equinox

The spring and fall equinoxes, when the lengths of day and night are equal, have apparently been natural festivals for human beings since prehistoric times. The spring equinox coincides with the end of the worst of winter, when flowers begin to grow, and the fall equinox, in most parts of the Northern Hemisphere, marks the time of harvest of important crops. The spring equinox is celebrated by the Sabbat of Eostar, and the fall equinox by the Sabbat of Mabon—the names now generally used in the United States.

See Also: Eostar; Sabbats
Further Reading
Campanelli, Pauline. *Wheel of the Year: Living the Magical Life*. St. Paul, MN: Llewellyn, 1989.
Kelly, Aidan A. *Religious Holidays and Calendars: An Encyclopedic Handbook*. Detroit, MI: Omnigraphics, 1991.

Esbat

The Esbat is a monthly meeting, usually during a full moon, of a coven of Neopagan Witches. The term is derived from Margaret Murray, who asserted that the Esbat was the meeting of a small local group of Witches, whereas a Sabbat was a meeting of a much larger group for one of the eight Pagan holidays that make up the Wheel of the Year (though she did not use the latter term). Whether she was right about all this or not, her terminology has been adopted by Neopagan Witches.

The Esbat is the occasion when a coven will work practical magic or an initiation, since these almost never are done at Sabbats. The ritual worked at Esbats has now become a very flexible and adaptable procedure for covens that do not feel bound to read old scripts as scripture.

See Also: Moon; Sabbats
Further Reading

Campanelli, Pauline. *Wheel of the Year: Living the Magical Life*. St. Paul, MN: Llewellyn, 1989.

Kelly, Aidan A. *Religious Holidays and Calendars: An Encyclopedic Handbook*. Detroit, MI: Omnigraphics, 1991.

Evocation and Invocation

The terms *evocation* and *invocation* refer to two methods to call spirits and deities into magical and religious rituals. Evocations, used in ceremonial magic and sorcery, are elaborate commands, comprised of detailed gestures directed to an entity that appears and does whatever the magician asks. The entities are usually spirits that are evoked to appear in a triangle outside the magician's protective magic circle. The magician is supposed to purify him- or herself through fasting and prayer and is supposed to purify the magical tools beforehand.

Invocations, on the other hand, are used in religious ceremonies as well as in some magic and Neopagan rites. They invite an entity to be present and to protect the rite. The details of such a ritual may vary, in that entities can be invoked by name as well as by the visual and sensory perceptions associated with them. In modern Witchcraft, common entities are the Guardians of the Watchtowers (the spirits ruling the cardinal points), and the Goddess and the Horned God, who are sometimes drawn down into the High Priestess or High Priest. Invocations are also used in Vodun to effect a trance possession.

See Also: Aspecting; Drawing Down the Moon; Magic; Sorcery
Further Reading

Green, Marian. *The Elements of Ritual Magic*. Longmead, Shaftesbury, Dorset, U.K.: Element, 1990.

Stewart, R. J. *Advanced Magical Arts*. Longmead, Shaftesbury, Dorset, U.K.: Element, 1988.

Exorcism

Exorcism is the expulsion of otherwise disembodied spirits who have taken over control of ("possessed") a human being. This driving out can be a for-

Investigator Mr. Price draws chalk rings around vases to see whether they will move during an investigation (and possible exorcism) of a haunted house. (Corbis/Hulton-Deutsch Collection)

mal, ritual procedure, or a less formal process, depending on the tradition. Notions of possession and exorcism practices are found worldwide, in every major religious and cultural tradition. In Western monotheistic religions, the possessing spirit is almost invariably considered an evil demon. Because Witches were also viewed as agents of Satan, it was natural that demonic possession should be attributed to the activity of Witches. No modern Witch, however, would engage in such activity because it would violate the central tenet of contemporary Wiccan ethics, which is "to harm none." Neopagan Witches do not typically engage in personal exorcisms. Exorcism is, however, an important part of such contemporary Afro-Caribbean religious systems as Vodun ("Voodoo").

Exorcism derives from *exousia*, Greek for "oath." Thus, to exorcise means something like placing the possessing spirit under oath—invoking a higher authority to compel the spirit to leave—rather than an actual "casting out" of the spirit. This placement under oath implies that a kind of binding takes place.

In Western religions, possession and exorcism are associated with evil. In this tradition, priests and ministers perform most exorcisms, and the process is often dramatic and even violent. Exorcism is also mentioned in Hebrew scriptures (the Old Testament) in Samuel I where Saul becomes possessed and David exorcises the spirit by playing his harp. Early Rabbinical literature also makes reference to exorcism. As recorded in the Gospels, exorcism played a significant role in Jesus's ministry. Perhaps the best known of his exorcisms was when Jesus was said to cast out unclean spirits from a madman. These spirits then possessed a herd of pigs, who charged over a cliff to drown in the waters below.

In modern times, there has been a revival of interest in possession and exorcism, although current perspectives on such phenomena are more moderate than the traditional, Christian views were. For example, the American psychologist and doctor Carl Wickland felt that such spirits were more confused than demonic and were simply "caught" in the energy of the person whom they appeared to afflict. As a result of this entrapment within the human, the spirit caused what appeared to be schizoid symptoms and other types of aberration in behavior. Wickland found simple persuasion was often enough to effect an exorcism. He described his findings in *Thirty Years among the Dead* (1924).

A contemporary term for exorcism is *releasement*, a word that seems to imply Wickland's view that discarnate spirits become trapped in the possessed person's aura. Some therapists and mediums who deal with such problems prefer the term *releasement* because it does not bear the same connotations with evil as does *exorcism*. Releasement also has been termed *depossession*, a term coined in the field of past-life therapy (dealing with current psychological problems by tracing their roots to previous incarnations). Clients engaged in this form of therapy are sometimes exorcised from the influence of spirits that can cause a wide range of physical, emotional, and mental problems. As with other contemporary therapists, most of the obsessing spirits are not viewed as demonic.

The Western, Christian Tradition does not have formal rituals for exorcising spirits from *spaces* (for example, there are no rites for ridding spirits from "haunted houses"). In traditional China, by way of contrast, there were highly developed rites for clearing spaces bothered by unhappy or mischievous spirits. Contemporary Witches sometimes are called upon to help clear a haunted house of unwanted spirits. This "exorcism of space" can take the form of a clearing ritual. Alternately, a psychically sensitive Witch can attempt to contact and persuade the troubled spirit to vacate the premises, much as a depossession therapist would in the case of spirit obsession.

See Also: Binding; Demons; Possession; Vodun

Further Reading

Crabtree, Adam. *Multiple Man: Explorations in Possession and Multiple Personality.* New York: Praeger, 1985.

Ebon, Martin. *The Devil's Bride, Exorcism: Past and Present.* New York: Harper and Row, 1974.

Eliade, Mircea. *Shamanism: Archaic Techniques of Ecstasy.* Trans. by W. Trask. Princeton, NJ: Princeton University Press, 1964.

Wickland, Carl A. *Thirty Years among the Dead.* North Hollywood, CA: Newcastle Publishing Co., 1974 [1924].

Extrasensory Perception (ESP)

The term *extrasensory perception*, or ESP, has been used since the nineteenth century to refer to any case or situation in which a person acquires information or exercises talents in ways that do not seem explainable in terms of known human abilities. ESP is usually assumed to be the major focus of the discipline of parapsychology. Traditional parapsychology focused on what kind of information or talents were manifested and tried to separate the phenomena of ESP into clairvoyance (seeing at a distance), clairaudience (hearing at a distance), telepathy (mind-reading), psychometry (perceiving the history of an object), and telekinetics (moving an object without physically touching it). Current research tends to focus on the *psychology* of ESP and attempts to interpret ESP in terms of the intuitive or holistic functions of the mind.

One of the academic controversies surrounding ESP is the question of whether it exists at all. The "proofs" of its existence that have been offered never gained universal acceptance among scholars. Even if one discounts the opinions of devout Humanists, for whom it is virtually an article of faith that ESP cannot exist, the whole issue is still debatable.

Another approach to the study of ESP examines whether all human abilities are actually *known*. Many have argued that the accumulated evidence of the existence of anomalous experiences indicates that the human mind is much more complex than we ordinarily imagine, or perhaps are capable of imagining. This theory reaches back at least to William James's classic *The Varieties of Religious Experience,* and continues on through the work of Carl Jung.

Many current attempts to explain the phenomena of ESP do so by asking how the Collective Unconscious or Deep Mind may be communicating information to the ordinary, egoistic mind in an individual. Although there are still problems with this sort of approach, it is at least consonant with, rather than contradicted by, the most recent discoveries in modern physics concerning what the ultimate nature of reality may be.

This idea is perhaps expressed most clearly in the essays of Professor John Archibald Wheeler of Princeton, famous as an expert on general relativity and as the inventor of the concept of the Black Hole. Wheeler tried to have parapsychologists expelled from the American Association for the Advancement of Science on the grounds that parapsychology was not a science at all. His own writings, however, emphasize that physical reality is actually shaped by our perception of it, and that time is not innate, but is merely an aspect of how we unconsciously structure our own experience.

In Wheeler's understanding and as many other writers (such as Robert Anton Wilson) have emphasized, it is possible for information to travel faster than the speed of light, for an effect to precede a cause, or for consciousness to be ultimately "more real" than physical matter. Given this assumption, the speculations of parapsychologists, Witches, Shamans, and occultists seem far more realistic in their way than those that assume that reality is nothing more than what it seems *to them.* The assumption itself creates the reality (called "consensus reality" by sociologist Peter Berger) that they perceive. Currently, the concept that perception is not passively receiving objective, fixed data, but is an interaction between the human mind and the world that partially creates and shapes the data perceived, is a popular notion.

See Also: Hypnosis; Parapsychology
Further Reading
Pratt, J. Gaither. *ESP Research Today: A Study of Developments in Parapsychology since 1960.* Metuchen, NJ: The Scarecrow Press, 1973.
Shepard, Leslie A., ed. *Encyclopedia of Occultism and Parapsychology.* Detroit, MI: Gale Research Inc., 1991.

F

Fairies

Fairies are nature spirits that, under different names and guises, are found in every part of the world. Often pictured as small humanoid beings with wings, they appear to be miniangels. Unlike angels, however, fairies have always been thought to have a mixed relationship with humanity. As nature spirits concerned with natural processes, they do not normally seek out human contact. On the other hand, they have been pictured as mischievous beings who enjoy playing pranks on people. Because the Catholic Church did not have room in its worldview for morally neutral spiritual beings who were neither good nor evil, fairies were rejected as agents of Satan.

The contemporary Neopagan view of fairies has been influenced by Theosophy (the Theosophical Society was founded by Madame Helena Blavatsky in New York in 1875). Theosophy synthesizes ideas from the philosophical systems of China and India as well as the works of Gnostics, Neoplatonists, and Cabalists. At the core of Theosophy is the concept of "spiritual *evolution*," which teaches that human souls can develop their inner potential and then return to the Source of All with increased consciousness.

Theosophists believe that the cosmos is populated with innumerable spiritual entities. A significant class of these entities are

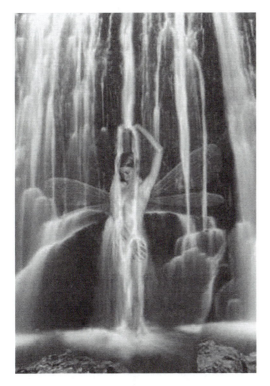

An imaginative illustration of a fairy, embodiment of nature's elemental forces. (North Wind Picture Archive)

what Theosophists call the *devas*, a Sanskrit term for the demigods of Hinduism and Buddhism. These devas are the Theosophical equivalents of angels. Devas oversee natural forces and are responsible for building forms on inner spiritual planes as well as on the physical plane. Some strands of Theosophy view devas as human souls who have, through the process of reincarnation, evolved into higher, spiritual beings. Other strands place the devas on a separate evolutionary path, viewing devas as having developed from elemental spirits and fairies, rather than from human forms. As such, fairies are the prototypes of angels.

The word *fairies*—*fayes* in old English—is thought to be derived from *fatae*, the ancient Greek Fates who were pictured as three-winged women. *Fay-erie* was originally the "erie" state of enchantment that could be induced by the fays, and the word only later became interchangeable with the beings themselves. The fays were originally but one class of spirit being, and it was perhaps the general association of "little people" with enchantment that enabled the term *fairy* to become generic for fays, brownies, elves, pixies, and the like.

Folklorists advance a number of theories to explain the source of belief in fairies. One plausible notion is that, particularly in pre-Christian Europe, fairies were originally the spirits of the dead. After Christianity came onto the scene, the Christian notion of what happened to the souls of the dead supplanted earlier beliefs. Rather than disappearing, however, the older folklore associated with the dead persisted, with the modification that the fairy spirits became entities independent of humans, rather than spirits of dead human beings.

Another theory is that fairy lore represents a distant memory of an earlier and more primitive race (for example, the aboriginal Picts of the British Isles) who continued to interact with the dominant invaders (the Celts) for many centuries before their race disappeared altogether. Yet another idea put forth to explain belief in fairies is that they are the gods of pre-Christian Europe, not spirits of the dead, and that these fairies were reduced to the diminished status of nature spirits after being supplanted by Christianity.

These theories tend to ignore that similar ideas regarding nature spirits are found in traditional, tribal societies all over the world where none of the above conditions, like that of the aboriginal Picts, exist. On the other hand, in non-European traditional societies nature spirits are not thought to interact as intensively with humanity as they do in European folklore, which indicates that one or more of these theories may at least partially explain some aspects of fairy belief.

Examples of this intensive interaction thought to exist between humans and fairies are explored in the themes of Katherine Briggs's comprehensive fairy encyclopedia: for example, in the themes of fairy borrowing, fairy thefts, dependence of fairies upon mortals, fairy brides, and fairy loans. A close examination of this folklore lends plausibility to some of these theories because these stories sound like residues of real interactions. It may be possible that fairy lore is a residual memory of interactions with a more primitive race.

There are a number of alternative names for fairies that describe other characteristics of this type of spirit. Pixies (Pigsies or Piskies), for example, are said to be small, winged fairies with large heads, pointed ears and noses, and arched eyebrows. They wear hats made from the tops of toadstools or foxglove plants, and are attracted to gardens in bloom. They also love coming together for large gatherings—known in northern England as Pixie Fairs—at which they play and dance.

Like other inhabitants of the fairy realm, they are not necessarily either good or bad. Pixies do not normally seek out human contact, but, when they take a liking to someone, they will help her or him in various ways, such as doing work around the house or farm. On the other hand, they enjoy playing pranks on people and are especially fond of misleading travelers. The latter habit has given rise to the expression "Pixie-led," a state in which one wanders in circles and cannot seem to find the way back to the beaten path. It was said that the Pixie-led spell could be broken when one turned his or her coat inside-out.

It has been speculated that the name *Pixie* comes from Pict, which refers to the aboriginal peoples of the British Isles. This idea would explain some traits attributed to Pixies, such as their tendency to avoid people (as when they avoided the dominant Celts) and their occasional aid to people (as when they would help Celtic farmers who fed them). The Picts also were said to work in gold, silver, and bronze, and the metal dust generated by their work may be the prototype for the idea of Pixie dust—the magical powder associated with the popular character Tinker Bell, Peter Pan's comrade.

Another type of fairy, the Brownie, was said to be short (about three feet tall) and ragged, with pointed ears, brown complexions, and brown clothes. For the most part they were considered beneficent beings that took care of the house or farm in which the humans they adopted lived. Brownies are traditionally portrayed as intelligent beings who seek out deserving people to serve. They are also supposed to be nocturnal beings—one piece of folklore is that the cock crows not in order to awaken humans but to tell Brownies that it is time to retire. Because they were helpful spirits, it was traditional to set out milk and cakes for the house Brownies. This had to be done carefully because, according to Brownie folklore, a fairy could be offended by the offer of payment.

Though the term *Leprechaun* has come to be a general term for all Irish fairies, it originally seems to have been reserved for a particular species of *solitary fairies*, often seen working on one shoe. Leprechauns are known as tricksters who like to play pranks on humans. They are fond of dancing, whiskey, and Irish folk music. Some of the folklore associated with the Leprechaun is well-known, such as the crock of gold which one can obtain by tricking him. Various methods, such as an unblinking stare, are supposed to give one power over Leprechauns.

Dwarfs are a form of German fairies. Because of the diminutive size of most fairies, and because the term *dwarf* itself has come to mean "tiny," many other species of little spiritual beings have been referred to as dwarfs. It is said that the Isle of Rügen is inhabited by dwarfs that are white and black in color. More generally, many *solitary fairies* are considered dwarfish, but it is questionable whether the term is properly applied to them.

Gremlins are technological fairies, associated particularly, but not exclusively, with airplanes. Traditional fairies, who are usually thought of as connected with nature, are said to dislike technology, but Gremlins seem to have adapted to the modern age. Some claim that Gremlins are spirits of the air, others that they live underground around airfields. While descriptions vary, they are usually pictured as being about a foot tall, green in color, and having large fuzzy ears and webbed feet (with which to cling to airplane wings). They sometimes go about naked, while at other times they are clothed like aviators, with suction cups on the bottoms of their boots.

At the beginning of the age of air flight, aircraft struck the human imagination as quasi-mystical devices, at once representing the Earth and the celestial regions. Aviators' fears regarding flight stimulated overactive imaginations to perceive prankish spirits who let air out of tires, stalled engines, bored holes in the side of airplanes, bit through cables, and emptied gas tanks (Gremlins were said to drink petrol).

The term *Gremlin* originated from Grimm's *Fairy Tales*. While first thought to exist aboard British military aircraft, they were not given their name until 1939. During that year, a British bomber squadron stationed in India experienced a rash of what seemed like sabotage against their aircraft. Unable to locate human culprits, the crew resorted to blaming the damage on the pranks of spirits they came to call Gremlins. Gremlins did not, however, always work against the best interests of the craft on which they stowed away—for instance, some incidents of miraculous rescue have been attributed to the action of these technological fairies. It should also be noted that Gremlins have moved well beyond the aviation field and into other areas of technological activity, from factories to computers.

See Also: Gnomes; Salamanders; Sylphs; Undines

Further Reading

Briggs, Katharine. *An Encyclopedia of Fairies*. New York: Pantheon, 1976.
Masello, Robert. *Fallen Angels and Spirits of the Dark*. New York: Perigee, 1994.
McCoy, Edwin. *A Witch's Guide to Faery Folk*. St. Paul, MN: Llewellyn, 1994.

Fairy Tradition

Prior to 1939, a small number of people in the United States (and probably in England, although no hard data prove it) called themselves Witches, practiced Witchcraft, and may have considered their form of Witchcraft to be their religion. Although there were very few of them, their existence in the United States is well documented. However, their beliefs were utterly unlike what Gardner described for his "cult." The available books on American "Witchcraft" before 1939 focus on folk remedies for healing. The vocabulary and concepts in them are strictly Jewish or Christian in background.

Current members of these traditions, despite the contempt they may feel toward Gardnerians as "newcomers," have, for the most part (with the eclecticism typical of true Pagans), enthusiastically adopted the Gardnerian "reforms" because of their popularity and their usefulness. This has muddied whatever historical traces there may have been for the origins of these groups.

The most important of the pre-Gardnerian Witches was certainly Victor Anderson, a founder (or, as he claimed, a transmitter) of the Fairy Tradition, and, like Sara Cunningham, an influential teacher of Starhawk (Miriam Simos). Anderson was born on May 15, 1917, in New Mexico; his family moved to Bend, Oregon, when he was quite young. He claims that he underwent a sexual initiation by an old woman at age nine. Anderson relates that he was initiated into the Harpy Coven in Ashland, Oregon, in 1932; the High Priestess and High Priest were Maybelle and Jerome Warren, and other members included Jim Murdoch and Patricia Fern. The coven was quite eclectic, mixing Huna (a form of Shamanism) with varieties of folk magic more common in the continental United States. Anderson said that the coven's emphasis was on practical magic; there was little concern with worship, theology, ethics, or ritual. They did celebrate the Sabbats by getting together to work magic on those dates. Anderson said that the only time they met in a circle was when they were eating—and that this ordinary meal was, for them, part of the celebration of the Sabbat.

Anderson did say at one time that the Harpy Coven was not focused on worship of a goddess; rather, their concept of God was of a male god opposed to Christianity. This God was neither specifically equated with nor specifically distinguished from Satan. Their attitude apparently was much like that described in *The Black Arts* by Richard Cavendish, who pointed out that Satan had been made a heroic figure, a rebel against arbitrary authority and injustice, by Western poets and writers since the Reformation; so that modern literature-based Satanism is not at all a worship of evil, but a neo-Gnostic fighting against systemic injustice in the cosmos.

The Harpy Coven broke up around the time of World War II. At that time, Anderson met and married his wife, Cora, who came from a southern family that practiced a folk magic variety of Witchcraft. They practiced the Fairy Tradition by themselves until Anderson acquired his most important student, Thomas DeLong (1946–1982), when DeLong befriended Anderson's son in junior high school. He became a friend of the family and was initiated into the Craft. DeLong later wrote under the pen name Gwydion Pendderwen. After the publication of Gardner's *Witchcraft Today*, Anderson decided to form his own coven. He and DeLong wrote most of the rituals for the Faerie Tradition, named after the Faeries with whom Anderson had worked when young. After DeLong met Alex Sanders on a trip to Britain and received a copy of the Alexandrian Book of Shadows, some Alexandrian materials were incorporated into the Faerie Book of Shadows as well.

Pendderwen's work led to the founding of the Covenant of the Goddess. Anderson's authority as a traditional Witch was instrumental in the creation of the Covenant of the Goddess, and he served on the national and local boards of directors for several years. Despite advancing age and precarious health, Anderson continued teaching well into the 1990s. His most prominent, publicly identified students have included Gabriel Caradoc, Francesca Dubie, Alison Harlow, Aidan A. Kelly, Starhawk (Miriam Simos), and Valerie Voigt.

See Also: Tradition

Further Reading

Anderson, Cora. *Fifty Years in the Feri Tradition*. San Leandro, CA: n.p., 1995.
Anderson, Victor. "Faerie Shaman: An Interview with Victor Anderson." By Francesca Dubie. *Green Egg* 111 (winter 1995): 14–15.
———. *Thorns of the Blood Rose*. Edited by Thomas O. DeLong. San Leandro, CA: n.p., 1970.
Dubie, Francesca, and Victor Anderson. Interview by Ellen Evert Hopman and Lawrence Bond. In *People of the Earth: The New Pagans Speak Out*. Rochester, VT: Destiny Books, 1996.

Familiars

Familiars are spirits associated with Witches who are traditionally portrayed as serving their "masters" by carrying out their wishes. They usually take the form of animals and are sometimes thought to have the power to shapeshift. In terms of the older stereotype of Witches, cats were an especially favored form of familiar, which partially explains the periodic massacres of cats that swept through Europe during the Middle Ages.

Familiars were said to be given to Witches by the devil or by other Witches. They required blood, and their masters either sacrificed animals for them or provided blood directly through protuberances on the surface of their skin—termed "Witches' teats" or "Witches' marks." In addition to aiding Witches by carrying their bewitchments to the intended victims, familiars acted as the infernal equivalent of guardian angels, providing Witches with protection from attacks.

Among modern Neopagan Witches, familiars have been reinterpreted as animal companions who are psychically sensitive enough to aid Witches in their craft. Alternately, some Neopagans have reconceptualized the idea of familiars in light of Neoshamanic theories regarding "power animals" (the anthropological concept of "totems"). This interpretation of the Witch's familiar—which can be imaginary, in that one need not actually keep a living animal around as a pet—embodies certain traits and powers that a Witch taps by asking for help from a specific animal in her imagination.

Further Reading

Guiley, Rosemary. *The Encyclopedia of Witches and Witchcraft*. New York: Facts on File, 1989.
Valiente, Doreen. *An ABC of Witchcraft: Past and Present*. New York: St. Martin's Press, 1973.

Family Tradition

FamTrad Witches (also called "Clan Witches") are those whose form of Witchcraft has been passed down to them through their families. Many stories and claims about such family traditions have been exaggerated, especially when anachronisms can be detected, but there are nevertheless many cases of genuine family traditions—and the less they resemble Gardnerian-style Witchcraft, the more genuine they seem to be.

The content of these family traditions is almost never concerned with any kind of formal ritual and certainly not with any ritual scripts that must be followed. Rather, they focus on practical folk magic and developing the use of each individual's psychic abilities, however great or small. Members of a family may not think of themselves as "really" Christian, but will participate fully in the official church of the community in order to protect themselves from persecution. Such families may never refer to their own practices and beliefs as "Witchcraft," but will instead call them something like "the Old Ways."

See Also: Tradition
Further Reading

Adler, Margot. *Drawing Down the Moon: Witches, Pagans, Druids, and Other Goddess-Worshippers in America Today*, 2d ed. Boston, MA: Beacon Press, 1986 [New York: Viking, 1979].

Guiley, Rosemary. *The Encyclopedia of Witches and Witchcraft*. New York: Facts on File, 1989.

Festivals

It is not clear exactly how the phenomenon of Neopagan festivals began. It may be that they were inspired in part by Llewellyn Publications' Gnosticons, patterned after science fiction–fan conventions in the mid-1970s, which provided an annual gathering place where workshops, rituals, and general networking could take place. It may also be that the Church and School of Wicca's annual Samhain Seminar provided a model for a festival.

In any event, festivals began to take place by the mid-1970s and soon followed a standard format:

1. The typical festival lasts for two or three days, over a weekend close to one of the eight annual Sabbats, and is attended by several hundred people, mainly local, but some from great distances. The largest festivals may have up to 1,000 attendees and may last for a week. The festival may be held in a hotel; a rural retreat with cabins, dormitories, and cafeterias; or bare fields with latrines, tents, and campfires.

2. There are usually two or more nationally known Craft leaders or authors who give keynote addresses and something like "master-class" seminars. Local Craft leaders can give many more workshops and seminars.

3. Several large circles are scheduled; that is, there are the equivalent of organized worship services held during a festival. Usually there is one large circle scheduled to begin the festival, one (the most elaborate and well attended) on Saturday night, and another to formally end the festival. In addition, there are a great many smaller, Esbat-style circles conducted by covens or newly assembled clusters of Witches and Pagans.

4. There are usually many merchant booths set up in a convenient area, some run by merchants who make a living solely by traveling from festival to festival. The booths create a desired resemblance to a medieval trade fair.

5. The most important activity at each festival is the spontaneous networking that goes on, as Witches and Pagans from different areas get to know one another and begin to establish friendships and alliances. The festival is never a solemn affair, and some Pagans attend them just because there is almost always a lively party going on somewhere on the grounds.

Neopagan festivals have proliferated since the very first ones in the mid-1970s. Adler listed more than 50 in 1985, and the number now probably approaches 100. This phenomenon has further decentralized the Craft, making it more accessible to people in general. There are now many Neopagans whose primary activity consists of attendance at national and local festivals. They are not focused on a coven and are not subject to the authority of a High Priestess. In this sense, the festivals are one force (among others) working to create a genuine laity in the Neopagan Craft movement, alleviating a history of a movement that seemed "all chiefs and no braves."

In *Drawing Down the Moon*, Adler wrote, "Festivals have completely changed the face of the Pagan movement . . . have created a national Pagan community, a body of nationally shared chants, dances, stories, and ritual techniques. They have even led to the creation of a different type of ritual process—one that permits a large group to experience ecstatic states and a powerful sense of religious communion" (p. 422).

There is no set pattern for how to run and organize festivals. The most common and most successful pattern is for the festival to be organized by one of the large Neopagan networking associations, or else by a committee that exists solely to run the festival. It should be noted that festivals are always nonprofit, break-even affairs. Neopagans pride themselves on their refusal to make money off of their coreligionists, and they consider their labors to be a gift to their religious community.

See Also: Church and School of Wicca; Sabbats
Further Reading
Adler, Margot. *Drawing Down the Moon: Witches, Pagans, Druids, and Other Goddess-Worshippers in America Today*, 2d ed. Boston, MA: Beacon Press, 1987 [New York: Viking, 1979].

Oz. "An Insider's Look at Pagan Festivals." In Clifton, Charles S., ed., *Witchcraft Today, Book One: The Modern Craft Movement*. St. Paul, MN: Llewellyn, 1992.

Pike, Sarah M. "Forging Magical Selves: Gendered Bodies and Ritual Fires at Neo-Pagan Festivals." In Lewis, James R., ed., *Magical Religion and Modern Witchcraft*. Albany, NY: State University of New York Press, 1996, 121–140.

Fetch

The term *fetch* refers to the spirit double or apparition of a living person. According to Irish and British belief, the fetch, also known as the wraith, is a ghostly appearance resembling in every detail an individual whose death it predicts. More than one person may see the fetch at the same time, and sometimes the fetch may even appear to the individual it represents. If the fetch is seen in the morning, it indicates long life for the individual; if it is seen at night, it indicates proximate death. Fetches are the subjects of several Irish folktales, as well as of the accounts of more sophisticated writers.

See Also: Ghosts

Further Reading

Bletzer, June G. *The Donning International Encyclopedic Psychic Dictionary*. Norfolk, VA: Donning, 1986.

Shepard, Leslie A., ed. *Encyclopedia of Occultism and Parapsychology*. Detroit, MI: Gale Research Inc., 1991.

Fetish

Fetishes are wooden dolls or other objects that represent spirits. They protect and help their owner with their magical powers. The term *fetish* is particularly associated with West African religions. Fetishes were commonly owned by slaves who were kidnapped from Africa and were taken to the New World. Because they symbolized non-Christian gods, they were prohibited by white masters. Fetishes were also feared by whites, which led to their association with "black" magic.

See Also: African Religions; Amulet

Further Reading

Eliade, Mircea. *The Encyclopedia of Religion*. New York: Macmillan, 1987.

Shepard, Leslie A., ed. *Encyclopedia of Occultism and Parapsychology*. Detroit, MI: Gale Research Inc., 1991.

Fire

Fire is one of the four classical elements of nature thought to constitute the manifest universe. Along with air, it is also considered a male element. The

A fire dancer at the 1997 Pagan Spirit Gathering sponsored by Circle Sanctuary. (Photo by Jeff Koslow, Circle Sanctuary archives)

direction south, action, courage, struggle, animosity, jealousy, anger, the color orange, the metal gold, the sword (the Witches' tool), and the Tarot suit sword are all associated with fire. Fire was believed to be able to destroy evil, which was the reason that Witches were burned at the stake.

See Also: Air; Earth; Salamanders; Sword; Water
Further Reading
Cirlot, J. E. *A Dictionary of Symbols*. New York: Dorset Press, 1991.
Heisler, Roger. *Path to Power*. York Beach, ME: Weiser, 1990.

Fivefold Kiss

The Fivefold Kiss is an element in Gardnerian ritual that was apparently devised by Gardner himself. The oldest known ritual script for the Fivefold Kiss reads as follows:

> The Moon having been drawn down, that is, link established, Magus and other men give Fivefold Kiss:
> (kissing feet) "Blessed be thy feet, that have brought thee in these ways";
> (kissing knees) "Blessed be thy knees, that shall kneel at the sacred altar";
> (kissing womb) "Blessed be thy womb, without which we would not be";

(kissing breasts) "Blessed be thy breasts, formed in beauty and in strength";

(kissing lips) "Blessed be thy lips, that shall speak the sacred names." Women all bow.

As can be seen from the first line, this "Fivefold Kiss" is actually part of the procedure for "Drawing down the Moon" (it is followed by the High Priestess's recitation of the "Charge of the Goddess"), and it does not make as much sense when used as a ritual on its own. It seems that it was not used very much, even in strictly Gardnerian covens, and has certainly not been adopted widely by other traditions. However, it has inspired ritual developments in other traditions, some poetic, and some Tantric.

See Also: "Charge of the Goddess"; Drawing Down the Moon
Further Reading
Farrar, Stewart. *What Witches Do: The Modern Coven Revealed.* New York: Coward, McCann, 1971.
Guiley, Rosemary. *The Encyclopedia of Witches and Witchcraft.* New York: Facts on File, 1989.

Flying

Flying, or transvection, with the aid of a broomstick, fork, or shovel by demons and Witches was a popular belief during the Middle Ages and the Renaissance, when it was claimed that the devil, his demons, and Witches could fly and transport others through the air. Witches were also said to ride demons who were transformed into such animals as goats, cows, horses, and wolves, while the devil could carry people through the air with no visible means of transport.

The notion that Witches possessed the power to fly was rejected during the Witch hunts and, as early as the tenth century, the act of flying was proclaimed impossible by the Canon Episcopi. However, in the late fifteenth century, the *Malleus Maleficarum*, the "Bible" of Witch-hunters and judges, asserted that this view was erroneous. During the Inquisition, many Witches confessed to flying, either bodily or in their imagination. Although demonologists and inquisitors did not believe that Witches could fly, they regarded these confessions as incriminating, nevertheless.

Magical ointments were said to be used by Witches, sorcerers, and necromancers to be able to fly. These ointments supposedly consisted principally of the boiled baby fat of a young child that had been killed before baptism. The speed of flying broomsticks and forks was said to be very high, but church bells were supposed to ground them and keep Witches away, especially during festivals.

Magical and mystical flying, on the other hand, is a transcendent experience of the spirit, not the body, often attributed to alchemists, mystics, sorcerers, Shamans, medicine men, yogis, and fakirs, as well as Witches. Several modern Witches have attained mystical flight by blending Eastern and Shamanic spiritual elements into Neopagan Witchcraft.

See Also: Anointing Oil; Broom; Ointments
Further Reading

Adler, Margot. *Drawing Down the Moon: Witches, Pagans, Druids, and Other Goddess-Worshippers in America Today*, 2d ed. Boston, MA: Beacon Press, 1986 [New York: Viking, 1979].
Gordon, Stuart. *The Encyclopedia of Myths and Legends*. London: Headline, 1993.

Fortune-Telling

Fortune-telling is an alternative designation for divination. Traditional divinatory systems include astrology, runestone-reading, card-reading, palmistry, dream-interpretation, and scrying (crystal ball–gazing). Unlike divination, however, the expression *fortune-telling* has acquired a negative connotation. This is due in large degree to the many "gypsy" fortune-tellers who utilized card- and palm-readings to snare clients into schemes that enticed them to purchase various other, more expensive, "occult" services. In sharp distinction to such gypsy fortune-tellers, Neopagans who offer such services are almost always cautious and ethical.

Divination is often equated with foreseeing the future. However, the thrust of the occult arts has been significantly—though, for the most part, indirectly—influenced by the human potentials movement. As a result, traditional divinatory methods have been appropriated for the potential insights they offer into personal character as well as their potential as tools for personal transformation. Without dropping predictive "fortune-telling," contemporary Neopaganism has absorbed the ethic of personal transformation, and reinterpreted the divinatory arts in terms of this perspective.

Further Reading

Bletzer, June G. *The Donning International Encyclopedic Psychic Dictionary*. Norfolk, VA: Donning, 1986.
Shepard, Leslie A., ed. *Encyclopedia of Occultism and Parapsychology*. Detroit, MI: Gale Research Inc., 1991.

Fraternitas Rosae Crucis

The Fraternitas Rosae Crucis, founded in 1858 by the physician P. B. Randolph (1825–1875), is generally considered the oldest Rosicrucian order. The Grand Lodge, first established in San Francisco in 1861, closed and was

A seventeenth-century engraving of a mythical Temple of the Rosy Cross teems with Rosicrucian imagery. (North Wind Picture Archive)

reestablished first in Boston (1871), then in San Francisco (1874), and finally in Philadelphia (1895).

Among the teachings of the order is a system of occult sexuality. This system was called *Eulistic*, a term derived from the Greek Eleusinian mysteries, believed to be mysteries of sex. A Provisional Grand Lodge of Eulis was established in Tennessee, but internal problems among the members led to its clo-

A traditional image of the Fraternitas Rosae Crucis (North Wind Picture Archive)

sure. Randolph's teachings on occult sexuality soon became the source for the sex magic system developed by the Ordo Templi Orientis (OTO). OTO teachings have been denounced as "black" magic by twentieth-century followers of Randolph.

Among other teachings of the order are the basic ideas of the "secret schools," including reincarnation and karma, the Law of Justice, and noninterference with the rights of others. Members learn how to contact the hierarchies of the heavenly realm, the process of transmutation, and how to acquire health and strength by dismissing thoughts concerning weakness and age. They believe in the fatherhood of God and the ultimate sisterhood and brotherhood of humanity.

While the Aeth Priesthood represents the inner circle of the fraternity, the Church of Illumination constitutes the Outer-Court group that interacts with the public. The focus of the church is upon "manisism," which is the recognition of the equality of man and woman and is the name of the new world leader who teaches the fundamentals of the divine law. According to the church, the "Manistic" age began in the late nineteenth century, following the previous Egyptian and Christian ages.

After Randolph, the order was led respectively by Freeman B. Dowd; Edward H. Brown (1907); and R. Swinburne Clymer (1922), author of numerous books and recently succeeded by his son, Emerson M. Clymer. Authority of the order is represented by the Council of Three, whereas the highest office is held by the Hierarch of Eulis. The order's literature is distributed by the Beverly Hall Corporation in Quakertown, Pennsylvania.

See Also: Ordo Templi Orientis; Sex and Sex Magic
Further Reading
Lewis, James R. *The Encyclopedia of Cults, Sects, and New Religions.* Amherst, NY: Prometheus, 1998.
Melton, J. Gordon. *Encyclopedia of American Religions*, 5th ed. Detroit, MI: Gale Research, 1996.

Freemasonry

The teachings and practices of the Fraternal Order of Free and Accepted Masons is the world's largest "secret society"—although, these days, little about its membership or practices is kept secret. Many Masons believe that their order goes back to the medieval guilds of stonemasons who built the cathedrals of Europe, and to those who built the temple in Jerusalem. Gerald Gardner, founder of the modern Neopagan Witchcraft movement, adopted many elements of Freemasonry in his new synthesis.

Historically, it appears that Freemasonry began in England in the late seventeenth century. It may have been started by Royalists who worked to restore the monarchy, perhaps even by those who established the Royal Society under the sponsorship of Charles II in 1660. Even though some Scottish lodges have records that appear to date back to 1599, the beginning of the Masonic movement in practice was probably 1717, when four lodges met in London and established the Grand Lodge in order to "restore" Masonry. Freemasonry spread within the British Empire and then throughout Europe. Of the present six million Freemasons in the world, approximately four million are in the United States, one million are in the British Isles, and most of the rest are in British Commonwealth countries and in Europe.

The symbol of Freemasonry is built around the compass and the level, both traditional stonemason's tools. (North Wind Picture Archive)

Freemasonry has many religious elements—for example, its teachings emphasize morality, charity, and obeying the law of the land, and applicants must be adult males who believe in a Supreme Being and in the immortality of the soul. However, neither its members nor outsiders consider Freemasonry to be a religion. (The French Lodges under the Grand Orient were expelled by the Grand Lodge after they dropped the requirement that a member must believe in a Supreme Being.) Still, the Roman Catholic Church perceived Freemasonry as a possible rival, and forbade Catholics to be Masons early in the eighteenth century. This rule was simply ignored in Latin countries, where most Masons were freethinkers and anticlericalists, but was observed in northern countries, where Masons were almost entirely Protestants. Some lodges were charged with prejudice against Jews, Catholics, and nonwhites in previous decades, but such problems have tended to fade away in recent years. After the Second Vatican Council, the stricture on Catholic membership in Freemasonry was abolished.

The basic structure in most lodges is based on a Three-Degree System consisting of Entered Apprentice, Fellow of the Craft, and Master Mason. Although Freemasonry itself has become almost entirely exoteric, its rituals and terminology have been absorbed by many other movements, most notably by the Inner Temple rituals of the Mormon Church and the rituals of the Neopagan Witchcraft movement. The Degree System in many lodges has proliferated into many more Degrees; the lodges that amalgamated into the Scottish Rite have 33 separate degrees.

There are also some social groups, such as the Shriners, which draw their membership entirely from the higher Degrees of Masonry, as well as adjunct organizations for wives, sons, and daughters—these being the Orders of the Eastern Star, DeMolay, and Job's Daughters, respectively.

See Also: Co-Masonry; Craft, The; Degrees
Further Reading

Lewis, James R. *The Encyclopedia of Cults, Sects, and New Religions*. Amherst, NY: Prometheus, 1998.

Melton, J. Gordon. *Encyclopedia of American Religions*, 5th ed. Detroit, MI: Gale Research, 1996.

Waite, Arthur Edward. *A New Encyclopaedia of Freemasonry*. New York: Weathervane Books, 1970 [1921, 1898].

Gaia

Gaia, also known as Gaea or "Deep-Breasted One," was one of the oldest deities in the ancient Greek pantheon, representing Mother Earth. Gaia has been adopted as a generic name for the universal Great Goddess, known more popularly as Mother Nature. Gaia nurtures all beings on Earth; she rules the birth, death, and regeneration cycles of all living beings.

She was born out of the dark abyss of Chaos, whose son, Uranos, she married. From their union the first creatures, the Titans and Cyclops, were created. Gaia was served by the Pythoness Priestess at the Oracle at Delphi, and she was gradually assimilated into the deities Rhea, of Cretan origin, and Cybele, Goddess of Caverns.

In the 1970s, the Gaia Hypothesis, formulated by the British specialist in gas chromatography, James Lovelock, captured the interest of the media, the scientific community, the Neopagan community, and the environmental movement. According to this theory, all organic and inorganic matter on Earth is related in a single, complex organism, with self-regulating capabilities. Humankind is but one part of this complex organism. Lovelock asserted that Gaia created the conditions necessary to support life on the planet—conditions that are currently threatened by humankind's industrial pollution. If humans fail to maintain homeostasis, Gaia could regulate itself (the Earth) to compensate for the damage by eliminating humanity. According to Lovelock, environmental changes can be anticipated by the collective intelligence of humans, which constitutes a Gaian brain.

An earlier version of the Gaia Hypothesis was formulated by Otter Zell, founder of the Church of All Worlds, one of the earliest Neopagan groups. Zell said that, in a vision, he saw Earth as a single biological organism that had evolved from a single original cell, making all life-forms a single vast creature, which he named Terrebia. According to Zell, humans function as cells of Terrebia, serving as its brain and nervous system. He also claimed that humankind will awaken Terrebia, and a new biosphere will be born. However, the polluting cancer of the nervous system (humanity) threatens this awakening—the Omega Point awakening described by the theologian Teilhard de Chardin. A nuclear holocaust could be one way to control this cancer. Other forms of control could be natural phenomena such as plagues,

An imaginative illustration of Gaia, the Earth as a living being. (North Wind Picture Archive)

droughts, famines, and floods. Zell, who later changed the name of Terrebia to Gaea, said that the Omega Point awakening can be achieved by ending environmental exploitation and by developing alternative, nature-conscious lifestyles. Environmental consciousness is highly regarded by Neopaganism, and Witches cast spells for ecological healing.

See Also: Church of All Worlds; Goddess(es)
Further Reading

Lovelock, J. E. *Gaia*. New York: Oxford University Press, 1979.

Zell, Oberon. "Who on Earth Is the Goddess?" In James R. Lewis, ed., *Magical Religion and Modern Witchcraft*. Albany, NY: State University of New York Press, 1996, 25–33.

Gardner, Gerald

See Introduction

Garter, Order of the

The garter is used in Gardnerian covens as a badge of a Third-Degree High Priestess, who may add a silver buckle to the garter to represent every High Priestess to whom she is Queen. The garter has also been adopted as a Third-Degree badge by other traditions. The source of this usage is Margaret Murray's ingenious story in her books on the "Witch cult." She wrote that the garter was a badge of the Witch—a reason for the foundation of the Order of the Garter, which has 169 (that is, 13 multiplied by 13) members. Most historians doubt that she is right, but many Wiccans consider her story to be one of Wicca's foundational myths.

See Also: Degrees; Murray, Margaret
Further Reading

Murray, Margaret, A. *The God of the Witches*. Garden City, NJ: Doubleday Anchor, 1960 [Oxford: Oxford University Press, 1934].

———. *The Witch-Cult in Western Europe*. Oxford: Oxford University Press, 1962 [1921].

Gateway Circle

A gateway circle is a regular meeting that is open to newcomers so that they can see what a Neopagan circle is like and so that they can meet people who are active members of covens. Sometimes the gateway circle serves as a permanent Neopagan Outer Court, at least for some members; for others, it can be the first step toward their training and initiation into a coven. The existence of gateway circles is not widely advertised, but they can be tracked down now in most large metropolitan areas by reading bulletin boards in occult stores and asking questions at any sort of Neopagan gathering.

See Also: Coven; Pagan Way

Further Reading

Adler, Margot. *Drawing Down the Moon: Witches, Pagans, Druids, and Other Goddess-Worshippers in America Today*, 2d ed. Boston, MA: Beacon Press, 1986 [New York: Viking, 1979].

Roberts, Susan. *Witches USA*, 2d ed. Custer, WA: Phoenix, 1974 [New York: Dell, 1971].

Gematria

Gematria is the interpretation and codification of words after they have been converted into numbers. Its first known use was during the eighth century B.C. in Babylonia. In the following centuries, gematria was used in divination and magical ceremonies. It also was a means to interpret dreams and religious texts and, starting in the thirteenth century, a key to interpret the Old Testament.

This latter application was developed by Cabalists who believed that the Old Testament was written in a coded language; for them, gematria was a key in deciphering the hidden meaning of the text. Cabalists wrote numerous manuals on gematria. This activity eventually brought about different ways of applying the method.

In magic, gematria allowed the creation of words of power to be used in rituals, while others used it to interpret the holy names of God. Even before the development of Cabala, Christians and Hebrews applied gematria to the interpretation of religious terms.

See Also: Cabala; Magic; Numerology

Further Reading

Bletzer, June G. *The Donning International Encyclopedic Psychic Dictionary*. Norfolk, VA: Donning, 1986.

Shepard, Leslie A., ed. *Encyclopedia of Occultism and Parapsychology*. Detroit, MI: Gale Research Inc., 1991.

Genie

According to Islam, the *jinn*—from which we derive the English term *genie*—are invisible spirits made out of fire and were created 2,000 years before Adam. Islamic thinkers postulated three orders of existence beyond God: angels, jinn, and humanity. The angels, created out of light, were closest to God. The jinn, intermediate between angels and humanity, inhabited a subtly material or etheric realm. Like human beings, the jinn possessed intelligence and free will and were thus capable of being saved. For this reason, the Koran sometimes addresses itself explicitly to both humans and jinn. It is said that, one night, a group of jinn overheard the Prophet reciting the Koran and they became believers. The spot where Muhammad later met with the jinns' leaders and accepted their allegiance is the site of the "Mosque of the Jinn" in Mecca.

Iblis, the Islamic Satan, was transformed from an angel into a jinn when he refused God's command that he worship Adam (who was created out of mere clay). Subsequently, Iblis and other angels who shared his viewpoint were removed from their stations. Iblis and the jinn were exiled from Eden and subsequently became demons. (Also amongst the outcasts were five of Iblis's sons.) Ejected from the presence of God, these former angels turned to trickery and caused trouble for mortals. One example of good behavior by the jinn is when Aladdin, in the book *Arabian Nights*, is assisted by a friendly *jinni* (genie) when he rubs his magical lamp.

The stereotypical genie-in-the-bottle that contemporary popular culture has derived from the *Arabian Nights* represents a particular kind of spirit, one bound to a human being in a kind of slave-master relationship. Such relationships are more characteristic of the operation of ceremonial magic than of modern Wicca. As a system that is primarily religious and secondarily magical, a contemporary Witch honors, cooperates with, and attunes divinities, and does not compel divinities to do her or his bidding. Even Neopagan magic is conceptualized more in terms of directing *energy* than in terms of manipulating entities.

See Also: Demons; Fairies

Further Reading

Davidson, Gustav. *A Dictionary of Angels: Including the Fallen Angels*. New York: Free Press, 1971 [1967].

Glassé, Cyril. *The Concise Encyclopedia of Islam*. San Francisco, CA: HarperSan Francisco, 1989.

Ghosts

Belief in the existence of ghosts is found throughout history and in all cultures. Etymologically, *ghost* is linked to the German word *Geist* ("spirit"), thus indicating a broader connotation of the original word. In fact, ghosts have been viewed in different ways—as a soul, as a breath, as good and/or evil. Most typically, ghosts are believed to be the souls of the dead who return from their afterlife location to the living world for a variety of reasons, such as revenging their own unjust death, reclaiming their goods, accomplishing some unfinished task, revealing some sort of truth, or protecting their families.

Ghosts have been viewed differently in different civilizations. In more traditional cultures, particularly in Africa, ghosts are, at times, considered cruel spirits who steal children. A wandering, lonely ghost can be the restless soul of someone who has committed suicide or of a woman who died giving birth. Also, those who, for whatever reasons, did not receive the traditional burial rites remain in a wandering, restless status of a ghost. Where there is a

As part of Candomblé religion, worshipers wash the steps of the Bonfim Church in Salvador, Brazil, 1988, to clear away ghosts. (Corbis/Stephanie Maze)

cult of the ancestors, as in traditional Chinese culture, the existence of ghosts is taken for granted.

In the West, the appearance of ghosts was considered frightening, a source of evil, or a demonic force. In Eastern Europe, there was a good deal of popular lore about ghosts of the dead who came back to attack the living in the form of vampires. In Indian culture, both Hinduism and Buddhism acknowledge the existence of some sorts of ghosts. Ghosts, like evil spirits, haunt cemeteries and live in trees. The day of celebration of the Dipavali festival is used to cast off evil forces, such as those embodied by ghosts. Those who die a violent death need particular funeral rites to cast off the evil energy. In Burmese Buddhism, existence as a ghost is the third of four stages achieved by the dead (after first being an animal and, second, a demon) before the next reincarnation occurs.

Within Christianity, the Holy Ghost, often depicted as a dove, represents the spirit of God that empowers human beings. In contrast, the Catholic Church developed the practice of exorcism to cast out evil demonic spirits. Some of the practices of Shamans and other healers also aimed to cast out evil entities that possessed a sick person. A new approach to ghosts developed in the nineteenth century with the birth of Spiritualism. Mediums, intermediaries who communicated with the spirits, viewed ghosts as souls of the dead, often confused and trapped and in need of the medium's help to find their way.

While it is typically believed that ghosts appear at night, there are many traditions of daylight appearances or appearances during twilight. Various theories have explained the phenomenon that sees ghosts as tricks of light and shade, or as figments of the imagination. Psychological theories tend to explain the appearance of ghosts as the result of dreams, projections of one's subconscious, or hallucinations.

Ghosts are particularly associated with the haunting of houses. The term *haunting*, which has the same root as the word *home*, refers to the manifestation of unaccountable phenomena allegedly originated by spirits and ghosts. Haunting usually occurs where people and animals, to whom the spirits belong, used to live; in places merely frequented by the deceased; and in places of violent deaths.

Haunting includes the appearance of apparitions, noises, smells, tactile sensations, extremes in temperature, and movement of objects—all of which have no apparent reason. A place that is haunted is generally characterized by a heavy atmosphere, in which inexplicable phenomena, which can be perceived only by individuals with particular psychic qualities, can last from a short period to centuries. Some hauntings include the sight of apparitions, typically clothed in a period costume and usually wearing the same dress. Some apparitions change their appearance, and some others are horrific—such as missing some body parts.

There has been much scientific inquiry into the subject of ghosts over the last 100 years, since the first investigations of the founders of the Society for Psychical Research, whose members proposed definitions of haunting. Frederic W. H. Myers, for instance, defined a ghost as a manifestation of a persistent personal energy, while Eleanor Sidgwick asserted that hauntings could be considered a form of psychometry—vibrations of events and emotions contained in a house, site, or object. Other theories refer to the incapability of the spirits of the deceased to leave the "Earth plane."

Various techniques are employed to investigate hauntings, usually including descriptions obtained from eyewitness accounts; experimentation involving a medium to corroborate the accounts; and detection, involving the observation or recording of phenomena. Despite the accuracy of new technologies used by investigators, including various electronic devices, the interpretation of the results of investigations about ghosts is often subjective and inconclusive. Very little is really known about the nature of hauntings and why they happen.

Contemporary Witches are sometimes called upon to help "clear" a haunted house. This might take the form of a clearing ritual. Alternatively, a psychically sensitive Witch might attempt to contact and persuade the troubled spirit to vacate the premises, much as a depossession therapist would do in the case of spirit obsession.

See Also: Fetch; Parapsychology; Spirit; Spiritualism

Further Reading

Bletzer, June G. *The Donning International Encyclopedic Psychic Dictionary*. Norfolk, VA: Donning, 1986.

Cavendish, Richard, ed. *Encyclopedia of the Unexplained. Magic, Occultism, and Parapsychology*. London: Arkana Penguin Books, 1989.

Fodor, Nandor. *An Encyclopaedia of Psychic Science*. Secaucus, NJ: The Citadel Press, 1966 [1933].

Gnomes

Gnomes are a form of dwarf fairy, associated with the element earth. They are said to reside in deep forests and in roots of ancient oak trees; they are traditionally said to be occupied with the healing and protection of wild animals. They reach maturity early and are thus often pictured as quite old. In the Occult Tradition, earth is traditionally associated with the physical body, and earth elementals (Gnomes) are said to work with human beings to maintain the health of the body.

Gnomes are the archetypal spirits of the earth element and, as such, are occupied with maintaining the physical structure of the planet. In magic, the Gnomes are the earth elementals of one of the directions (usually north) invoked in rituals. The task of the elementals is to build forms in the natural world. While some writers view elementals as soulless entities that simply disappear at death, others view them as spirits who eventually evolve into devas (angels). Due to their association with earth, Gnomes are under the rule of the archangel Uriel.

See Also: Earth; Salamanders; Sylphs; Undines
Further Reading
Andrews, Ted. *Enchantment of the Faerie Realm: Communicate with Nature Spirits and Elementals*. St. Paul, MN: Llewellyn Publications, 1993.
McCoy, Edwin. *A Witch's Guide to Faery Folk*. St. Paul, MN: Llewellyn, 1994.

Gnosticism

Gnosticism is a generic name given to various "nonmainstream" (as they later appeared after "orthodoxy" was established) forms of Christianity that were established in the second century A.D. These nonmainstream forms gradually died out after the fourth century when the Christian Church became the only legal religion in the former Roman Empire. *Gnosticism* is also a general term for a type of theology ("knowledge" or "enlightenment") that was developed by some of these early groups, and that has reappeared over and over again during medieval and modern times. One reason why the medieval Church reacted so violently to the Waldensians, Albigensians, and other "heretics" was the belief that these movements constituted a revival of the Gnosticism that the Church had struggled so long to eradicate in preceding centuries.

Gnosticism's core teaching was that this world, and especially the human body, were the products of an evil deity—the demiurge—who trapped human souls in the physical world. They believed that a human's true home was the absolute spirit, referred to as the *pleroma,* and, hence, humans should reject the pleasures of the flesh as an escape from this prison. Unlike Christianity, in which one was saved by faith, in this school of thought one was saved by a kind of intellectual insight, or Gnosis. Gnosticism, in the proper sense, died out before the Western Middle Ages, although the term continued to be used to refer to any deviations the Church deemed excessively world-denying (that is, denying worldly pleasures), or that stressed mental insight over faith as the essential mode of salvation.

While many mystery religions (such as the Eleusinian mysteries in Greece) and other religious movements in antiquity emphasized a dualism between the body and the soul, none took this concept to the extreme that Gnosticism did. Rather than yearning for immortality in the present life as everybody else seemed to, living in the world was viewed as a kind of hell (from the Gnostic viewpoint). Like the South Asian religions, which may have influenced this school of thought, Gnosticism saw human beings as trapped in a cycle of reincarnation, so that even suicide would not release one from bondage to the flesh. Some Neopagan groups have adopted ideas from Gnostic documents, but the basic orientation of modern Neopaganism is antagonistic to the Gnostic worldview.

See Also: Heresy, Heretic
Further Reading

Eliade, Mircea, ed. *Encyclopedia of Religion*. 16 vols. New York: Macmillan, 1987.
Shepard, Leslie A., ed. *Encyclopedia of Occultism and Parapsychology*. Detroit, MI: Gale Research Inc., 1991.

Goddess(es)

Goddesses in general are of great interest to Witches, and it is difficult to find a goddess, however obscure, who has not been the focus of a coven's workings at some time. What Witches "know" about goddesses is, to be sure, entirely derived from literature, and especially from Robert Graves's *The White Goddess*— a questionable source of information.

The major thealogical (feminine form of the word *theology*) concept in the Craft is of *the* Goddess, that is, the ultimate divinity conceived of as essentially female. Some traditions and covens operate with a duotheistic thealogy, in which the Goddess and the God are equal, but most conceive of the Goddess as the more fundamental reality. It became obvious by the 1970s that one of the most attractive features of Neopagan Witchcraft was its insistence that divinity is at least as much female as male, since this shift in emphasis provided a way to eliminate characteristics that most Pagans (and others) disliked about most churches. Thealogical discussion in the Neopagan movement, therefore, often involves debates about the nature and characteristics of the Goddess and whether all goddesses are one Goddess. Dion Fortune said (and most classical scholars deny) that the concept of the Goddess empowers women to improve their status in a very male-oriented world.

See Also: Graves, Robert; Women's Spirituality Movement
Further Reading
Adler, Margot. *Drawing Down the Moon: Witches, Pagans, Druids, and Other Goddess-Worshippers in America Today*, 2d ed. Boston, MA: Beacon Press, 1986 [New York: Viking, 1979].
Downing, Christine. *The Goddess: Mythological Images of the Feminine*. New York: Continuum, 1996.
Edwards, C. Taliesin. "She Touched Me; or, How I Achieved a Personal Relationship with the Goddess." *Gnostica* (December 1974).
Graves, Robert. *The White Goddess: A Historical Grammar of Poetic Myth*, 3d ed. London: Farrar, Straus, 1966 [2d ed., 1956; 1st ed., 1948].

Grail

The story of the Holy Grail was originally a Pagan story that became Christianized and mixed with Arthurian legend. In its Christian version, the Holy Grail is a spiritual mystery representing regeneration through Christ's teachings. The Grail is viewed as a gateway to Paradise and as a connection to a supernatural and spiritual realm—making a direct knowledge of God possible. It is also believed to possess unlimited healing power. In Pagan imagery, the Grail, or *Graal*, is a cup of plenty and regeneration, a vessel in which the life of the world is preserved. It symbolizes the body of the Goddess, or the Great Mother.

In its Christianized form, the Grail represents the chalice from which Jesus Christ drank during the Last Supper, and which held his blood after the crucifixion. According to medieval belief, blood embodied both the soul and the divinity of Christ. The notion of the Grail was never completely accepted by the Church because it could not be identified with an actual relic, but it was never considered heretical. Its symbolism was eventually absorbed by Rosicrucianism.

The Grail has been the subject of several legends since the end of the twelfth century, although it is generally believed that the story existed earlier in oral tradition. Attributed to the sixth-century bard Taliesin, the first Grail legend was Pagan. However, as new versions emerged, it came to embody elements of classical and Celtic mythology, Christian iconography, Arabic poetry, and Sufism. The original story of the Grail was about a magic cauldron kept by nine maidens in *Annwn*, "the otherworld," and sought by King Arthur's men.

The ancient motif of a sacred vessel as a symbol of power and a source of miracles is the ultimate source of the Grail legend. Vessels, which are feminine symbols, can be found in Vedic, Egyptian, classical, and Celtic mythology. They also can be found in a number of mystery traditions, where vessels are depicted as cups or cauldrons of inspiration, rebirth, and regeneration. Alchemy associates the Grail with the Philosopher's Stone, whereas Tibetan Buddhism associates such chalices with human skulls, which represent vessels of transformation. Other feminine symbols, such as a dish, womb, or stone, can have the same symbolic meaning as the Grail.

According to Christian legend, Joseph, who was charged with the preparation of Christ's dead body for the tomb, obtained the cup used during the Last Supper and used it to catch the blood flowing from Christ's wounds. He was accused of stealing Christ's body after its disappearance and was jailed without food. He was able to remain alive in prison until after the appearance of Christ, who gave him the cup and taught him a number of mysteries, such as the Mass. The legend says that a mysterious dove appeared every day, leaving a wafer in the cup, and that, upon his release in A.D. 70, Joseph founded the first Christian Church at Glastonbury, Britain, in which the Grail was preserved.

In another version of the story, Joseph gave the Grail to his sister's husband, Bron, who eventually became the biblical "rich fisher" who fed many people from the cup with a single fish. It was believed that the Grail was preserved in a temple on Muntsalvach—the Mountain of Salvation—where it was guarded by an Order of Grail Knights. The king who kept the Grail was said to be wounded in the thighs or genitals by a spear, and subsequently his kingdom became a wasteland, which could only be restored when the king healed.

According to Arthurian tradition, a vision of the Grail appeared at Pentecost to the Knights of the Round Table, who promised to find it. The only knights to find the Grail were Galahad the pure, Perceval the fool, and Bors the humble. After finding the Grail, they traveled east to Sarras, the Heavenly City, where they celebrated the mysteries of the Grail. In modern times, the Grail quest has been interpreted by psychiatrist Carl G. Jung as a search for truth and the real Self. Also, according to lore, the Grail may be seen only by those who have raised themselves above human limitations, thus attaining a particular state of spiritual consciousness.

See Also: Cup; Goddess(es)
Further Reading
Gordon, Stuart. *The Encyclopedia of Myths and Legends.* London: Headline, 1993.
Leach, Maria. *Standard Dictionary of Folklore, Mythology, and Legend.* San Francisco, CA: HarperSan Francisco, 1984 [1949].

Graves, Robert

One major source of current enthusiasm about an ancient matriarchal period in history is Robert Graves's *The White Goddess.* Indeed, most feminist writing on the subject attempts to bolster Graves's argument. However, the evidence and arguments he used in the book simply did not lead to the conclusions he made. In fact, Graves's approach was entirely one of special pleading: He emphasized the evidence that favors the idea of an ancient Goddess religion and tried to explain away all the contrary evidence. As a result, al-

The celebrated British author Robert Graves in 1968. (Corbis/Bettmann)

though about half the information in *The White Goddess* is valid, the other half is distorted by Graves's efforts to fit the information into his preconceived theory. As a result, *The White Goddess* cannot be used to truthfully reconstruct ancient religions of any sort.

Looked at objectively, *The White Goddess*, like Graves's attempts to reconstruct Christian history, is a compilation of ideas that were proposed by scholars in the nineteenth and early twentieth centuries. Eventually these theories were tested, found inadequate, and discarded. Some feminist writers imply (and sometimes even state) that these scholars rejected "feminist" ideas because the scholars were, consciously or unconsciously, suppressing the true importance of women in history.

Graves did his best to disguise the fact that he was working with theories that most mainstream scholars had discarded. It is true that when *The White Goddess* was first written, in the 1940s, there was still an outside chance that the pre-Greek culture of Greece might have been the sort of matriarchal, matrilocal, and matrilineal culture Graves imagined. However, during the next three decades, modern archaeology in the Mediterranean and allied disciplines made great advances in proving that Greece, during the period of 2500–1500 B.C., was an outpost of Mesopotamian culture. This culture shared the languages, architecture, economics, and, no doubt, social structures of the societies uncovered at Ugarit and other circum-Mediterranean sites. Given these data, we must suppose that the Greeks had the same sort of polytheistic beliefs we know inhabitants of these other sites had—goddesses were certainly important, but there is no indication that a single goddess was the dominant deity.

Anyone familiar with the work of Georges Dumezil might notice that Graves was right to perceive that a tripartite pattern existed in myths about goddesses, but Graves was wrong in thinking that this pattern was pre–Indo European. A threefold goddess was surely a member of the Indo-European pantheon.

Furthermore, the theory that a wonderful, matriarchal, agricultural period in Europe was destroyed by dreadful patriarchal invaders who spoke Indo-European languages during the second millennium B.C. has now been laid to rest. Sir Colin Renfrew's article "The Origins of Indo-European Languages," in the October 1989 issue of *Scientific American*, reports that the consensus among prehistorians is that the language spoken by the people who spread agriculture across Europe between 8000 and 2000 B.C. was most probably Indo-European. Thus, if the Indo-Europeans brought agriculture to Europe, the pre-Indo-Europeans could not have been agriculturalists.

Witches generally think, incorrectly, that *The White Goddess* provides independent evidence for the existence of "Murray-ite" Witch cults during the Middle Ages. Few references to Murray appeared in the original, and much shorter, 1948 first edition of *The White Goddess*. Finally, one should note that Graves was not an independent authority, but was part of the tight circle that surrounded Gardner; Graves was a good friend of Idries Shah, who may even have been an initiate of the London Coven.

See Also: Goddess(es); Murray, Margaret
Further Reading
Graves, Robert. "An Appointment for Candlemas." *Magazine of Fantasy and Science Fiction* (February 1957). The existence of this story shows that Graves was part of Gardner's mythmaking campaign by 1956.
———. *The White Goddess: A Historical Grammar of Poetic Myth*, 3d ed. New York: Farrar, Straus and Giroux, 1968 [1948].

Hutton, Ronald. *The Pagan Religions of the Ancient British Isles: Their Nature and Legacy*. Cambridge, MA: Blackwell, 1991.

Renfrew, Colin. "The Origins of Indo-European Languages." *Scientific American* (October 1989): 106–114.

Great Rite

The Great Rite in Neopagan Witchcraft is sex—but it is always *sacred* sex or *symbolic* sex. The concept of sacred sex is, of course, difficult for many people in Western society to grasp, given the puritan biases of the past, but it is intuitively understood by people in some other cultures.

The Great Rite is almost synonymous with the Third-Degree initiation: If the two parties to the initiation are consenting adults and are free to do so (in terms of their other relationships), they may consummate the initiation with actual sexual intercourse—but whether they do so is known only to them, since this part of the initiation is always private. The initiation can also be magically completed by the "symbolic Great Rite," which is the dipping of the tip of the athame into the cup, as during the consecration of cakes and wine. After this third stage of initiation, the Great Rite can still be used by Third-Degree Witches, but here it begins to merge into the categories of sex magic and of Tantra. Most current literature that describes actual practices within covens provides a fair amount of theorizing and practical advice about use and abuse of the Great Rite and about sex in general.

See Also: Sex and Sex Magic

Further Reading

Farrar, Stewart, and Janet Farrar. *The Witches' Way: Principles, Rituals, and Beliefs of Modern Witchcraft*. With notes and appendix by Doreen Valiente. London: Robert Hale, 1985.

Frost, Gavin, and Yvonne Frost. *Tantric Yoga: The Royal Path to Raising Kundalini Power*. York Beach, ME: Weiser, 1989.

Starhawk [Miriam Simos]. *Dreaming the Dark: Magic, Sex, and Politics*. Boston, MA: Beacon Press, 1982.

Green Man

The Green Man, also known as Green Jack, Jack-in-the-Green, and Green George, is a Pagan God of the Woodlands. Popular in Europe and the British Isles, he is associated with forest-dwelling fairies, called Greenies and Greencoaties. He personifies the spirits of the trees, plants, and foliage, and is described as a horned man peering out from a mask of foliage, generally the sacred oak. He has the power to make rain and foster livestock with lush meadows. The Green Man leads the festival procession of spring Pagan rites as a young man clad from head to foot in greenery, and sometimes is dunked into a river or pond to guarantee rain for the fields and meadows.

See Also: Horned God
Further Reading
Farrar, Stewart, and Janet Farrar. With notes and appendix by Doreen Valiente. *The Witches' Way: Principles, Rituals, and Beliefs of Modern Witchcraft*. London: Robert Hale, 1985.
Gordon, Stuart. *The Encyclopedia of Myths and Legends*. London: Headline, 1993.

An image of the Green Man, European deity of the woodlands. (Dover Pictorial Archive Series)

Grimoire

Through the centuries, a large number of handbooks have offered instructions on how to perform different kinds of magic. Among these books, usually referred to as grimoires, the oldest and best known is *The Key of Solomon*, which is believed to have been written by the legendary King Solomon. A copy of the book was in circulation as early as the first century A.D. Countless versions, often with additions, have followed that first-century edition, making it impossible to identify the original text.

Besides *The Key of Solomon* and its derivations, many other grimoires circulated in the Middle Ages. Some of these are still used as references in modern Witchcraft. The intent of the majority of grimoires was to teach magicians how to summon and control the power of spirits and demons. The sources of the grimoires were ancient Egyptian, Greek, Hebrew, and Latin texts.

The rituals illustrated in grimoires were usually very complicated. They suggested ways of dressing and of behaving during and prior to evocation ceremonies. They contained prayers and incantations, directions for the creation of amulets, instructions on how to sacrifice animals, and lists of demons and spirits who could be summoned through the grimoire.

Grimoires' users were not necessarily worshippers of the devil. Very often, their intent was to summon a demon and, after making a pact with him, to deceive him and take advantage of his powers. These handbooks gave readers the instructions necessary to carry out this trick.

Grimoires have often come under attack by religious authorities, and some of them have been condemned as dangerous or have been publicly destroyed. Nevertheless, they continued to circulate in various versions throughout the Middle Ages. Some material from traditional grimoires appears in modern Books of Shadows—handbooks used by contemporary Witches.

See Also: Book of Shadows; Demons; Spirit
Further Reading
Lady Sheba. *Book of Shadows*. St. Paul, MN: Llewellyn, 1971.

Gris-gris

While the etymology of the word *gris-gris* is uncertain, there is no doubt about its West African origins. The practice of using dolls and cloth bags (gris-gris) was to keep away evil or to attract good luck. Shaping dolls in the image of Gods was an ancient practice, more recently replaced by filling cloth bags with various kinds of objects and personal items.

In Vodun (Voodoo), gris-gris are very common in places like New Orleans, America's Vodun capital, where people carry them for many reasons. They are believed to protect the carrier and his or her belongings, to attract richness and love, or to maintain health.

The preparation of gris-gris is a complicated process, and varies according to the person and the purposes for which it is made. Marie Laveau was one of the most famous gris-gris makers in New Orleans. The number of items in the cloth bag always was between 1 and 13, but was an odd number only. These items were carefully chosen for their symbolic value, as were the kind and color of the cloth that held them. Gamblers were common clients of Marie Laveau, and she could prepare bad-luck or warning gris-gris that could be flung in front of the house or in the path of a victim.

Gris-gris are also common in the religion Santeria: *Mayomberos*, "black" Witches, prepare bags called *resquardos*, "protectors," and *gurunfindas*, a variation on the cloth gris-gris. These are made with a hollowed-out fruit named *guiro*, which is first filled with ritual objects, then buried, and finally hung from a tree to repel evil spirits.

See Also: Amulet; Santeria; Vodun
Further Reading
Hinnells, John R., ed. *A New Dictionary of Religions*, 2d ed. London: Blackwell, 1997.
Miller, Timothy, ed. *America's Alternative Religions*. Albany, NY: State University of New York Press, 1995.
Rigaud, Milo. *Secrets of Voodoo*. San Francisco, CA: City Lights Books, 1985 [1953].

Grounding

At the end of every Neopagan ritual or magical working, it is necessary for all participants to be "grounded." This is often done by touching one's hands to the ground with a chant or mantra asking that the power, or energy, be taken back by the Earth. There are some good reasons for such a "grounding" procedure.

1. Any sort of ritual or working will produce a somewhat altered state of consciousness—and some would argue that this is their whole purpose. Hence, at the end of a ritual, the participants must be returned to an ordinary state of consciousness so that, for example, it will be safe for them to drive home.
2. If a ritual has created sacred space and sacred time, in Eliade's vocabulary, then the participants must be returned to ordinary time and space in order to reach closure.
3. If a Priest or Priestess has been aspecting, he or she will need to be carefully and thoroughly grounded in order to be returned from divine to human status. Witches generally feel that, whatever might be true in the circle, it is not prudent to have someone out on the streets still thinking that he or she has divine powers.
4. Finally, the failure to ground energy is the equivalent of a failure to draw a protective circle or pentacle when evoking spirits or exorcising ghosts. It could leave strange phenomena trailing behind for a while.

See Also: Aspecting; Rite, Ritual
Further Reading
Farrar, Stewart. *What Witches Do: The Modern Coven Revealed*. New York: Coward McCann, 1971.
Starhawk [Miriam Simos]. *The Spiral Dance: A Rebirth of the Ancient Religion of the Great Goddess*, 2d ed. San Francisco, CA: HarperSan Francisco, 1989 [1979].

Grove

Grove is one name used for a local group of Neopagans who choose not to call themselves Witches. The term is used most often by members of the various Druid Orders. It is also sometimes used for an Outer Court or training circle associated with a coven, especially if it has some organizational independence. Finally, some covens choose "Grove of (something)" as their formal name. Hence, the only way to be sure what *grove* means for a particular group is to ask.

See Also: Druids; Gateway Circle
Further Reading
Guiley, Rosemary. *The Encyclopedia of Witches and Witchcraft*. New York: Facts on File, 1989.

Guardians

The guardians in a Craft circle are the entities invoked to guard the four cardinal directions during the overall casting of the circle. How they are conceived can differ widely. In some covens guardians are thought of as little more than elementals; in others they may be among the deities of the highest pantheon that the group honors. Generally, they have a status somewhat like that of a Greek demigod or hero, and it is guardians of this status who are known as the Lords of the Watchtowers. The basic concept is clearly derived from the angels who guard the four quarters in ceremonial magic. However, it should be pointed out that, in a nondualistic theology (such as with Jewish writers between 500 and 200 B.C.), *angeloi*, "messengers," and gods are all in the same category of superhuman entities who mediate between humans and the ultimate divinity.

See Also: Cast; Circle, Magic; Quarters

Further Reading

Green, Marian. *The Elements of Ritual Magic*. Longmead, Shaftesbury, Dorset, U.K.: Element, 1990.

Stewart, R. J. *Advanced Magical Arts*. Longmead, Shaftesbury, Dorset, U.K.: Element, 1988.

H

Handfasting

Sex, like death and food, is a topic about which all people have beliefs. Human beings never eat any and all kinds of food without distinctions or rules. Likewise human beings rarely have sex without regard to society's rules on the subject.

Certainly a great many, perhaps most, adherents of New Age and other new religions were raised in sexually restrictive churches and cultures. Hence, they are generally very interested in finding sexual lifestyles that meet their needs and in minimizing the number of rules about sexuality with which they must be burdened. If formal church structures exist in these new religions, they typically include women, gays, and other minorities normally excluded by mainstream churches and ensure that these minorities are eligible for ordination as Priests, Priestesses, or ministers.

One area of resistance to rules for these groups is on the issue of monogamy. More and more New Agers are unwilling to assume that a lifelong marriage between two people is the ideal for all psychological and physical types. In fact, *lifelong* marriage meant something very different 200 years ago, when the life expectancy was only 35.

Concern about these issues is a major problem for some people in America, including the millions of immigrants who are unaccustomed to the regulation of their private lives that is determined by the beliefs of a single religious persuasion. There is now, as there has been since the early nineteenth century, a vast amount of experimentation with forms of complex marriage, communal living arrangements, multiple relationships, sacramental sexuality, sex magic, and sensual freedom among members of new religions. Whatever their differences in theology, which are profound, many are united in the belief in their right to religious freedom in these areas.

Neopagan Witchcraft offers an alternative to the usual concept of marriage in its concept of handfasting. It is often said that handfasting is the Wiccan equivalent of marriage, but that is not a very accurate statement. Handfasting creates a *magical* partnership between two people, for the purpose of working magic, and especially sexual magic, together. During the ceremony the couple's hands are tied together, hence the name. It differs from marriage in the following ways:

Selena Fox and Dennis Carpenter wed Kyra and Cygnus in a handfasting rite at the 1997 Pagan Spirit Gathering in Ohio. (Photo by Jeff Koslow, Circle Sanctuary archives)

1. The "vows" that define the relationship entered into by the handfasting ritual are not defined by law, but are completely flexible and are limited only by the imaginations of the partners.
2. Handfasting is not exclusive and it is independent of legal marriage. Two people who are handfasted as magical partners in a circle may each have legal spouses as well, who may or may not be members of that circle. People of the same sex can be handfasted. People may have multiple handfasting partners, for whatever magical reasons seem appropriate. As a result, many Pagans who have attempted some sort of complex marriage have used handfasting as a way to formalize and solidify their relationships with one another. The Neopagan Witchcraft movement recognizes all these forms of "marriage" as equally valid, but does not define the partners involved as belonging to one another.
3. A handfasting can be for a set period of time—a day, a month, a year, and seven years are the lengths of time often used—or handfasting can be dependent on some condition, such as "so long as our love shall last" or "so long as we continue to grow, each in our own way." And, when the handfasting is over, no one needs to enrich any lawyers or courts.

Sexual experimentation is not universal in the Craft or among Neopagans; instead, it is the path followed by a minority. The vast majority of Neopagans follow the norms of monogamy.

See Also: Sex and Sex Magic
Further Reading

Adler, Margot. *Drawing Down the Moon: Witches, Pagans, Druids, and Other Goddess-Worshippers in America Today*, 2d ed. Boston, MA: Beacon Press, 1986 [New York: Viking, 1979].
Lewis, James R., ed. *Magical Religion and Modern Witchcraft*. Albany, NY: State University of New York Press, 1996.

Healing

The practice of healing has had a long tradition, far older than modern medicine as a science has had, and contemporary Witchcraft considers healing one of its most important fields of activity. Witches use healing techniques and knowledge that derive from current and ancient cultures.

Probably the most ancient documented healing performance is seen in cave paintings found in the Pyrenees that show an example of healing by touch. The paintings date back 15 millenniums. There also exist written references to this kind of healing that are 5,000 years old, and the practice was known in China, India, Egypt, and Tibet. The Old Testament also has references on this subject. Within the Christian Tradition, the only authorized form of contact healing was the king's touch, which was performed by various monarchs throughout the seventeenth century to treat a form of the disease scrofula.

Modern healing by touch is based on the concept of the use of a subtle energy, referred to as *prana* by yogis, and the complementary notion of the existence of an aura, a subtle energy field that surrounds and permeates living beings. The aura is an energy layer, visible only to clairvoyants, which can be weak from illness. Healers can direct their own energy, the prana, to restore weak areas of another's aura. By simply running one's hands through the field, the healer can revitalize the aura and revitalize or cure the patient.

The use of herbs is another common way of healing. In his *Natural History*, Pliny gives the first large-scale description of the medicinal use of plants and herbs. Although his work was a milestone on which others elaborated for centuries, there is no doubt that a high level of knowledge on herbalism had been attained earlier by the Assyrians, Babylonians, Sumerians, and Egyptians.

Along with herbal remedies, crystals and gems have long been popular among healers. In recent years, New Age groups have revived their use as healing, meditational, and divination tools. The properties of stones vary according to their shape, magnetism, and colors, and stones can be worn or placed on specific parts of the body, particularly on the energy centers called *chakras*.

Other methods of healing used in modern Witchcraft are magical spells. Witches deploy such spells during rituals that often involve the personal belongings of the patient. The spells are formulated according to the type of patient and ailment in question.

In some cases, healing can coincide with exorcism, particularly when the illness is attributed to the negative influence of a low spirit. In such cases, an entranced healer can sometimes succeed in driving away the evil spirit from the victim. Although not common within Neopagan Witchcraft, this method has roots in Shamanism and, as such, is studied by Witches interested in non-Western healing techniques. Other methods of healing sometimes utilized by contemporary Neopagans—methods such as acupuncture, shiatsu, and reflexology—originated in Asia and have been imported to the West.

See Also: Aura; Exorcism; Spells
Further Reading
Grossman, Richard. *The Other Medicines*. Garden City, NJ: Doubleday, 1985.
Walker, Benjamin. *Encyclopedia of Metaphysical Medicine*. London: Routledge and Kegan Paul, 1978.

Hecate

The Greek Goddess Hecate is the patron of magic and Witchcraft. She is Goddess of Fertility and Plenty, Goddess of the Moon—as part of the Triple Goddess with Selene and Diana—and queen of the night, ghosts, and shades. As part of the lunar trinity, Hecate rules over the waning phase of the moon, which lasts two weeks, during which magic dealing with banishing, releasing, planning, and introspection is at its best.

William Blake's famous painting of the Goddess Hecate. (Tate Gallery, London/Art Resource, New York)

As the Goddess of the Dark of the Moon, Hecate is the destroyer or restorer of life. She roams the Earth at night, when she is said to be visible only to dogs. Known also as "The Nameless One," she is related to nightmares and terror. Hecate is also the Goddess of Crossroads; she looks in three directions at the same time and has been variously associated with incantations, sacrifices, and rituals practiced in front of homes and at crossroads in several cultures. In ancient times, Hecate was considered more important than the mythical sorceress Circe or the Witch Medea, both of whom were said to be her daughters. Hecate is also invoked for justice.

See Also: Diana; Goddess(es)
Further Reading
Gordon, Stuart. *The Encyclopedia of Myths and Legends.* London: Headline, 1993.
Grant, Michael, and John Hazel. *Who's Who: Classical Mythology.* New York: Oxford University Press, 1993.

Heresy, Heretic

The Greek word *hairesis* meant "choice" and, by extension, a sect or subvariety of a school of philosophy. In Christian usage in the second century it came to mean "a member of a variety of Christianity (especially Gnostic Christianity) different from that of the speaker"; Irenaeus of Lyon was probably the first writer to use it in this sense. As the historical mainstream of Christian belief took shape during the following centuries, the term *hairesis* took on a disparaging connotation. Once Christianity had become the official and only legal religion, people who belonged to sects not recognized by the religious authorities were criminals by definition. Despite their legal advantage, the official church was not able to eliminate the last Gnostic communities until the eighth century.

It was the memory of that struggle that explains the Church's violent reaction to the discovery of new heresies in Europe in the eleventh century. The Roman establishment feared that the Gnostics had returned (and it is possible that there was a historical connection between some Gnostics and the Cathars). Pope Lucius III established the Holy Office of the Inquisition in 1088 to search out these heretics, which it did with diligence, but also with some measure of reason. It was not until after Pope Innocent VIII's bull against Witchcraft in 1488 equated Witches with heretics that the great Witch hunts began. These Witch hunts were in modern, not medieval, times and had more to do with the war between Catholics and Protestants, the traditional nobility and the new merchants, than with any aspect of religion. The furor died down as Europe approached the period of Enlightenment and the Witch hunts ended.

See Also: Burning Times; Gnosticism
Further Reading
Eliade, Mircea, ed. *Encyclopedia of Religion*. New York: Macmillan, 1987.
Shepard, Leslie A., ed. *Encyclopedia of Occultism and Parapsychology*. Detroit, MI: Gale Research Inc., 1991.

Hermetic Order of the Golden Dawn (and its offshoots)

The magical system used by Neopagan Witchcraft is not anything inherited from a secret tradition. Instead, all Neopagan Witches and ritual magicians use what is essentially the same system of ceremonial magic. This system can be traced back to the Hermetic Order of the Golden Dawn (HOGD), which was an offshoot of a Masonic-Rosicrucian organization, the Societas Rosicruciana in Anglia (SRIA). The Societas Rosicruciana was founded by Robert Wentworth Little in 1865 and was supposedly based on old manuscripts (apparently owned by the psychic Fred Hockley) found in Freemasons' Hall in England. In 1887, Dr. William Wynn Westcott, a London coroner and a member of the SRIA, obtained part of a manuscript, written in a cipher code, from the Reverend A. F. A. Woodford. In 1885, Woodford, a Mason, inherited the magical manuscripts owned by Hockley. Westcott claimed to have "decoded" the manuscript and to have discovered that it contained fragments of rituals for the "Golden Dawn," a secret organization that apparently admitted both men and women as full members—a radical idea in Victorian London.

Westcott then asked an occultist friend, Samuel Liddell MacGregor Mathers (1854–1918), to "flesh out" the fragments of the manuscript into full-scale rituals that could be carried out by members of a magical lodge. Mathers did so, using largely Masonic materials. He was uniquely qualified for this work, being a gifted classical scholar from a scholarly family. Mathers was a relative of Alice Liddell, whose father coauthored the most important Greek dictionary of the nineteenth century, and whose adventures in Wonderland were chronicled by the Reverend Charles Ludwidge Dodgson (Lewis Carroll). Mathers's translations of *The Greater Key of Solomon* (the basic text of ritual magic) and of the Zohar (the basic text of Cabalism) are still standard texts; his book on the Tarot is still in use.

At this time Westcott (or perhaps someone else) may have simply forged papers claiming to trace the "Golden Dawn" back to a Rosicrucian organization in Germany. These papers included the Nuremberg address of Anna Sprenger, a Rosicrucian Adept in touch with the Masters in the East. Mathers and Westcott claimed to have written to her and to have received a great mass of information and rituals. Among this information was a charter for the Isis-Urania Temple of the Hermetic Order of the Golden Dawn, founded in London with Westcott, Mathers, and W. R. Woodman, Supreme Magus of the SRIA, as its ruling triumvirate.

The London Lodge of the Theosophical Society opened in 1883, and members of both it and the SRIA were among the early members of the Isis-Urania Temple. For some reason the Hermetic Order of the Golden Dawn suited the temper of the times. During the first eight years of the lodge's existence, more than 300 members were initiated, and these included some of the greatest literary and artistic figures of the times. HOGD members (as revealed by Ithel Colquhoun's appendixes of *Sword of Wisdom: MacGregor Mathers and the "Golden Dawn"*)

William Butler Yeats was one of many famous members of the Hermetic Order of the Golden Dawn. (North Wind Picture Archive)

included Arthur Machen, Arthur Edward Waite, James M. Barrie, Sir E. A. Wallis Budge, Hugh Schonfield, Florence Farr (at one time George Bernard Shaw's lover), Maud Gonne (mother of Sean McBride, the founder of Amnesty International), and, most famous, William Butler Yeats (Maud Gonne's lover).

An elaborate system of magical lessons and initiations was created and divided into ten magical grades corresponding to the ten sephiroth of the Cabalistic Tree of Life, plus a "zeroth" grade for the neophytes. The grades also were grouped into three orders: Outer, Inner, and Third (or Secret). Initiates advanced through the Outer Order by passing a series of written examinations and undergoing a corresponding series of elaborate initiations. At some point, Mathers took the notebooks of Dr. John Dee, Elizabeth I's advisor, and turned the information into a usable system that is now generally called Enochian Magic; it is, oddly enough, a strictly Christian magical system. Note that all of this was financed by the HOGD members' annual dues of 100 pounds sterling apiece—more than the annual earnings of an average British workman at that time. The Hermetic Order of the Golden Dawn was very much a rich person's club.

At first, the only members of the Inner Order were Mathers, Westcott, and Woodman, and they claimed to be directed by the Secret Chiefs of the Third Order, entities on the Astral Plane rather like the Secret Masters of theosophical belief. In 1891, Woodman died and was not replaced in his post within the Inner Order. At this time, Mathers created the initiation ritual for the Adeptus Minor grade, the first within the Inner Order, and gave the Inner Order a new name: *Ordo Rosae et Aureae Crucis* ("Order of the Ruby Rose and Cross of Gold"). Membership was by invitation only.

Mathers married Moina Bergson, daughter of the philosopher Henri Bergson. It is said that they never physically consummated their marriage. Moina was very much Mathers's partner in his magical work, as he was about to receive teachings from the Secret Chiefs through clairaudience, that is, hearing voices.

Mathers, though brilliant, was eccentric and financially incompetent. His devotion to the HOGD had, by 1891, left him and Moina penniless. Fortunately, a wealthy member of the order, Annie Horniman, decided to become their benefactor in order to enable them to continue their work. Hence, in 1891, the couple was able to move to Paris, where they set up a second lodge. Mathers continued to write teaching materials and send them to London. He became increasingly jealous of Westcott, and increasingly autocratic. He concentrated on translating another major magical treatise, *The Book of the Sacred Magic of Abra-Melin the Mage*, which was published in 1898.

In 1896, Mathers claimed that the Secret Chiefs had initiated him into the Third Order and that he therefore had supreme authority over the entire Hermetic Order of the Golden Dawn. Horniman disputed his claims and was subsequently expelled from the society; so, of course, she cut off her financial support. The Matherses' situation became increasingly more desperate.

By 1897, the members of the HOGD had begun to suspect Westcott's role in "creating" the organization and accused him of forgery. His resigned from his position and was replaced by Florence Farr. The stage was now set for the battle that soon ensued.

In 1898, young Aleister Crowley was initiated, and he rose rapidly in the organization, passing the examinations almost as fast as they could be administered. Impatient with the slow procedures in London, in 1899 he went to Paris and insisted that Mathers initiate him into the Second Order. Mathers complied, but the London lodge, under Farr's direction, refused to accept his initiation as valid. Crowley, who was fairly wealthy at the time, and Mathers now became allies. In 1900, Mathers sent Crowley to London to attempt to take over the London temple. According to Virginia Moore (in *The Unicorn: William Butler Yeats' Search for Reality*), when Crowley attempted to open the file cabinet in the office, Yeats, who was over six feet tall, picked Crowley up, held him overhead, walked to the front door, and threw Crowley down the stairs into the gutter of a London street. When Crowley returned, there was a constable standing on each side of Yeats's desk.

Crowley retaliated by publishing some of the lodge's secret rituals in his magazine, *The Equinox*. Crowley and Mathers engaged in a magical war with each other, and also parted ways. Crowley went on to found a rival organization, the Astrum Argentinum ("Silver Star"), and later joined and took over the Ordo Templi Orientis (OTO).

In 1900, with all of the original triumvirate gone, Yeats, who joined in 1890, was elected head of the Inner Order and tried to restore peace and unity. Unfortunately, the schisms were deep enough after a dozen years that the Hermetic Order of the Golden Dawn soon split into several separate organizations. Followers of Mathers formed the Alpha et Omega Temple, which Moina continued to direct after Mathers's death. In 1903, A. E. Waite and his followers broke away, forming a group that kept the Golden Dawn name but emphasized mysticism more than magic; after Waite left in 1915, the group went into a decline.

In 1905, the majority of the remaining members of the Isis-Urania Temple reorganized themselves as the Stella Matutina, or Order of the Morning Star, with Yeats as their Grand Master. Yeats served in this position until 1917, when he married his young secretary, Georgie, settled down finally to married life, and, under Georgie's influence, gave up the active magical work in order to concentrate on his poetry. The work Yeats produced during the last two decades of his life is generally acknowledged to be among the greatest literary work ever produced.

With Yeats's departure, the Isis-Urania Temple was resurrected as the Merlin Temple of the Stella Matutina, which remained active into the 1940s. The temple then went into a decline after its secret rituals were published by Israel Regardie, who had, at one time, been Aleister Crowley's secretary. However, it is interesting to note that Regardie did not publish any of the Christian magical materials used by the HOGD members.

There do not seem to be any HOGD lodges in North America that were chartered directly by either the original Hermetic Order of the Golden Dawn or the Stella Matutina. Instead, the American lodges trace their lineage back to the OTO or have begun "from scratch," working with the copious information that has been published in recent decades on exactly how the lodges functioned at every level.

See Also: Mathers; Samuel Liddell; Ordo Templi Orientis
Further Reading
Colquhoun, Ithell. *Sword of Wisdom: MacGregor Mathers and the "Golden Dawn."* New York: Putnam's, 1975.
King, Francis. *Ritual Magic in England, 1887 to the Present.* London: Spearman, 1970.
Mathers, S. L. MacGregor, ed. and trans. *The Greater Key of Solomon.* Chicago: De Laurence, Scott, 1914.
Moore, Virginia. *The Unicorn: William Butler Yeats' Search for Reality.* New York: Macmillan, 1954.
Regardie, Israel. *The Golden Dawn: An Account of the Teachings, Rites, and Ceremonies of the Order of the Golden Dawn, 1937–1940,* 2d ed. River Falls, WI: Hazel Hills, 1969.

Herne the Hunter

Of the many ways in which this character of the English tradition is portrayed, Herne the Hunter is most associated with the dead and with night activities. He leads the mythological Wild Hunt wearing a horned headdress, a feature that associates him with other horned gods, such as Pan and Cernunnos. Similar figures exist in the German and French traditions, and sightings of Herne the Hunter are reported in English forests.

See Also: Cernunnos; Horned God
Further Reading
Gordon, Stuart. *The Encyclopedia of Myths and Legends.* London: Headline, 1993.
Leach, Maria. *Standard Dictionary of Folklore, Mythology, and Legend.* San Francisco, CA: HarperSan Francisco, 1984 [1949].

Hex

Hex refers to a spell laid through Witchcraft. It derives from a German word adopted by the Pennsylvania Dutch. Although in common usage it is a close synonym of *curse*, the Pennsylvania Dutch use it to designate good, as well as evil, spells.

See Also: Curses; Spells
Further Reading
Guiley, Rosemary. *The Encyclopedia of Witches and Witchcraft.* New York: Facts on File, 1989.

Hex Signs

The long tradition of inscribing good-omen signs on houses and on tools dates to the Bronze Age and has made its way through Europe to the Pennsylvania Dutch, who have used them throughout the nineteenth century. Hex signs are usually of circular shape and represent flowers, stars, hearts, swastikas, wheels, and many other symbols. Each carries a specific meaning and provides a particular type of protection or enhancement of certain qualities. Some hex signs are designed and used to favor courage, fertility, or virility. Others are placed on cradles, or on the doors of houses and stables to prevent bewitchment.

See Also: Amulet; Talismans
Further Reading
Valiente, Doreen. *An ABC of Witchcraft: Past and Present.* New York: St. Martin's Press, 1973.

Hieros Gamos

The Greek *hieros gamos* (meaning "sacred marriage," "sacred wedding feast," or "sacred sexual intercourse") refers to the mythical or ritual union between a god and a goddess. It can also refer to the union of a deity with a human being, particularly between a king and a goddess. More generally, the term can represent the union of a set of opposites—such as east and west, north and south, or sky and Earth—expressed through the symbol of sexual union. In various myths, for example, Earth and sky are depicted as having been one in the beginning (as in a sexual embrace) and were separated during the act of creation. Agriculture and the ritual work on the land have been endowed with sexual symbolism, since tilling the soil can be interpreted as a male act performed on the female Earth. Thus, the work of the farmer can be depicted as a sexual ritual. During the ritual of agricultural work, the seasons acquire a new significance.

As far back as the ancient Indus Valley civilization, goddesses seem to have been associated with the expression of the power of vegetation on the Earth. The power of the goddess, the most striking theme in the mythology and rituals of sacred marriage, is the ability to generate everything—with a secondary, almost irrelevant participation of the male. This power was usually associated with war and destructive anger, and with irresistible life and love. Various images of prehistoric, protohistoric, and traditional goddesses show the ancient significance of nudity, symbolically associated with prosperity, abundance, and increased harvest.

Sexual rituals associated with agricultural life have drawn the attention of a number of scholars, not only to rites in ancient societies but also to continuing folk customs. Such scholars as Wilhelm Mannhardt (1831–1880) and James G. Frazer (1854–1941) recorded many instances in which the sex act was believed to have a magical effect to induce fertility in people, animals, and fields.

Hieros gamos rituals were also associated with the creation of early city-states built on the wealth provided by agriculture. These rituals derived from earlier symbolism, although in an expanded and stylized form. One of these was the *hieros gamos* rite celebrated in various cultic centers in Mesopotamia during the New Year Festival. The rite usually consisted of a sexual union of the king of the city and the city's goddess, sometimes represented by the king's wife, but more often a female servant of the sanctuary, a Priestess. During the ceremony, sacrifices were offered, representing wedding gifts, and the ritual wedding was seen as a visible representation of the celestial union.

Among the earliest prototypes of this ritual was the Sumerian story of the Goddess Inanna and her relation to Dumuzi, a shepherd boy. Comparable sacred marriage symbologies can be found in other culture areas, such as Mexico and India. These systems of symbols always share an agricultural context and generally appear in a tropical or temperate region more or less close to the equator.

See Also: Great Rite; Ordo Templi Orientis; Sex and Sex Magic
Further Reading
Eliade, Mircea, ed. *The Encyclopedia of Religion.* 16 vols. New York: Macmillan, 1987.
Matthews, Caitlín, and John Matthews. *The Western Way: A Practical Guide to the Western Mystery Tradition.* London: Arkana, 1994.

High Priest(ess)

A High Priest or High Priestess is generally understood to be a person who has received Third-Degree initiation (or the highest available degree) in his or her tradition and who is the leader of a coven. In a coven with group leadership rather than individual leadership, the role of the High Priestess may be rotated among the members.

See Also: Coven; Degrees
Further Reading
Farrar, Stewart. *What Witches Do: The Modern Coven Revealed.* New York: Coward McCann, 1971.
Valiente, Doreen. *The Rebirth of Witchcraft.* London: Robert Hale, 1989.

Hiving Off

When a coven has become too large to function well as a group, or when a High Priestess raises another woman in her coven to the Third Degree, it is often wise for some members to resign from the original coven and form a new one of their own. This process is called "hiving off," in reference to the way a swarm of bees divides when a new queen bee is hatched. How peaceful such a process is depends upon the coven's particular circumstances—but, in general, the growth of the Craft has been peaceful more often than not.

See Also: Coven
Further Reading
Starhawk [Miriam Simos]. *The Spiral Dance: A Rebirth of the Ancient Religion of the Great Goddess,* 2d ed. San Francisco, CA: HarperSan Francisco, 1989 [1979].

Hocus Pocus

The etymology of this magical phrase is not clear. Various magicians with the name *Hocus Pocus* or a similar name have been credited with the origination of the words, although Hocus Pocus is not related to Witchcraft or magic. The most accepted interpretations consider the phrase either alliterative nonsense or a corruption of a line in the Catholic Mass, *hoc est enim corpus meum,* which means "this is indeed my body."

See Also: Magic
Further Reading
Grant, R. M. *Gnosticism and Early Christianity.* New York: Columbia University Press, 1959.
The Oxford Dictionary of English Etymology, s.v. "Hocus Pocus." New York: Oxford University Press, 1985 [1966].

Hod

The eighth sephira of the Cabala is splendor, or majesty. It is the left leg of Adam Kadmon, the primal human. Hod is the realm of the mind and science and it influences the rules and logic of the material realm.

See Also: Cabala
Further Reading
Fortune, Dion. *The Mystical Qabalah.* York Beach, ME: Weiser, 1994 [1935].
Myers, Stuart. *Between the Worlds: Witchcraft and the Tree of Life—A Program of Spiritual Development.* St. Paul, MN: Llewellyn, 1995.

Holly King

The Holly King was one of the more popular figures in premodern Pagan cultures as well as in contemporary folklore. He was associated with a worldview inspired by the cycles of nature and particularly by the cycles of the sun and the moon, to which calendars and seasonal festivals are linked. The solar cycle is characterized by eight Sabbats, or sacred times, known also as the Wheel of the Year: the solstices, the equinoxes, and the four points between, or cross quarters. The Holly King was part of a dual divine image associated with the waxing and waning of the days of the year. The Holly King ruled and represented withdrawal and rest during the waning half of the year, when the days grow shorter. The Oak King, on the other hand, ruled and represented expansion and growth during the waxing phase of the calendar year, when the days grow longer.

See Also: Oak King
Further Reading
Leach, Maria. *Standard Dictionary of Folklore, Mythology, and Legend*. San Francisco, CA: HarperSan Francisco, 1984 [1949].

Horned God

In the Neopagan Tradition, the Horned God is the consort of the Goddess and represents the male principle of the supreme deity. He is the lord of the woodlands, the hunt, and animals. He is also associated with death, the underworld, sexuality, vitality, logic, and power, and is portrayed as gentle, tender, and compassionate. The Horned God personifies the Sun, in contrast to the Goddess's Moon, with whom he alternates in ruling the fertility cycle of birth-death-rebirth. His birthday is at the winter solstice, whereas his marriage with the Goddess is at Beltane (May 1). The Horned God's death represents a sacrifice to life. His horns are associated with his domain of the woodlands, with the bull and the ram, and with the crescent moon.

Several deities have been associated with the Horned God, whose origin dates back to Paleolithic times. Among them are Cernunnos, Celtic God of Fertility, Animals, and the Underworld; Herne the Hunter; Pan, Greek God of the Woodlands; Janus, Roman God of Good Beginnings; Tammuz and Damuzi, son-lover-consorts of Ishtar and Inanna; Osiris, Egyptian God of the Underworld; and Dionysus, Greek God of Vegetation and the Vine. The Horned God has also been associated with the devil. In modern Witchcraft, the Horned God is not emphasized as much as the Goddess is, although he is considered equally important and is worshipped in magic rites, during which he is personified by the High Priest.

See Also: Cernunnos; Green Man; Herne the Hunter
Further Reading
Gordon, Stuart. *The Encyclopedia of Myths and Legends*. London: Headline, 1993.

High Priestess crowning the High Priest with the symbol of the Horned God during a Samhain ceremony. (Raymond Buckland/Fortean Picture Library)

Horseshoe

In European and Arabic cultures the horseshoe has a long tradition as an amulet. It is believed to keep away evil spirits when its ends point downward. It can also bring good luck, with the ends pointing upward, although the two functions cannot coexist. It is commonly placed at the entrance of or inside households, often attached to pieces of furniture or chimneys. In the latter case it will scare away flying Witches. In order to preserve its effectiveness, it must not be removed from where it has been placed or nailed.

See Also: Amulet; Talismans

Further Reading

Bletzer, June G. *The Donning International Encyclopedic Psychic Dictionary*. Norfolk, VA: Donning, 1986.

Shepard, Leslie A., ed. *Encyclopedia of Occultism and Parapsychology*. Detroit, MI: Gale Research Inc., 1991.

Hypnosis

What is now called hypnotism has been known to exist in almost all societies in the past, though its nature was hardly understood or appreciated. Hypnotic phenomena began to be studied in Europe in the sixteenth century, when the phenomena were attributed to "magnetism" (a subtle influence exerted by every object in the universe onto every other object). From this concept Paracelsus constructed the "sympathetic" theory of medicine, and he apparently used iron magnets in some treatments, as did J. B. van Helmont. This theory of magnetism was also advocated by Robert Fludd, the English hermeticist, and by a Scottish physician, William Maxwell. In the seventeenth century, several healers appeared who used hypnotic suggestion. Two of these healers were the Irishman Valentine Greatrakes (1629–1683) and a Swabian Priest named John Joseph Gassner (1727–1779), who passed his hands over a patient's body to drive out evil spirits that caused illness, and who considered this to be a type of exorcism. At about this time, Emanuel Swedenborg (1688–1772) tied the phenomena of "magnetism" together with his theories of the spiritual world in a manner that laid the grounds for spiritualism.

The next stage in the development of hypnotism arose with Franz Anton Mesmer, who was born on May 23, 1733, at Wiel, near Lake Constance in Germany, and who died on March 5, 1815, at Meersburg, Switzerland. Mesmer proposed that phenomena were caused by a "universal fluid" that he called "animal magnetism." His success as a practitioner gave rise to the term *mesmerism*. Mesmer was greatly influenced by his reading of Paracelsus during his studies at the University of Vienna. Like Paracelsus, he believed that the microcosm of the human body reflected the macrocosm of the universe; he also believed that the corresponding parts of the body and the universe are tied together by the universal magnetic fluid. In 1773, he effected his first cure by means of such a magnetic pass. In 1776, he met Gassner, who achieved the same results with his bare hands. This led Mesmer to wonder whether healing power might reside in the human body itself, rather than in magnets; dispensing with the magnets, he, too, began to pass his hands without magnets over patients' bodies.

For the next few years Mesmer practiced in various European cities and tried to win official recognition for his theories, but without success. In 1778, he moved to Paris and became wildly successful among the fashionable and the literati, although the learned societies still shunned him. He saw hundreds of wealthy patients and developed a procedure using a *baquet*, or magnetic tub, that allowed many patients to be treated simultaneously.

Among his pupils was Charles D'Eslon, a prominent physician and medical advisor to the Count d'Artois. D'Eslon presented Mesmer's theories before the Faculty of Medicine (an academic group much like the British Royal Academy) in September 1780, but did not win Mesmer a hearing, and was himself threatened with expulsion from the faculty unless he recanted his views. In 1784, the French government appointed a commission, whose 13 members included Benjamin Franklin as its president, the chemist Antoine-Laurent Lavoisier, J. K. Lavater, and Jean Sylvain Bailly, to investigate the magnetic phenomena. The commission chose to investigate the experiments of D'Eslon, rather than of Mesmer himself. They observed the phenomena, especially the rapport between patient and physician, but concluded that imagination and suggestibility could account for all the observed phenomena and that there was no evidence for the existence of a magnetic fluid. The report quenched most of the public enthusiasm for mesmerism. Despite the decline in public enthusiasm, Mesmer and his followers continued to practice, and formed the "Societies of Harmony" until the political terror after the French Revolution drove them out of existence. Mesmer himself fled to England.

The modern era in the history of hypnotism began in 1813, when Abbé Faria ascribed all "magnetic phenomena" to the power of suggestion. This hypothesis was the foundation for the works of Alexandre Bertrand (1795–1831), whose explanation of the important role played by suggestion in the various known forms of trance and mesmeric phenomena revived the flagging public interest in the subject. In 1841, a British surgeon, James Braid (1795–1860), read a paper in which he described hypnotism as a special condition of the nervous system characterized by an abnormal exaltation of suggestibility. In his paper, he introduced the term *hypnotism*, from the Greek *hypnos* ("sleep"), since the subjects appeared to be asleep or sleepwalking. During the nineteenth century, more and more medical uses for hypnosis were found, though many doctors were suspicious of it because of its association with Spiritualism. Sigmund Freud investigated hypnosis, but found it did not work as well as other techniques for his purposes.

The altered state of consciousness, known as the hypnotic state, is easily and reliably achieved, whether by a hypnotist or self-induced. It is also quite versatile and has been put to many uses within new religious movements. The hypnotic state is often characterized by increased suggestibility in the subject, or patient. It can proceed along a wide spectrum of characteristics, from a light trance to complete catalepsy, with varying degrees of anesthesia, amnesia, suggestibility, and personality dissociation.

An important product of hypnosis is the condition called *hyperaesthesia,* in which all or some of the body's senses become acutely sensitive to any and all sensations: A piece of wire laid on the hands may feel as heavy as a bar of iron, or every sound can be heard, no matter how faint. It is becoming clear that the human mind is vastly more complex than most people assume and that the mental mechanisms revealed by the hypnotic state are not in any way occult, peripheral, or abnormal, but are instead part of the underpinnings of all mental functioning. That is, hyperaesthesia seems to function all the time, but in the hypnotic trance, the distractions that usually disguise it are stripped away or shunted aside.

The hypnotic state can be self-induced by any person trained to do so. The system of autosuggestion devised by Emile Coué (1857–1926) allows a subject to benefit from his or her own suggestions and has become part of the basis for many other popular systems of healing—including psychosynthesis, Gestalt therapy, meditation, psychodrama, and hypnotic therapies in general. Carl Jung coined the term *active imagination* to refer to a process in which the mind makes use of mental pictures to modify misperceptions of one's inner and outer circumstances; this procedure is now more often called "guided meditation," and serves as the basis for many psychic training courses.

There has been an ongoing argument over whether the hypnotic state can amplify or augment any psychic abilities that a subject may have. At the least, a hypnotized subject is easily persuaded to believe, or act as if he or she believes, that he or she has powers of telepathy, clairvoyance, precognition, or astral flight and is able to give convincing (and sometimes verifiable) performances of these talents. Hence, hypnotic techniques are now widely used by Neopagan Witches to train their students in the development and use of psychic abilities.

In a hypnotized state, a person can be asked to recall what he or she was doing on a specific date in the past, say, in early childhood, and almost all subjects will then tell of detailed memories, often spoken in a childish manner. If subjects are asked to recall a date before they were born, they will often "remember" memories from the life of a person living at that time. In 1954, reincarnation received a boost from Morey Bernstein's best-selling *The Search for Bridey Murphy* (1956), based on his experiences with Mrs. Virginia Tighe, who "remembered" her previous life as an Irish girl named Bridey Murphy.

The interpretation of past-life regression remains controversial. Those who believe in reincarnation offer it as evidence in favor of their belief. However, skeptics argue that the human mind, in the hypnotic state, is uncritical and eager to please and will fabricate a plausible story if asked to do so. Believers argue that many past lives have been verified by objective research: The person from the past who was remembered by a subject under hypnosis, though not at all famous, turns out to have existed. Skeptics argue that plausible accounts of past lives will appear to be verified by sheer chance: One only has to search for a person with a common Irish name, such as Bridget Murphy or Aidan Kelly, somewhere in Ireland in the nineteenth century, and one will surely turn up. Furthermore, skeptics argue, vast numbers of people claim to remember being *the same* famous person—Cleopatra or Napoleon, for example. These subjects cannot all be correct unless a personality is something like a holograph and can be reproduced from a small piece of itself. But such an argument violates the logical principle of Occam's Razor, the skeptics say, and is certainly not a sort of survival of a personality, with its sense of identity and memories intact.

The historical truth of a past life is probably inherently neither provable nor disprovable. The reality of the past life as a psychological construct is indubitable, however, and, in the hands of a skilled therapist, can provide clues to incidents buried in a person's past that are the key to successful therapy. For the most part, though, a past-life regression is experienced as something like a sacrament by those who believe in reincarnation. Hypnotists who offer to perform past-life regressions often function more as ministers than as therapists; and some of them advertise their services as ministry, rather than as psychotherapy.

See Also: Extrasensory Perception; Healing; Parapsychology
Further Reading
Ambrose, G., and G. Newbold. *A Handbook of Medical Hypnosis,* 4th ed. New York: Macmillan, 1980.
Bernheim, H. *Hypnosis and Suggestion in Psychotherapy.* New Hyde Park, NJ: University Books, 1964 [1888].
Bernstein, Morey. *The Search for Bridey Murphy.* Garden City, NJ: Doubleday, 1956.
Erickson, Milton. *Hypnotic Realities.* New York: Irvington, 1976.

I

I Ching

The *I Ching*, or Book of Changes, is one of the Chinese classics whose authorship is ascribed (most probably incorrectly) to Master K'ung, better known in the West as Confucius. It is a straightforward system of divination, popular among Neopagans. It is used as follows:

The person asks a question, then either throws yarrow sticks or tosses coins in order to generate a series of six whole or broken lines. All of the possible combinations of these lines comprise 64 hexagrams, whose meanings are written out in the Book, along with lengthy traditional commentaries on the meanings of the hexagrams. Some of the lines are considered "changing lines": These generate a second hexagram, which indicates the final outcome of the situation under consideration. As with all divination systems, the tendency today is to understand them in terms of Jung's theories about the collective unconscious or deep mind, which will, in his view, use any means available to communicate with the ordinary ego.

See Also: Divination; Fortune-Telling
Further Reading
Fox, Judy, Karen Hughes, and John Tampion. *An Illuminated I Ching*. New York: Arco, 1984.

Ifa

Ifa is the principal Yoruba system of divination. It originated in the city of Ife and eventually spread throughout such West African societies as Benin, Fon, and the Ewe of Togo, and then to eastern Ghana, as well as Brazil and Cuba. Ifa's divination is based upon the manipulation of 16 palm-nuts, or the toss of a chain by which 16 basic permutations are possible, and on which 256 figures depend. Ifa is believed to provide several verses for each figure, recited by the diviner until the client chooses one. These verses are part of a considerable corpus of unwritten scripture, known as *odu* or *orisa*, providing guidance and instructions to offer sacrifices at the shrine of Eshu.

The *babalawo*, the Ifa diviner and "father of ancient wisdom," is always a man and a Priest of Orunmila. He is required to memorize the verses and may rise in honor through various initiations. In Ifa, sacrifice generally deals with death as well as the avoidance of experiences of loss, disease, famine, sterility, isolation, and poverty. It can also be regarded as the reversal of death into life. It constitutes the food of the orisa and other spirits, and through the sacrificial act the creative power of the orisa, the ancestors, or the mothers is brought to the worshipper.

See Also: African Religions; Divination
Further Reading
Hunt, Carl M. *Oyotunji Village*. Washington, D.C.: University Press of America, 1979.
Murphy, Joseph M. "Santeria and Vodou in the United States." In Miller, Timothy, ed., *America's Alternative Religions*. Albany, NY: State University of New York Press, 1995.

Incantation

Incantation, or chanting, refers to the rhythmic repetition of words and phrases during both religious and magic ceremonies. Magicians, ministers, and sorcerers can achieve altered states of consciousness and enhance the effectiveness of their rituals through the prolonged and often accelerating repetition of chants.

Chants are often accompanied by dances and forms of beat-keeping such as music, drumming, or simple hand-clapping. The practice of incantation has existed since ancient times in many cultures around the world. Besides a widespread use of incantation in ancient Greece and in medieval rituals, chanting is documented in Shamanistic traditions, such as among American Indians.

Today's Witches use chants to enhance the power of spells. Chants can be derived from magical texts, although Witches often create their own rhyming or alliterative phrases and dedicate them to the gods and/or goddesses of their particular tradition.

See Also: Rite, Ritual; Spells
Further Reading
Eliade, Mircea. *The Encyclopedia of Religion*. New York: Macmillan, 1987.
Farrar, Stewart. *What Witches Do: The Modern Coven Revealed*. New York: Coward McCann, 1971.

Incense

The word *incense*, derived from the Latin *incendere*—"to burn or to kindle"—refers, like the word *perfume*, to the aroma emanated by the smoke of an odoriferous substance when burned. Generally, the substances used in incense produce a pleasant odor and may include various aromatic woods, barks, resins, and herbs. Aloe, camphor, cloves, sandalwood, myrrh, frankincense, cedar, juniper, balsam, galbanum, and turpentine are among the most popular substances used to produce incense. In contemporary Neopagan rituals, incense represents the presence of the element of air.

Incense has been an important element in religious rites and practices since ancient times. It has been used to please the gods, sanctify a place or an object, show respect, honor commitments and promises, or tie bonds and friendships. Since it is associated with concepts of purity *and* pollution, as well as with the transforming powers of fire and sweet smells, it is also used in purification rites and customs as well as in ceremonies of offering, prayer, and intercession. Incense is often used to establish a connection with a deity and to scare and exorcise evil forces. Fairies were also thought to be kept away by strong odors, such as that of garlic.

The burning of sweet-smelling substances is common to many peoples, and seems to have spread southeast and west from the Semitic lands. Incense was taken from Egypt and Babylonia to Greece and the Roman Empire. It has never been used in Muslim religious rites, but incense was used in Islamic countries for magical purposes, such as to repel the Evil Eye. In China, incense was often used in association with aesthetic activities such as reading, writing, and performing music. In Chinese Taoism, incense was used to banish evil and to satisfy the gods, as well as to cure diseases brought on by evil deeds. In India, incense is used in both Hindu and Buddhist rituals. Incense also plays an important part in Buddhist ceremonies in Korea, where it is used in ancestor worship as well.

In ancient Egypt, incense was often used. According to Plutarch, it was burned as an offering to the Sun three times a day. Incense was also burned before the pharaoh during the coronation procession, and it was an important element of funerary practices, as the soul of the dead was claimed to ascend to heaven by means of the smoke of burning incense. In the Mesopotamian *Epic of Gilgamesh,* Gilgamesh's mother, Ninsuna, burned incense and offered it to the God of Creation, Shamash, to display her reverence for him and to receive his blessings.

In ancient Israel, incense was regarded as a holy substance to be reserved for Yahweh. It was not used in public worship ceremonies of the early Christian Church. The Church Fathers severely condemned its use as an offering, as they associated it with Pagan practices. Christians were identified by their refusal to burn incense before a statue of the emperor, and those who succumbed in order to avoid execution were called *turificati,* or "burners of incense." However, the use of incense later became part of the liturgical services of both Eastern Orthodox and other Western churches.

See Also: Air; Rite, Ritual
Further Reading
Chevalier, Jean, and Alain Gheerbrant. *The Penguin Dictionary of Symbols.* London: Penguin, 1996.

Valiente, Doreen. *An ABC of Witchcraft: Past and Present*. New York: St. Martin's Press, 1973.

Incubus and Succubus

The ancient idea that spirit beings or demons could appear in human form in order to have sex with mortal beings bears little resemblance to the notions of fallen angels, incubi and succubi, that populated the overheated imaginations of the late Middle Ages. Especially during the Inquisition, when the clergy as well as the popular mind seemed obsessed with devils and demons of all sorts, a fairly elaborate folklore developed around fallen angels. Succubi could take the form of beautiful women and seduce men, whereas incubi took the form of handsome men and seduced women. Although sterile themselves, incubi could supposedly impregnate women with seed taken by succubi from men—a belief that was sometimes used to explain the pregnancy of a woman resulting from a secret affair. This type of explanation not only absolved the woman from charges of licentiousness, but, because the sperm was taken from a man, it also saved the child from being slain as an offspring of a demon.

In Western "angel lore," speculation on such ideas grew out of two short verses in chapter 6 of Genesis: "The sons of God saw that the daughters of men were fair; and they took to wife such of them as they chose" (6:2) and "The Nephilim were on the Earth in those days, and also afterward, when the sons of God came in to the daughters of men, and they bore children to them. These were the mighty men that were of old, the men of renown" (6:4). In these rather strange verses, the expression "sons of God" was thought to indicate angels. And while Scripture does not condemn angels bedding humans, the traditional interpretation of these passages is that these sons of God are *fallen* angels. This interpretation provided biblical legitimation for the elaborate notions of incubi and succubi that later developed in the Western Middle Ages.

There were, however, other medieval traditions that asserted that incubi *could* impregnate mortal women, and that succubi *could* become pregnant by mortal men. It was, for instance, rumored that Merlin the magician was the offspring of such a union. This notion of semidemonic children was useful for explaining such phenomena as deformed babies. Incubi were sometimes referred to as *demon lovers*. Also, some writers asserted that succubi were the same as the wood nymphs of European folklore.

While these demons did some of their work in the waking state, they were particularly useful for explaining sexual dreams in a society where any form of illicit sex was viewed as demonic. One can imagine the dismay of celibate clergy, monks, and nuns who awakened with vivid memories of erotic dreams. By attributing such dream images to evil spirits who seduced them in their sleep, they could absolve themselves of responsibility for such dreams.

Mortals who willingly responded to the seductive wiles of these beings risked damnation. A papal bull issued by Pope Innocent in 1484, for instance, asserted that "many persons of both sexes, forgetful of their own salvation, have abused incubi and succubi." Some of the Church Fathers, such as St. Anthony, asserted that demons could take the form of seductive naked women who would try to lure them away from their devotions. These experiences were later taken as evidence for the real existence of succubi.

See Also: Sex and Sex Magic; Spirit
Further Reading
Baskin, Wade. *Dictionary of Satanism*. New York: Philosophical Library, 1962.
Lewis, James R. *Encyclopedia of Dreams*. Detroit, MI: Gale Research Inc., 1995.

Initiation

Initiation is an integral part of every secret society and of every religion, if one defines "initiation" as what a person must do or experience in order to become a member of that religion. To become a Christian, one must be baptized; to become a Muslim, one must submit to the will of God; and to become a Witch, one must be initiated. Witches, however, have the right to perform a self-initiation in order to become a member of the Wiccan religion. Almost all Wiccan initiations are modeled on or simply are borrowed from Gardnerian initiations.

See Also: Coven; Degrees

White Witch Kevin Carlyon performs an environmental ritual and initiation of a new Witch at Stonehenge, 1991. (Kevin Carlyon/Fortean Picture Library)

Further Reading

Crowley, Vivianne. "Wicca as a Modern-Day Mystery Religion." In Harvey, Graham, and Charlotte Hardman, eds., *Paganism Today: Wiccans, Druids, the Goddess, and Ancient Earth Traditions for the Twenty-First Century*. London and San Francisco: Thorsons, 1996, 81–93.

Farrar, Stewart. *What Witches Do: The Modern Coven Revealed*. New York: Coward McCann, 1971.

Gardner, Gerald B. *High Magic's Aid*. New York: Michael Houghton, 1949.

Kelly, Aidan A. *Crafting the Art of Magic, Book I: A History of Modern Witchcraft, 1939–1964*. St. Paul, MN: Llewellyn, 1991.

Inner Planes

The idea that one or more spirit worlds exist alongside the world of our ordinary, everyday experience is taken for granted in almost every religious and cultural tradition outside of the modern West. For many of these traditions, the spirit realm is as important and real as the physical realm. Cross-culturally and across many different historical periods there is widespread agreement on this point.

Modern Neopaganism's understanding of the nature of reality is rooted in a traditional worldview that perceives the physical world of our everyday experience to be but one facet—one "story," so to speak—of a multidimensional cosmos. Neopagan thinking about these other realms is rooted in the Western occult tradition, which postulates many levels of reality. The most familiar of these, the so-called astral level, or astral plane, is very close to the tangible, physical realm, intermediate between the physical and other, more inward planes. According to some writers, magic works by setting in motion astral forces. Various metaphors for this vision of reality could be that of a ladder (Jacob's Ladder, for instance), a many-storied building, or a terraced hillside.

Another analogy to explain this multilevel reality is a comparison of different states of matter: Molecules in a solid object, such as a block of ice, can vibrate at different rates (for instance, at different temperatures) without changing the nature of the ice block as a solid substance. However, if the molecules begin to vibrate fast enough, the solid changes into a liquid. In the case of H_2O, the block of ice will eventually be transformed into a puddle of water. Water can vary considerably in temperature and remain a liquid. However, at the boiling point of water, it transforms once again, this time into gas. Similarly, the fundamental substance of which the various planes are composed is basically the same. However, at the increasingly rarified vibration of higher levels of being, this material transforms into a subtler substance.

In terms of these levels, reincarnation can be thought of as a process in which the individual loses her or his outermost layer at death, disappears from the physical level, and then reacquires a body at rebirth. We might think of this as a sponge diver. Sponge divers put on bulky, spacesuit-like diving suits while collecting sponges. These suits are, in a figurative sense, an additional "body." Divers put on this extra body in order to be able to operate at the "liquid" level. After finishing their task in the water and returning to the surface, they divest themselves of their outermost sheath until the next time they need to undertake further work at the "liquid level." *Summerland* is the common Neopagan term for the realm in which the souls of the departed reside while awaiting reincarnation.

See Also: Astral Plane; Summerland
Further Reading
Lewis, James R. *Encyclopedia of Afterlife Beliefs and Phenomena*. Detroit, MI: Gale Research, 1994.
Matthews, Caitlín, and John Matthews. *The Western Way: A Practical Guide to the Western Mystery Tradition*. London: Arkana, 1994.

Isis

The Goddess Isis originated in ancient Egypt and was subsequently adopted into Greek and Roman mythology. Some of the stories relating to her origins and characteristics have transformed across time and in the passage from one culture to the other, but her principal attributes have remained unchanged.

The Egyptians worshipped her as the Mother Goddess. The moon and the star Sirius were her symbols. She attained immortality through a trick played on Ra, the Sun God, and she was married to Osiris, king of the underworld. In ancient legends, her son Horus was born from a virgin birth after Osiris's death, which links her to the myth surrounding virginity that was later adopted by Christianity.

Among ancient, classical writers, Isis took on further symbolic attributes: While preserving her role as universal Mother, she was also considered the inspirator of wisdom and progress for mankind. According to the Hermetic Tradition, she was the daughter and pupil of Hermes. She revealed her wisdom to initiates, who were never to talk about the knowledge they acquired. Among magicians, Isis is considered a goddess who can heal the sick with her incantations.

See Also: Goddess(es); Healing
Further Reading
Barrett, Clive. *The Egyptian Gods and Goddesses: The Mythology and Beliefs of Ancient Egypt*. London: Aquarian Press, 1991.
Regula, Traci de. *The Mysteries of Isis*. St. Paul, MN: Llewellyn, 1996.

Isis, one of the most popular forms of the Goddess in both modern and ancient Witchcraft. (Denver Art Museum)

J

Jewelry and Degrees of Initiation

Neopagans wear jewelry for the same reasons that anybody else might, but there is a specific category of jewelry that has special meaning within the Craft. This category consists of types of jewelry that indicate something about personal rank or office within a coven or the Craft in general. For the most part, this type of jewelry is used only by Gardnerians.

Necklace

In a Gardnerian circle, all women are supposed to wear a necklace made of large, "lumpy" semiprecious stones. This rule is stated in Gardner's *Witchcraft Today*, in a note at the end of the text. As a result, this necklace has always allowed female Gardnerian Witches to identify one another when they happen to meet at a festival or elsewhere in public. There do not seem to be any universal (or reported) patterns on how necklaces are used in other traditions, although Witches in general will wear a necklace, chain, or cord with a metal pentacle on it and this is considered a badge of membership in the Wiccan religion.

Bracelet

As Gerald Gardner also states in *Witchcraft Today*, in a Gardnerian coven, a female Witch is entitled to wear a wide, silver bracelet inscribed with her Craft name and the symbol for her degree of initiation. An upright pentacle indicates the First Degree; an inverse (two points up) pentacle indicates the Second Degree; and an encircled pentacle indicates the Third Degree. In writing letters signed with their Craft names (and sometimes their ordinary names), Gardnerians draw the symbol of their degree after their name, much as one might write "M.A." or "Ph.D." after one's name in a formal letter.

Garter

Again in *Witchcraft Today*, Gardner states that the garter is the badge of a High Priestess. Not usually considered jewelry, this garter is made with a silver buckle, and a Gardnerian High Priestess is entitled to add another silver buckle for every coven for which she is the Queen or the High Priestess.

Moon Crown

When a High Priestess (actually, the High Priest who is her working partner) elevates another woman in the coven to the Third Degree, and that woman hives off and begins another coven, then the High Priestess of the mother coven attains the status and responsibilities of a Queen in the Gardnerian Tradition. At this point she is entitled to wear a moon crown, which is a metal band or a tiara on which a crescent moon is mounted. This crown can be as elegant as the Queen chooses. In a fair number of other traditions, the moon crown is just used as a badge of a High Priestess and, sometimes, in covens where the role of High Priestess rotates among the members, the moon crown is used to show who is "on duty" during the specific working.

Horned Helmet

Little has been said about men in the preceding text—partly because men play a secondary role in traditional Gardnerian circles and do not wear much jewelry. There is one exception, however: The working partner of a Queen becomes known as a Magus, and he is entitled to wear a horned helmet, much like a medieval Viking helmet. It is worn in the circle rather rarely, however—usually only when the sun has been "drawn down" upon the Magus.

See Also: Degrees; Garter, Order of the; Initiation
Further Reading
Guiley, Rosemary. *The Encyclopedia of Witches and Witchcraft*. New York: Facts on File, 1989.

Jewish Wicca, Jewish Pagans

Some surveys of Neopagans have shown that they are more than twice as likely to be of Jewish background than of any other. As a result, in New York City, which has a population of about one-third Jews, the Neopagan movement at first looks much like a Jewish subculture. Many Jewish Neopagans have been dissatisfied with the general focus among Neopagan Witches on Greek, Egyptian, or Celtic divinities and have begun to look back at their own traditions for inspiration. Thus, the effort to define a Jewish Paganism that respects the essence of both traditions has been quietly growing for many years. It has arisen out of the historically accurate perception that Judaism was not monotheistic when it was founded and out of the fact that one does not have to reject one's original heritage in order to be a Neopagan.

Neither Mordecai Kaplan's Reconstructionist Judaism, which became the fourth branch of Judaism, nor Rabbi Sherwin Wine's Humanistic Judaism, which has become the fifth branch, defines Judaism in terms of monotheism or even any theism, but instead in terms of the history of the Jewish people. This history extends far back, before the invention of monotheism by the "Second Isaiah" in about 550 B.C. It is not widely known that there was a "heterodox" Jewish temple in Elephantine, Egypt, founded by refugees from the destruction of Jerusalem in 586 B.C. For centuries, this "heterodox" temple continued to be an alternative to the "newfangled" variety of Judaism that became "orthodox" during the captivity in Babylon. It is an indisputable fact that this temple had a three-pronged altar for the cult statues of Yahweh and both his wives, Asherah and Astarte. Hence it is to the Hebrew and Canaanite gods and goddesses of this period that the Judeo-Pagans look back. It does not seem too early to predict that this Judeo-Paganism may become the sixth branch of Judaism.

Among current Jewish-Pagan groups is Michael and Penny Novack's Step by Step Farm. The Novacks were among the most important organizers of the Pagan Way while they were in Philadelphia in the early 1970s, and Penny Novack is still widely regarded as one of the best poets in the Neopagan community. Her poetry has been widely published under her own name and her pen name, Molly Bloom. After moving to rural Massachusetts, the Novacks concentrated on raising their family and quietly developed a Judeo-Pagan family tradition, one that blends what they consider to be the best elements from premonotheistic Judaism, Neopaganism, and folk traditions.

One of the first completely public Pagan synagogues was Beit Asherah, "the house of the Goddess Asherah," in Minneapolis, Minnesota. Founded in the early 1990s by Stephanie Fox, Steven Posch, and Magenta Griffiths (Lady Magenta), it serves a growing congregation in the Twin Cities area and publishes an excellent journal called *Di Schmatteh* (which means "the dishrag"; one presumes this is false modesty). This synagogue and its activities are widely admired and are becoming a model for new Judeo-Pagan synagogues around the country. Fox has been active in the Neopagan movement for many years and has founded several organizations, from Oregon to Wisconsin. Steven Posch is well regarded as a writer, and his theological articles in *Di Schmatteh* are among its most interesting attributes. Lady Magenta has been High Priestess of her own coven for many years and has served as an officer on the board of directors of the Northern Dawn Local Council of the Covenant of the Goddess (CoG) and on CoG's national board.

Another Judeo-Pagan group is the Tuatha Cymry in Kansas City. Founded in 1990, they had 40 members (counting children) by 1995, organized into eight clans. Although their focus is primarily Celtic, they also incorporate such things as a Pagan Seder into their regular round of holiday celebrations. A good source of information about this entire movement is the *Michtav-Habiru: Newsletter of the Jewish-Pagan Network*, edited by Eliezer Ibn-Raphael.

Further Reading

Elie. Interview by Ellen Evert Hopman and Lawrence Bond. In *People of the Earth: The New Pagans Speak Out*. Rochester, VT: Destiny Books, 1996.

Fox, Stephanie, and Stephen Posch. "Funny, You Don't Look Jewitch: An Interview with Stephanie Fox and Stephen Posch." By Stephen Wise. *Green Egg* 99 (winter 1992–1993): 18–19.

K

Kabala

See Cabala

Karma

Most contemporary Neopagans accept the notion of reincarnation as well as the related notion of karma. A wide variety of different religious systems, particularly those in or originating in South Asia (India), all assume the basic validity of the law of karma. In its simplest form, this law operates impersonally like a natural law, ensuring that every good or bad deed eventually returns to the individual in the form of reward or punishment commensurate with the original deed. The term derives from the Sanskrit root word *kr*, which means "to act, do, or make."

Karma originally referred to ritual action, which in the Hindu Tradition produces concrete results if properly performed (the Priest controlled the Gods if his rituals were correctly carried out). Traditionally some of the discourse about karma was carried out in terms of agricultural imagery—in which the original action is the "seed" of later "fruit"—suggesting that India's long-standing agrarian economy was a source for the notion. The meaning of karma was later extended to refer to proper action in general.

The notion that one's actions set loose forces that eventually return to the actor can be interpreted on more than one level. When initially transferred from the ritual to the moral sphere, the notion of karma operated independently of the actor's intentions. Thus, if a pedestrian stepped out in front of a speeding truck (or a speeding chariot, in the ancient Indian context) and was killed, the driver incurred the same negative karma as if he or she had *intentionally* murdered the pedestrian. However, as a staple of Indian thought, centuries of reflection on karma resulted in more sophisticated notions, so that earlier ideas about karmic reactions that are created by unintended actions have been discarded.

Karma also refers to both the personality patterns that result from past actions as well as the forces at large in the cosmos that bring reward or

A traditional Tibetan image of the cycle of existences to which we are bound by karma.
(American Museum of Natural History)

retribution to the human individual. In yogic psychology, the personality patterns shaped by karma—in the sense of the subconscious motivators of action—are referred to as *samskaras*. Karma ties in with notions of the afterlife in the South Asian tradition that compels human beings to be reborn (to reincarnate) in successive lifetimes. In other words, if one dies before reaping the effects of one's actions (as most people do), the karmic process demands that one be reborn in another life. This next lifetime allows karmic forces to reward or punish the person by affecting the circumstance in which he or she is born. For example, an individual who was generous in one lifetime might be reborn as a wealthy person in her or his next incarnation.

For the most part, the mainstream of South Asian thinking does not view the cycle of death and rebirth as attractive. The ultimate goal of most Indian religions is to escape the cycle of death and rebirth (*samara*). While the traditional South Asian view is that returning to live another life is distinctly undesirable, many contemporary Westerners, including Neopagans, view the prospects of reincarnation positively. Rather than a burden, life in the body is viewed as good, and physical pleasure is a blessing that should be sought rather than avoided. Hence, this view sees reincarnation as a *reward* rather than a *punishment*.

In line with this more positive view of reincarnation, karma becomes less a system of reward and punishment and more a process of *learning*. The importance of learning as a spiritual metaphor is reflected in a host of educational images and forms that embody essentially religious meanings in the Neopagan subculture. In other words, many of the more important gatherings found in this subculture are workshops, lectures, seminars, and classes. These educational settings reflect a view of the human condition that sees spiritual development as a gradual learning process, rather than as the kind of abrupt conversion experience that occurs in the midst of traditional Protestant revivals. Karma becomes a way of bringing the individual face-to-face with certain life *lessons* ("karmic lessons"), rather than a process of rewarding or punishing good and bad actions.

See Also: Reincarnation
Further Reading
Lewis, James R. *Magical Religion and Modern Witchcraft*. Albany, NY: State
    University of New York Press, 1996.
Zimmer, Heinrich. *Philosophies of India*. New York: Bollingen, 1951.

Keepers of the Ancient Mysteries (KAM) Tradition

Keepers of the Ancient Mysteries (KAM) was founded by Elders of five different Craft traditions, including Gardnerian and Alexandrian. This was done largely because they needed a way to handle those who sought to join the Craft in the Washington, D.C., area by referral of Lady Theos, Mary Nesnick, Jim B., and others in the early 1970s. The five Elders pooled their Sabbat scripts to create ones with which they could all be comfortable. In the course of this work, one of them commented, "Well, whatever else we may be doing, we are keeping the ancient mysteries"—and so they acquired their name. KAM then proceeded to evolve into a Craft tradition in its own right in the following years. It became incorporated as a nonprofit religious corporation in Maryland in May 1976, but did not seek tax-exempt status.

On June 22, 1977, Lady Morganna turned KAM over to her daughter, Lady Ayeisha (Carolyn K.), who was initiated by Mary Nesnick and Jim B. in 1971, in a circle attended by Lady Morganna and Roy Dymond, among others. Lady Ayeisha is still active as the High Priestess of the mother coven. Lady Morganna remains active as an Elder of the Foxmoore Temple in Laurel, Maryland, and, having been cross-initiated into Lady Gwen Thompson's Welsh Tradition, also served as High Priestess of the Coven of Minerva in Providence, Rhode Island, in 1995.

KAM celebrates the usual Esbats, Sabbats, and rites of passage of Neopagan Witchcraft. KAM is a teaching coven and holds regular classes at several locations in the Baltimore, Maryland, area. Its specific policy of broadening knowledge of the Craft by its members and members of other groups (through participation in rituals of other Craft traditions) is also encouraged by inviting members of other traditions to share in KAM rituals.

Further Reading
Lewis, James R. *The Encyclopedia of Cults, Sects and New Religions*. Amherst, NY: Prometheus Books, 1998.
Melton, J. Gordon. *Encyclopedia of American Religions*, 5th ed. Detroit, MI: Gale Research Inc., 1996.

Keridwen
See Cerridwen

Kether
Kether is the first sephira of the Cabala. *Kether* means "crown" in Hebrew. It is a crown on the head of Adam Qadmon, the primordial Adam. Kether is also called *ayin*, or "nothing," because nothing can be known of it. Kether is God in his primal state, from which everything else flows. In the Tree of Life, Kether is the root of roots. Along with Chokhmah and Binah, it makes up the upper, or supernal, triangle of the ten sephiroth.

See Also: Cabala
Further Reading
Fortune, Dion. *The Mystical Qabalah*. York Beach, ME: Weiser, 1994 [1935].
Myers, Stuart. *Between the Worlds: Witchcraft and the Tree of Life—A Program of Spiritual Development*. St. Paul, MN: Llewellyn, 1995.

Knife, White

A white-handled knife is usually included among the working tools of a Neo-pagan Witch. Like the black-handled knife, now called an athame, the white-handled knife is derived from the specifications for tools in Mathers's *The Greater Key of Solomon*. The white knife is not itself used symbolically in rituals. Rather, it has a very practical purpose and is used to cut objects, whereas the athame is rarely used to cut anything, so that it will not lose its built-up magical charge. The white knife has no charge of its own, but it is kept magically clean so that the energy of what it cuts is not altered. It is sometimes called a bolline, but the word *bolline* can also refer to a small sickle for cutting herbs. In terms of magic, the white knife and bolline are considered equivalents.

See Also: Athame; Tools, Witches'
Further Reading
Farrar, Stewart. *What Witches Do: The Modern Coven Revealed*. New York: Coward McCann, 1971.
K., Amber. *True Magick: A Beginner's Guide*. St. Paul, MN: Lllewellyn, 1991.

Knot Magic

Since ancient times, knots have carried symbolic and magical values in numerous cultures. In ancient Rome knots symbolized impotency, and, under the right circumstances, were viewed as responsible for causing impotency in men. The tying or untying of knots was also seen as a way to prevent or facilitate pregnancy. In the legends of ancient Greece and through the Middle Ages, sailors believed that knots allowed them to control the winds. Magicians and Witches have used knots, individually or in a series, to symbolize the releasing of energy during rituals and spells. In major religions, such as Islam and Christianity, knots play a negative role, as they represent entanglement and confusion. For example, a passage in the Koran condemns knots. Also, Christian ministers wear collars, but never ties.

See Also: Binding; Cords
Further Reading
Chevalier, Jean, and Alain Gheerbrant. *The Penguin Dictionary of Symbols*. London: Penguin, 1996.
Gordon, Stuart. *The Encyclopedia of Myths and Legends*. London: Headline, 1993.

Kundalini

Kundalini, in Hindu, is considered the raw energy underlying both sexuality and the higher functions of consciousness. It is usually depicted as a serpent dwelling in the first chakra at the root of the spine. The kundalini energy can be awakened through the practice of kundalini yoga, which helps this energy to rise up through the rest of the chakras, until the seventh chakra, which is located at the crown of the head. At this point, the blissful state of *samadhi* is reached. *Samadhi* is pictured as the sexual union between the Hindu God Shiva and Shakti—the personification of energy as a goddess. The kundalini energy also has been depicted as the personification of the Hindu Goddesses Durga and Kali.

The practices of *pranayama*—"breath control"—and meditation, as well as the moral code established by Patanjali (ca. 200 B.C.) requiring sexual purity or abstinence, are usually adopted in order to raise the kundalini energy.

The fourteenth-century Indian writer Lalla Yogishwari authored the most evocative literary report of kundalini energy. She studied with a Sufi master and is considered one of the greatest women poets of history.

Pandit Gopi Krishna (born in 1903), on the other hand, is regarded as an important modern kundalini researcher. Author of several books, he asserts that the kundalini constitutes an evolutionary force playing a considerable role in the development of human society. A number of important spiritual teachers, such as the late Swami Muktananda, claimed to be able to awaken the kundalini energy through a touch, referred to as *shaktipat*.

See Also: Aura; Chakras

Further Reading

Frost, Gavin, and Yvonne Frost. *Tantric Yoga: The Royal Path to Raising Kundalini Power*. York Beach, ME: Weiser, 1989.

Mookerjee, Ajit, and M. Khanna. *The Tantric Way: Art, Science, Ritual*. New York: Graphic, 1977.

Levi, Eliphas

Eliphas Levi was the pseudonym of Alphonse-Louis Constant (1810–1875), a French occultist and writer who was a major influence on the development of modern magical practices. Educated in the church, he became a priest but was expelled because of his left-wing political opinions (his writings earned him three short jail terms) and because he did not keep his inability to be celibate a secret. He became a follower of a man named Ganneau, who claimed to be the reincarnation of Louis XVII, and began serious study of the occult, which had always interested him. In 1861 his most important book, *The Dogma and Ritual of High Magic*, was published. Based on the work of Francis Barrett in *The Magus*, the book attempted to create a unified magical system of all occult knowledge, and this effort was continued in his later books. His system was then adopted and improved by the Hermetic Order of the Golden Dawn (HOGD), and so became the source of all modern systems of magic. Levi's work also influenced the English occult writer Sir Edward Bulwer-Lytton; they both joined an occult organization (which Bulwer-Lytton may have founded) and studied together. This organization may also have influenced the formation of the Hermetic Order of the Golden Dawn. Levi's works were translated into English by A. E. Waite, a very prominent member of the HOGD, and have been kept in print by occult publishers ever since.

See Also: Hermetic Order of the Golden Dawn
Further Reading
Levi, Eliphas [Alphonse-Louis Constant]. *The Dogma and Ritual of High Magic*.
———. *History of Magic*. York Beach, ME: Weiser, 1969.
———. *Key to the Great Mysteries*. York Beach, ME: Weiser, 1970.
———. *Transcendental Magic*. York Beach, ME: Weiser, 1970.

Levitation

Levitation can assume passive or active forms. In the former case, people can be lifted from the Earth's surface by the effect of a possession or bewitchment.

A painting of occultist and magician Eliphas Levi by Gordon Wain. (Fortean Picture Library)

Witches were traditionally said to fly, and contemporary Wiccans tend to view this tradition as a figurative reference to altered states of consciousness.

See Also: Flying
Further Reading
Gordon, Stuart. *The Encyclopedia of Myths and Legends.* London: Headline, 1993.

Leys

Leys are invisible lines of power linking sacred and natural places. A ley center is an area charged with energy and radiating over seven lines. The energy at a ley center is labeled either male or female, natural or man-made. Stones used in building holy structures are charged with energy by the shaping with hammers and chisels. Energies can be masked at a site or in a stone by certain woods, iron, salt, and quartz.

See Also: Power Spots
Further Reading
Hawkins, Gerald S. *Stonehenge Decoded.* New York: Dorset Press, 1965.

Libation

The term *libation* derives from the Latin *libatio* and refers to the sacrificial offering of drink. It is one of the oldest of religious rituals—the sacrificial pouring out of liquid. Libation, which originated at least as early as the Bronze Age, can be found in almost every culture and geographical area. Its precise practice varies depending on the location, sacrificial materials, relations to other rituals, and the meaning of the libation. The liquids that are poured out may be wine, milk, honey, water, oil, and sometimes even blood. Libations may be poured out on the ground, on an altar, on a sacrificial victim, or into a sacrificial bowl.

The original meaning of the libation is uncertain, although it is generally believed that libations were initially separate gift offerings. In Babylonian and Assyrian religions, libations were a part of meals, offered to the gods. In purification rituals and magic their purpose was different. According to Greek magical papyruses, libations of wine, honey, milk, water, and oil were offered in most religious rites and were originally separate from animal sacrifices. Libations were part of the communication with the divine sphere of life through the exchange of gifts, as they were offered to the deity in return for benefits received. The gods themselves were believed to offer libations.

In Greek religion, libations were common as early as the Minoan-Mycenaean period (ca. 2000 B.C.). The separate gift offerings eventually became associated with animal sacrifice, which had libations of wine as part of its preliminary sacrifice as well as in its conclusion—wine was poured into the fire that consumed the remains of the victim. Libations could be offered for protection prior to sea voyages, for legal agreements, and for the dead. The latter was more magically oriented, although the specific function of libations for the dead is still obscure. It seems that the soul of the dead received nourishment from libation.

Water libations, on the other hand, were considered mostly as purifications. Israelite libations, as is known from the Hebrew scriptures and the Mishnah, were similar to ancient Greek rituals. Other religions and cultures, such as Zoroastrianism, Vedic Hinduism, and ancient Chinese religion, have developed special forms of libation offerings. The Vikings of Scandinavia, for instance, conducted a ceremonial beer-drinking ritual, known as *drykkeoffer*, during which three ceremonial cups of mead were offered to Odin, Thor, and Frigga.

See Also: Rite, Ritual; Sacrifice
Further Reading
Eliade, Mircea, ed. *The Encyclopedia of Religion*, 16 vols. New York: Macmillan, 1987.

Lilith

The Night Goddess Lilith is the archetypal seductress and the personification of the dangerous feminine glamour of the moon. Lilith was said to search for newborn children to kidnap or strangle, and she would seduce sleeping men in order to produce demon sons. She is a patron of Witches and is usually depicted as a beautiful vampire with great claws as feet. Lilith can be found in Iranian, Babylonian, Mexican, Greek, Arab, English, German, Oriental, and North American Indian legends, and she is often associated with other characters, such as the Queen of Sheba and Helen of Troy.

A terra-cotta plaque depicting the malevolent female spirit of the Sumerians and prototype of the Hebrew Lilith. (Art Resource)

According to Muslim legend, Lilith slept with Satan. In Jewish legend, she was the first wife of Adam, before Eve was given to him. She allegedly coupled with him in his dreams, thus giving birth to all the uncanny invisible beings known as fairy races or the *jinn*. She was regarded as a queen of evil spirits, from whom Jews protected themselves by the use of amulets engraved with the names and images of the three angels—Sanvi, Sansavi, and Semangelaf. Supposedly, God sent the angels to bring Lilith back to Eden after she deserted Adam. During the eighteenth century, a common practice was to protect new mothers against Lilith with such amulets. Sometimes magic circles were drawn around the bed in order to protect a newborn child. It was believed that if a child laughed in his or her sleep, it meant that Lilith was present. She could be sent away by tapping the child on the nose. It was further claimed that Lilith was assisted by succubi and by her demon lover Samael, whose name means "left" or "sinister." According to the Zohar, the source of the Cabala, Lilith is at the height of her power when the moon is in its waning phase.

See Also: Amulets; Fairies; Genie; Seal of Solomon
Further Reading
Masello, Robert. *Fallen Angels and Spirits of the Dark*. New York: Perigee, 1994.
Sykes, Egerton. *Who's Who: Non-Classical Mythology*. New York: Oxford University Press, 1993.

Lineage

A lineage is a pathway up and down a Gardnerian family tree created by the continuing relationship between a Gardnerian Queen and the High Priestesses she has trained and helped initiate. Except for the final link to Gardner, orthodox Gardnerian lineages are traced only through the female line. Covens that consider themselves to be "reformed" Gardnerian have abandoned this rule. The concept of lineage is not as emphasized in other traditions, since they are less hierarchic than the Gardnerians are. Nevertheless, members of many traditions can trace their family tree back several generations—and usually to the tradition's earliest known founder.

See Also: Coven; Tradition
Further Reading
Kelly, Aidan A. *Crafting the Art of Magic, Book I: A History of Modern Witchcraft, 1939–1964*. St. Paul, MN: Llewellyn, 1991.
———. *Inventing Witchcraft: A Case Study in the Creation of a New Religion*. Los Angeles, CA: Art Magickal Publications, 1996.

Litha

Litha is one of the Lesser Sabbats that, with the four Greater Sabbats, make up the "Wheel of the Year"—major holidays celebrated by the Neopagan

Honoring each of the sacred directions is an essential part of Wiccan rituals. Participants at the Morning Ritual of the 1997 Pagan Spirit Gathering, a Summer Solstice celebration sponsored by Circle Sanctuary. (Photo by Jeff Koslow, Circle Sanctuary archives)

Witches in the United States and elsewhere. The Lesser Sabbats comprise the English quarter days, that is, the solstices and equinoxes. The most common names used by Witches for the Lesser Sabbats are Eostar (spring equinox, about March 22), Litha (summer solstice, about June 22), Mabon (fall equinox, about September 22), and Yule (winter solstice, about December 22).

Litha, or "Midsummer Eve," is noted for festivities, revivals of ancient rituals, and the burning of bonfires in the British Isles. It is observed by the Ancient Order of Druids (founded 1781) and various other British Druid orders, some of whom stay up all night to observe the midsummer sunrise at Stonehenge. Litha marks the night celebrated in Shakespeare's *A Midsummer Night's Eve*, and as many folk customs center about Litha as are centered about May Day. Most Neopagans celebrate Sabbats or festivals at this time of year.

See Also: Sabbats; Wheel of the Year

Further Reading

Campanelli, Pauline. *Wheel of the Year: Living the Magical Life*. St. Paul, MN: Llewellyn, 1989.

Kelly, Aidan A. *Religious Holidays and Calendars: An Encyclopedic Handbook*. Detroit, MI: Omnigraphics, 1991.

Lithomancy

Lithomancy is a mode of divination that uses a set of 13 stones. The stones are tossed and a prophecy is drawn from the arrangement in which the stones land. The stones symbolize love, the home, magic, luck, news, and the signs of Jupiter, Mars, Mercury, Saturn, Venus, the Sun, and the Moon. The stones used in lithomancy are handpicked and are generally around the same size.

See Also: Astrology; Divination
Further Reading
Shepard, Leslie A., ed. *Encyclopedia of Occultism and Parapsychology.* Detroit, MI: Gale Research Inc., 1991.

Love Spells

Among the purposes of spells is love, one of the strongest human emotions. Love spells, like charms and potions, have been used since antiquity and are still popular in folklore. Traditional spells, contained in old books on fortune-telling, played a significant part in many old-country magical practices, which, according to legend, were recommended to village girls by the local Witch.

The love spell often consists of words or incantations containing the name of a lover. The incantations are verbalized in conjunction with a set of actions that must be repeated for a number of consecutive nights upon going to bed. The spell's power and success are based upon a combination of willpower, concentration, visualization, identification, and incantation. It is claimed that, if the love spell works, it is by the power of thought. An herb-filled poppet or cloth doll is often used during a love ritual. The doll is identified with the individual who is the object of the love spell, so that it becomes that person during the ritual. The doll may be marked with the name, astrological sign, or hair of the person, whose photographs may also be used. If no actual object is available, a thought-form or mental image is created during the ritual. Spontaneous rhyming words of incantation are generally used during a spell to help with the buildup of energy. The purpose of some love spells, which can be considered forms of divination, is to see one's future lover in a dream.

See Also: Incantation; Philtre; Spells
Further Reading
Leach, Maria, ed. *Standard Dictionary of Folklore, Mythology, and Legend.* San Francisco, CA: HarperSan Francisco, 1984 [1949].
Valiente, Doreen. *An ABC of Witchcraft: Past and Present.* Custer, WA: Phoenix, 1973.

Lughnasad

Lughnasad, or the "Games of Lugh," is the current name used by most Neopagans to mean the Sabbat celebration that begins at sunset on July 31. The name is derived from what once was apparently an extremely popular Irish holiday. Lughnasad is one of the eight Sabbats of the "Wheel of the Year." It is usually celebrated outdoors, during a weekend camp-out, if possible, during which the ancient "Games of Tara" are reenacted. A ritual drama that the members feel is appropriate to the season can also be performed as part of the major ritual of the weekend.

The same Celtic festival is also called by a Saxon name, *Lammas*—from *hlafmasse*, a word meaning "loaf Mass," that is, harvest festival. The first Monday in August is observed as a holiday from work throughout the British Commonwealth. Lammas Fair Day has been celebrated for more than 350 years on the last Tuesday in August at Ballycastle, Ireland. Summer Holiday is celebrated on the last Monday of August in the United Kingdom, but not in Scotland. All of these celebrations appear to be relics of the traditional cross-quarter day of Lughnasad. There are many surviving local Scottish Lammas Fairs, which were once famous for their "handfast marriages," trial unions that either party could end, without any social stigma, after a year and a day. Modern Neopagan Witches have derived their own concept of "handfasting" as "Craft marriage" from this custom. Lammas, in the midst of the most popular period for vacations in American society, is also the occasion for some of the largest and most popular Neopagan festivals.

See Also: Sabbats; Wheel of the Year
Further Reading
Campanelli, Pauline. *Wheel of the Year: Living the Magical Life*. St. Paul, MN: Llewellyn, 1989.
Kelly, Aidan A. *Religious Holidays and Calendars: An Encyclopedic Handbook*. Detroit, MI: Omnigraphics, 1991.

Lycanthropy

Lycanthropy is the metamorphosis of a human being into a wolf. There have been many legends concerning werewolves throughout history. The most popular is the tale of a man (rarely a woman) who is under a curse that changes him into a man-eating wolf (werewolf) during a full moon. The werewolf can later be identified when the wolf is injured and his wound is found on the human's body. Sorcerers and magicians supposedly have been able to transform themselves into werewolves with the intent of wreaking havoc on their enemies. Lycanthropy is described on two separate levels; the first is when a person imagines himself to be a wolf and the second is when the actual shapeshifting of man into wolf occurs, aided by magical powers and ointments. Belief in lycanthropy peaked in Europe during the Middle Ages and werewolf trials began to evolve. By the fifteenth and sixteenth centuries, werewolves and Witches were categorized as the devil's servants.

See Also: Shapeshifting
Further Reading

Gordon, Stuart. *The Encyclopedia of Myths and Legends.* London: Headline, 1993.
Leach, Maria, ed. *Standard Dictionary of Folklore, Mythology, and Legend.* San Francisco, CA: HarperSan Francisco, 1984 [1949].

M

Mabon

Mabon is the fall-equinox Sabbat of Neopagan Witches. The date on which Mabon falls is especially likely to be changed from its traditional date so that the holiday will fall closer to the date for a favored Pagan festival. For example, the Eleusinian Mysteries in Greece were celebrated just after the full moon that fell closest to the fall equinox; hence, if September 22 falls midweek, many covens that favor the Greeks will move their Mabon Sabbat to a weekend nearer the full moon.

The Christian feast of St. Michael the Archangel on September 29 is a traditional English quarter day. Customs associated with this day include bringing herds down from the summer high pastures, eating roast goose, lighting bonfires, and returning to school. Many of these customs appear to be related to the fall equinox.

See Also: Sabbats; Wheel of the Year
Further Reading
Campanelli, Pauline. *Wheel of the Year: Living the Magical Life*. St. Paul, MN: Llewellyn, 1989.
Kelly, Aidan A. *Religious Holidays and Calendars: An Encyclopedic Handbook*. Detroit, MI: Omnigraphics, 1991.

Macumba

Macumba, an Afro-Brazilian group found in Rio de Janeiro, is based—like Santeria and Vodun—on the worship of the ancient African gods, and it involves spirit possession and magic. Macumba itself is not a religious organization, but rather an umbrella term for the two principal Afro-Brazilian groups: Candomblé and Umbanda. The *macumba* were the possessed elders of the Macumba movement in its early form.

Initially, the macumba consisted of the introduction of certain orisha into the Bantu cult known as *caboula*, and gradually became a syncretism of elements from African and American Indian religions, popular Catholicism, and the spiritism of Allan Kardec. The followers of macumba become medi-

A High Priest of a Macumba temple (in a private home) and his assistant sacrifice animals and prepare food for the orishas (gods). (Corbis/Stephanie Maze)

ums. Singing and dancing are used to induce possession by the spirits of the dead rather than the orisha (deities). Spirits are divided into such categories as suffering spirits, malevolent furies, and benevolent spirits. Reincarnation is regarded as the return of souls of the dead in order to atone for the sins of their previous existence.

See Also: African Religions; Candomblé; Santeria; Vodun

Further Reading

Hess, David J. *Samba in the Night: Spiritism in Brazil.* New York: Columbia University Press, 1994.

Hinnells, John R., ed. *A New Dictionary of Religions.* London: Blackwell, 1997.

Magic

Many current new religions believe in working magic (Aleister Crowley spelled the word *magick* in order to distinguish it from stage magic, but the common spelling *magic* is used in this book). Many of these groups have not only adopted Crowley's spelling but also have adopted his definition of magic—the ability to make changes in physical reality by nonphysical means, especially by sheer willpower. Beyond African American syncretisms, such as Santeria, the most popular new religion to endorse working magic is certainly Neopaganism. The procedure used to work magic in Neopagan practice can be described generally as follows.

1. A magical circle is "cast" (traced) with a consecrated athame (knife) or sword, perhaps with symbols of all four classical elements (fire, air, water, and earth). The circle is intended to serve as a container for the magical energy that will be raised and used during the ritual.
2. The guardian spirits of the four cardinal directions are invoked and invited to guard the proceedings. These spirits are often called the Lords of the Watchtowers, and there are many different theological interpretations of their nature within Neopaganism, ranging from elementals to members of the highest polytheistic pantheon.
3. One or more deities (a god, a goddess, or perhaps "The God" or "The Goddess," by whatever name) are usually invoked. The magical work is done in that deity's name and will be understood as a way to venerate that deity.
4. Magical energy is raised by some means—dancing, chanting, and sex-magic techniques being among the more common. (This energy can be thought of as something like mana, chi, ki, or prana.) A coven, at this point, works an initiation ritual.
5. The energy is put to some magical use: healing a person or helping someone find a job, for example. Generally, Neopagan Witches are leery of engaging in anything that might be perceived as "black magic." To avoid even definitional gray areas, many Witches have

adopted the rule that one may not work magic without the permission of the person(s) who might be affected by it.

6. There is a little feast of "cakes and ale"; this may be followed by group discussion or working of folk magic, depending on the group's purpose for the magic.

7. Finally, the deities and spirits are thanked and invited to depart. The circle is taken down according to ritual.

The preceding procedure is not something that Neopagan Witchcraft inherited from a secret tradition, but instead goes back, by several different pathways, to the practices of magical groups such as the Hermetic Order of the Golden Dawn, Ordo Templi Orientis, and, most directly, through Dion Fortune's Society of the Inner Light. This Society of the Inner Light was divided into at least two autonomous inner sections, one of which was avowedly "Pagan"—that is, non-Christian. Other magical groups can have utterly different origins and theologies.

See Also: Hermetic Order of the Golden Dawn; Rite, Ritual
Further Reading
Ashcroft-Nowicki, Dolores. *Highways of the Mind: The Art and History of Pathworking.* Wellingborough, Northamptonshire, U.K.: Aquarian Press, 1987.
Bonewits, P. E. I. *Real Magic*, 3d ed. York Beach, ME: Weiser, 1991.
Cavendish, Richard. *The Black Arts.* New York: Putnam's, 1967.
———. *A History of Magic.* London: Weidenfeld and Nicolson, 1977.
Crowley, Aleister. *Magick in Theory and Practice.* New York: Dover, 1976 [1929].
Green, Marian. *Magic for the Aquarian Age.* Wellingborough, Northamptonshire, U.K.: Aquarian Press, 1983.
Knight, Gareth. *A History of White Magic.* London: Mowbray, 1978; York Beach, ME: Weiser, 1979.
———. *A Practical Guide to Qabalistic Symbolism.* York Beach, ME: Weiser, 1978.
Luhrmann, T. M. *Persuasions of the Witch's Craft: Ritual Magic in Contemporary England.* Cambridge, MA: Harvard University Press, 1989.
Regardie, Israel, ed. *Gems from the Equinox: Selected Writings of Aleister Crowley.* St. Paul, MN: Llewellyn, 1974.

Magus

In ancient times, a magus was a Priest of the neo-Babylonian state religion, which focused on worship of the "visible gods," the *planetoi* ("wanderers") in the night sky. Hence, the term *magus* originally meant "astrologer." Though not used much in the Neopagan movement, it does turn up in one specific context: When a Gardnerian High Priestess hives off a new coven, becoming a Queen, then her working consort is entitled to be called a Magus. The only additional benefit the title of Magus confers in the orthodox Gardnerian system is the right to wear a horned helmet when the sun is drawn down upon the consort.

See Also: Hiving Off
Further Reading
Gardner, Gerald B. *Witchcraft Today*. London: Jarrolds, 1954.
Gordon, Stuart. *The Encyclopedia of Myths and Legends*. London: Headline, 1993.

Maiden

The term *maiden* was used by Margaret Murray as a title for an officer in a coven. Over the years the Maiden has become a specific office in an orthodox Gardnerian coven—a Second-Degree Priestess who serves as Assistant High Priestess in the circle and serves as Acting High Priestess if the High Priestess is absent from a circle. In the Gardnerian system, such a Maiden is empowered to do everything a Third-Degree High Priestess can except to cast the circle for an initiation. Since the term was used frequently by Murray, it has been picked up by many covens and traditions other than the Gardnerian Tradition, but exactly what privileges and responsibilities are associated with a Maiden in any particular tradition can be discovered only by inquiry.

See Also: Degrees; Murray, Margaret
Further Reading
Murray, Margaret A. *The Witch-Cult in Western Europe*. Oxford: Oxford University Press, 1962 [1921].
Starhawk [Miriam Simos]. *The Spiral Dance: A Rebirth of the Ancient Religion of the Great Goddess*, 2d ed. San Francisco, CA: HarperSan Francisco, 1989 [1979].

Malkuth

Malkuth, the tenth sephira of the Cabala, means "kingdom." Another name for this is *Shekhinah*, that is, "God is immanent in the world"—the feminine principle of the Divine. Malkuth, the Moon, is the bride of Tiferet, the Sun, and out of their sacred union comes the world of creation. The world contains the root, the essence, of the entire Cabala within.

See Also: Cabala
Further Reading
Fortune, Dion. *The Mystical Qabalah*. York Beach, ME: Weiser, 1994 [1935].
Myers, Stuart. *Between the Worlds: Witchcraft and the Tree of Life—A Program of Spiritual Development*. St. Paul, MN: Llewellyn, 1995.

Man in Black

In her books, Margaret Murray presented the concept of a mysterious "Man in Black" who is mentioned in various transcripts of English Witch trials. According to Murray, this man was actually the local head of the "Dianic cult" and, therefore, was not the devil. Whether Murray was right or not, the term has been adopted as a title in some Neopagan traditions. In the New Reformed Orthodox Order of the Golden Dawn, for example, the term *Black Man* is used in the ritual scripts for Sabbats and most Esbats, since many male members did not want to be called a Priest, high or otherwise.

See Also: Murray, Margaret; Sabbats

Further Reading

Murray, Margaret A. *The God of the Witches*. Oxford: Oxford University Press, 1934; New York: Doubleday Anchor, 1960.

———. *The Witch-Cult in Western Europe*. Oxford: Oxford University Press, 1962 [1921].

Mathers, Samuel Liddell

Samuel Mathers (January 8, 1854–November 20, 1918), a founder of the Hermetic Order of the Golden Dawn, was born into a Scottish family in London, England, and later gave himself the first name of MacGregor to reflect his Scottish heritage. His father died when he was young and his mother then supported the family as a clerk in the town of Bournemouth.

Mathers remained at home, reading widely and participating in the Masonic Society and the Rosicrucian Society in Anglia until 1885. At that time he moved to London and joined the Theosophical Society. In 1887, he published *The Kabbalah Unveiled*, establishing himself as an occult scholar. During this time he met with Wynn Westcott and others to decode and rework a number of magical manuscripts. These manuscripts became the basis of the Hermetic Order of the Golden Dawn (HOGD), founded in 1888. Westcott soon left the group and Mathers gained complete control. In 1890, he married Moina Bergson, the daughter of the famous philosopher Henri Bergson.

In 1891 or 1892 Mathers moved to Paris and established a temple of the HOGD, adding it to the temples in London, Edinburgh, and Bradford (which he also established). The organizing idea of the HOGD was the Hermetic principle of correspondence between the microcosm (human being) and the macrocosm (the universe). Through the proper magical procedures, a person can access or make manifest any powers or characteristics present in the macrocosm.

In 1903, Mathers overrode the objections of the London officers of the HOGD and initiated Aleister Crowley into its higher levels—an act that caused a split among the British adherents. More importantly, although Crowley soon left the HOGD, he used what he had learned with the group, a significant factor in what became Crowley's twentieth-century revival of magic. After Mathers's death, his widow moved to London and led a temple herself, but the HOGD eventually became defunct.

Samuel Liddell Mathers, flamboyant founder of the Hermetic Order of the Golden Dawn. (Hulton Getty/Liaison Agency)

See Also: Hermetic Order of the Golden Dawn
Further Reading
Colquhoun, Ithell. *Sword of Wisdom: MacGregor Mathers and the "Golden Dawn."* New York: Putnam's, 1975.

May Pole

The May pole is a specially selected young tree, cut down and then shorn of its branches and leaves and set up in the middle of a clearing, where it becomes a key part of a magical celebration. The May pole is elaborately decorated with ribbons and garlands, attached at the top. The May pole received its name from May Eve, the day on which Beltane is celebrated. Beltane is the fertility Sabbat of modern Witches and Neopagans. During this festival, a group surrounds the May pole, alternating the order between the sexes, and each person takes up a ribbon, dancing in a circular motion around the pole. By the end of the dance, the ribbons are plaited around the pole. The dance is altered slightly in France, where only women dance; in Bavaria a man is wrapped in straw and is the dancer. In Scandinavia, where the ceremony is celebrated in the middle of summer, May poles are set up at each house.

See Also: Beltane

Further Reading

Campanelli, Pauline. *Wheel of the Year: Living the Magical Life*. St. Paul, MN: Llewellyn, 1989.

Kelly, Aidan A. *Religious Holidays and Calendars: An Encyclopedic Handbook*. Detroit, MI: Omnigraphics, 1991.

McFarland Dianic Tradition

Morgan McFarland and Mark Roberts founded their Dianic Tradition (which includes men) in the late 1960s in Dallas, Texas. It is not clear whether there was any contact between McFarland and Z. Budapest by about 1970—there may have been. In 1972, McFarland and Roberts began publishing the periodical *The New Broom*; although well-liked, it was, like almost all Craft periodicals, not a financial success and it folded after producing about four issues in four years.

However, because *The New Broom* made her well-known, McFarland was invited by women in the Craft community in Boston to perform the opening ritual for a women's conference. On April 23, 1976, Morgan McFarland led 1,000 women in a Goddess ritual in Boston's Arlington Street Church, beginning the three-day Women's Spirituality Conference, which introduced most attendees to the Craft. The women's spirituality movement was never the same again. McFarland soon faded from national prominence and Roberts began another periodical, *The Harp*, but it, too, soon disappeared.

Issues of *The New Broom* and *The Harp* may be found in the American Religion special collection at the University of California, Santa Barbara.

See Also: Dianic Wicca/Goddess Religion

Meditation

Meditation has been used for religious, mystical, and magical purposes in various ways and with different goals for centuries. It is generally regarded as a spiritual exercise during which mental activity becomes detached from one's physical sensations by focusing on predetermined thoughts, images, sounds, objects, or entities. A differentiation is generally made between Eastern and Western types of meditation. In Eastern religions meditation tends to be inwardly focused, while an outward focus characterizes Western meditation.

Compared to Western religions, Eastern systems placed a greater emphasis on meditation and developed a number of sophisticated meditation techniques. As a result, many Eastern techniques made their way to the West. In their passage to the West, Eastern meditation techniques lost some of their mystical connotations. The deployment of meditation as merely a remedy for the dissatisfactions and frustrations of modern life has often been criticized by those interested in the original goal of meditation.

Within the metaphysical subculture of the West (such as alternative medicine), the importance of meditation techniques as means for the advancement and growth within the individual is stressed. Body positions, breathing, and relaxation play a fundamental role in most kinds of meditation. Magic rituals also use meditation, usually as a way for individuals to achieve a state of maximum relaxation that favors the visualization and evocation of spirits or entities. The focus developed during meditation also helps one avoid distractions that can be dangerous during certain rituals.

See Also: Rite, Ritual
Further Reading
Smith, Bradford. *Meditation*. Philadelphia, PA: J. B. Lippincott, 1963.

Meet

The verb *to meet* is used in a special sense by Neopagan Witches: It can mean "to meet in order to circle." That is, it can mean to hold a ritual, work magic, and so on. It is an innocuous term that can be used in public; the special meaning is deduced from the context.

See Also: Circle, Magic
Further Reading
Guiley, Rosemary. *The Encyclopedia of Witches and Witchcraft*. New York: Facts on File, 1989.

Moon

The moon is associated with female fertility, the monthly cycle, and the powers of nurturing. Traditionally, it is also seen as connected with the powers of darkness, the night, and the mysteries of the dark. It embodies wetness, moisture, intuition, emotion, tides, the psychic, moods, and madness. The moon also represents time, as the earliest calendars are based on its phases.

The moon has always been regarded as feminine, although there are moon gods as well as moon goddesses. The association of the moon with the feminine seems to be based on the similarity between the 28-day lunar cycle and the length of a woman's menstrual cycle. In a number of cultures, the words for *moon* and *menstruation* are the same or very similar. The moon has been regarded as the source of fertility since antiquity, and moonlight has been considered responsible for abundant harvests and human fecundity.

The lunar cycle is characterized by three phases, which have been said to rule all aspects of life: the waxing moon, during which the moon expands toward fullness; the full moon; and the waning moon, during which it grows smaller in the sky. It is frequently believed that the waxing moon is auspicious for crop-planting, luck, and general growth; whereas the waning moon represents a time of diminishment and destruction. The lunar gods and goddesses of antiquity were often portrayed with crescent moons, the auspicious symbol of the waxing, lucky moon.

In modern Witchcraft, worship of the Goddess is associated with the moon, and the magic activities of Witches or covens are generally scheduled according to the phases of the moon. Witches usually meet during a full or new moon. The Great Goddess—the giver of all things in the waxing phase and the destroyer of all in her waning phase—is often conceptualized by Witches in a tripartite way, according to the phases of the moon. Diana, the Maiden, rules the new and waxing moon; Selene, the Matron, rules the full moon; and Hecate, the Crone or old wise woman, rules the waning and dark moon.

Witches are said to draw down the power of the moon from the sky. This usually takes place during a trance ritual, in which a High Priestess asks the spirit of the Goddess to come into her in order to speak to those present. During the Renaissance and Reformation, alchemy, high magic, and folk magic activities were based on the phases of the moon in order to create and consecrate magical tools, summon the spirits, prepare remedies and charms, and cast spells. Magic for healing, gain, luck, and increase is said to be the most powerful during the waxing moon. The full moon represents the best moment for magical power. Magic for binding, banishing, and eliminating is generally done during the moon's waning phase.

The moon was also believed to govern the humours, the moisture in the body and brain. The light of the moon, especially the midsummer moon, has been believed to have an unsettling effect upon the mind (the word *lunatic* generally refers to the mentally disturbed). It was also claimed that children born during the full moon would never be healthy, thus risking moon madness, or lunacy. The moon also rules the tides, which are highest at the new moon and full moon. The metal silver, enhancer of psychic powers, is associated with the moon.

See Also: Diana; Drawing Down the Moon; Goddess(es); Hecate

Further Reading
Lewis, James R. *Magical Religion and Modern Witchcraft*. Albany, NY: State University of New York Press, 1996.
Paungger, Johanna. *Moon Time: The Art of Harmony with Nature and Lunar Cycles*. New York: Barnes and Noble, 1995.

Murray, Margaret

Margaret Murray was an English classicist and Egyptologist who became interested in the European Witch trials around the end of World War I. In reading through the transcripts of the Witch trials, especially those in England, she became convinced that what she perceived was the survival of a Pagan religion that the religious establishment was attempting to exterminate. Murray assembled what she considered the evidence for this theory in the book *The Witch-Cult in Western Europe*, which was published by Oxford University Press in 1921 and immediately became the subject of controversy.

In any event, whether she was right or not about European history, she did give a reasonably detailed description of a Pagan religion that she called Witchcraft—and it was only a matter of time until someone would attempt to re-create that religion. Apparently, no such efforts were actually made in the 1920s, but the appearance of her next book, *The God of the Witches*, in 1933 seems to have tipped the scale. A student group at Cambridge in the mid-1930s began the attempt, and their work influenced at least one other group in particular, later known as the New Forest Coven.

About 20 years after the publication of *God of the Witches*, Murray, who had become a good friend of Gerald Gardner's at meetings of the Folklore Society, wrote the introduction for Gardner's book *Witchcraft Today*, hailing it as vindication of her views—but, this wasn't the case. In fact, what few readers notice is that the religion described by Gardner in his book had evolved *away* from the one described by Murray; she merely provided a starting point for a highly creative process. She wrote her autobiography at age 100.

See Also: Graves, Robert; Maiden; Man in Black
Further Reading
Gardner, Gerald B. *Witchcraft Today*. London: Jarrolds, 1954.
Murray, Margaret A. *The God of the Witches*. Oxford: Oxford University Press, 1933; Doubleday Anchor, 1960.
———. *The Witch-Cult in Western Europe*. Oxford: Oxford University Press, 1962 [1921].

Music, Pagan

The first album of songs specifically intended for the Neopagan community was *Songs of the Old Religion*, written and performed (with the California

Famous Pagan traveling musician Kenny Klein. (Courtesy of Kenny Klein)

Wicca Blues Band) by Thomas DeLong (Gwydion Pendderwen), released in 1973. Some years later came *The Fairie Shaman*. Both continue to sell steadily.

The next such recording to be produced was *Circle Magic Music* by Circle's founders, Jim Alan and Selena Fox. This was homespun music, recorded (as many early Pagan cassettes were) on rudimentary recording equipment, but it served a need. Not only did the music sell well, but it inspired many others to create songs for Pagans.

In 1981, Kenny Klein played punk-rock music in after-hours clubs in New York City, but made a living playing country music in various New Jersey honky-tonk bars. He met Tzipora Dufner in an occult bookstore on the Lower East Side of Manhattan, and she spoke to him about a musical project she and her covenmate Tina had planned for some time. Their concept was to create a recording that would portray a Pagan ritual entirely in song.

To familiarize Klein with the state of Pagan music, Dufner played for him the only Pagan recordings available at that time: those by Pendderwen and by Jim and Selena Fox. Dufner, Tina, and Klein worked in late 1982 and early 1983 on *Moon Hooves in the Sand*, the Pagan ritual in song, which was probably the third recording released specifically for a Pagan audience. After that album, Dufner and Klein began a musical career together. In 1984, they released *Songs of the Otherworld*. These first two tapes, like most Pagan recordings, were self-produced. Music for Pagans probably would not exist today if it had not been for 1980s technology that provided easily manufactured cassette recording. In 1985, Dufner and Klein were picked up by a small folk music label, Kicking Mule Records, and released *Wineskin, Tinkers, and Tears* on that label.

Kicking Mule Records was also home to a pair of Pagan women who sang and played dulcimers beautifully. Playing as the group Aeolus, Ruth Barrett and Cynthia Smith recorded two albums for Kicking Mule, *Aeolus* and *Music of the Rolling World*. Their third album, *Deepening*, was self-produced and is considered to be some of their best work together. The duo continues to record music, and Ruth Barrett has performed on solo projects and recordings with other partners. Her *Parthenogenesis* is widely popular.

Lady Isadora's first album, *The Witching Hour*, also was released at about that time, and she joined the roster of nationally popular Pagan artists. Her later projects included *Priestess of the Pentacle*.

In 1986, Isaac Bonewits's *Pagan Once Again* was released and is now considered a classic. Another new band, Pomegranate, consisted of several women who sang Goddess-oriented material. Some of the band's members left to form the band Kiva, which became one of the more active touring bands on the Pagan musical circuit.

The late 1980s gave rise to the prominence of Ian Corrigan, whose bellowing voice did justice to traditional British tunes, and Angie Remedi, formerly of the Pallas Society, who sings chants that many consider lovely. During that decade, Jim Alan, formerly of Circle, returned as a solo performer with *Tales of the Songsmith* and *Dragon Tracks*.

In 1989, Dufner and Klein were involved in two landmark projects. Gypsy, co-owner of White Light Pentacles (a Pagan distribution firm) contacted them about a recording on which she was working. They played several tracks on *Enchantress*, which was the first Pagan dance rock tape, and broke ground in this genre. That same year, they worked with Gail Perigo on a tape called *Never Again the Burning*, which featured complex poems recited to a background of rock and folk music.

In 1992, Klein and Dufner's marriage and working partnership ended. Klein was signed by Blackthorn Records in Kansas City and he spent the year recording *Gold of the Autumn* for that label.

Leigh Anne Hussey, High Priestess of Black Oak Coven (NROOGD) for many years, was a noted composer and performer with her ensemble, Annwn; she also served as National Publications Officer of the Covenant of the Goddess, 1988–1989.

Another well-liked new performer was Charlie Murphy, who, although not a Neopagan himself, sang Neopagan songs and was very much in tune with Neopagan, as well as gay, issues. Yet another performer, Todd Allen, created the band The Quest, which may be the first de facto Pagan rock band. By the early 1980s, there was a nationally known collection of songs and chants that people learned and repeated at festivals. Some of the most popular of these chants were composed by Starhawk, who was considered rather a genius at this specialized task.

Thus, the Neopagan community has evolved what amounts to a standard hymnal, one of the elements that hold religious communities together. Pagan music is a growing market. Pagan-sponsored coffeehouses are opening in several cities, giving Pagan musical acts a venue in which to perform. Non-Pagan groups record music for Pagan markets, such as Robert Gass and On Wings of Song's *From the Goddess*, a recording of Goddess-inspired tunes. On Wings of Song also recorded Christian and Native American music. Likewise, the non-Pagan group Libana recorded *A Circle Is Cast*, a project targeted for Goddess-worshippers.

The compact-disc (CD) recording format has opened a larger market for Pagan acts in New Age retail outlets, and the widening Pagan audience may entice more Pagans to perform for other Pagans. (There are well-known performers who do not openly profess to endorse Paganism, though they leak information that they do.) Pagans still face the problem of distribution and availability of their music: Many Pagans had no idea that Pagan music was available because there were relatively few retail outlets that carry this type of music. But magazines like *Circle Network News* and *Green Egg*, with their wide audiences, educated Pagans about the diversity of available recordings. Other artists listed in *Circle Network News*'s two-page spread on Pagan music in every issue have included Andras and Deirdre Arthen, and EarthSpirit Community's choral group, Mother Tongue; Anne Williams; Kay Gardner; Reclaiming; Deborah and Rick Hamouris; Lisa Thiel; and Gaia's Voice, a San Francisco–area choral group that Deborah Hamouris directs. A listing of Pagan recordings is available from *Circle Network News*, P.O. Box 219, Mount Horeb, WI 53572.

Mysteries

The term *Mysteries* is the name for the esoteric teachings and rites of secret societies outside the classical world. The secretive religious groups known as the Mysteries prospered during the Hellenistic period and were characterized by the adoration of a number of deities from Greece, Syria, Anatolia, Egypt, and Persia, and by rites of spiritual transformation and rebirth. The word *mystery*, from the Greek *myein*—"to close the mouth or the eyes"—relates both to the esoteric content of the Mysteries themselves as well as to the silence kept by its initiates. The Mysteries groups were usually limited to men or women, although some, such as the Eleusinian Mysteries, admitted both sexes.

Mysteries generally focused upon a divine female as the vessel of transformation. Their purpose was to secure eternal life in the afterworld by means of rebirth or redemption. An erotic-sexual element of union with the primal mother was common to many Mysteries, as were elements of magic and ecstasy. The transformative process usually featured the preparation and consumption of special food and drink. Some rites also featured blood sacrifices. The initiates generally received knowledge and were asked to keep the instructions of the religion secret. Dramas of the deities, reenactments of the *hieros gamos*, and the death and rebirth of a deity constituted the rites of the Mysteries.

The Hellenistic Mysteries came to an end with Christianity, although Christian rites of circumcision, baptism, and anointing the forehead with oil are similar to the ancient Mystery rites of initiation. The Eucharist, the Cross, and the baptism are the fundamental Christian Mysteries, and the cult of Mary has associations with the Goddess and with the ancient Mysteries. A number of elements and purposes of the ancient mysteries have been maintained in the practices of such secret societies as the Freemasons and Rosicrucians. Neopagan groups that refer to their divinities using Greek names also tend to make use of elements drawn from the Mysteries.

See Also: Freemasonry; Rite, Ritual; Sacrifice
Further Reading
Guiley, Rosemary Ellen. *Harper's Encyclopedia of Mystical and Paranormal Experience*. San Francisco, CA: HarperCollins, 1991.
Matthews, Caitlín, and John Matthews. *The Western Way: A Practical Guide to the Western Mystery Tradition*. London: Arkana, 1994 [1985].

Mythology

In the most general sense, scholars these days use the term *mythology* to mean both all myths collectively and the study of myths (stories intended to convey theological beliefs or values rather than factual history). Most myths, however, are told as if they were historical, and the distinction between myth and history remains both subtle and controversial.

The study of myths, at least of some classic texts, began as classical scholarship during the Renaissance and has continued since. The modern understanding of myths began only around 1800, when the first folklorists, most notably the brothers Jacob and Wilhelm Grimm, began to collect folktales and subsequently discovered these stories closely resembled ancient myths. The study of folklore and mythology has developed into an academic discipline in its own right, with an immense literature.

The current importance of mythology for new religious movements is related to, but not identical with, classical and folkloric scholarship. Neopagans are interested in such scholarship as a resource for creating modern versions of ancient Pagan religions. Members of many New Age groups are interested in myths as a resource of self-understanding.

Neopagans, by definition, attempt to recover and re-create ancient Pagan religions and adapt them to the modern world; hence, they are interested in stories about the gods and goddesses of nonmonotheistic religions, ancient and modern. Much of the Neopagan effort to recover and re-create, shared by many members of the women's religion movement, focuses on recovering the imputed Paleolithic cult of the Great Earth Goddess.

Neopagan Witches, whose religion is based on the Gardnerian model (whether acknowledged or not) and who are now the majority among Neopagans, generally use a "duotheistic" theology of a Horned God and a Great Goddess. The underlying concept here, however, is not of a specific god and goddess, but rather one asserted by Dion Fortune, founder of the Society of the Inner Light in England in the 1930s—all gods are one God and all goddesses are one Goddess. That is, Neopagans generally conceive of all gods and goddesses of all religions as manifestations of a single, underlying, bipolar, divine reality.

In a typical Neopagan ritual, at least six deities are invoked; more is not unusual. The most popular pantheons for this purpose are the Greco-Roman and the Celtic, with Hindu deities gaining popularity as well. In addition, Egyptian, Mesopotamian, and Sumerian deities are sometimes called. When all gods and goddesses are equated (as Robert Graves does in his highly influential *The White Goddess*), the deities invoked can be all from one historical pantheon, and, occasionally, a very diverse crowd of deities may be called into the circle. However, Nordic deities are usually invoked only by groups specifically dedicated to re-creating Nordic religion; and the invocation of Native American divinities is generally avoided altogether these days out of respect for Native Americans' recent angry assertions that their religions are exploited by outsiders.

It should also be observed that this use of mythology is a creative effort to meet people's current religious needs and is not antiquarianism for its own sake. Much of the mythology used by Neopagans for their reconstructions is taken from secondary sources, such as from Robert Graves and Barbara Walker, but, for practical purposes, this lack of historical fact does not matter.

The other major use of mythology is in terms of the psychology of Carl Jung, who proposed that similarities among myths and pantheons could be explained if they arose from archetypal structures in the Collective Unconscious or Deep Mind that is common to all human beings. If this is so, myths represent another way in which the Deep Mind attempts to communicate with the individual ego, and the study of myths can give insight into one's own psychic structure.

A very similar approach to Jung's is the use of mythology to develop one's intuitive or psychic abilities. In the last several decades, many texts and workbooks have been written that explore and seek to strengthen the reader's internal structures—some of the best and most typical are those written by Jean Houston.

See Also: Goddess(es); Graves, Robert

Further Reading

Bolen, Jean Shinoda. *Goddesses in Everywoman: A New Psychology of Women.* New York: Harper and Row, 1984.

Farrar, Janet, and Stewart Farrar. *The Witches' Goddess: The Feminine Principle of Divinity.* London: Robert Hale, 1987; Custer, WA: Phoenix Publishing, 1988.

Houston, Jean. *The Search for the Beloved: Journeys in Mythology and Sacred Psychology.* Los Angeles, CA: Jeremy P. Tarcher, 1987.

N

Names of Power

Names of power are the secret names of gods or goddesses. These names are used to invoke power to assist in magical practices. In Western magic, when names of power, words, or certain sounds are chanted from within a magic circle, the desired power is raised. Power can be associated with a name if it rates highly in numerology. Grimoires contain many ancient names of power, some so old that they no longer have meaning. The strongest name of power is Tetragrammaton or YHWH (Yahweh), the personal name of the god in Hebrew Scriptures.

See Also: Evocation and Invocation; Grimoire; Numerology
Further Reading
Green, Marian. *The Elements of Ritual Magic*. Longmead, Shaftesbury, Dorset, U.K.: Element, 1990.
Stewart, R. J. *Advanced Magical Arts*. Longmead, Shaftesbury, Dorset, U.K.: Element, 1988.

Necromancy

Necromancy means "divination with the aid of the dead." Its use dates back to ancient Persia, Egypt, and Rome, and this type of divination is still practiced in some cultures (Haiti, for example). In Greece, necromancy signified the descent into Hades to consult the dead, who supposedly had great prophetic powers. During the Middle Ages, when necromancy was a part of what was called "sorcery," it was believed to be widely practiced by magicians and Witches. When, for instance, a great persecution of Witches occurred between the late Middle Ages and the beginning of the Renaissance, necromancy was one of the crimes that Witches were accused of committing. Numerous accounts of necromancy are mentioned in the Bible and in the Talmud, as well as in myths, legends, and literary works in cultures around the globe. One of the best-known necromancers was the biblical "Witch" of Endor, who summoned the shade of the dead prophet Samuel for King Saul.

A seventeenth-century painting by Salvador Rosa of Saul and the Witch of Endor, one of the best-known necromancers. (Scala/Art Resource)

Because the word *necromancy* is derived from the Greek *nekros* ("dead") and *manteia* ("divination"), it refers to divination by the spirits of the dead and/or divination through the use of corpses. The concept presupposes belief in a form of life after death, and it involves either a call to a corpse to come back to life or, more commonly, summoning a spirit in order to persuade it to provide information, usually information about the future. The practice of necromancy is also based on the assumption that the dead, no longer bound by the limitations of mortality, are in some sense all-knowing and all-seeing. According to occult theory, the departing soul leaves some of the body's energy in what is called the astral corpse. The astral corpse can sometimes be induced to return to the physical world by the power of magic, because of the corpse's great desire to live again. It has also been suggested that the soul, in ascending to a higher level of existence, moves on a shadowy plane that surrounds the physical plane, from which it can see everything. In the Western magical tradition of necromancy, the period during which a soul supposedly remains in the vicinity of its grave (and, consequently, the period during which necromantic practices can be performed) is the 12 months that follow the death of the body.

The rituals of necromancy in traditional Western magic also presuppose the conviction that the dead return only for some special reason and that a communication with them can be achieved only through particular techniques and precautions, which are very similar to those employed for conjuring demons. These methods involve magic circles, incantations, wearing clothes stolen from corpses, meditations upon death, preparations that last for days or weeks, and the choice of the proper time and a suitable place for the practice.

See Also: Divination; Spiritualism
Further Reading
Cavendish, Richard. *The Black Arts*. New York: G. P. Putnam's Sons, 1967.
Lewis, James R. *Encyclopedia of Afterlife Beliefs and Phenomena*. Detroit, MI: Gale Research Inc., 1994.

Nemeton

Nemeton means "sacred grove" in Welsh. It is the name chosen for a group founded in 1970 in Oakland, California, by Thomas DeLong (Gwydion Pendderwen) and Alison Harlow, a fellow initiate of the Faery Tradition and a fellow member of the Society for Creative Anachronism that was founded by Diana Paxson. This group originally served as a Neopagan networking organization; it was intended to be the West Coast equivalent of the Pagan Way, primarily active in the East and Midwest. In 1974, Nemeton published three issues of *Nemeton* magazine, which subsequently folded. (Issues of *Nemeton* may be found in the American Religion special collection at the University of California, Santa Barbara.) Regional secretariats of the Nemeton organization spread across the United States, playing a key role in early Wiccan and Pagan networking and growth there. In 1978, Nemeton merged with the Church of All Worlds and became that church's publishing arm.

In 1981, Pendderwen's Forever Forests sponsored an immense Midsummer Pagan Festival at the Big Trees Meadow campground of the East Bay Regional Park System in Contra Costa County, California (the Oakland hills); there were 150 people in the New, Reformed, Orthodox Order of the Golden Dawn circle. However, it turned out to be a one-time event instead of the community he imagined Nemeton could become. Pendderwen tried to establish an extended Witchcraft family on Annwfn, his retreat property, but personal differences with friends and a constant shortage of money impeded him. On November 9, 1982, returning home after an evening out visiting friends, his truck went off the winding dirt road at Annwfn and over the side of a steep hill. He was thrown out and the truck rolled over him, crushing him to death.

Netzach

Netzach, the seventh sefira of the Cabala, represents eternity or victory. It is the right leg of Adam Kadmon, the primordial person. Netzach influences all forms of love, beauty, and harmony that exist in the material world.

See Also: Cabala
Further Reading
Fortune, Dion. *The Mystical Qabalah*. York Beach, ME: Weiser, 1994 [1935].
Myers, Stuart. *Between the Worlds: Witchcraft and the Tree of Life—A Program of Spiritual Development*. St. Paul, MN: Llewellyn, 1995.

New Reformed Orthodox Order of the Golden Dawn

The New Reformed Orthodox Order of the Golden Dawn (NROOGD) began as a project for a graduate class in ritual at San Francisco State University in 1967 (it was named in honor of the Hermetic Order of the Golden Dawn, and especially in honor of William Butler Yeats). The group of friends who worked on the project transformed themselves into an occult study group during the next year and, by the end of 1969, into a Gardnerianistic coven, which later was called the Full Moon Coven.

By 1972, the Full Moon Coven began to train candidates for a new coven; its members decided to call themselves the Spiral Dance Coven (from which Starhawk derived the name for her book). In 1973, when the five surviving members of this training coven were invested with the Red Cord (the badge of full initiation in the NROOGD system), there were Red-Cord Witches in two different covens. Hence, the members of the Full Moon Coven decided to form a Red-Cord Council—to consist of all those with Red Cords—and to allow *it*, rather than the Full Moon Coven, to direct the overall affairs of the Order. The Full Moon Coven, relieved of its original function, then dwindled in size until it was disbanded in December 1974. The Spiral Dance Coven continued to exist until 1978.

Another coven, the Stone Moon Coven (later the Moonlit Cauldron Coven), hived off from the Full Moon Coven in 1972. It was headed by Glenn A. Turner, who is still the reigning High Priestess of the NROOGD covens.

By 1976, there were so many covens, and so many Elders holding the Red Cord, that the meetings of the Red-Cord Council became thoroughly unwieldy. In May 1976, rather than create yet another level of government, the Elders dissolved the NROOGD as an organization, deciding that it was only a "tradition" with which covens could be affiliated if they were descended from the original Full Moon Coven and met a few other criteria.

The coven operated largely by consensus and with a collective authority; there was no High Priest or High Priestess as such; rather, ritual roles were rotated among members of this group, and newer initiates were brought in to be trained.

Further Reading

Lewis, James R. *The Encyclopedia of Cults, Sects, and New Religions.* Amherst, NY: Prometheus Books, 1998.

Melton, J. Gordon. *Encyclopedia of American Religions*, 5th ed. Detroit, MI: Gale Research Inc., 1996.

New Thought Movement

New Thought is not so much a religion as a type of teaching that has influenced a number of groups—including, ultimately, Neopaganism. New Thought proper includes such churches as the Church of Religious Science, the Church of Divine Science, and Unity. Major New Thought writers include Phineas Quimby (*Immanuel*), Ralph Waldo Trine (*In Tune with the Infinite*), Horatio Dresser (*A History of the New Thought Movement, Spiritual Health and Healing,* and *The Quimby Manuscripts*), and Ernest Holmes (*Creative Mind* and *The Science of Mind*). Belief in the supreme reality and power of the human mind is fundamental to New Thought, which links New Thought with contemporary magical practices.

Like Theosophy (and unlike Neopaganism), the New Thought movement asserts that the inner reality of the universe is the mind and the idea. However, the movement differs from Theosophy in that it does not point to Masters as the minds that make things happen, but to the mental potential of every individual. New Thought teachers strive to show how thoughts of health, wholeness, and success can create corresponding material realities.

The "mind cure" movement of Phineas Parkhurst Quimby (1802–1866) of Belfast, Maine, set down roots that would later evolve into New Thought. Quimby was exposed to hypnosis at a lecture-demonstration by mesmerist Dr.

Collyer in 1838. Quimby then began to experiment with mesmerism. One of Quimby's subjects, while hypnotized, frequently diagnosed and prescribed treatments for illnesses that people brought before him even though he wasn't a doctor. Quimby noted on several occasions that people were healed when they took a prescribed medicine with no real medicinal value. He began to believe that sickness was the result of erroneous thinking and that a cure could consist of changing one's belief system. He eventually dropped hypnosis as a therapeutic tool and began to speak directly with each patient about the need to link the individual's spiritual nature with the divine spirit. Quimby felt that priests and doctors were benefactors of human misery and had wicked and unethical holds on the minds of people. Rather than healers, he considered priests and doctors to be major sources of error and therefore major sources of illness. Quimby's students included Warren Felt Evans, Annetta and Julius Dresser, and Mary Baker Eddy, all of whom influenced the New Thought movement.

Warren Felt Evans (1817–1887) was a devotee of Emanuel Swedenborg. Evans was a former Methodist minister who forsook his Methodist training and became a minister in the Church of the New Jerusalem. In 1863, Evans became a client of Quimby's practice and was healed by his methods. After Quimby's death, Evans moved to a Boston suburb and opened a healing practice. Evans brought his Swedenborgian thinking to his practice. He wrote prolifically from 1869 and onward about spiritual healing methods. Evans stressed that disease is a result of a disturbance in the human spiritual body that adversely affects the physical body.

In 1862, Mary Baker Eddy traveled to Portland, Maine, to receive treatment from Quimby. Within a month she was cured and wrote in praise of Quimby to the newspaper in Portland. On February 1, 1866, less than a month after Quimby's death, Eddy fell on some ice. The next day she suffered from severe internal spasms. She was confined to bed and some doubted if she would recover. Three days later, she was given a Bible to read and was left to meditate alone. She became overwhelmed with the conviction that her life was in God and that God was the only life, the sole reality of existence. With that realization, she was healed. She got out of bed, dressed, and walked into the next room, to the astonishment of all in attendance.

During the following decade, Eddy engaged in intensive Bible study and struggled to understand the implication of God as a healer versus Quimby's notion of the mind as a healer. In 1870, she held her first class and began writing *Science and Health*, which was published in 1875. Eddy's book attracted readers who previously had read Warren Felt Evans's works. In 1879, the Church of Christ, Scientist was organized. In 1882, Eddy opened the Massachusetts Metaphysical College in Boston. She taught basic classes that students needed to become Christian Science practitioners. Graduates of the college began to open offices around the country.

There were accusations that Mary Baker Eddy had taken Quimby's ideas and had published them under her name. Although Quimby had an undeniable influence on Eddy, there were great differences between her outlook and his. Eddy had trouble accepting Quimby's concept of the mind as spiritual matter. She could not reconcile Quimby's hostility toward religion with her own Christian faith.

On October 23, 1881, eight students resigned from the Christian Scientist Association, among them Elizabeth Stuart. Stuart continued to practice what she had been taught throughout New England and is most remembered as the teacher of some of the most prominent of the New Thought leaders, including Charles Brodie Patterson, who influenced the founders of the Christ Truth League.

In 1885, Eddy excommunicated Emma Curtis Hopkins from the Church of Christ, Scientist, who then went on to found the New Thought movement. Hopkins had studied with Eddy and had edited the *Christian Science Journal* in 1884 and 1885. After her break with Eddy, Hopkins founded the Emma Curtis Hopkins College of Christian Science in 1886.

In the mid-1880s there was an array of healers related to Christian Science in some manner throughout the United States. Many of them interacted with other unconventional healers such as Spiritualists, Theosophists, and Christian healers. As word about Hopkins's work spread, students began to travel to Chicago to study with her and she began to travel to other places to teach. By the end of 1887, she was organizing the independent Christian Science practitioners and her students into associated centers across the country.

In 1888, Hopkins transformed her Emma Hopkins College of Metaphysical Science into the Christian Science Theological Seminary and offered advanced training for students planning to enter the Christian Science ministry. This was never possible within the Church of Christ, Scientist as Eddy was the only person ordained. Since her death the church has been led by laypeople. In January 1889, Hopkins held the first graduation ceremonies from the seminary and, assuming the office of bishop, she became the first woman to ordain others to the ministry in modern times. Her first graduating class consisted of 20 women and 2 men (both of whom were husbands of other members of the graduating class). Hopkins added an innovation to Christian Science by identifying the Holy Spirit as female, an idea that originated with Joachim of Flore (1145–1202). After ordaining her students, Hopkins sent them to create new churches and ministries throughout the country.

In 1895, after ordaining more than 100 ministers, Hopkins retired, closed the seminary, and moved to New York City. She spent the rest of her life teaching students on a one-on-one basis.

As Hopkins's students established their own centers, they began to differentiate themselves from Christian Science. Myrtle and Charles Fillmore in Kansas City, Missouri, adopted the name Unity. Melinda Cramer and Nona E. Brooks in Denver named their work Divine Science. Faculty member Helen Van Anderson moved to Boston after the seminary closed and formed the Church of the Higher Life. Faculty member Annie Rix Militz established the Homes of Truth on the West Coast. George and Mary Burnell formed the Burnell Foundation in Los Angeles. Albert C. Grier founded the Church of the

Truth in Spokane, Washington. Ernest S. Holmes, one of Hopkins's last students, founded the Institute of Religious Science in Los Angeles, later called the Church of Religious Science. These were the New Thought churches.

Thomas Troward, a retired judge, developed a second career as a New Thought lecturer. He introduced new psychological concepts into the movement in the early twentieth century. He argued for the differentiation of the mind into its objective (waking consciousness) and its subjective (unconscious) aspects. In doing so he opened the movement to the new concept of the dynamic subconscious, a concept missing from the theology of both Eddy and Hopkins. Holmes took Troward's main insights and used them in creating the Church of Religious Science.

The International New Thought Alliance (INTA) was formed in 1914. It produced a statement of agreement, which became its first Declaration of Principles. The statement affirmed the Alliance's belief in God as Universal Wisdom, Love, Life, Truth, Power, Peace, Beauty, and Joy; that the universe is the body of God; that the human is an invisible spiritual dweller inhabiting a body; and that human beings continue to grow and change after death. An important feature of the INTA has been its ability to allow individualism among its members.

The New Thought movement distinguishes itself from the Christian Science from which it developed in the following ways:

1. The movement is led by ordained ministry, although there are many teachers and writers among the laity.
2. It developed a decentralized movement that celebrates its diversity of opinion.
3. It developed an emphasis on prosperity. New Thought leaders reason that poverty is as unreal as disease and they teach students to live out of the abundance of God.
4. Rather than retaining an exclusively Christian emphasis, the movement as a whole has moved to what it sees as a more universal position that acknowledges all religious traditions as valuable.

Since the emergence of this movement, independent New Thought teachers have been the single most important force responsible for the widespread acceptance of the "power of the mind" in the West's occult/metaphysical subculture. Via this widespread idea, it is possible to reinterpret the methodology of traditional magic psychologically—as providing a focus of attention for mind power. And it is precisely this line of interpretation that many contemporary Neopagans have adopted when explaining the workings of magic.

See Also: Magic
Further Reading
Lewis, James R. *The Encyclopedia of Cults, Sects, and New Religions.* Amherst, NY: Prometheus, 1998.

Melton, J. Gordon. *Encyclopedia of American Religions*, 5th ed. Detroit, MI: Gale Research Inc., 1996.

Norse Neopagans

Norse Paganism constitutes a branch of Neopaganism devoted to the Norse deities. These deities are generally classified into two major categories: the Aesir—the sky gods, including Odin and his wife Frigga, Thor, Loki, Balder, and others; and the Vanir—gods concerned with earth agriculture, fertility, and the cycle of death and rebirth. Values of honor, honesty, courage, and duty to one's family, kin, and friends are particularly emphasized by Norse Pagans.

A number of independent Norse Pagan groups were formed in the 1970s almost simultaneously in America, England, and Iceland. The largest group was the now-defunct Asatru Free Assembly, formed in 1972 by Stephen Mc-Nallen, which embraced both categories of deities. Another form of Norse Paganism is known as Odinism, recognizing only the Aesir deities. Norse Paganism is influenced by elements in the Sami tradition, which is the Lappish Shamanic way, particularly in the northern areas of Norway and Sweden. Adherents do not necessarily have High Priests and High Priestesses; rather, they have guides. Several Norse adherents emphasize blood ties and genetics, the warrior ethic, and the Norse symbology, which is composed of Norse and Germanic elements, and includes runes, spears, warriors, and the swastika.

The runes, a magical alphabet of symbols used for healing, divination, and on several charms and in invocations, originated in the Fresia area of southern Denmark. Diffused throughout Europe, Britain, and Russia by the Saxons, Norse, Danes, and Vikings, runes were used during the Middle Ages. According to Norse mythology, they were created by the God Odin, who gained knowledge of the runes by impaling himself with his own spear onto Yggdrasil, the World Tree, for nine days and nights.

The runes are believed to possess significant magical power, and one important use of runes is divination. In the late nineteenth and early twentieth centuries, German occultists became very interested in runes, associating them with racial supremacy. The Nazis adopted two runes that became the most feared symbols on Earth: the swastika, an ancient symbol representing the hammer of Thor (god of thunder) and the wheel of the sun; and the *sig* or "S" rune, representing the trademark of Heinrich Himmler's *Schutzstaffel*, or SS.

The warrior imagery has a certain "macho" appeal, and the Norse Pagan religion is heavily patriarchal, although the Norse goddesses are strong and assertive. One of these goddesses is Freya, Goddess of Fertility, who does not shrink from a battle. Norse religion is used as a way of identifying oneself with Scandinavian or German ancestral roots. Norse Pagans have often been accused of white-supremacy racism. Many Norse groups are based on the writings of Guido Von List, a white supremacist who, in the 1700s, discovered the runes. Some right-wing Norse Pagan groups believe they have founded a religion suited to the Aryan race. Some of these groups include neo-Nazis, though most Norse Pagans do not support Nazism. Norse festivals are usually held on the seasonal equinoxes and solstices. Among other Norse holidays is Ragnar's Day (March 28), commemorating Viking Ragnar Lodbrok's sacking of Paris in 845.

See Also: Asatru; Odinists; Runes

Further Reading

Davidson, H. R. Ellis. *Myths and Symbols in Pagan Europe*. Syracuse, NY: Syracuse University Press, 1988.

Fitch, Ed. *The Rites of Odin*. St. Paul, MN: Llewellyn, 1993.

Kaplan, Jeffrey. "The Reconstruction of the Asatru and Odinist Traditions." In Lewis, James R., ed., *Magical Religion and Modern Witchcraft*. Albany, NY: State University of New York Press, 1996, 193–236.

North, Dolores

Dolores North (who died in 1982) was an English psychic and writer who used the pen name Madeline Montalban. Gerald Gardner and others called her "The Witch of St. Giles," because she lived in St. Giles High Street, London, and because she was considered a Witch whether she belonged to Gardner's coven or not. She was well-known as a regular contributor to the popular occult magazine *Prediction*.

As one of the occult circle around Gardner, she was almost certainly a member of the New Forest Coven from the very beginning. An oral history taken from Rolla Nordic by the New Moon New York Oral History Project confirms North's Craft activity during World War II. North introduced Nordic to a meeting of 200 "Witches" who sent psychic energy out to aid the war effort—held every Tuesday night at a church in London (here Nordic apparently used the term *Witches* to describe persons who could—or claimed to—use paranormal abilities).

According to Doreen Valiente, North's family had some connection with Lord Louis Mountbatten's estate, Broadlands, in the New Forest area. During the war, North wore the uniform of an officer in the Women's Royal Naval Service as a cover; Mountbatten (who knew her because of her family's connection) had retained her as his personal clairvoyant and psychic advisor. Readers of Katherine Kurtz's novel *Lammas Night* will recognize this scenario.

Valiente also claimed that it was North who typed out for Gardner the manuscript of his book *High Magic's Aid*, apparently cleaning up Gardner's somewhat dyslexic spelling as she did so. Valiente gave a very curious account of what may have been a magical working with Gardner and North in a book by Kenneth Grant entitled *Nightside of Eden*; this ritual would have taken place in 1949. Apparently, North occasionally worked with Gardner up until the 1950s. She later founded the Order of the Morning Star, in which she trained Michael Howard, who received Gardnerian initiation in 1969. This fact by itself should settle the question of whether she had been a member of Gardner's coven.

Further Reading

Kelly, Aidan A. *Crafting the Art of Magic, Book I: A History of Modern Witchcraft, 1939–1964*. St. Paul, MN: Llewellyn, 1991.
———. *Inventing Witchcraft: A Case Study in the Creation of a New Religion*. Los Angeles, CA: Art Magickal Publications, 1996.
Kurtz, Katherine. *Lammas Night*. New York: Ballantine, 1983.
Valiente, Doreen. *The Rebirth of Witchcraft*. London: Robert Hale, 1989.

Numerology

The term *numerology* denotes the system of divination developed out of the philosophy of Pythagoras, who believed that the universe is built upon the power of numbers. In numerology all words, names, and numbers may be reduced to a single digit with occult properties and associations. Numerology can be used for various purposes, such as to analyze a person's character; assess a person's weaknesses, strengths, and natural gifts; predict the future; determine the best place to live; discover the best times to make choices; and select partners in one's business, marital, and social lives.

In the sixth century, Pythagoras, who had discovered that the four musical notes known at the time could be expressed in numbers, drew the conclusion that all of creation could be expressed in numbers as well. He inferred that the universe could be expressed by the numbers 1 through 4. The sum of these numbers is 10, a holy number that represented the material and metaphysical perfection of the universe.

It was also believed that numbers were characterized by individual, sublime qualities. For instance, even numbers represented wholeness, stability, or weakness. Because they could be divided in two, they featured the feminine quality of "opening." Odd numbers, on the other hand, represented assertion, power, and creativity. Because they could not be split in two, they were thought of as featuring a masculine "generative part."

Numbers were used in magical squares—numbers arranged in a square that add up to the same sum in all directions—by the Cabalists for a number of amuletic and talismanic purposes and in order to compose names of power that could be used in magic rituals. In the modern system of numerology, the nine primary numbers are associated with letters in the alphabet. According to this system, the numerical digits corresponding to the letters of a name or word can be added together, totaling a single primary number.

Each primary number features particular characteristics that can be interpreted by numerologists. The number 1, associated with God and the sun, denotes creation, unity, intellect, and uniqueness. The number 2 represents duality; the number 3 denotes sexual potency and procreation. Associated with the Trinity, in Neopagan Witchcraft 3 represents the Triple Goddess aspects of the moon. The number 4 represents the foundation and root of all numbers, and 5 is the first number comprised of the sum of both even and odd numbers (3 and 2), representing male sexuality, pleasure, adventure, and impulsiveness. Wholeness, perfection, tranquillity, and female love are represented by the number 6. The number 7 represents wisdom, knowledge, mysticism, secrets, the occult, and the psychic. The number 8 means justice and fullness. Finally, the number 9 is the symbol of completeness and the highest attainment of mental and spiritual achievements, representing the ideal diameter for the magic circle.

Among the numbers with particular importance in traditional lore and Witchcraft are the 13 and 7. The number 13 corresponds to the 13 lunar months of the year. According to tradition, the seventh son or daughter of a seventh son or daughter is a born Witch.

See Also: Cabala; Gematria; Names of Power
Further Reading
Jeanne. *Numerology: Spiritual Light Vibrations*. Salem, OR: Your Center for Truth Press, 1987.
Valiente, Doreen. *An ABC of Witchcraft: Past and Present*. Custer, WA: Phoenix, 1973.

Oak King

The Oak King is one of the more popular figures in premodern Pagan cultures and in contemporary folklore. He was associated with a worldview inspired by the cycles of nature and particularly by the cycles of the sun and the moon, to which calendars and seasonal festivals are still linked. The solar cycle is characterized by eight Sabbats, or sacred times—known also as the Wheel of the Year: the solstices, the equinoxes, and the four points between, or cross quarters. The Oak King was a dual, divine image associated with the waxing and waning of the sun. He ruled and represented expansion and growth during the waxing half of the calendar year, when the days grew longer. In contrast, the Holly King ruled and represented withdrawal and rest during the waning half of the year, when the days grew shorter.

See Also: Holly King; Wheel of the Year
Further Reading
Gordon, Stuart. *The Encyclopedia of Myths and Legends*. London: Headline, 1993.
Leach, Maria. *Standard Dictionary of Folklore, Mythology, and Legend*. San Francisco, CA: HarperSan Francisco, 1984 [1949].

Odinists

The term *Odinism* derives from the name of the Norse God Odin, and it denotes a form of Norse Pagan religion that worships the various deities classified as the Aesir. Besides Odin, these deities include his wife Frigga, Thor, Loki, and Balder. Odinism traces its origins to the social and political crises of the Weimar Republic, when some members of the German Youth movement made sacrifices to Wotan. Many of these young people eventually helped build Adolf Hitler's Third Reich. At that time, a literature focused on the mystical endeavors of Nazi leaders and on pre-Christian religious forms began to appear. Several mystics outside of Germany, such as the Australian Alexander Rud Mills, were interested in the occult aspects of the Third Reich. In the 1930s Mills, a Nazi sympathizer and believer in racial mysticism, began to consider the possibility of rebuilding the pre-Christian,

Anglo-Saxon society in the contemporary age. His book, *The Odinist Religion: Overcoming Jewish Christianity* (1930), represented the first of a series of writings on a new form of Pagan philosophy. It portrayed Europe as the true birthplace of civilization. White men were depicted as descending from a common ancestor, George, or Sigge. His progeny built the Egyptian pyramids and founded empires. Mills's Anglecyn Church of Odin won only few converts.

However, in the early 1960s, Mills's writings were rediscovered by Else Christensen and her husband and, in 1971, became the inspiration for the Odinist Fellowship in Crystal River, Florida. Else Christensen disseminated Mills's thought through the pages of her publication, *The Odinist*, which contained a conspiratorial view of history, a pronounced warrior ethic, a strong racial mysticism, and a reductionist emphasis upon an idealized form of the tribal ethical values of the Germanic and Norse peoples. Readers were called upon to rebuild the religious, communal, and magical practices of the golden age (the romanticized era when Odin was worshiped in the past) in the context of the modern world. Among the major recent exponents of Odinism is George Dietz—a German immigrant and longtime figure in American neo-Nazi circles—who distributes anti-Semitic and racist literature through his Liberty Bell Publications. With Ron Hand, he created the Odinist Study Group as a front operation for his own National Socialist movement.

Thus, Odinism has been described as the religion of the Aryans. The Odinist faith is opposed to Christianity and promotes the family unit, self-respect, and loyalty to the ancestral heritage. Immortality is believed to be achieved through the improvement of a future generation.

See Also: Asatru; Norse Neopagans; Runes

Further Reading

Davidson, H. R. Ellis. *Myths and Symbols in Pagan Europe*. Syracuse, NY: Syracuse University Press, 1988.

Fitch, Ed. *The Rites of Odin*. St. Paul, MN: Llewellyn, 1993.

Kaplan, Jeffrey. "The Reconstruction of the Asatru and Odinist Traditions." In Lewis, James R., ed., *Magical Religion and Modern Witchcraft*. Albany, NY: State University of New York Press, 1996, 193–236.

Mills, A. Rud. *The Odinist Religion: Overcoming Jewish Christianity*. Melbourne, Australia: n.p., 1930.

Ointments

Since ancient times, ointments have aided in processes of healing, magic, and prophecy. Ointments are concoctions created with specific recipes and are intended for specific purposes. In ancient Egypt, ointments were used to promote oracular dreams and in the embalming process. Witches use ointments to fly, to shapeshift, and have received many ancient recipes from grimoires. Ointments can contain a wide variety of ingredients—from herbs to toxic drugs.

The ointments and balms used by Witches to fly and to shapeshift are thought to have possessed hallucinogenic drugs that created the illusion that the user flew to a Witches' revelry or changed into a wolf and roamed in the night. It has also been suggested by Gerald Gardner, the founder of twentieth-century Witchcraft, that medieval Witches utilized ointments as a method of retaining heat at their Sabbats, which were held outside at night, even during cold weather.

See Also: Anointing Oil; Flying
Further Reading
Chevalier, Jean, and Alain Gheerbrant. *The Penguin Dictionary of Symbols*. London: Penguin, 1996.
Guiley, Rosemary. *The Encyclopedia of Witches and Witchcraft*. New York: Facts on File, 1989.

Old (name)

In reading about the Craft movement in England, one often runs across a somewhat peculiar use of the word *old* that looks like a title. The three most frequent occurrences of this use are in references to "Old George" Pickingill, "Old Dorothy" Clutterbuck Fordham, and "Old Gerald" Gardner. This is, in fact, an English dialectical usage, but it has been picked up to some degree in the Neopagan movement as an informal title for Elders in a community. *Old* is not used too widely, especially since Americans generally object to being called "old."

Further Reading
Valiente, Doreen. *An ABC of Witchcraft: Past and Present*. Custer, WA: Phoenix, 1973.

Oneiromancy

Oneiromancy is the technical term for divination (*manteia*) by means of dreams (*oneiros*). It is related to more familiar words, such as *chiromancy* (literally: "hand divination" as in palmistry) and *necromancy* (literally: "dead divination" as in divination through a medium). The term is Greek, which is fitting in that, perhaps more than any ancient people, the Greeks were fascinated by dreams.

In contrast to modern dream interpretation, which is psychologically oriented, ancient dream interpretation was concerned with discovering clues to the future. Approaching dreams as omens of the future characterized the interpretation of dreams in both ancient Egypt and Mesopotamia. While guides to dream divination have been found in the remains of both of these civilizations, a complete dream dictionary, the *Oneirocritica* by Artemidorus of

Daldis, has survived from second-century Greece. As an example of a dream omen, Artemidorus asserts that a dream about discharging tapeworms through the rectum or the mouth signifies that the dreamer will discover that he is being wronged by members of his household, by those who live with him, or, for the most part, by those who share the same table. He will subsequently drive the wrongdoers away or get rid of them in some other way (Artemidorus, *Oneirocritica*, p. 161).

How expelling tapeworms could be taken to symbolize the need to expel someone from one's house should be clear enough (a person inhabits a house as a tapeworm inhabits a body). This kind of interpretation by symbolic association is characteristic of most forms of divination. Contemporary dream interpretation utilizes the same sort of symbolic associations, but the goal of the interpretation is to discover clues to the dreamer's mental and emotional state rather than to predict the future.

See Also: Divination
Further Reading
Artemidorus. *The Interpretation of Dreams (Oneirocritica)*, 2d ed. Translated by
    Robert J. White. Torrance, CA: Original Books, 1990 [1975].
Van de Castle, Robert. *Our Dreaming Mind.* New York: Ballantine, 1994.

Oracle

An oracle is a person or animal that acts as a medium between humans and deities. In the ancient world, the oracle was generally a Priestess who entered into a trance and prophesied on issues concerning the state. The oracle provided not only prophecy but also advice. In ancient Greece and Rome, the most powerful oracles were the sibyls. The sibyl was placed in a temple and a limited number of people were allowed to consult with her. A question was posed and the sibyl removed herself to a separate chamber where she entered a trance. Her answer to the question was generally obscure and had to be interpreted by Priests. It is believed that Priests manipulated the prophecies.

The ancient Egyptians consulted a variety of oracles. Their primary source of prophecy was through oracular dreams but there were also Priestesses—women from upper-class families who served as oracles. The Egyptians of the New Kingdom consulted statues through which the gods were supposed to be able to communicate.

Present-day oracles are consulted throughout the world. In Africa, chickens are poisoned and their reactions are monitored in order to obtain a prophecy. Tibetan oracles are men who are recognized in their youth as having psychic powers and therefore become mouthpieces of the deities.

See Also: Aspecting; Divination
Further Reading
Cavendish, Richard. *The Black Arts.* New York: G. P. Putnam's Sons, 1967.

Shepard, Leslie A., ed. *Encyclopedia of Occultism and Parapsychology*. Detroit: Gale Research Inc., 1991.

Ordo Templi Orientis (and its offshoots)

Aleister Crowley (1875–1947), while a student at Trinity College in Cambridge, England, joined the Hermetic Order of the Golden Dawn at age 23 and rapidly became one of its most famous members. He was expelled in 1900 after he attempted to attack William Butler Yeats.

In 1903, he married Rose Kelly, who bore him a child, and he began to receive messages from a being called Aiwass. In April 1904, Aiwass manifested as a voice and dictated to Crowley *The Book of the Law*, one of the most important modern magical treatises and the basis of all Thelemic magic. Crowley then founded his own organization, the Astrum Argentinum ("Silver Star") in 1907 and, in order to spread his ideas, published *The Equinox* semiannually from 1909 to 1913. He published descriptions of many rituals of the Hermetic Order of the Golden Dawn in *The Equinox*. Samuel MacGregor Mathers tried, but failed, to get an injunction to stop Crowley from doing so. The ten large volumes of this series have been kept in print by several publishers, most notably Samuel Weiser.

The Ordo Templi Orientis (OTO) was founded in the 1890s by a German named Karl Keller. Crowley joined the British branch of the OTO and was made its head somewhere between 1904 and 1912. When Theodor Reuss died in 1922, Crowley became the OHO, the Outer Head of the Order, and essentially made the OTO the "outer order" for his AA (Astrum Argentinum, or Silver Star)—a secret society based on *The Book of the Law*.

The OTO taught a system of sex magic that was based, in part, on Oriental practices and, in part, on the secret sex-magic teachings of P. B. Randolph (founder of the Fraternitas Rosae Crucis, a major Rosicrucian society in America). Crowley perfected this system between 1920 and 1922 at his Abbey of Thelema in Sicily. Public notoriety over his activities caused the OTO to be disbanded and banned in England in 1923.

Crowley was recognized as head of the OTO by a majority of its members in 1924 and 1925, but the organization then divided in two over whether to accept Crowley's *Book of the Law* as authoritative. (Rudolf Steiner headed an OTO chapter early in the twentieth century, before he founded the Anthroposophical League. It is this common background in magic that seems to explains why Steiner's Waldorf schools celebrate the same eight Sabbats as Neopagan Witches.)

The OTO spread to the United States with Crowley's visit there in 1905 and from 1915 to 1919, when he lived there. In 1914, Charles Stansfield Jones (Frater Achad) opened OTO branches in Vancouver, Los Angeles, and (perhaps) Washington, D.C. Crowley visited the Vancouver Lodge in 1915, at which time he met Winifred T. Smith (Frater 132) and gave him permis-

British occultist Aleister Crowley as a Hierophant in the Order of the Golden Dawn when he was about 25. (Corbis/Bettmann-UPI)

sion to open a lodge. Smith moved to Pasadena, California, opened a lodge there, and, when Jones fell into disfavor with Crowley in 1919, became head of the OTO in America.

In Pasadena, Smith entered into what was apparently an experiment in group marriage with Jack and Helen Parsons and Helen's younger sister, Betty. At some point, Parsons became the head of the lodge, which was called the Agape Lodge. With the OTO in Germany outlawed and disbanded in 1934, with the English OTO discredited and disbanded in 1923, the Agape Lodge apparently constituted the entire active membership of the OTO during the late 1930s and the 1940s.

Another OTO offshoot was founded in Chicago in 1931 by C. F. Russell, who was with Crowley at the Abbey of Thelema, but split from him to found the Chonzon Club, or Great Brotherhood of God (GBG). One member of the GBG, and head of its San Diego Lodge, was Louis T. Culling, who left the GBG in 1938 to join the OTO. This system also focused heavily on sex magic.

One of Jack Parsons's associates at California Institute of Technology (Cal-Tech) in Pasadena, California, was the eminent Hungarian aerodynamicist Dr. Theodore Von Karman. During the early 1940s, Von Karman and Parsons were both members of "the suicide club" at Cal-Tech, a group of engineers and scientists who tried to develop rocketry in the United States. Their initial projects involved the development of RATO (Rocket-Assisted Take-Off) units for conventionally powered aircraft, but, fairly soon, their area of interest expanded to include high-altitude sounding rockets like the WAC-Corporal. In 1939, this team formally constituted as GALCIT (the Guggenheim Aeronautical Laboratory at the California Institute of Technology). GALCIT was later reorganized into a private aerospace research company, Aerojet General, and later it was, in turn, reorganized into the Jet Propulsion Laboratory, now commonly known as the JPL. In his autobiography, Von Karman wrote:

> Parsons, for example, was an excellent chemist, and a delightful screwball. He loved to recite Pagan poetry to the sky while stamping his feet. The son of a one-time tycoon, he stood six-foot-one, with dark wavy hair, a small mustache, and penetrating black eyes which appealed to the ladies.
>
> When Parsons wasn't working with explosives, for which he had an uncanny talent, he headed a local chapter of a religious sect called the Thelemites. Occasionally I would hear strange tales about this sect. It had been founded in Europe by an English ex-mountain climber named Aleister Crowley, who was once labeled by the press the World's Most Evil Man because of his strange practices. His life is described in a book, *The Great Beast*. The members met in a mansion on Millionaire's Row in Pasadena in a room with walls of carved leather. The membership was sworn to obey the law: "There is no law beyond do what thou wilt. Do what thou wilt shall be the whole of the law." In practice, this was translated among other things, into sex rituals, which I learned about many months later when the FBI questioned me about Parsons. (pp. 257–258)

During the 1940s, the Federal Bureau of Investigation investigated Parsons and the Agape Lodge; its findings were considered risqué. The Agape Lodge continued to exist until 1952, when Parsons was killed in an explosion in his home laboratory.

Aleister Crowley's advancing years had dramatically curbed his aptitude for sex magic during the 1930s, and, by 1945, he was 69 years old and had lost his legendary libido. Crowley was angry with Parsons for his "debauchery" and also because, as Crowley saw it, Parsons allowed himself to be conned out of all his money. These two revelations were the causes for the warrant that Crowley issued to the young Grady McMurtry in 1946.

Aleister Crowley ran very short of money during the last few years of his life. His last big projects were his Thoth Tarot, produced under his supervision by Lady Frieda Harris; his *Book of Thoth* on that Tarot deck; and the stream of letters written between him and some initiates—later edited into the book *Magic without Tears*. The original paintings of the Tarot deck were exhibited in London in July 1942. The events in the background of *Magic without Tears* took place from about 1941 to 1944, and the *Book of Thoth* was completed about March 1944. Crowley apparently did not qualify for any sort of pension, and an initiate in New York City, Karl Germer, was his primary source of income.

A young Army corporal, Grady McMurtry, an initiate of the Pasadena Lodge, visited and attended to Crowley from 1943 to 1945 and, in 1946, was given an emergency warrant to take command of the OTO in the United States and to correct the problems that had been caused by Jack Parsons's questionable administration of the American OTO. For the next 20 years, this emergency warrant was all but forgotten.

In March 1945, Crowley moved to a decrepit boardinghouse in Hastings, England, which is not far from Southampton or, for that matter, from the New Forest area. The OTO and the AA always took pride in their Rosicrucian affinities; so it is very likely that Crowley would have gravitated to the Rosicrucian Theatre and its members. Crowley could easily have known Dorothy Clutterbuck Fordham, Gerald Gardner, and other members of the New Forest Coven during this period.

What was the nature of the relationship, if any, between Gardner and Crowley? It is clear that they did know one another. The files of the Wiccan Church of Canada, which bought the contents of Gardner's Castletown museum from Ripley's International, contain handwritten notes from Crowley to Gardner, informing Gardner of OTO events—so apparently there were some such activities between May and June 1947. Also among the former Ripley's holdings is a warrant, issued by Crowley, that awarded Gardner the magical name Scire and the grade 7 = 4 in the OTO; it was on display in the Ripley's Museum of Witchcraft at Fisherman's Wharf in San Francisco in 1974.

But what does "7 = 4" mean? To begin with, despite the warrant and the title page, 7 = 4 is not an OTO grade. The OTO's Degrees began with the probational 0th-Degree (Minerval) and ran up to a Ninth Degree that was concerned with sex magic. (There are two more Degrees, the Tenth Degree—the Supreme and Holy King, who is international head of the Order—and the Eleventh Degree, which has no organizational significance, but is concerned with a specific type of sex magic.) There is no specific attribution of any OTO grade to a Sephiroth on the Tree of Life; the OTO is mostly a public organization (much like the Masons) and has always had large ceremonies. Much of its doctrine is summarized openly in the writings of Aleister Crowley.

In *Magic in Theory and Practice*, Crowley explains his other Order, the Silver Star (Argentinum Astrum), which certainly does have such a degree. The AA is a totally secret occult organization in which any member should know only the person who initiated him or her and those whom he or she has initiated. There are no large ceremonies and no complete and public declaration of its teachings, although there are some hints and partial declarations in the writings of Aleister Crowley. These members of AA are, in short, "Secret Chiefs" or "Secret Chiefs-In-Training." The grade 7 = 4 in the AA is called an "Exempt Adept," and it is attributed to the Fourth Sephiroth, which is called Chesed. The most significant function of an "Exempt Adept" is to declare a new magical formula and/or a new religion to mankind as a whole. In *Magic in Theory and Practice* (Dover edition, p. 236), Crowley wrote, "The adept must prepare and publish a thesis setting forth his knowledge of the Universe and his proposals for its welfare and progress. He will thus be known as a leader of a school of thought."

Gardner was only about 10 years younger than Crowley; he was about 60 in 1945. Designation of Gardner as an Exempt Adept in the AA is not something that Crowley would have done without substantial firsthand knowledge of Gardner. Designation as an Exempt Adept implies that, in Crowley's view, Gardner had already attained a dialogue with his higher self. In the AA, this is known as "Knowledge and Conversation of the Holy Guardian Angel" and it is associated with the Degree 5 = 6, called Adeptus Minor. In addition, being above the Degree 6 = 5 (Adeptus Major), the Exempt Adept degree would have implied a broad range of magical powers on Gardner's part. The warrant that Crowley gave Gardner would therefore, in Crowley's mind at least, have given Gardner an official warrant to establish a new religion of an unspecified type. This may cast new light on Gardner's motives during the 1940s. In any event, a longtime Craft leader, Allen Greenfield, has recently argued that the entire Neopagan Witchcraft movement makes sense magically as an actualization of Crowley's warrant.

In 1947, Gardner wrote *High Magic's Aid*, which went into print two years later. In the first edition of this book, he identified himself simply as "Scire, 7 = 4." In 1947, Gardner may not have seen *High Magic's Aid* as a recruiting aid for his own coven, but by the time he wrote *Witchcraft Today* (1954), things were starting to change. Gardner was willing to allege—under his given name—that Witchcraft influenced events *not* back in the late twelfth century, but in 1940. He described how several old Witches had danced skyclad (naked) at Lughnasad without protective grease and that their subsequent deaths were magically involved with Hitler's failure to invade England.

The first Tenth Degree to be awarded after Crowley's death in 1947 was to Karl Johannes Germer, who had worked with Crowley in England, but had returned to his native Germany in the 1930s. Arrested and placed in a concentration camp during a Nazi purge of occultists, Germer was fortunate enough to be deported from Germany in 1941. Arriving in the United States, he sold heavy equipment in New York City. He lived on a fraction of his salary, sending the lion's share of it to Crowley in England so that Crowley could have money with which to survive in his last couple of years. Crowley made him a high initiate in the AA for this, and, at Crowley's death in December 1947, Karl Germer became the heir of his literary estate and the Supreme and Holy King of the OTO. At this point, Parsons refused to recognize Germer's authority and defected from the OTO.

During the 16 years that Germer was the head of the OTO, he apparently did not initiate anyone, and the organization faded—almost to extinction. Kenneth Grant formed the Nu-Isis Lodge of the OTO in London that was, during the 1950s, a hotbed of Thelemic activity. This eventually sent Germer into a paranoid fit, and he expelled Grant from the Order in 1952. The Nu-Isis Lodge continued to prosper on its own.

Germer died in 1962, and did not designate a successor. Karl Metzger (Frater Paraganus) of Basil, Switzerland, was a very respectable member of the OTO and the ranking member of the Order. He became known as the head of the Order, although he was never designated the Supreme and Holy King (Tenth Degree) by anyone, even himself. Germer's wife, Svetlana, presented herself as the head of the Order at this time, but, aside from her marriage to Germer, she had no qualifications for this office. Around 1966, Grady McMurtry retired from the Army and lived modestly on his pension until his death in 1985. Once freed from the regimentation of military life—he worked in the Pentagon for a while—he began to openly promote the OTO. Using the warrant from Crowley given to him in 1946, Grady declared himself head of the Order in the United States in 1969. He rejected the claims of Kenneth Grant, who reemerged as an OTO leader in England in the 1970s, pointing out that Grant had been legally expelled from the Order by Germer in 1952. He also rejected the claims of Metzger in Switzerland, on the grounds that Metzger's election had been spurious according to the OTO rules then in effect.

From around 1976 to 1979, McMurtry performed "battlefield promotions" of several younger protégés to the exalted Ninth Degree of the OTO, although they had not been through the long series of initiations and training generally required. While this created problems within the Order, the OTO in California grew and prospered as never before. By the time of McMurtry's death, there were chapters and lodges across the United States and Canada, as well as in ten other countries. The initial warrant from Crowley may not have quite justified Grady's assumption of the Tenth Degree (Supreme and Holy King), but most OTO members feel that his later actions clearly demonstrated his fitness for it. When Grady declared himself head of the OTO, the Order was virtually dead and had been since Jack Parsons's defection in 1947.

Yet another claimant desiring the office of OHO was Marcelo Ramos Motta, a Brazilian initiate who claimed an essentially spiritual rather than legal authority and who defamed McMurtry and all other OTO members in his new volumes of *The Equinox*. McMurtry sued Motta for libel. The case ended up in the United States Supreme Court, which, in 1985, ruled that McMurtry was, in fact, the legal OHO and owned the copyrights to all of Crowley's writings; the Court threw out all other claims. A key piece of evidence in this legal battle was the fact that the original manuscript of Crowley's *Book of the Law* turned up in a box in a basement in Berkeley.

By the time he died in 1985, Grady had turned the OTO into a dynamic organization with an active membership of several hundred individuals, about half of them in California. One manifestation of this was the Nuit-Urania Coven of the New Reformed Orthodox Order of the Golden Dawn, which practiced "Thelemic Wicca" under the leadership of (among others) the Lady Chandria, who succumbed to cancer in 1988. By then, the OTO reported a membership of 700 in the United States and 1,400 worldwide.

At several points, the OTO developed internal organizations that were, to some extent, "secret" and claimed to carry on the traditions of the old AA. In July 1981, this internal "secret society," called "The Knights of Baphomet," was described as the Caliph's Praetorian Guard. Three or four years later, The Knights of Baphomet fell apart, and the new "inner court" society was called the AA. Lon Milo DuQuette was one of Grady's "battlefield promotion" Ninth Degrees and the head of Heru-Ra-Ha Lodge in Costa Mesa, California, from 1978 on. (In the 1990s, he still was the official head of the lodge, but it has been inactive since about 1988.) DuQuette was given the title "First Emir" by the Caliph (Grady McMurtry) and was, at one point, the prime contender for the next Caliph and the next head of the Order.

Another contender for this position was William Heidrick of Berkeley, California. The contest between DuQuette and Heidrick threatened to tear the organization to shreds. In September 1985 (about three or four months after Grady's death), a compromise candidate who prefers to be known only as Hymenaeus Beta was made head of the OTO, and its headquarters moved to Manhattan. Since that time, the AA became more secretive, and the OTO became "squeaky clean" in its public image. The OTO thoroughly (or at least publicly) de-emphasized the practice of any sort of magic, sexual or otherwise.

In England there are now two major OTO groupings, the "Caliphate" and the "Typhonian," both of which claim to be authentic. The Caliphate is an English branch of the American OTO headed by Hymenaeus Beta. The Typhonian group is headed by Kenneth Grant and produces a periodical, *Starfire*, which is published about once every year or two.

See Also: Fraternitas Rosae Crucis; Hermetic Order of the Golden Dawn; Sex and Sex Magic

Further Reading
Crowley, Aleister. *Magic in Theory and Practice*. New York: Castle, n.d. [ca. 1929].
Hymenaeus Beta, ed. *Equinox*. Vol. III, no. 10. York Beach, ME: Weiser, 1991. This presents the data on recent history, court rulings, and so on.
King, Francis. *Sexuality, Magic, and Perversion*. London: New English Library, 1971.
Parsons, Jack. "The Woman Girt with a Sword." *Green Egg* 100: 25.
Randolph, Paschal Beverly. *Eulis: Affectional Alchemy*, 5th ed. Quakertown, PA: Beverly Hall, Confederation of Initiates, 1930.
Regardie, Israel, ed. *Gems from the Equinox: Selected Writings of Aleister Crowley*. St. Paul, MN: Llewellyn, 1974.
Von Karman, Theodore, with Lee Edson. *The Wind and Beyond: Theodore Von Karman, Pioneer in Aviation and Pathfinder in Space*. Boston, MA: Little, Brown and Co., 1967.

Orishas

Orishas are spiritual beings found in traditional Yoruba (African) religions as well as in several Yoruba-influenced religions, such as Santeria, in the Americas. Like Hinduism, the basic Yoruba worldview is ultimately monistic, postulating a single divine energy behind the apparent diversity of the perceived world. Also like the Hindus, the Yoruba are simultaneously polytheistic, postulating a pantheon of some 400 gods called *orisha*. The Yoruba believe that the orisha were once human beings who led notable lives and who became gods at death. The term *orisha* also can refer to one's individual destiny or "soul" (specifically, one's spiritual double in the other world).

In the syncretistic religious systems of the Western Hemisphere—systems such as Santeria (Cuba) and Candomblé (Brazil) that mix the Yoruba tradition with Catholicism and other religious elements—orishas are retained as important demigods. Catholic saints and angels supplied important models for the role orishas played in these new religions. For example, among the Candomblé it is believed that each person receives two orishas (one male, one female) at birth and these orishas play the role of "guardian angels" for the newly born person. This is clearly a reformulation of the Yoruba Tradition in terms of Western religion.

See Also: African Religions; Candomblé; Fairies; Santeria

Further Reading
Eliade, Mircea. *Encyclopedia of Religion*. Vol. 15. New York: Macmillan, 1987.
Parisen, Maria. *Angels and Mortals: Their Co-Creative Power*. Wheaton, IL: Quest, 1990.

Pagan Academic Networking

In the mid-1990s, after three decades of growth in the United States, and four decades of growth in the United Kingdom, the Neopagan movement began to develop a significant number of younger scholars—with faculty positions at colleges and universities—who are themselves practicing Neopagans of some sort. As a result, scholarly methodology and theological concepts developed in the study of other religions were being applied to Neopaganism and other new religions, with the slightly skeptical but generally favorable attitude toward Neopaganism as a religious movement—just as toward other, more established religions.

For example, Dennis Carpenter (of Circle) neared completion of his Ph.D. program at Saybrook Institute and became steadily more active in the American Academy of Religion (AAR), where his consort, Selena Fox, was already presenting papers. They organized a Pagan Academic Network that met both at Circle's annual Pagan Spirit Gathering and as an adjunct to the annual meeting of the AAR; the first AAR meeting was held in 1993. By 1996, these meetings achieved the first level of recognition as actual AAR meetings themselves.

As another example, Nature Religions Today, the world's first international and interdisciplinary conference on Pagan studies, took place April 9 to 13, 1996, at Charlotte Mason College, the Lake District Campus of Lancaster University in Cumbria, northwestern England. The conference was organized by the Religious Studies Department of Lancaster University, and the 130 participants came from 8 countries in addition to the United Kingdom. The U.S. representatives included Selena Fox and Dennis Carpenter. The conference was inspired by previous conferences at Bath in 1993, and at Newcastle-on-Tyne in 1994, which inspired publication of the recent anthology *Paganism Today*.

See Also: Circle, Magic
Further Reading

Harvey, Graham, and Charlotte Hardman, eds. *Paganism Today: Wiccans, Druids, the Goddess, and Ancient Earth Traditions for the Twenty-First Century*. London and San Francisco: Thorsons, 1996.

Lewis, James R., ed. *Magical Religion and Modern Witchcraft*. Albany, NY: State University of New York Press, 1996.

Pagan Way

The Pagan Way emerged in the United States specifically because various coven leaders anticipated a flood of inquiries spurred by the publication of Susan Roberts's *Witches U.S.A.* in 1971. Existing Witchcraft covens, with traditional intensive screening programs and "year-and-a-day" probationary periods, could not have accommodated a large number of inquiries and applicants. The Pagan Way provided an alternative to the traditional covens, with an open, nature-oriented system that emphasized the celebration of nature over magic and that had no formal initiation or membership requirements.

The three most important figures in the creation of the Pagan Way were probably Joseph B. Wilson, Ed Fitch, and Thomas Giles. Wilson was an American Witch who founded the first Craft journal in America, *The Waxing Moon*, in 1965. While stationed with the U.S. Air Force in England in 1969, Wilson began and coordinated correspondence between 15 to 20 groups and persons interested in establishing an exoteric form of Paganism. The timeliness of his proposal became clear as the implications of Roberts's forthcoming book were examined.

Ed Fitch was a High Priest in the Gardnerian Tradition (easily one of the most important of Raymond and Rosemary Buckland's initiates), at the time stationed with the U.S. Air Force in North Dakota. While serving in the Air Force in Thailand, Fitch wrote two books that were never formally published but that later circulated in the Pagan community and became underground classics: *The Grimoire of the Shadows*, a book of magical training techniques, and *The Outer Court Book of Shadows*, which integrated his knowledge of the magical and seasonal rituals of ancient Crete, Greece, and Druidic Europe with the basic Gardnerian influence. Twenty years later, material from these books still surfaced in new traditions and rituals, sometimes labeled as an "ancient Celtic Tradition from Ireland and Scotland."

Thomas Giles was a Witch of a homegrown American Tradition that began with Olney Richmond, founder of the Order of the Magi in Chicago in the 1890s, and that was passed on to Giles by his mentor, the Chicago bookseller Donald Nelson. In his own practice, Giles began to blend the folk-magic practices of his own tradition with the Gardnerian procedures that came to light—moving more and more toward Gardnerianism because of its usefulness, as apparently all traditional American Witches did.

These three men were apparently also responsible for creating the American Tradition, a form of Witchcraft that was Gardnerian in all but a few oath-bound details and that could serve as a middle ground between the noninitiate religion of the Pagan Way and the rigorous rules of the strict Gardnerians.

Among other key figures on the Committee of Correspondence that created the Pagan Way were Fred and Martha Adler, Witches of the American Tradition in California; John Score (also known as M) of England, who wielded considerable influence on both sides of the Atlantic through his newsletter *The Wiccan*; Thomas DeLong (Gwydion Pendderwen) in California; the leaders of the Regency and Plant Bran (1734 Tradition) covens in Britain; Tony Kelly, a British poet; and Susan Roberts, journalist and author of *Witches U.S.A.*

After four to five months of correspondence, these founders decided on basic principles for the new movement and conceived ideas for rituals. Fitch composed group and solitary rituals based on Celtic and European folk traditions, with some Gardnerian influence, and with Kelly wrote introductory materials. In addition, he composed material for an Outer Court Book of Shadows, to serve as an introduction to Witchcraft, based on the materials he had already written while in Thailand. The material first appeared in *The Waxing Moon*, publication of which Wilson turned over to Fitch and Giles in 1969, when he was transferred to England.

Wilson thought it would be helpful if they had an organization to help get things rolling. The others agreed, but they disagreed on how to do this. Eventually they divided into three "sister" groups: DeLong started Nemeton on the West Coast, Giles and Fitch formed the Pagan Way on the East Coast, and Wilson was the first leader of the Pagan movement in Britain and Ireland.

Fitch and Giles set up mailing centers in Minot, North Dakota, and in Philadelphia, Pennsylvania. The Pagan Way material was so enthusiastically received that they approved the establishment of additional, independent mailing centers. Giles, because he traveled on business, became the "point man"—carrying word of this new development directly to the covens he was in contact with across the United States. The rituals, lore, and background material were never copyrighted but were placed in the public domain in order to gain the widest possible distribution. Over the years, Fitch and Giles have been republished several times by various occult houses under the titles *The Rituals of the Pagan Way* and *A Book of Pagan Rituals*, and perhaps under other titles as well.

The Pagan Way movement received a strong boost in the United States from two of Fitch's colleagues, Lady Morda and Herman Enderle, Gardnerian Witches in Chicago. Morda and Enderle adapted Fitch's material and formed the first formal grove (chapter) in Chicago, Illinois. In Philadelphia, Penny and Michael Novack took over from Giles and formed other groves, which rapidly expanded and spawned more groves in the eastern United States. In the 1970s, Pagan Way groves continued to spread across the United States, primarily in major cities, but also in some small communities. The founders and early organizers let the movement take its own course. No central organization was formed; the groves and mailing centers remained autonomous and loosely affiliated.

There were many solitary followers of the Pagan Way, as it appealed to two main audiences. The first audience was composed of those just getting started in Witchcraft, and the second audience was composed of those interested in attending Pagan ceremonies and structuring social and civic activities around them, much as mainstream churches did.

Some covens of Witches ran Pagan Way groups as training circles for interested persons and potential initiates. Candidates for initiation spent the traditional year and a day in probation, studying the Craft and undergoing evaluation by coven leaders. Not everyone who joined a Pagan Way training circle was initiated into Witchcraft. Those who were not remained in Pagan Way groups for as long as they chose, worked as solitary followers, or formed their own Pagan Way groups.

With the formation of the Covenant of the Goddess in 1975 and with the spread of the festival movement (each festival run by an autonomous local committee), there came to be less and less need for the Pagan Way as an intake device for the Neopagan Witch initiates. By 1980, what little was left of the organization had fallen apart, and groves dwindled in size and number. An ever-changing array of new groups emerged out of Pagan Way and the Pagan Way rituals endured and continue to be used and adapted by those new groups. According to Fitch, the Pagan Way movement was never intended to address the *esoteric* audience of those who wanted initiation and training in the Craft itself. Eventually, adaptations of Pagan Way materials were made for those who wanted more esoteric aspects: Initiation rites were added by Lady Morda, Enderle, and others, and secret, closed Outer Courts were formed that placed more emphasis on magic.

See Also: American Tradition; Gateway Circle

Further Reading

Adler, Margot. *Drawing Down the Moon: Witches, Pagans, Druids, and Other Goddess-Worshippers in America Today*, 2d ed. Boston, MA: Beacon Press, 1986 [1987].

Fitch, Ed, and Janine Renee. *Magical Rites from the Crystal Well*. St. Paul, MN: Llewellyn, 1984.

Roberts, Susan. *Witches U.S.A.* Custer, WA: Phoenix House, 1974 [1971].

Palmistry

The term *palmistry*, also known as *cheiromancy* or *chiromancy*, refers to the art of divination based on the reading of hands. Palmistry is said to reveal character as well as predict an individual's future and is one of the oldest divinatory systems attributed to Witches, village wise women, and gypsies.

Palmistry is closely associated with astrology. Each sign of the Zodiac corresponds to a particular digit, and various parts of the human palm are named after planets. Through the examination of the shape and size of the hand and digits—as well as of the fleshy mounts and the lines on the palms, wrists, and digits—a palmist can "read" a person's character, life expectancy, and destiny.

At birth, the left hand is said to indicate a person's destiny, whereas the right hand shows what has been altered by decisions and actions later in life. The palm of a hand is characterized by several major lines, including the line of the heart (emotions), the line of the head (intellect), the line of Saturn (fate), and the line of health. Numerous smaller lines can represent marriage, and the wristlets or bracelets (the lines around the wrist), denote happiness. Compassion and warmth are indicated by the Mount of Venus, whereas the Mount of the Moon reveals psychic ability.

It is believed that the origins of palmistry can be traced back to 3000 B.C. in China and India, from where the practice spread to Greek and Roman culture. During the Middle Ages, palmistry was regarded as a scientific discipline. It grew in popularity when gypsies arrived in Europe in the fifteenth century. However, by the end of the fifteenth century, palmistry was condemned by the Church because of its widespread use and the deception that often characterized its practitioners. By the early seventeenth century, palmistry had fallen into disgrace as a form of wooly-headed occultism and became a parlor art. The practice of palmistry experienced a revival of interest in the West during the 1960s, and it is practiced by some modern Witches.

See Also: Astrology; Divination
Further Reading
Campbell, Edward D. *The Encyclopedia of Palmistry*. New York: Perigee, 1996.

Parapsychology

The term *parapsychology,* coined in 1889 by the German psychologist Max Dessoir, refers to the scientific study of paranormal and mediumistic phenomena. These phenomena include practically everything beyond those normally understood in terms of physical cause and effect, such as telepathy, clairvoyance, precognition, and psychokinesis. Witchcraft is frequently associated with parapsychology in the popular mind. This association is partly historical—traditionally, anyone manifesting parapsychological powers was regarded as a "Witch." The association is also contemporary, in that modern Witches aim to develop their paranormal abilities.

Among traditional parapsychology's subjects of investigation is the problem of survival—the continuation of the personality after death—which, during the first half of parapsychology's history, was given more attention by investigators than any other issue. This focus was inherited from Spiritualism, a religious movement built around spirit communication that originated in early nineteenth-century America. Interest in spirit communication has always been part of popular culture. In the nineteenth century, the practice of Mesmerism popularized the trance state, encouraging the idea of a psychical ability to communicate with spirits of the deceased during such altered states. Thought transference, hypnosis, and experiments in telepathy provided the first scientific support of the contention that the mind can exist independently of the brain.

See Also: Extrasensory Perception; Hypnosis

A fortune-teller gazes into a crystal ball, one of many phenomena studied by parapsychologists. (Corbis/Hulton-Deutsch Collection)

Further Reading

Cavendish, Richard, ed. *Encyclopedia of the Unexplained. Magic, Occultism, and Parapsychology*. London: Arkana Penguin Books, 1989.
Pratt, J. Gaither. *ESP Research Today: A Study of Developments in Parapsychology since 1960*. Metuchen, NJ: The Scarecrow Press, 1973.

Shepard, Leslie A., ed. *Encyclopedia of Occultism and Parapsychology.* Detroit, MI: Gale Research Inc., 1991.

Zolar's Book of the Spirit. New York: Prentice Hall Press, 1987.

Pendulum

A pendulum is a rod-like device from which a weight is hung by a thread, string, or wire. The suspended weight can be any object, such as a metal plumb, a button, or a coin. It is claimed that the pendulum can "read" energy patterns emanating from beings and objects and communicate that information by swinging back and forth or in circles. This belief is based on the principle that every being and object is characterized by both positive and negative energies. The pendulum can be used by human beings to sense these energies and, consequently, to use the positive energy and avoid the negative energy.

In earlier ages, the pendulum was particularly used in divination. Among the various uses of the pendulum were dowsing or water-witching, a form of divination that is presently employed to find water, minerals, and objects buried in the ground. Pendulums can be used in the search for lost objects, thieves, missing persons, and hidden treasure, as well as in medical diagnosis—termed radiesthesia—and treatment, since pendulums seem to sense the negative energies associated with disease. The pendulum is first adjusted over a healthy part of the body; when moved to an unhealthy area, its movement changes.

Another use of the pendulum is simply to answer questions. Teleradiesthesia, or Superpendulism, is the practice of finding water, lost objects, and so forth by holding a pendulum over a map. This procedure is based on the link that is believed to exist between a location and its symbolic representation on a map. Other uses of the pendulum include geological prospecting and military activities. In World War II, British intelligence forces used pendulums to try to divine Hitler's next moves. Pendulums were also used during the Vietnam War to locate underground mines and tunnels.

See Also: Divination; Dowsing

Further Reading

Shepard, Leslie A., ed. *Encyclopedia of Occultism and Parapsychology.* Detroit: Gale Research Inc., 1991.

Pentagram

The pentagram is a written or drawn five-pointed star. The symbol dates back to ancient Babylon. It is a Cabalistic sign known to occult fraternities derived from the Rosicrucians. Pentagrams were inscribed on doors and windows to keep out evil. Some old Celtic coins had pentagrams on them. The pentagram is regarded as a symbol of magic because its five points represent the four elements of life (water, air, earth, and fire) plus spirit. The point of spirit is the upper point of the star, presiding over the other four. When the pentagram is drawn with its point down it is used for "black magic," representing spirit hidden in matter.

See Also: Amulet; Talismans
Further Reading
Chevalier, Jean, and Alain Gheerbrant. *The Penguin Dictionary of Symbols*. London: Penguin, 1996.

Philtre

A philtre is a love potion. The ingredients of a philtre can range from herbs and plants to the organs of an animal. The most common plant used in a philtre is the root of the mandrake, a member of the poisonous nightshade family. Love potions have been consumed throughout myth and history. Their popularity peaked in the Middle Ages and dwindled through the seventeenth and eighteenth centuries. Every region of the world has its own unique set of ingredients for the potion—from fern seed in England to *shang-luh* in China. Many love potions contain vile-tasting elements and can be difficult to administer; this may be a cause for their waning popularity. Philtres are still used in folk magic, but not in Neopagan Witchcraft. Neopagan Witches consider them to be venal and will only use love potions as a catalyst to a love that already exists.

See Also: Love Spells; Spells
Further Reading
Valiente, Doreen. *An ABC of Witchcraft: Past and Present*. Custer, WA: Phoenix, 1973.

Polarity

The human mind organizes its comprehension of the world into dyadic structures, such that any given concept "makes sense" only in terms of a contrast with its opposite. In other words, "up" has meaning only in contrast with "down" or "dark" in contrast with "light." Thus, there is a close connection between polar opposites, at least at the conceptual level.

Such connections can become the basis for magical operations. With the principle of similarity, for example, the perceived relationship between a person and her or his image in a photograph is the foundation for the belief that doing certain things to the photo will have an impact on the living person. This relationship, which might be expressed as "Lookalikes *are* alike," is the basis for one of the "laws" of magic, the Law of Similarity.

The perceived relationship between opposites is the basis for a "law," the Law of Polarity. In his book on magic, *Real Magic*, Isaac Bonewits discusses polarity in the context of other magical principles, summarizing the Law of Polarity as "everything contains its opposite."

Contemporary Wiccans perceive the broader world in terms of the dynamic relationship between opposites, much like classic Taoism. This stands in contrast to the dominant worldview of the modern West that tends to draw hard, disjunctive boundaries between opposites. Particularly with respect to natural phenomena, Neopagans see events such as night and day or winter and summer as the complementary poles of larger cycles, rather than as mutually exclusive opposites.

See Also: Correspondences; Magic

Further Reading

Bonewits, Isaac. *Real Magic*, 3d ed. York Beach, ME: Weiser, 1989 [1971].
Starhawk [Miriam Simos]. *The Spiral Dance: A Rebirth of the Ancient Religion of the Great Goddess*, 2d ed. San Francisco, CA: HarperSan Francisco, 1989 [1979].

Possession

Possession refers to a state in which a disembodied spiritual entity—whether divinity, demon, or deceased human being—takes control of the body of a living human being. The closest thing to possession in contemporary Neopaganism is a form of ritual mediumship in which the Priest or Priestess acts as an oracle for the god or goddess. Because monotheistic religious traditions tended to view possession as invariably evil, Westerners are most familiar with the concept of demonic possession. However, most other societies that accept the reality of spirit possession believe that one may be possessed by more beneficent beings. In fact, contemporary Witches reject the very notion of demonic possession.

Enthusiasmós (from the Greek *en theos*, "to be in God") and ecstasy characterized the initiation and purification process of the cult of Dionysus in ancient Greece. Women, and to a lesser extent men, who were possessed by the god and surrendered to the possessed state could become free forever. This ritual was widespread in the ancient Hellenistic world and became so popular that in ancient Rome it was legally suppressed in 186 B.C.

This type of phenomenon, known as possession, was not limited to the Mediterranean world. Spirit possession can be found in different forms throughout history and across the world, with somewhat more emphasis in traditional Pacific and indigenous American cultures. But the practice of spirit possession was also widespread in the Western world (famous in medieval times), the Mediterranean region, and Africa. The different social and cultural backgrounds of civilizations determined the variations in ritualization and the values attributed to such an experience from country to country. Being possessed is a phenomenon difficult to define because of its fluidity and

This woman has become possessed after hypnotic chants, dancing, and drumming. The men on either side are assistants to the High Priest, or Houngan, and help guide the woman through the unseen world. (Corbis/Bradley Smith)

many facets. Possession is related to certain forms of dissociation, ritual trance, and similar altered states of consciousness, and it has drawn much attention from anthropologists, psychologists, and religious authorities.

Typically, spirit possession involves a dramatic change in the physiognomy and behavior of the person who hosts the spirit and, historically, it has occurred more among women and the lower classes. Spirit possession was and still is widespread, for example, among South Asian women (who tend to explain their problems as a result of evil spirits) and in the ancestor worship of Vodun ("Voodoo"), Santeria, and certain African religions. In Shamanic cultures, possession is viewed as an integral part of the healing power of the Shaman. When sickness is diagnosed as caused by the loss of the soul in the netherworld, the Shaman performs a ritual in which he or she enters a trance state in order to seek out the lost soul—which has frequently "wandered off" to the realm of the dead (often an underworld). If the rite is successful, the wandering spirit will be persuaded to return, and the ill person will recover.

The ritual trance that leads to spirit possession can be induced through various techniques, such as inhaling the fumes of certain substances (as with the Oracle of Delphi), by ingesting drugs (for example, peyote is used among certain Native American groups) or wine (in Dionysus cults), by rituals involving body techniques (such as hyperventilation, monotonous drumming, dancing, or chanting), or by fasting. Once this altered state of consciousness is created, the host is no longer in a regular state of wakefulness and might, at times, not even remember the experience of possession (the somnambulistic type of possession).

Where possession was viewed as an evil phenomenon, as in traditional Christianity, the practice of exorcism developed to expel the spirit from the host. Outside the Christian Tradition, the possessing spirit was viewed as a neutral entity that could be made benign through specific rituals and religious practices. In modern times, the idea of spirit possession has not been entirely eclipsed by scientific and technological progress and is no longer viewed with the negative connotation of a devilish or destructive force.

In particular, in the mid-nineteenth century a movement known as Spiritualism was based on the consultation of spirits of the dead through seances and mediums. Spiritualism, built on what seemed to be a very scientific methodology (the seances), became a true scientific religion to such reflective individuals as Sir Arthur Conan Doyle (author of *Sherlock Holmes*). Similarly, Spiritism, developed in France by Allan Kardec, emphasized the invocation of spirit guides who could help with the healing of diseases that originated out of a spiritual need.

In more recent times, especially in the New Age milieu, mediums have become channels. There are a number of religious movements that are based on the authority of channeled messages, such as the I AM Religious Activity and the Church Universal and Triumphant (though they would not call their mediumship "channeling"). Since the 1970s a variety of literature has been produced that is directly inspired by spirits, such as *Emmanuel* and *Bartholomew*, which present their perspective on the afterlife and the future of humankind.

Within Christianity, the ecstatic experience of possession by the Holy Spirit (which began with the descent of the Holy Spirit in the form of flames over the apostles after Christ's crucifixion and resurrection in the day of the Pentecost) has been reinstituted by the Pentecostal movement, which recognizes such phenomena as the ability to speak in tongues (glossolalia)—a gift of the Holy Spirit. A residue of the belief in spirit possession is still preserved in the English language in the word *inspired*, from Latin *in spirito*, "being in spirit."

In psychology and psychiatry, spirit possession has been explained in terms of multiple-personality disorders or related disturbances, such as schizophrenia, paranoia, hysteria, and compulsive behaviors. But medicine has not been able to demonstrate psychological problems in all cases of multiple personalities. In fact, in some cases doctors actually admitted that spirit possession may be responsible for multiple-personality disturbances.

One of the more familiar ceremonies in Neopagan Witchcraft is *calling*, or *drawing down the moon*, a ritual in which a coven's High Priestess is "possessed" by the spirit of the Goddess (the moon) and becomes the mouthpiece for the Goddess. The image of drawing down the moon is Greek in origin, and this Neopagan rite is in many ways similar to the activity of the Delphic Oracle, who served as the mouthpiece of Apollo while in a state of trance. Contemporary Neopagan Priests can also be possessed by the God. Parallel to the Priestess, they "draw down the sun."

See Also: Aspecting; Drawing Down the Moon; Exorcism
Further Reading
Bletzer, June G. *The Donning International Encyclopedic Psychic Dictionary*. Norfolk, VA: Donning, 1986.
Guiley, Rosemary Ellen. *The Encyclopedia of Ghost and Spirits*. New York: Facts on File, 1992.
Lewis, James R. *Encyclopedia of Afterlife Beliefs and Phenomena*. Detroit, MI: Gale Research, 1994.

Power Doctor

Power doctor is the name used to describe a faith healer in the Ozark region of the United States. They use magic (charms, potions, amulets, and chants) to heal their clients. Power doctors are consulted for cures of minor illnesses, such as warts, colds, and body aches. Each individual power doctor has a set of favorite cures, with certain potions, rituals, and chants that can be tied to the Bible. Power doctors are similar to the "powwowers" of the Pennsylvania Dutch except for their mode of transferring knowledge of their craft. Power doctors learn their trade from a person of the opposite sex who has no hereditary link to them. The power doctors can only teach a few people or their power begins to wane.

See Also: Amulet; Healing; Magic
Further Reading
Randolph, Vance. *Ozark Magic and Folklore*. New York: Dover, 1964 [Reprint of *Ozark Superstition*. New York: Columbia University Press, 1947].

Power Spots

Among the beliefs common to the New Age movement as well as the occult community is the conviction that particular spots on the Earth possess an excess of spiritual energy that facilitates the practice of disciplines such as medi-

Stonehenge, located in Wiltshire, England, is widely regarded as one of our planet's power spots. (Corbis)

tation and magic. The energy released at the power spots can intensify whatever is brought to their location, and this energy can facilitate transformation.

The origins of the theory of power spots can be traced to occult speculation on the ancient British monolithic culture. In *The Old Straight Track*, Alfred Watkins described a system of straight lines that crossed various parts of the world, aligned with the sun and several star paths. These lines were viewed by later occultists as made of psychic energy, capable of connecting ancient sites of Pagan worship. In more recent years, sites with a strong magnetic deviation have been considered power spots.

There are three categories in which power spots are placed:

1. Spots characterized by an impressive natural scenery, such as Mount Shasta in Northern California, Maui, the Black Hills of South Dakota, and the Grand Tetons.
2. A number of ancient worship sites, such as the ancient Andean town of Machu Picchu, and the nearby Nasca Line on the desert of Peru, as well as Stonehenge, Glastonbury, the Egyptian pyramids, and Chichen Itza in Yucatan.
3. Places considered power spots by the psychic–New Age community, such as Sedona, Arizona, which has become a center of New Age speculation. New Agers consider power spots as places of personal transformation, and a popular activity for New Age groups is to make pilgrimages to sites such as Egypt, Peru, and England.

See Also: Leys
Further Reading
Guiley, Rosemary Ellen. *The Encyclopedia of Witches and Witchcraft*. New York: Facts on File, 1989.

Powwowing

Powwowing is the word chosen by the Pennsylvania Dutch to describe their form of Witchcraft. The Pennsylvania Dutch are German immigrants who came to the United States in the 1700s and 1800s and settled in Pennsylvania. They maintained their culture by remaining reclusive, thus preserving their set of beliefs, including Witchcraft and magic.

They acquired the term *powwowing* from Native Americans, whose powwows they observed and whose way of life they respected. When they first arrived in the United States, the Pennsylvania Dutch received help from Native Americans regarding the flora and fauna of the area.

Powwowing is an ancient Witchcraft mixed with elements from the Bible and Cabala. The powwower's power is a hereditary gift, passed on to both men and women. Legend maintains that the seventh son of the seventh son will carry the powers of extrasensory perception, precognition, and healing. There are two books used as guides to powwowing: The first is *Pow-wows or Long Lost Friend* by John George Hohman. This volume contains recipes for cures, remedies, and charms, some dating back to ancient times. The second book, titled *Seventh Book of Moses*, was written anonymously and contains information from the Talmud, Cabala, and the Old Testament.

Powwowing is against the law in Pennsylvania today—however, it is still practiced. Some powwowers pursue their craft full-time and others pursue it simply as a moonlighting activity. Charging a fee for services is considered unethical, but a powwower can suggest that a contribution be made. Powwowers have different methods of carrying out their work. Some use powders, incantations, or special charms.

See Also: Cabala; Extrasensory Perception; Healing; Magic
Further Reading
Hohman, John George. *Pow-wows or Long Lost Friend*. Brooklyn, NY: Fulton Religious Supply Co., n.d. (first published 1820).
RavenWolf, Silver. *To Ride a Silver Broomstick: New Generation Witchcraft*. St. Paul, MN: Llewellyn, 1996.

Q

Qabalah
See Cabala

Quarter Days

Quarter days were the traditional days in the British Isles (during the Middle Ages and on into early modern times) when quarterly rent was due. The Scottish quarter days were Imbolg or Brigid (February 2), Whitmonday or Lammas (August 1), and Martinmas (November 11). The English quarter days were Lady Day (Feast of the Annunciation on March 25, which was New Year's Day in England until 1752), Midsummer Day, Michaelmas (September 29), and Yule. Currently in the United States, the quarter days are important to Neopagan Witches, who hold their Lesser Sabbats on them. The most common names used by Witches for the Lesser Sabbats are Eostar (spring equinox, about March 22), Litha (summer solstice, about June 22), Mabon (fall equinox, about September 22), and Yule (winter solstice, about December 22). Notice that in either England or Scotland, there were only four quarter days per year. The current Neopagan system of the eight Sabbats that make up the Wheel of the Year cannot be traced back farther than 1957.

See Also: Sabbats; Wheel of the Year
Further Reading
Campanelli, Pauline. *Wheel of the Year: Living the Magical Life*. St. Paul, MN: Llewellyn, 1989.
Kelly, Aidan A. *Religious Holidays and Calendars: An Encyclopedic Handbook*. Detroit, MI: Omnigraphics, 1991.

Quarters

The quarters are the four cardinal directions. In a Neopagan circle, they are often marked by quarter candles. A ritual always begins, after the drawing of the circle with a sword or athame, with the "calling of the quarters," that is, the invocation of the guardian spirits (usually called the Mighty Ones, or the Lords of the Watchtowers) who preside over those directions. The quarters are always included in a coven's system of correspondences.

See Also: Cast; Circle, Magic; Guardians
Further Reading
RavenWolf, Silver. *To Ride a Silver Broomstick: New Generation Witchcraft*. St. Paul, MN: Llewellyn, 1996.

Queen

In the orthodox Gardnerian system, a High Priestess becomes a Queen when she has successfully hived off her first new coven under a new Third-Degree High Priestess. She then becomes eligible to wear the Moon Crown. The sequence of High Priestesses and Queens traced back to Gerald Gardner is known as a lineage, and every orthodox Gardnerian High Priestess has a set of "lineage papers" proving the authenticity of her status.

The bond between a High Priestess and her Queen in the Gardnerian system can be quite strong and provides the tradition with an element of stability that other traditions lack. However, a High Priestess's loyalty to her Queen is voluntary—she is fully empowered to manage her own coven as she sees fit without asking permission from anyone, even her Queen. Hence, a Queen can maintain her leadership over the lineage she has established only by discussion, persuasion, and other noncoercive means. There is no punishment that she can inflict to enforce her authority—aside from "banishing" a person from the Gardnerian Tradition entirely, which destroys her ability to influence that person further in the future.

See Also: Jewelry and Degrees of Initiation; Tradition
Further Reading
Valiente, Doreen. *The Rebirth of Witchcraft*. London: Robert Hale, 1989.
———. *Where Witchcraft Lives*. Wellingborough, Northampshire, U.K.: Aquarian Press, 1962.

A depiction of the Goddess Artemis wearing the Moon Crown associated with the Witch Queen. (North Wind Picture Archive)

R

Radical Faeries

The Radical Faeries are not so much a formal organization or tradition as a network. This network is a manifestation of the perception within the Neopagan movement that gay and lesbian Neopagans have not only the right, but the need, to be as outrageous as they want in order to compensate for the emotional repression they must endure in "straight" society. There is always an element of "costume ball" at a Neopagan festival, and the Radical Faeries take this to an extreme.

One founder of the Radical Faerie movement within Neopaganism is Sparky T. Rabbit of Rock Island, Illinois. Rabbit is half of the duo "Lunacy," whose two cassettes are among what Neopagans generally consider the finest Pagan music produced to date.

Recently, some Radical Faerie Communalists and other Neopagans have worked to create a church sanctuary near Roscoe, New York. There are also the Radical Faeries of Arizona, who can be contacted through *PAN Pipes*, the journal of the Pagan Arizona Network. To avoid confusion, it should be emphasized that the Radical Faeries as such have no relationship to the Fairy Tradition of Victor Anderson.

Further Reading

Adler, Margot. *Drawing Down the Moon: Witches, Pagans, Druids, and Other Goddess-Worshippers in America Today*, 2d ed. Boston, MA: Beacon Press, 1986 [1979].

Reclaiming Tradition

Starhawk is perhaps the best known of the current leaders of the Neopagan movement and is especially noted for having provided the movement with a theory of political action that is, in its way, comparable to the "Social Gospel" movement in American Christianity. She was born Miriam Simos on June 17, 1951, in St. Paul, Minnesota, to Jack and Bertha Simos. She married Edwin W. Rahsman on January 22, 1977. She pursued her undergraduate education at the University of California, Los Angeles (UCLA), receiving a B.A. (*cum laude*) in 1972, with a major in art. She did her graduate study at

A recent photograph of Starhawk, a founder of Reclaiming and one of the best known of the current leaders of the Neopagan movement. (Courtesy of Starhawk)

UCLA in 1973. While in Los Angeles, she studied Witchcraft with Sara Cunningham and Z. Budapest.

Arriving in the San Francisco area in 1973 or 1974, she gave workshops for women in photography, writing, poetry, and feminist thought, and she studied Fairy Tradition Witchcraft with Victor Anderson, who is the source of much of the information in her first book, *The Spiral Dance*. Starhawk remained solitary in her practice of Witchcraft for years before forming her first coven, Compost, from a group of men and women who attended a class in Witchcraft that she taught at the Bay Area Center for Alternative Education in San Francisco from 1975 to 1977. After organizing, the coven performed a formal initiation ceremony. Later, she formed another coven with others, Honeysuckle, which consisted entirely of women. Rituals for both covens were based on the Fairy Tradition.

Compost Coven was one of the original signers of the Covenant of the Goddess in 1975; Starhawk was elected national first officer (president) for the term 1976–1977; Alison Harlow held that position during the first year of the organization's existence. Starhawk taught and was a freelance film writer for industrial training films from 1978 to 1980.

On October 31, 1979, *The Spiral Dance* was published in California on the same day that Margot Adler's *Drawing Down the Moon* was published in New York.

In about 1980, Starhawk was one of the founders of Reclaiming: A Center for Feminist Spirituality and Counseling, in Berkeley, California, a feminist collective that offers classes, workshops, public rituals, and private counseling in the tradition of Goddess religion, and she has served as a director, teacher, and counselor for the collective since then. Starhawk returned to graduate study at Antioch West University from 1980 to 1982, receiving her M.A. in the feminist therapy program, which combined women's studies and psychology. Matthew Fox appointed her as a faculty member of his Institute for Culture and Creation Spirituality at Holy Names College in Oakland, California.

Starhawk described her first book, *The Spiral Dance: A Rebirth of the Ancient Religion of the Great Goddess*, as "an overview of the growth, suppression, and modern-day reemergence of the Old Religion of the Goddess, the pre-Christian tradition known as Paganism, Wicca, or Witchcraft. The book presents the history, philosophy, theology, and practice of this serious and much misunderstood religion, and explores its growing influence on the feminist and ecology movements." It is evident from this statement that she subscribes to the Gardnerian myth of the Craft as a survival from the Witchcraft of medieval times; however, she does not mention Gerald B. Gardner in her book, except in the bibliography, and in general neglects to give credit to many sources of her information.

Starhawk has also said, "*Dreaming the Dark* is a further exploration of the Goddess as a catalyzing symbol of the immanent consciousness that challenges the present social order. My motivation in most of my work has been the integration of a strong feminist vision and commitment to social justice with a strong spiritual search. I was born and raised Jewish, with a strong Hebrew education. Presently, I am a leader of the religion of the Great Goddess, the life force manifest in nature, human beings, and the world. To me the Goddess is a symbol that evokes women's strength and men's nurturing capabilities, and restores deep value to nature, sexuality, and the ecological balance."

See Also: Women's Spirituality Movement
Further Reading

Starhawk [Miriam Simos]. *Dreaming the Dark: Magic, Sex, and Politics*. Boston, MA: Beacon Press, 1982.
———. Interview by Ellen Evert Hopman and Lawrence Bond. In *People of the Earth: The New Pagans Speak Out*. Rochester, VT: Destiny Books, 1996.
———. *The Spiral Dance: A Rebirth of the Ancient Religion of the Great Goddess*, 2d ed. San Francisco, CA: HarperSan Francisco, 1989 [1979].
———. *Truth or Dare: Encounters of Power, Authority, and Mystery*. San Francisco: HarperSan Francisco, 1987.

Reincarnation

There are two basic varieties of belief in immortality: One is based on belief in the concept of an immortal soul; the other on belief in a physical resurrection of the body. Either concept can allow belief in some form of reincarnation, but does not require it.

In order to believe in reincarnation in the sense of rebirth of the personality in a new body, one must logically first believe in the existence of an *immortal soul*, that is, in something that can carry on the personality, memories, or other unique characteristics of the individual to be reborn. If the soul is immortal, one can believe either that the soul comes into existence at a certain moment and then exists forever afterward; or one can believe that the soul has always existed, will always exist, and is simply part of the fabric of reality. Similarly, one can believe that the goal of reincarnation is to stop being reborn—to go on finally to some other state of existence; or one can believe that the process of reincarnation is unending. Furthermore, one can believe that the soul is reincarnated immediately or only after a period of time has passed or that during such a period the soul may remain on Earth or may instead dwell in some other world or plane of existence. Also, one can believe that reincarnation is automatic and mechanical or is controlled by higher beings (or the gods or God)—with the circumstances of rebirth intended to reward the virtues or punish the vices of the previous life. These virtues and vices are sometimes believed to be documented in the akashic records on the akashic plane, one of perhaps many higher planes of existence.

Not all reincarnationists accept that the ultimate goal of reincarnation is to be freed from the "wheel of rebirth." Neopagans, for example, generally believe in reincarnation as a reward for siding with the gods—specifically, that one is reborn among people she or he loves, and that one will remember them and love them again. Some Neopagans believe that there probably are two kinds of souls, both mortal and immortal. According to this belief, all souls begin as mortal, but can be transformed into immortal souls by certain kinds of initiatory experiences and spiritual growth; when the uninitiated die, their mortal souls simply cease to exist.

See Also: Karma
Further Reading

Head, Joseph, and S. L. Cranston, eds. *Reincarnation in World Thought*. New York: Julian Press, 1967.
Lewis, James R. *The Encyclopedia of Afterlife Beliefs and Phenomena*. Detroit, MI: Gale Research Inc., 1994.
Osborn, Arthur. *Superphysical: A Review of the Evidence for Continued Existence, Reincarnation, and Mystical States of Consciousness*. New York: Barnes and Noble, 1974.

Rings

Rings have been symbols of power and protection since ancient Babylon. Ancient Egyptians and Hebrews wore signet rings inscribed with specific phrases, words, or symbols. This tradition was passed on to secular and religious authorities throughout Europe. During the medieval era, rings were blessed by the monarch and were doled out to prevent illness. This idea originated in England and eventually spread through most of Europe. Witches wear rings, usually made of silver, with inscriptions of runes, names of power, symbols of gods and goddesses, or other related images. Rings made of precious metals inlaid with a precious stone take on the characteristics of the stone. These rings can protect against death and evil doings and promote good health.

See Also: Amulet; Talismans

Further Reading

Chevalier, Jean, and Alain Gheerbrant. *The Penguin Dictionary of Symbols*. London: Penguin, 1996.

Cooper, J. C. *An Illustrated Encyclopedia of Traditional Symbols*. London: Thames and Hudson, 1992 [1978].

Rite, Ritual

One of the characteristics of Neopaganism that sets it apart from other new religious movements is its explicit emphasis on ritual. It would, in fact, be difficult to imagine contemporary Neopaganism without rituals. This emphasis on ritual appears to derive primarily from the centrality that Margaret Murray gave to magic and magical workings in her attempt to reconstruct a picture of the pre-Christian religion of Europe from Inquisition records. Based on their familiarity with ceremonial magic and the rituals of Freemasonry, it would have been natural for the New Forest group from which modern Wicca derives to have drawn from these ritualistic models in their efforts to re-create the "Old Religion."

For a variety of different reasons, however, the word *ritual* has acquired negative connotations. Specifically, a "ritual" is a dead relic from the past— something that is performed only because it is a tradition, without feeling, enthusiasm, or even an understanding of the meanings that the ritual is supposed to convey. This negative definition of ritual seems to have derived at least partially from the Protestant Reformation, which criticized Roman Catholicism as being "ritualistic." This connection is implicit in the remarks of some critical observers of Neopagan Witchcraft, who asserted that a disproportionate number of Neopagans come from Roman Catholic backgrounds (an assertion that has been disproven by empirical studies) because of their need for a *ritualistic* religion. However, the rituals of the modern Neopagan movement are evocative and meaningful for participants—rather than the "dead rituals" of the popular stereotype.

The components of a typical Wiccan ritual are discussed in such popular books as Starhawk's *The Spiral Path* and Silver RavenWolf's *To Ride a Silver*

Broomstick (see also the introduction to this book). Almost all such rituals are framed by the construction ("casting") of a circle of sacred space. This typically involves invoking the directions and charging the circle with the four elements (earth, air, fire, and water). The group then proceeds to invoke the deities; to carry out acts of magic, worship, or initiation; to dismiss and thank the divinities; and then to deconstruct the circle.

Although the sometimes elaborate process of casting and closing the circle may strike observers as excessive and unnecessary, this process represents the construction and taking down of the Witches' portable temple, involving considerably less time and resources than a permanent church or synagogue. One should also note that, unlike most traditional rituals, Neopagans generally feel free to innovate, particularly in the spoken part of the liturgy (with the exception of orthodox Gardnerians). Rituals thus represent a kind of art form for the Neopagan movement.

See Also: Book of Shadows; Cast; Freemasonry
Further Reading

RavenWolf, Silver. *To Ride a Silver Broomstick: New Generation Witchcraft.* St. Paul, MN: Llewellyn, 1996.
Starhawk [Miriam Simos]. *The Spiral Dance: A Rebirth of the Ancient Religion of the Great Goddess,* 2d ed. San Francisco, CA: HarperSan Francisco, 1989 [1979].

Runes

The term *runes* usually refers to the alphabets devised in northern Europe by the Nordic and Celtic peoples. The Norse runes are sometimes called the F-U-T-H-A-R-K, those being the first letters in that alphabet. The Irish runes are usually called Ogham, and were said to have been devised by Ogma Sunface, the Celtic culture hero similar to the Egyptian Thoth. Despite claims about the originality of these systems of writing, current scholars tend to agree that, like the systematizing of the Irish and Nordic myths, these systems were based directly on imitation of Greek and Latin models.

The major interest in the runes these days is not, however, in terms of their history, but in terms of how they can be used as a system of divination. The classical authors who mention the runes state that they were used for divination, but give no details of how that was carried out. This unfortunate gap in our knowledge has been filled during the last 20 years by numerous authors, who have advanced detailed and immensely practical systems for divination by means of the runes. Sets of runes carved on small wooden or stone blocks, plus an instruction manual explaining how to cast and interpret them, can now be purchased in most chain bookstores in shopping malls. Those whose intuitive gifts are consistent with the runes say they are just as useful as astrology, palmistry, clairvoyance, or any other system that peers into another's soul in order to give that person spiritual counseling.

See Also: Asatru; Norse Neopagans

Further Reading

Davidson, H. R. Ellis. *Myths and Symbols in Pagan Europe*. Syracuse, NY: Syracuse University Press, 1988.

Guiley, Rosemary. *The Encyclopedia of Witches and Witchcraft*. New York: Facts on File, 1989.

Sabbats

The eight Sabbats of the "Wheel of the Year" are the major holidays celebrated by members of the various Neopagan religions (by far the largest of which is the Gardnerian-style Witch Tradition). These Sabbats have emerged in the United States since the mid-1960s. They are usually supplemented with a few of the most important holidays peculiar to the (usually) ancient Pagan religion to which a local coven or family of covens is partial. The most popular ancient religious traditions are the Celtic, Greek, Mesopotamian, Egyptian, and Nordic, in roughly that order.

The eight Sabbats fall into two subgroups: the Greater Sabbats (the Celtic cross-quarter days) and the Lesser Sabbats (the English quarter days—that is, the solstices and equinoxes). The most common names used by Witches for the Greater Sabbats are Brigid (February 1), Beltane (May 1), Lughnasad (August 1), and Samhain (pronounced "sa-oo-en," November 1), and those for the Lesser Sabbats are Eostar (spring equinox, about March 22), Litha (summer solstice, about June 22), Mabon (fall equinox, about September 22), and Yule (winter solstice, about December 22).

In a Gardnerian-type coven, which meets for an Esbat at each full moon during the year, each Sabbat is observed by means of a special ritual that is inserted in the middle of the coven's ordinary working ritual. Hence, there is a set of eight such special rituals in a coven's Book of Shadows (in effect, its liturgical manual); the other four or five Esbats during the year use the basic ritual.

Almost every religious body in the world (except for the Muslims, whose calendar is totally unrelated to the solar year) has at least one major holiday that falls on or fairly near a solstice or equinox. The changes in the sun during the course of each year are fairly dramatic in most latitudes, and are therefore discussed in the myths and rituals of most cultures. Stonehenge proves that formal marking of the solstices goes back about 5,000 years in Britain. It is in this sense that modern Witches claim that their Sabbats are the "original" or "oldest" holidays known to humankind.

See Also: Book of Shadows; Esbat; Wheel of the Year

Goya's famous painting of a Witches' Sabbath. (Giraudon/Art Resource, NY)

Further Reading

Farrar, Stewart, and Janet Farrar. With notes by Doreen Valiente. *Eight Sabbats for Witches*. London: Robert Hale, 1981.

Rees, Aylwin, and Brinsley Rees. *Celtic Heritage: Ancient Tradition in Ireland and Wales*. London: Thames and Hudson, 1961. On the nature of Celtic beliefs about time, see esp. pp. 83–94 and 342–351.

Sacrifice

The word *sacrifice* derives from the Latin *sacrificium*—a victim killed and consumed on the altar. The victim is an object or animal that has been made *sacer*—holy—by being entirely devoted to a god. Therefore, a sacrifice is something consecrated to a deity, as a mode of communication between humanity and the unseen powers and an expression of intentions in relation to those powers. A sacrifice may be offered as a gift, as an act of atonement, or as an act of fellowship and communion. In some religions sacrifices are also made to the elements, the sun and the moon, the cardinal points, sacred landmarks, ghosts, and other supernatural beings.

Among the most popular gifts are food, drink, fruits of harvest, and the blood sacrifice of animals and fowl. The sacrifice of human life is now rare—contemporary Neopagans regard blood sacrifice as an abomination. In Neopagan Witchcraft, gifts are represented by such "nonbloody" offerings as cakes, drinks, fruit, flowers, poems, handicrafts, incense, and nuts. These offerings are generally presented at the altar or sprinkled about outdoors.

The locations of sacrifices vary greatly. In traditional cultures, for instance, they were performed by natural sites of peculiar sanctity, such as caves, hills, and groves, or tombs of the powerful dead. However, with the advent of urban civilization, the necessity to find a sacred place in the city led to the construction of temples, where the gods were worshipped and sacrifices were offered.

In Christian liturgy, the Eucharist and Communion services symbolize the sacrifice of the body and blood of Jesus Christ. Blood sacrifice has been practiced in most ancient religious rites as a form of propitiation to the gods and to secure generous harvests. The association of blood with sacrifice is significant, since blood has always been regarded as the bearer of life. Thus, special measures were sought to consecrate the blood of a sacrificial animal to the deity. In Viking sacrifices, blood was frequently spread on the participants.

Similar practices are found in many other religions, even in ancient Israel, where sprinkling blood on the altar was preliminary to burning a sacrificial animal. The sacrificial practices of the early Hebrews are familiar to the West through the Hebrew Scriptures (the Old Testament). The Paschal Lamb, eaten at Passover, represents a sacrifice celebrating the rescue of the Israelites from Egypt.

Blood from animals, fowl, or humans was believed to give one who drank it the soul and features of the sacrificed being. In ceremonial magic, blood sacrifices are believed to release a flash of power that can be used by a magician for a spell or conjuration. In order to release the maximum energy, an animal offered to a god or various demons should be young, healthy, and a virgin.

Among those who sacrificed human beings were the Celts and Druids, who drank the blood of their victims; Aztecs, who often ate the dismembered body of the victims as an act of ritual cannibalism; and Khonds of southern India, who fertilized the soil with pieces of the bodies of the victims. The sacrifice of firstborn children was common in several cultures, such as among the nobility of Carthage during the Punic Wars. The sacrifice of unbaptized children to the devil was part of the negative stereotype of Witches during the Witch hunts of the Renaissance and Reformation. Witches also were charged with the cannibalism of infants and children.

Animals are sacrificed in a number of contemporary tribal religions, as well as such contemporary syncretisms as Vodun and Santeria. Santerians, who traditionally sacrifice fowl, lambs, and goats and leave the remains in public places, have been harshly criticized by animal-rights groups. Various attempts have been made to forbid animal sacrifices. Santerians have justified the performance of animal sacrifice by the fact that the act is both ancient and ubiquitous in world culture. Finally, it should be noted that part of the negative stereotype of Satanists (and, in the minds of some conservative Christians, contemporary Witches as well) is that they practice blood sacrifices of both animals and humans. However, no group of organized Satanists, much less of Neopagan Witches, has ever been apprehended for carrying out such sacrifices.

See Also: Santeria; Satanism; Vodun
Further Reading

Eliade, Mircea, ed. *The Encyclopedia of Religion*. 16 vols. New York: Macmillan, 1987.
Miller, Timothy, ed. *America's Alternative Religions*. Albany, NY: State University of New York Press, 1995.

Salamanders

Salamanders, not to be confused with the amphibians by the same name, are fairy-like creatures associated with the element of fire. They are said to be "fiery" beings who appear as lizards and are said to reside deep in the Earth and in fires. They are responsible for all fires, from the tiniest match strike to the most dramatic volcano eruption. In the Occult Tradition, fire is associated with activity and with the quality of inspiration, and fire elementals (Salamanders) are said to work with human beings to maintain their vitality, inspiration, and enthusiasm.

Salamanders are the archetypal spirits of the fire element and, as such, are occupied with maintaining the heat of the Earth. In magic, Salamanders are the fire elementals of one of the directions (usually south) that are invoked in rituals. The task of the elementals is to build forms in the natural world. While some occultists view elementals as soulless entities that simply disappear at death, others view them as spirits who eventually evolve into devas (angels). Due to their association with fire, Salamanders are under the rule of the archangel Michael.

See Also: Fire; Gnomes; Sylphs; Undines
Further Reading
Andrews, Ted. *Enchantment of the Faerie Realm: Communicate with Nature Spirits and Elementals*. St. Paul, MN: Llewellyn, 1993.
McCoy, Edwin. *A Witch's Guide to Faery Folk*. St. Paul, MN: Llewellyn, 1994.

Salem Witches

The so-called Salem Witches were the protagonists of one of the last episodes of Witchcraft hysteria. The relevant events took place in Salem—now Danvers—Massachusetts, from 1692 to 1693.

Upon his return from Barbados, where he had worked as a merchant, the Reverend Samuel Parris, minister of the Puritan Church of Salem, brought back a slave couple, John and Tituba, to Massachusetts. Tituba, who cared for Parris's 9-year-old daughter, Elizabeth, and his 11-year-old niece, Abigail Williams, soon began to tell them stories about her native Barbados, including tales of "voodoo." The girls were fascinated with the subject and were joined by other girls in the village, ranging from age 12 to 20. They told each other's fortunes and tried to discover what the trades would be of their future husbands through a primitive crystal ball (made by floating an egg white in a glass of water). It was said that one little girl saw the likeness of a coffin in the crystal ball, representing death. Beginning with Betty Parris in January 1692, the girls began having fits, crawling into holes, making strange noises, and contorting their bodies.

The Reverend Parris consulted the village physician, Dr. William Griggs, who could find no medical precedent for the girls' condition. He diagnosed the girls as bewitched, since it was believed that Witchcraft was among the causes of illness and death. It was also believed that Witches derived their power from the devil. Thus, it became necessary to find the Witch or Witches responsible for the girls' strange behavior, exterminate the Witches, and thus cure the girls. Unwilling to admit their own complicity with Tituba's magic, the girls gave the names of other supposed Witches.

Tituba, who was afraid to reveal the story sessions and conjurings, confessed to being a Witch. She also claimed that a black dog had threatened her and ordered her to hurt the girls, and that there was a coven of Witches in Massachusetts, about six in number, led by a tall, white-haired man dressed all in black. The Witch hunts began as soon as more Witches were named. Among them were Martha Corey, a member of the Salem village congrega-

The Salem Witch panic began innocently enough when the slave woman Tituba taught a few "magic tricks" to several young girls in her care. (North Wind Picture Archive)

tion; Rebecca Nurse, one of the most respected members of her community and church; and John and Elizabeth Proctor, tavern-keepers and vocal opponents of the proceedings.

The accused remained in prison, often languishing in irons, without a formal trial, until May 1692, when the new Royal Governor Sir William Phips established a Court of Oyer and Terminer to try the Witches. During the course of the trials, 141 people were arrested as suspects, 19 were hanged, and 1 was pressed to death. The bodies of the sentenced Witches were casually placed in shallow graves on Salem's Gallows Hills because, it was believed, Witches did not deserve Christian burials. According to legend, the ghosts of the victims still haunt the area even today. The causes of the Salem Witch-hunt trials, examined by a number of studies, have variously been attributed to the political and social problems of Salem village.

Further Reading

Cahill, Robert Ellis. *The Horrors of Salem's Witch Dungeon*. Peabody, MA: Chandler-Smith, 1986.

Demos, John Putnam. *Entertaining Satan*. New York: Oxford University Press, 1982.

Salt

Salt has long been used as a symbol of purity and as a substance to ward away evil spirits. In Christianity, salt is associated with eternity and divine protection. Salt and holy water are used to bless church sites, to baptize a person, to protect unbaptized babies prior to baptism, and to protect the dead in their journey from Earth to the next world.

Witches and demons were traditionally said to be repelled by the presence of salt. It was used as protection against Witchcraft and the evil eye, and was even said to have the power to break evil spells. When trying to conjure demons or spirits, it was recommended that one avoid salt, as it could interfere with the connection. Salt has been utilized in regard to those accused or suspected of being Witches. Feeding the accused heavy doses of salt was used as a form of torture. Women were suspected of being Witches when they complained that their food was overly salty.

When one spills, borrows, or runs out of salt, it is considered unlucky and is said to make one susceptible to the powers of the devil. It is believed possible to negate this situation by pinching salt in the right hand and tossing it over the left shoulder.

See Also: Earth; Spirit
Further Reading

Chevalier, Jean, and Alain Gheerbrant. *The Penguin Dictionary of Symbols*. London: Penguin, 1996.
Cooper, J. C. *An Illustrated Encyclopedia of Traditional Symbols*. London: Thames and Hudson, 1992 [1978].

Samhain

Samhain (pronounced "sa-oo-en") is the Gaelic name for the month of November. It is also the ancient Celtic New Year's Eve and Festival of the Dead, as well as one of the cross-quarter days, on which the Greater Sabbats are celebrated.

The Celtic belief was that the boundary between this world and the other world—the world of fairies, gods, spirits, and magic—was at its weakest on this night. Hence, they believed that all manner of nonhuman beings could slip through the boundary into this world on this evening. The spirits of one's own departed ancestors, as well as divine, semidivine, semi-demidivine, or perhaps just hellish beings (none of whose intentions toward the living could be trusted) might appear on Samhain. All the customs of this night were directed toward understanding and propitiating these spirits by divining their wills, by giving them what they wanted, by identifying with them, and by protecting one's family and friends against them.

These customs are duplicated in the Hallowe'en ritual of "trick-or-treat": Children go from door to door, signaled that they are welcome by the lit "jack-o'-lantern" placed in front of the house. They wear costumes resembling these untrustworthy spirits and demand to be appeased with candy. The children will work some trick—some "magic trick"—on anyone who turns them away without the required loot.

All Hallows' Eve, or Hallowe'en (that is, the evening before All Saints' Day), on October 31, is one of the best-known holidays in the United States. The tricks and practical jokes once associated with this date are generally things of a past generation, save perhaps among college fraternities. In British Commonwealth countries, these customs were replaced by Guy Fawkes's Day in the seventeenth century.

The Sabbats of Neopagan Witches on this night now tend to honor the dead: calling out the names of those who have passed on, remembering what they did in life, asking the gods to grant them a worthy rebirth. It is not totally different in purpose from honoring All Saints and All Souls.

Several important festivals take place annually at Samhain. These include the Samhain Festival sponsored by the Council of the Magical Arts, held in Bellaire, Texas, on the weekend nearest November 1; and the Samhain Seminar, sponsored by the Church and School of Wicca and held in Durham, North Carolina (usually), every year since 1972. The Reclaiming Coven's Spiral Dance, in San Francisco, California, is possibly the largest open (public) Sabbat in the United States, with more than 2,000 participants each year.

See Also: Sabbats; Wheel of the Year
Further Reading
Edwards, Leila Dudley. "Tradition and Ritual: Hallowe'en and Contemporary
    Paganism." In Harvey, Graham, and Charlotte Hardman, eds., *Paganism Today:*
    Wiccans, Druids, the Goddess, and Ancient Earth Traditions for the Twenty-First
    Century. London and San Francisco: Thorsons, 1996, 224–241.

Sanctuaries and Temples

There is an important trend in the Neopagan movement toward the establishment of sanctuaries and temples. There are a small but growing number (now about a dozen) of nature sanctuaries: land permanently dedicated for no other purpose than the worship of nature deities. These sanctuaries are not open to the general public, but can be used by visiting Neopagans and friends who have been properly introduced with the proper credentials. (The general public is generally excluded from entry to these sanctuaries by the "by invitation only" policy in an effort to keep out certain conservative Christians who do not respect these "sacred spaces." Instances of disrespect and even wanton destruction of these places of worship are not unheard of.) The major use of the land is the celebration of the Sabbats during warm weather, but the sanctuaries are available for uses compatible with the Neopagan ethos: for example, for spiritual-development retreats. Some groups that maintain such sanctuaries attempt to reconstruct Greek, Roman, or other ancient Pagan religious observances.

Temples are actually what most Americans would call a church: a building dedicated for use as a place of worship and where there is a weekly liturgy (usually on Friday or Saturday night, rather than Sunday morning) that is open to the public. The use of temples is considered a radical innovation, and not necessarily a welcome one, by many in the Craft. To understand this, consider the preexisting situation. The Esbat of a coven is utterly private; in order even to hear that one is going to occur, a person needs to know members of a coven well enough that he or she could be considered for membership. This person could be invited to an Esbat only with the permission of the coven's reigning elders. The rules for a coven's Sabbat celebration are not much different.

Some Sabbats are more public. Such a Sabbat might be held in a rented hall or out in a park, many Witches would invite friends to it, and it would mainly be a gathering of the local covens—it would typically (these days) be sponsored by the local Neopagan association to which the various covens belong. Often, one member coven will take responsibility for the creation and performance of the liturgy at a Sabbat, and this task rotates through the local covens each year. Most of the local councils of the Covenant of the Goddess carry out this function.

These "open" Sabbats are not advertised. To be invited to one, a person must already be in contact with the sponsoring network. Similarly, the national festivals are not advertised except through the network of Neopagan publications, which are normally available only by subscription, though a few are beginning to be sold through bookstores. The *Green Egg* mailing list includes more than 500 periodicals at last count.

Hence, finding a Neopagan temple in the Yellow Pages and simply walking in to participate in the weekly liturgy is a vastly different experience from that of traditional Neopagans. Neopagan temples (even more than the festivals) seem to be creating a Neopagan laity: people who consider themselves members of the religion, but not the clergy, and who do not call themselves Witches. And whatever the word *Witch* might mean to people in other contexts, it is clear that, to the members of the Neopagan movement, a Witch is a Neopagan clergyperson (although they may also use another term for this); and they do not use the word *Witch* with any other meaning.

See Also: Sabbats; Rite, Ritual
Further Reading
Harvey, Graham, and Charlotte Hardman, eds. *Paganism Today: Wiccans, Druids, the Goddess, and Ancient Earth Traditions for the Twenty-First Century.* London and San Francisco: Thorsons, 1996.

Santeria

Santeria is a magical religion that had its origins among the Yoruba people of West Africa. In the early nineteenth century, the Yoruba were enslaved in great numbers and taken to Cuba and Brazil, where they formed Yoruba-speaking communities. Yoruba Priests and Priestesses created new lineages of initiates dedicated to the Yoruba spirits, called orishas (from the Spanish *santos*). Thus, Yoruba traditions in Cuba were called *Santeria*, "the way of the saints."

Since the Cuban revolution of 1959, over one million Cubans have come to the United States, many of them Priests and Priestesses of Santeria. Particularly in New York and Miami, but also in other large North American cities, Cuban immigrants have reestablished houses for the veneration of the African spirits.

Santeria recognizes a remote and almighty Supreme Being who is best understood as a personification of fate or destiny. In Santeria, God is invoked by the Yoruba title *Olodumare*, the "Owner of all Destinies." Individuals are given their own destinies by Olodumare. In order to fulfill these destinies with grace and power, an individual requires guidance from a variety of orishas. Trained Priests and Priestesses consult oracles to determine the sacrificial foods and actions necessary to secure the power and presence of an orisha. One particular orisha will begin to assert itself as an individual devotee's patron. If the spirit wills it, the devotee will undergo an irrevocable initiation into the mysteries of his or her patron spirit. This initiation constitutes the member's entry into the Priesthood of Santeria and gives the authority to the member to found his or her own house and consecrate other Priests and Priestesses.

The spirits are venerated through a variety of symbolic media. The most dramatic media for the orishas are the bodies of their human devotees, who, in the midst of the proper combination of rhythms and songs, lose individual consciousness and manifest the divine personalities of the spirits.

When Santeria first was brought to the United States by Cuban immigrants, the appeal of the religion was primarily to fellow immigrants who were familiar with the traditions in their homeland. The traditions were maintained primarily by poor and black Cubans despite brutal campaigns of suppression.

In the United States, the houses of the spirits offered cultural survival, mutual aid, and spiritual fulfillment. Santeria houses provided natural community centers where Priests and Priestesses trained as diagnosticians and herbalists and created avenues for health care in the new environment. The houses offered ways of aligning the individual with the force of the orishas in order to secure a job, win a lover, or take revenge on an injustice. The houses also offered spiritual opportunities to a variety of outsiders who came in contact with the traditions for the first time in the United States.

One influential nonimmigrant initiate of African traditions is an African American whose name at birth was Walter Eugene King. King rejected the Baptist Church in which he was raised. He was involved in the African Nationalist movements in New York City in the 1950s and was looking for a spirituality that would speak to black men and women. He found it among his Cuban neighbors in Harlem. In 1955, King founded the Order of Damballah Hwedo Ancestor Priests. He went to Cuba in 1959 and was initiated into the Orisha-Vodun African Priesthood. Upon his return to the United States, the Order of Damballah became the Shango Temple, later renamed the Yoruba Temple.

In 1970, King Efuntola, as Walter King was known by then, moved with most of the temple members to rural South Carolina, where the Yoruba village of Oyotunji was established. He began to reform the Orisha-Vodun Priesthood along Nigerian lines. In 1972, King Efuntola traveled to Nigeria and was initiated into the Ifa Priesthood. When he returned he was proclaimed oba-king of Oyotunji. In 1973, King opened the first parliament of Oyotunji chiefs and landowners and founded the Priests' Council. These two groups made the rules for the entire community and attempt to adhere to African patterns. A palace for the King and his seven wives and many children was constructed. In addition, there are temples dedicated to several deities. Only Yoruban is spoken before noon each day. In 1981, King was invited to a convention of Orisha-Vodun Priests at Ile-Ife, Nigeria, and was coronated by the King of Ife.

Practices of the Yoruba system include animal sacrifice, polygamy, ecstatic dancing, and the appeasement of the gods by various offerings. Worship venerates the deities and is also directed toward ancestors, the closest level of spiritual forces to individuals. There are over 50 residents of Oyotunji, with 19 affiliated centers in the Unites States and 10,000 reported members.

Santeria has been taught orally in the face-to-face context of initiation. The teachings are secret and available only to those who have been chosen by elders to receive them. With the arrival of the traditions in the mobile and unstable social environment of North American cities, more and more charlatans are pretending to be Priests and Priestesses. They often demand large sums of money for bogus services. As a solution to this problem, an increasing number of Santeria houses produce texts for the instruction of their initiates and for the education of outsiders.

The most controversial element of Santeria in the eyes of outsiders is the slaughter of animals as part of feasts for the orishas. Most of the more important ceremonies require a feast to be prepared for the spirits and to be enjoyed by the assembled community. In order to prepare the meal to the spirit's specifications, the food must be prepared and cooked according to strict recipes and must be properly consecrated with certain prayers and chants. Animals for the feast must be slaughtered by a Priest or Priestess (initiated specially for this task) in the presence of the community and to the accompaniment of the correct chants. This insistence on animal slaughter caused a number of problems in the urban centers of the United States, particularly in the crowded neighborhoods of New York and Miami. Problems with the storage of the animals before the ceremony and the disposal of the remains afterward spurred concerns on the part of municipal authorities.

In 1987, the city of Hialeah, Florida, enacted a ban against animal sacrifice directly aimed at the growing Santeria community of the city. One Santeria house decided to challenge the ban and brought the case before the Supreme Court in 1992. In June 1993, the Supreme Court unanimously declared the Hialeah ordinances unconstitutional.

Santeria has taken a different course in Brazil than in the United States. Umbanda is a syncretic religion in Brazil that uses the images of the orishas to construct and unify the theology of the European, African, and Indian heritages of Brazil. Since its formulation in Rio de Janeiro in the 1920, Umbanda has grown to be considered the national religion of Brazil, with thousands of independent houses throughout the country. Umbanda's rituals are much-simplified versions of the corresponding African rituals. Umbanda eschews the more controversial elements of other African-derived traditions, such as secret teachings and animal sacrifice. Umbanda's rejection of animal sacrifice is already being adopted by reformist houses in the United States.

See Also: African Religions; Candomblé; Macumba; Vodun
Further Reading
Hunt, Carl M. *Oyotunji Village*. Washington, D.C.: University Press of America, 1979.
Murphy, Joseph M. "Santeria and Vodou in the United States." In Miller, Timothy, ed., *America's Alternative Religions*. Albany, NY: State University of New York Press, 1995.

Satanism

Satanism, the worship of the Christian devil, has traditionally been associated with a number of practices that parody Roman Catholic Christianity. Among its rituals is the black mass, which usually includes the profaning of the central acts of worship, the repeating of the Lord's Prayer backwards, the use of a host that has been dyed black, and the slaughter of an animal. The worship usually culminates with the invocation of Satan for the working of malevolent magic.

Satanism, as described above, appeared in the fifteenth century, when its practitioners became subject to the Inquisition's action. The first well-documented case of a devil-worshipping group refers to the courtiers around Louis XIV, who used "black magic" in an attempt to remain in favor with the king. The practice almost brought down the government when it was discovered.

Although Satanist groups were quite rare prior to the 1960s, Satanism provided a rich variety of imaginative material for novels and horror movies. Among the most famous are those by British novelist Dennis Wheatley, who developed the theme of an ancient, worldwide, secret, and powerful Satanic society that regularly gathered its conspiratorial forces to attack the structures of order and goodness. However, such novels do not reflect an existing social phenomenon; no large organized Satanist movement or group exists, as an examination of all evidence shows.

Although Satanists produced almost no literature prior to the 1970s, their tradition was created and sustained by generation after generation of anti-Satanist writers—above all conservative Christians—who authored a number of books about Satanism, describing its practices in great detail (although none of those authors had ever seen a Satanist ritual or met a real Satanist). The Satanism portrayed in the Christian literature has been reproduced by groups and individuals over the last two centuries.

Since the early 1970s, the number of incidences of ritual remains found in graveyards, churches vandalized, and mutilated bodies of animals discovered increased, indicating a rise in the amount of Satanic activities. During the 1980s, emphasis shifted to the "New Satanism" and the emergence of the accounts by several hundred women who claimed to have been survivors of Satanic ritual abuse.

The forms of Satanism existing in the 1990s include a traditional Satanism—consisting of ephemeral groups of teenagers and young adults—and a new form of Satanism initiated by Anton LaVey and developed in various directions by several groups that split off from his Church of Satan. The Church of Satan originated from an attempt to reorganize modern occult and magical teachings around a Satanic motif. The Church of Satan preaches a philosophy of individual pragmatism and hedonism, rather than emphasizing the worship of Satan. It promotes the development of strong individuals who seek gratification out of life and who practice the selfish virtues without the intention of harming others.

All the formal trappings of an organized religion were created for the movement by its founder, Anton LaVey (born in 1930), who read occult books as a teenager. He developed a deep fascination for magic, such as the creation of change in the world through the use of cosmic powers that were controlled by an individual's will. He worked in the circus and, in the 1960s, he held informal meetings on magic. Finally, on April 30, 1966, he announced the formation of the Church of Satan, with some members of the magic groups among its first members.

In 1967, the church received the attention of the media when LaVey performed the first Satanic wedding and a funeral for a sailor. Membership grew rapidly, though the active membership was rarely over 1,000. In 1969, LaVey published the first of three books, *The Satanic Bible*, containing the perspective of the Church of Satan. It was followed by *The Compleat Witch* (1970) and *The Satanic Rituals* (1972). He also worked as a consultant for the movie industry, becoming the occult advisor on several films, such as *Rosemary's Baby*, in which he appears briefly as the devil.

In the Church of Satan the most important date on the calendar is an individual's birthday. By the 1970s, the Church of Satan had a national membership, with groups in many cities around the United States. At one time it was considered the largest occult organization in America, counting its active membership in the hundreds. *The Cloven Hoof*, edited by LaVey, was the newsletter of the church.

The Church of Satan was a rich source of splinter groups. In 1973, the Church of Satanic Brotherhood was formed by group leaders in Michigan, Ohio, and Florida. This church lasted only until 1974, when one of the founders announced his conversion to Christianity in a dramatic incident staged for the press in St. Petersburg, Florida. Other members of the Church of Satan in Kentucky and Indiana left to form the Ordo Templi Satanis, also short-lived.

As more schisms occurred, LaVey disbanded the remaining grottos, the local units of the Church of Satan, and decided to reorganize the church as a fellowship of individuals. The active membership has not grown beyond the level reached in the 1970s. There are many presently existing groups that derive from the Church of Satan, the most important of which are the Temple of Set, the Church of Satanic Liberation (founded in 1986 by Paul Douglas Valentine), and the Temple of Nepthys, founded in the late 1980s.

At the present time, the most active group of organized Satanists is the Temple of Set. The temple was established by Michael A. Aquino (born in 1946), a Magister Templi with the Church of Satan, and Lilith Sinclair, head of the largest of the grottos, in Spottswood, New Jersey. The Temple of Set is a group dedicated to the ancient Egyptian deity believed to have become the model for the Christian Satan. The group affirms that Satan is a real being.

In 1975, Aquino invoked Satan to receive a new mandate to continue the Church of Satan apart from LaVey. According to Aquino, Satan appeared to him as Set, giving him the content for his book *The Book of Coming Forth by Night*. Aquino holds a Ph.D. from the University of California at Santa Barbara and is a lieutenant colonel in the U.S. Army.

The main purpose of the Temple of Set is to awaken the divine power of the individual through the deliberate exercise of will and intelligence. Its members believe that, over the centuries, Set has manipulated human evolution in order to create a new species possessing unnatural intelligence. Its program is directed to an intellectual elite, who must undertake the reading of a lengthy list of required material.

The temple, which includes approximately 500 members in North America and some additional members in Europe, is headed by a Council of Nine, which appoints a High Priest of Set and the executive director. Aquino became well-known as a Satanist and was the subject of a variety of media coverage by the end of the 1970s. In 1987–1988 he was briefly charged with sexually molesting a young girl at the Army base in San Francisco, but was later exonerated of all charges.

See Also: Demons; Exorcism; Sacrifice

Further Reading

Lewis, James R. *The Encyclopedia of Cults, Sects, and New Religions*. Amherst, NY: Prometheus Books, 1998.

Richardson, James T., Joel Best, and David G. Bromley, eds. *The Satanism Scare*. New York: Aldine de Gruyter, 1991.

Scourge

The scourge is similar to a cord in that it is made of a light material. It is similar to a whip, but its purpose is only to stimulate the blood in an area of the body in order to direct it away from the brain, thus causing drowsiness and an altered state of consciousness. The scourge is the most controversial of the tools kept on the altar of a Neopagan Witch and is to be found primarily in Gardnerian and Alexandrian Traditions. It was Gardner who believed that one could learn through suffering and by exciting the body and spirit.

It is of no use in most circles except for initiations, and not all covens use it even for that purpose. On the other hand, orthodox Gardnerian covens are traditionally supposed to use it to begin every ritual, because the procedure for casting a circle that became standard for American Gardnerians includes these lines: "Then each girl should bind her man, hands behind back and cable Tow to neck. He should kneel at altar, and be scourged. When all men are thus 'purified,' they purify the girls in turn. No one may be in the circle without being thus purified" (Gardnerian Book of Shadows).

These lines were not added to the casting procedure by Gardner until about 1961. They were not in the casting procedure used by the London coven at the point that Doreen Valiente's coven hived off in February 1957, and not too long after Gardner dropped out himself. However, they *were* discussed in the Book of Shadows passed on to American Gardnerians.

See Also: Cast; Tools, Witches'
Further Reading

Gardner, Gerald B. "Ye Book of ye Art Magical." Unpublished manuscript, written between about 1945 (or earlier) and 1953, formerly owned by Ripley's International, Ltd., now owned by the Wiccan Church of Canada in Toronto.
Valiente, Doreen. *The Rebirth of Witchcraft*. London: Robert Hale, 1989.

A traditional Greek image, taken from the Villa of the Mysteries at Pompeii, of an initiate being scourged. (Reprinted from Valiente, Doreen, The Rebirth of Witchcraft, *Phoenix Publishing, 1989)*

Scrying

The term *scrying*, deriving from the English *descry*—"to make out dimly" or "to reveal"—denotes an ancient art of clairvoyance: concentrating on an object until visions appear. Scrying has been practiced by magicians and Witches through the ages. Among the purposes of scrying are predictions of the future, answers to questions, solutions to problems, help in finding lost objects, and help in tracking down criminals.

The object on which to concentrate is usually a shiny, smooth surface that makes a good speculum, such as the crystal ball used by Gypsy fortune-tellers or the still water of a lake or pond into which many early scryers gazed. Some of the most frequently used objects are mirrors, polished stones or metals, and bowls of liquid. Ink, blood, and other dark liquids were used by the Egyptians for centuries. Bowls of water were used by Nostradamus. A crystal egg and a piece of obsidian were used by John Dee, the royal court magician in sixteenth-century England. Aleister Crowley, on the other hand, used a precious topaz set in a wooden cross.

Traditional Witches were said to have favored the magic mirror, usually characterized by a concave side painted black, with a cauldron painted black on the inside. Other common scrying tools, especially in England, include glass-ball fishing floats and "Witch balls"—colored glass balls intended to be hung in houses in order to keep away Witches and the evil eye.

Contemporary Witches commonly scry within a magic circle, especially at night, when the reception of psychic vibrations is said to be clearer. The visions received during the practice are usually symbolic, requiring interpretation.

See Also: Divination
Further Reading
Valiente, Doreen. *An ABC of Witchcraft: Past and Present.* New York: St. Martin's Press, 1973.

Seal of Solomon (hexagram)

The Seal of Solomon, the six-sided star, is a design that has been documented as being used as early as the Bronze Age, when it had decorative functions. Its name comes from King Solomon who, according to Arabic legend, could command demons with the power he drew from the hexagram etched on his ring. Another name for the Seal of Solomon is the Star of David, which links it to the Jewish tradition. For the Jews, the hexagram is used as an amulet that protects against the demon named Lilith. The amuletic functions of the seal became popular in the Middle Ages. It can be found in many inscriptions and was widely used in alchemy, in the Cabala, and in magic. The name of God was often inscribed within the symbol. Several handbooks for magicians describe the Seal of Solomon and its relationship to the Magic Circle.

See Also: Amulet; Circle, Magic; Lilith
Further Reading
Chevalier, Jean, and Alain Gheerbrant. *The Penguin Dictionary of Symbols*. London: Penguin, 1996.
Cooper, J. C. An *Illustrated Encyclopedia of Traditional Symbols*. London: Thames and Hudson, 1992 [1978].

1734 Tradition

Joseph B. Wilson founded *The Waxing Moon*, apparently the very first Neopagan periodical in America, in 1964 in Topeka, Kansas. Among the resulting correspondence, he received about 30 letters from people in England who had read his advertisement. He recognized one of them, Robert Cochrane, as a regular contributor to *Pentagram*. (Cochrane was also the "magister" who gave Justine Glass a great deal of peculiar information for her book *Witchcraft, the Sixth Sense—and Us*.) Cochrane's writings were mystical and at odds with what he said was the simplistic approach that Gardnerian Wicca writers had. He claimed to be a member of a family that had secretly kept the knowledge of Witchcraft practices since before the persecutions of non-Christians in the Dark Ages. He called his group the Order of 1734. At the time, Wilson believed Cochrane's claims, although he later came to doubt them. They corresponded for about a year before Cochrane died by his own hand.

Cochrane, whose real name was Roy Bowers, agreed to teach Wilson as much as he could by mail. During their correspondence Wilson learned that Bowers's viewpoint was similar to that of Mac, the American folk Witch who originally initiated Wilson. In fact, except for the fact that it was oriented to English soil, Wilson found that Bowers's views blended with and supplemented Mac's teachings quite well. Much of the way Bowers taught was by posing mystical questions, such as "What two words were not spoken from the Cauldron?" "How many steps in a ladder?" "How many beans make five?" and the like. The answers to the questions were less important than the *process* of answering them, and he was relentless about emphasizing the importance of that work.

His mythos included a combination of mixed theological references, some from the Book of Genesis (Tubal Cain and Naamah), some from the Anglo-Saxon history of the British Isles (Weyland Smith and Goda), and some whose origins Wilson could not identify with any certainty (Lucet, Carenos, Node, Tettens—these might be Etruscan). His pattern of beliefs included use of hammer, tongs, and other implements more closely related to a blacksmith's trade than to ceremonial magic. While studying with Bowers, Wilson finally dropped his quest for magical powers, he said, and concentrated on mystical experience and spiritual growth.

When the Air Force sent Wilson, who was a sergeant, to England, another correspondent, the actress Ruth Wynn-Owen (who followed a family tradition of the Craft that she called Plant Bran, because the family's origin myth was that they were descendants of the God Bran) introduced him to Norman Giles, a man who lived in Oxford. Giles was a friend of Bowers's who had been with him on the evening that Bowers ritually drank a potion of poisonous herbs and thus took his own life.

Giles lived in a house that had been in his family for over 300 years. He insisted that he could photograph fairy spirits under the right conditions. He showed Wilson his pictures, and the images he interpreted as fairies Wilson saw as dirt on his camera lens. Nevertheless, Wilson went to talk with him once a week, and Giles taught him a lot about Bowers's orientation, the 1734 Tradition, journeying and visionary techniques, psychometry, and some palmistry. Giles gave Wilson the letters that Bowers had written to him. He also let Wilson know that sometimes Bowers was mixing truth with falsehood, and Giles showed Wilson how certain things that Bowers had furnished Wilson were obvious forgeries. Wilson was hurt and disappointed, but he said he grew from the experience.

After his return from Europe, Wilson lived in Missouri during 1973, then moved to Tujunga, California, in about 1974. There he began teaching the 1734 Tradition in his Gliocas Tuatha Coven, then later in the Temple of the Elder Gods (TOTEG). The various 1734 Tradition covens currently active in the Los Angeles area all descend from either Gliocas Tuatha or TOTEG.

Ann and Dave Finnin, seeking to trace the 1734 Tradition's roots, made several trips to England, where they met Evan Jones, who had worked in Bowers's coven with Doreen Valiente in the mid-1960s. Their conclusion was that 1734, as an organized tradition, simply did not exist in England, although Bowers did apparently have access to some pre-Gardnerian family traditions about magical workings. Instead, Bowers seems to have evoked these traditions out of Wilson by the way Bowers taught him. Thus, the 1734 Tradition came into existence and has served its members well.

Further Reading

Melton, J. Gordon. *Encyclopedia of American Religions*, 5th ed. Detroit, MI: Gale Research Inc., 1996.

Sex and Sex Magic

The topics of sex and sex magic are so intertwined in Neopagan thought and belief that they merit being discussed together. The opinions of Neopagans about sex range from extremely conservative to extremely radical, in terms of personal behavior. However, Neopagans are nearly unanimous in the belief that matters regarding sex should be left to an individual's conscience, that there should be minimal legal interference with the private lives of consenting adults, and that those who wish to pursue sex and sex magic as a spiritual pathway should have every right to do so without any sort of social penalty.

Neopagans, therefore, believe that any sort of sex between consenting adults is no one else's business (but "safe sex" is highly endorsed due to the spread of the AIDS disease worldwide). Neopagans also tend to believe that forms of marriage other than monogamy between a man and a woman are private, not public, issues. Probably the majority of Neopagans are monogamous, since they are demographically typical middle-class Americans. Nevertheless, Neopagans are far more likely than people chosen in a random sample to be seriously interested in or to be engaged in some sort of complex marriage, expanded family, communal living situation, or other Utopian scheme—thus continuing an old American tradition of utopian experiments.

Similarly, sex magic is of general interest to Neopagans, who practice or learn about it without discussing it in public. However, training in sex magic takes place only within the innermost oath-bound coven or other central working group in a Neopagan association. It is always considered very advanced and potentially explosive magic. Many books are available on sex magic, not all of which are influenced by Neopagan thought.

See Also: Fraternitas Rosae Crucis; Great Rite; Handfasting; Ordo Templi Orientis
Further Reading
Darling, Diane. "Aphrodite: In Her Majesty's Sacred Service—'All Acts of Love and Pleasure Are My Rituals,'" *Green Egg* 100 (spring 1993): 26–28.
D'vora and Annie Sprinkle. Interview by Ellen Evert Hopman and Lawrence Bond. In *People of the Earth: The New Pagans Speak Out.* Rochester, VT: Destiny Books, 1996.
Farren, David. *Sex and Magic.* New York: Simon and Schuster, 1975.
Frost, Gavin, and Yvonne Frost. *Tantric Yoga: The Royal Path to Raising Kundalini Power.* York Beach, ME: Weiser, 1989.
Randolph, Paschal Beverly. *Eulis: Affectional Alchemy,* 5th ed. Quakertown, PA: Beverly Hall, Confederation of Initiates, 1930.
Starhawk [Miriam Simos]. *Dreaming the Dark: Magic, Sex, and Politics.* Boston, MA: Beacon Press, 1982.

Shamanism

Shamans are the religious specialists of hunter-and-gatherer cultures. They are particularly associated with the aboriginal peoples of central Asia and the Americas and are perhaps most familiar to us as the "medicine men" of traditional Native American cultures. Contemporary Neopagan Witches often associate themselves with Shamanism, identifying contemporary Witchcraft as the lineal descendant of pre-Christian European Shamans.

Although the terms *Shaman* and *Shamanism* have come to be used quite loosely, in the disciplines of anthropology and comparative religion Shamanism refers to a fairly specific set of ideas and practices that can be found in many, but not all, world cultures. Characteristically, the Shaman is a healer, a psychopomp (someone who guides the souls of the dead to their home in the afterlife), and more generally a mediator between her or his community and the world of spirits (most often animal spirits and the spirits of the forces of nature).

A Hunza Bitan Shaman, with the aid of juniper smoke, dancing, and blood sacrifice, puts himself into a trance to hear what the "mountain fairies" are saying; Altit, Gojal, Pakistan. (Corbis/Jonathan Blair)

For smaller-scale societies, especially for hunting and gathering groups, Shamans perform all of the functions that doctors, Priests, and therapists (and sometimes mystics and artists as well) perform in contemporary Western societies. The religious specialists of traditional American Indian societies that people sometimes refer to as "medicine men" are examples of Shamans. True Shamans are more characteristic of hunting societies than of pastoral or farming societies, although one can often find segments of the Shamanic pattern in nonhunting cultures. Shamanism in the strict sense is not found in certain culture areas, such as in Africa, although there are religious specialists that fill the same "slot" in traditional African societies.

As a system, Shamanism frequently emphasizes contact and communication with spirits in the other world, healing practices in which Shamans search for lost souls of the living, and rituals in which Shamans guide the spirits of the deceased to the realm of the dead. Shamanism thus has certain parallels with Spiritualism. The word *Shaman* comes from the Tungusic term for this type of religious specialist, *saman*. The term *Shaman* was originally coined by an earlier generation of scholars who studied societies in Siberia and central Asia, and it was later extended to similar religious complexes found elsewhere in the world. Depending on how archeological evidence is interpreted, Shamanism is many thousands of years old.

In recent years, Shamanism has become somewhat of a fad in the West's occult-metaphysical subculture due to the recent development of interest in

Native American religions. While there is a long tradition that romanticizes Native Americans and their spiritual traditions, Anglos have rarely engaged in Native American religious practices. This changed in the 1960s, when certain groups of counterculturists made an effort to adopt what they conceived of as "tribal" lifestyles. In the late 1980s, the occult-metaphysical subculture began focusing attention on Native American religions when Shamanism— and, more particularly, the phenomenon that has come to be known as "neo-Shamanism"—became popular.

Neo-Shamanism has clearly impacted certain aspects of modern Neopagans. For example, some Neopagans have reconceptualized the idea of familiars in light of Neoshamanic theories about "power animals" (the anthropological concept of "totems"). In terms of this line of interpretation, the Witch's familiar—which can be imaginary, in that one need not actually keep a living animal around as a kind of pet—embodies certain traits and powers that the Witch taps by asking it for help.

See Also: Healing; Shapeshifting; Spirit
Further Reading
Barnouw, Victor. "Siberian Shamanism and Western Spiritualism." *Journal of the Society of Psychical Research* 36 (1942): 140–168.
Eliade, Mircea. *Shamanism: Archaic Techniques of Ecstasy.* Translated by W. Trask. Princeton, NJ: Princeton University Press, 1964.
Grim, John A. *The Shaman: Patterns of Siberian and Ojibway Healing.* Norman, OK: University of Oklahoma Press, 1983.
Hultkrantz, Ake. "A Definition of Shamanism." *Temenos* 9 (1973): 25–37.

Shapeshifting

Throughout history, it has been believed that people engaged in magical practices have the ability to change their physical form—in other words, to shapeshift. Shapeshifting generally involves a Witch changing into a creature from the animal kingdom, a mammal, a bird, or an insect. Witches have been accused of changing form for diabolical purposes. During the Middle Ages and Renaissance Witch trials, Witches were accused of or admitted to shapeshifting with the intent to torment a specific individual. Numerous stories were told about the metamorphosis of Witches into man-eating wolves.

Speculation and alternate hypotheses have arisen surrounding the issue of shapeshifting. It is said that Witches rubbed themselves down with hallucinogenic ointments prior to Sabbat ceremonies. Persons observed after such a process have been reported to sleep deeply for hours and, upon awaking, have fabulous stories of their travels in beast form. In reality, the body never left its original position.

The concept of shapeshifting is prevalent in Shamanism. The Shaman is able to spiritually transform into his guardian animal spirit. This transformation is achieved by the consumption of hallucinogenic drugs or after a period of drumming and dancing that would be sufficient to alter the consciousness.

See Also: Lycanthropy; Ointments; Shamanism
Further Reading
Eliade, Mircea, ed. *The Encyclopedia of Religion.* 16 vols. New York: Macmillan, 1987.
Leach, Maria. *Standard Dictionary of Folklore, Mythology, and Legend.* San Francisco, CA: HarperSan Francisco, 1984 [1949].

Sidhe

The word *sidhe*—also spelled *sidh, sithide, sid, sith, sitche*—is the standard term for "fairy" in the Gaelic tongue of Scotland and Ireland. Gaelic records speak of the fairies as the *fir sidhe*, that is, "the sidhe-folk." Although in modern Irish tradition the term refers to many species of supernatural creatures—it can be translated as "divine," "unearthly," or "supernatural"—in Gaelic the word *sidhe* also implies a mound or hill, the dwelling place of elves.

According to mythological tradition, when the Milesians invaded Ireland, they defeated the ancient gods—*Tuatha Dé Danann*—driving them underground below the hills, where they established otherworldly kingdoms. The Irish Happy Otherworld is generally described as a place of feasting, hunting, and revelry; there is no pain, disease, or old age.

Each of the gods was assigned a mound, or *sidhe*, by the Dagdha before he gave up leadership. Thus Nuadu became lord of the sidhe of Almu, whereas Midhir was lord of the sidhe of Bri Léith. The legend describes the Morrigan—the War Goddess—as emerging from her sidhe to destroy Cu Chulainn. The sidhe of the Dagdha is characterized by three trees that perpetually bear fruit, a pig that is always alive, and an inexhaustible supply of drink. During the festival of Samhain, which takes place on November 1, the boundaries between the natural and the supernatural worlds are temporarily negated, and spirits moved freely from their own sidhe.

See Also: Fairy; Samhain; Spirit
Further Reading
Ellis, Peter Berresford. *Dictionary of Celtic Mythology.* Santa Barbara, CA: ABC-CLIO, 1992.
Green, Miranda J. *Dictionary of Celtic Myth and Legend.* London: Thames and Hudson, 1992.
Spence, Lewis. *The Fairy Tradition in Britain.* London: Rider and Company, 1948.

Sigil

A sigil is a physical symbol through which a spirit may be called. The symbols are taken from geometric shapes, letters (Runic or Thebian), crosses, or emblems related to gods and goddesses. To obtain the proper sigil of a spirit, a shiny object is placed on an altar. The spirit reveals its sigil by marking it in

The sigil, or vèvè of Legba in the Voodoo tradition. (Reprinted from Rigaud, Milo, Secrets of Voodoo, *San Francisco, 1914.)*

dew on the object. Sigils may also be divulged during meditation or through smoke patterns. *Sigil* is derived from the Latin word *sigillum*, meaning "seal." It can be chosen by someone as a personal logo to be inscribed on magic tools or amulets. One may also control a spirit with a sigil by exposing the sigil to fire or piercing it with the magic sword.

See Also: Amulet; Spirit
Further Reading
Guiley, Rosemary Ellen. *The Encyclopedia of Witches and Witchcraft.* New York: Facts on File, 1989.
RavenWolf, Silver. *To Ride a Silver Broomstick: New Generation Witchcraft.* St. Paul, MN: Llewellyn, 1996.

Skyclad

Skyclad is a term introduced by Gerald Gardner to describe the practice of working naked in a circle. He probably derived it from his knowledge of

Hindu and related religious practices, since it is a literal translation of a San-skrit word that also means "naked." Skyclad working is a distinguishing char-acteristic of Gardnerian Witches. It has been adopted also by traditions that imitate the Gardnerians and has been rejected by others that do not admit any dependence on Gardner. Most covens and traditions consider working skyclad as a matter of local option, and a decision about whether a specific working should be robed or skyclad would depend on its purpose.

See Also: Circle, Magic
Further Reading
Farrar, Stewart. *What Witches Do: The Modern Coven Revealed.* New York: Coward McCann, 1971.
Starhawk [Miriam Simos]. *The Spiral Dance: A Rebirth of the Ancient Religion of the Great Goddess*, 2d ed. San Francisco, CA: HarperSan Francisco, 1989 [1979].

Solitary

A solitary Witch is one who is self-initiated, or one who has withdrawn from group activity and is operating as an individual. There were discussions in the early 1970s about whether a solitary Witch, and especially a self-initiated one, could be considered equal in status and ability to a Witch initiated into and trained by a coven. The consensus now among Neopagans is an em-phatic "yes"—but every Witch, solitary or coven-trained, should have his or her abilities judged on their own individual merits.

See Also: Coven
Further Reading
Guiley, Rosemary Ellen. *The Encyclopedia of Witches and Witchcraft.* New York: Facts on File, 1989.
RavenWolf, Silver. *To Ride a Silver Broomstick: New Generation Witchcraft.* St. Paul, MN: Llewellyn, 1996.

Solstices

The solstices are the days when the sun reaches its extreme in its annual cycle, rising more toward the north every day for six months and then more toward the south every day for six months. (This happens because the Earth's equator is tilted relative to the plane of the solar system.) The summer sol-stice is the day when the hours of daylight are at a maximum; it falls about June 22 every year. The winter solstice is the day when the hours of daylight are at a minimum.

These patterns in the annual cycle have been obvious to human beings for as long as humans have observed the phenomena of the sky. Astronomers are certain that Stonehenge (and probably other stone circles), built around

5,000 years ago, was designed to determine the solstice days; so, most likely, solstices are the oldest known holidays. The summer solstice is observed by Neopagan Witches as the Litha Sabbat, as it is generally known in the United States, and the winter solstice is observed as the Yule Sabbat.

See Also: Sabbats; Wheel of the Year
Further Reading
Campanelli, Pauline. *Wheel of the Year: Living the Magical Life*. St. Paul, MN: Llewellyn, 1989.
Kelly, Aidan A. *Religious Holidays and Calendars: An Encyclopedic Handbook*. Detroit, MI: Omnigraphics, 1991.

Sorcery

The word *sorcery* originates from the French root *sors*, meaning "spell." Throughout history, a thin line exists between the definitions of sorcery and Witchcraft. Sorcery, however, refers directly to the casting of spells and the manipulation of natural forces for a particular goal. It contains no connection to a more intricate set of beliefs and therefore has been classified in the category of "low magic."

The concept of sorcery can be traced back to the time of prehistoric humanity. Neolithic cave paintings of humans, beasts, and half-human and half-beast creatures have been found in Europe. These discoveries have led to the proposal that the characters were drawn in hopes of influencing the success of a hunt.

When casting their spells, the ancient Greek sorcerers enlisted the aid of the *daimones*, spirits who roamed between Earth and Heaven. The *daimones* were originally believed to be capable of assisting good or evil plans; however, this view changed when Xenocrates labeled *daimones* as evil and the gods as good. With the evolution of Christianity, sorcery became associated with the workings of the devil. By the time of the Inquisition, sorcery was considered a serious crime by both secular and religious authorities. Sorcery was seen as a root from which European Witchcraft sprang (Witches being defined as those who executed harmful or evil acts for the devil). In 1486, the *Malleus Maleficarum* was released as the Witch-hunter's guidebook of the Inquisition. Throughout the end of the Middle Ages and the Renaissance, the term *sorcerer* was redefined and became associated with men of advanced learning. It no longer had negative connotations; sorcerers were men who were able to gain knowledge from demonic sources, whereas Witches were those who practiced magic for evil ends. In present-day Europe, modern Witches are still viewed as assistants to the devil.

In Africa, Witchcraft is separated from sorcery. Witchcraft is evil, whereas sorcery is a primary source of stability. The African sorcerer is able to protect the village from disaster such as famine, drought, or even against an outside curse.

See Also: African Religions; Magic
Further Reading
Marwick, Max, ed. *Witchcraft and Sorcery.* New York: Viking Penguin, 1982 [1972].
Rush, John A. *Witchcraft and Sorcery.* Springfield, IL: Charles C. Thomas, 1974.

Spells

A spell is a series of words or incantations accompanied by a ritual with the purpose of altering the outcome of events. Throughout time and place, those with supernatural powers have been able to cast spells for both harm and benefit to themselves and others. The successful casting of a spell has three essential components: the sorcerer, magician, or Witch who is to perform; the ritual; and the actual spell. The importance of the wording and pronunciation of the spell varies as one moves around the globe. For example, in ancient Egypt the words used were the most crucial elements in the casting of a spell. In Western Witchcraft, however, it is the level of power invoked by the *combination* of the spell and the ritual that provides a spell with strength. Witches raise levels of power through chanting, dancing, and hand-clapping. As the level of power reaches its peak, the Witch lets it go and focuses it on the objective of the spell.

See Also: Hex; Love Spells; Magic
Further Reading
Marlbrough, Ray L. *Charms, Spells, and Formulas.* St. Paul, MN: Llewellyn, 1987.
Mickaharic, Draja. *A Century of Spells.* York Beach, ME: Weiser, 1988.

Spirit

Most traditional religions postulate that one or more "spiritual" worlds exist alongside the world of our ordinary, everyday experience in what might be called a different "dimension." For most of these traditions, the spiritual realm is at least as real as the physical realm. Cross-culturally and through many different historical periods there is widespread agreement on certain important traits of this otherworld. One of the more significant points of agreement is that some essential part of the human being survives death and goes on to reside in this other realm. Contemporary Neopaganism generally endorses this traditional worldview, often accepting a complex view of an otherworld populated with a confusing variety of spiritual entities. These spirits run the gamut from elementals to angels to gods and goddesses.

In the West, belief in such entities began to gradually decline in the wake of the rise of modern science in the early modern period. The physical sciences undermined belief in the concrete reality of Heaven, Hell, gods and goddesses, and devils. The only important countervailing tendency was the emergence of depth psychology, which gave these entities new plausibility as mental phenomena. The psychologist Carl Jung, for instance, postulated the existence of a collective unconscious. He discussed mythology and religion in terms of the "primordial images," or "archetypes" existing in the collective unconscious that every human being inherits. Using this approach, it is possible to acknowledge demons, angels, and other spirits as the personifications of the unconscious, rather than as literal spiritual beings existing *independently* of the mind.

For the most part, Neopagans accept the notion of such entities as actual, literal beings. On this topic there is, however, a diversity of opinion. Some practicing Wiccans find themselves more aligned with the Jungian psychological perspective than with what might be called a realist or ontological perspective. Other Neopagans would locate themselves somewhere in the middle of the spectrum, viewing certain phenomena as psychological and other phenomena as resulting from the activity of "real" spirits. All Neopagans, however, reject the notion of so-called evil spirits, although Wiccans often accept the existence of mischievous "trickster" spirits.

See Also: Fairies; Spiritualism
Further Reading
Eliade, Mircea. *The Encyclopedia of Religion.* 16 vols. New York: Macmillan, 1987.
Lewis, James R. *Encyclopedia of Afterlife Beliefs and Phenomena.* Detroit, MI: Gale Research Inc., 1994.

Spiritism

After the end of the Napoleonic era in France, interest in the paranormal phenomena associated with hypnotism (known then as mesmerism) contributed to the rise of the new religious movement known as Spiritualism: Its major tenet was a belief in survival of the soul after death and often in reincarnation. In France, early proponents of Spiritualism included St. Simon, Prosper Enfantin, St. Martin, Fourier, Pierre Leroux, and Jean Reynaud. However, Spiritualism's major form in France became the religion Spiritism, as proclaimed by Allen Kardec (1804–1869), whose original name was Hypolyte Leon Denizard Rivail. Rivail took his pseudonym from two of his previous incarnations, as revealed to him by the medium Celina Bequet Japhet and by another named Rose. Rivail had been an exponent of mesmerism and phrenology before he was introduced into Japhet's circle in 1856 by Victorien Sardou. He was fascinated by Sardou's "scripts" (documents produced by automatic writing), in which the spirits communicated the doctrine of reincarnation. Rivail edited and published selections from them in 1856 under the title *Le Livre des esprits* (The Book of the Spirits), which would go through more than 20 editions and serve as the recognized textbook of Spiritism in France.

Kardec's teachings proved to be enormously popular and spread rapidly over the continent. The major tenet of Spiritism, and the one on which it differs from most Spiritualism, is that spiritual progress is effected by a series of compulsory reincarnations. Kardec became so dogmatic on this point that he disparaged and opposed physical mediumship, which very often produced data that contradicted his beliefs. Instead, he encouraged automatic writing, which tended to contradict him much less. As a result, experimental psychic research was retarded for many years in France, relative to what was being pursued elsewhere. Kardec founded a monthly magazine, *La Revue spirite*, in which he refused to mention the most prominent French mediums. Kardec's views were publicly disputed by A. T. Pierart, editor of *La Revue spiritualiste*, a spokesperson for the view that humans are born only once and that all other lives are lived on a spiritual plane of existence. The debate was so lively that, by 1864, there were no less than ten Spiritist journals being published in France. In 1864, Kardec published most of the rest of the Japhet scripts as *Le Livre des mediums* (The Book of Mediums). His following books were *The Gospel as Explained by Spirits* (1864), *Heaven and Hell* (1865), *Genesis* (1867), and *Experimental Spiritism and Spiritualist Philosophy*. After Kardec's death on March 31, 1869, leadership of the Spiritist movement passed to Léon Denis (1846–1927), who published eight books on Spiritism, one of which was published in English as *Christianity and Spiritualism* (1904). Leadership of the Spiritism movement was shared with Denis by Gabriel Delanne (1857–1926), a professional engineer and avocational psychic researcher, described by Flournoy as the most "scientific" of French Spiritists, who wrote more than half a dozen books on subjects psychic and Spiritualistic. Denis and Delanne found a powerful supporter in another psychical researcher, Dr. Gustav Geley (1868–1924), whose book *From the Unconscious to the Conscious* (1919) reads like a bible of reincarnationism.

In England, Kardec's most prominent supporter was Anna Kingsford, who believed she was the reincarnation of the Virgin Mary, and who translated Kardec's works into English. (Her follower Edward Maitland believed himself to be the reincarnation of St. John the Divine.) In 1881, the three volumes of *The Four Gospels*, a commentary on the esoteric aspects of the Gospels, were published under her auspices; it was a further development of Kardec's theology.

Spiritism was exported to South America in the nineteenth century and is one of the major religions of Brazil, often found in the form of an amalgam with popular varieties of Catholic piety. There are about four million Spiritists in Brazil—Brazil has honored Kardec at least three times on its commemorative postage stamps. Brazilian Spiritism also amalgamated with the African American religions that had evolved there since the European settlers began importing African slaves in the sixteenth century. The religion has since been imported into the United States by Latin-American immigrants, where it has amalgamated with yet other forms of Spiritualism and African American religions.

See Also: Reincarnation; Spiritualism

Further Reading

Doyle, Sir Arthur Conan. *The History of Spiritualism*. New York: Arno Press, 1975 [1926].

Hess, David J. *Samba in the Night: Spiritism in Brazil*. New York: Columbia University Press, 1994.

Spiritualism

Spiritualism is a religious movement that emphasizes the belief in survival after death—a belief Spiritualists claim is based on scientific proof—and on communication with the surviving personalities of deceased human beings by means of mediumship. As the religious movement responsible for reviving the ancient practice of mediumship, Spiritualism has had an important, though indirect, influence on contemporary Neopagan Witchcraft. Also, the word *Summerland*, the commonly used Neopagan term for the realm in which the souls of the departed reside while awaiting reincarnation, was adopted from nineteenth-century Spiritualism.

The continuity of the personality after death through a new birth into a spiritual body (not a new physical body) represents the important central tenet of Spiritualism. According to Spiritualists, at death the soul, which is composed of a sort of subtle matter, withdraws itself and remains near the Earth plane for a period of time. After this, the soul advances in knowledge and moral qualities and proceeds to higher planes, until it eventually reaches the sphere of pure spirit. The rapidity with which the soul advances is in direct proportion to the mental and moral faculties acquired in earthly life. Spiritualists originally conceived of planes as spheres encircling the Earth, one above the other, whereas now planes are more commonly thought to interpenetrate each other, coexisting at different rates of vibration.

The concepts of hell, the last judgment, and eternal damnation are not part of Spiritualist belief. Communication with the deceased, through the agency of mediums, represents the other central belief of Spiritualism. Spirits contacted by mediums are traditionally asked first to prove their identities by giving correct information about their earthly lives and concerns. Spiritualism is regarded by its adherents as a religion based on science, combined with elements from other religions and creeds.

See Also: Ghosts; Spirit; Spiritism

Further Reading

Doyle, Sir Arthur Conan. *The History of Spiritualism*. New York: Arno Press, 1975 [1926].

RavenWolf, Silver. *To Ride a Silver Broomstick: New Generation Witchcraft*. St. Paul, MN: Llewellyn, 1996.

Ward, Gary L., ed. *Spiritualism I: Spiritualist Thought*. New York: Garland Publishing, 1990.

A German Spiritualist fortune-teller, Madame Terfren Laila, ca. 1935. (Corbis/Hulton-Deutsch Collection)

Summerland

Summerland is the Neopagan term commonly used to refer to the realm in which the souls of the departed reside, rest, and integrate lessons from their earthly life while awaiting reincarnation. Neopagans adopted the term from nineteenth-century Celtic studies, where it was used to translate a Gaelic term for an otherworld where the souls of the departed rested after death. Alternatively, it is said to have originally been coined in 1845 by Andrew Jackson Davis, the "American Swedenborg." The pleasant name *Summerland* reflects the Spiritualist image of the *other side* as a radiant, harmonious home for the departed. Like contemporary Neopaganism, the Spiritualist tradition rejects the notion of hell. Less theologically significant than such alternate designations as *heaven*, it is easy to see why the term *Summerland* was adopted by Neopagans. Curiously, current Spiritualists rarely use the term.

See Also: Astral Plane; Spiritualism
Further Reading
Guiley, Rosemary. *The Encyclopedia of Witches and Witchcraft.* New York: Facts on File, 1989.
Lewis, James R. *Encyclopedia of Afterlife Beliefs and Phenomena.* Detroit, MI: Gale Research Inc., 1994.

Susan B. Anthony Coven

In Los Angeles, California, after what she called a lifetime of preparation, Zsusanna Budapest in 1971 collected six friends and held Sabbats that admitted only women. The coven was "born" on the winter solstice of 1971, named the Susan B. Anthony Coven, after the leader of the women's suffrage movement.

Word of mouth quickly drew more participants to the coven, and the expanding group was moved to the beach—a location that drew too many onlookers—and then to a mountaintop in Malibu. For ten years, Budapest led Sabbats and full-moon circles, initiating Priestesses and teaching women to bless each other and connect with the Goddess through Mother Nature. One of Budapest's pupils was Starhawk. In addition, Budapest opened a shop, The Feminist Wicca, in Venice, California, and self-published a book that became a basic text of Dianic Wicca, *The Feminist Book of Light and Shadows*. Her book was based on parts of the Gardnerian Book of Shadows that were publicly available by 1971; she rewrote them in order to eliminate all mention of males, both mortal and immortal, and then she added some new rituals, spells, and lore. The book was later expanded and published as the two-volume *The Holy Book of Women's Mysteries*.

During the 1970s, the Dianic Wicca movement grew to be a major force both in Witchcraft and in the feminist movement. Cerridwen Fallingstar, now known as a novelist, was a member of Susan B. Anthony Coven No. 1. The very concept of a form of Witchcraft that was for women only was controversial in the Craft movement and was strongly rejected by many conservative Gardnerians. The issue is no longer controversial in any way.

By 1976, the core of the Susan B. Anthony Coven consisted of 20–40 women; up to 300 participated in some of its activities. Related covens were formed in at least five other states. In the early 1980s, Budapest closed her shop, turned the Susan B. Anthony Coven over to another leader, and moved to Oakland, California, where she formed a new coven, The Laughing Goddess Coven. When the original Susan B. Anthony Coven disbanded in Los Angeles, Budapest formed a new coven of that name in Oakland.

See Also: Dianic Wicca/Goddess Religion; Goddess(es); Women's Spirituality
    Movement

Further Reading

Budapest, Z. [Zsusanna]. *Grandmother Moon: Lunar Magic in Our Lives—Spells, Rituals, Goddesses, Legends, and Emotions under the Moon.* San Francisco, CA: HarperSan Francisco, 1991.

———. *The Grandmother of Time.* San Francisco, CA: HarperSan Francisco, 1989.

———. *The Holy Book of Women's Mysteries,* 2d ed. 2 vols. Oakland, CA: Thesmophoria, 1986. The Book of Shadows on Dianic Wicca and consensus governance of covens.

Budapest, Z. [Zsusanna], and Cerridwen Fallingstar. Interview by Ellen Evert Hopman and Lawrence Bond. In *People of the Earth: The New Pagans Speak Out.* Rochester, VT: Destiny Books, 1996, 352.

Sword

The sword is a basic magical tool used by many Neopagan Witches. It is associated with the element of air. Before it can be used in rituals, a sword must be consecrated in rites that involve its exposure to all four elements: by immersing it or sprinkling it with water, passing it through or over a flame (fire), passing it through incense smoke (air), and plunging it into the earth.

Magical swords are customarily inscribed with symbols. Ideally, the sword is handmade by the Witch, which imbues it with his or her own personal power. Gerald Gardner, the man chiefly responsible for reviving Witchcraft in the modern West, made his own swords. However, most contemporary Witches buy a sword and personalize it by inscription and consecration. Some covens have a single sword for use by the entire group.

The sword is used for ritual purposes, such as the casting of a circle in which all rites, magical work, and ceremonies are conducted. The Witch traces the circle on the floor or ground with the sword. The sword is not used for cutting. The doom suit of the Tarot deck was the suit of swords, which evolved into the modern suit of spades, from the Spanish *espada*, meaning "sword." The suit of swords is associated with the element of air.

The sword is a phallic symbol. Swords belonged to men in Pagan Europe when most other things—fields, houses, furniture, and utensils—belonged to women. Upon the death of the owner, his sword was either buried with him or was flung into water. A Norse wedding custom was for a bridegroom to plunge a sword into the main beam of his house as a symbol of his virility. The sword also represents the cardinal virtue of courage.

See Also: Air; Athame; Cast

Further Reading

Chevalier, Jean, and Alain Gheerbrant. *The Penguin Dictionary of Symbols*. London: Penguin, 1996.
Cooper, J. C. *An Illustrated Encyclopedia of Traditional Symbols*. London: Thames and Hudson, 1992 [1978].

Sylphs

Sylphs are small, winged fairies, associated with the element of air. They are said to be light, "airy," almost transparent beings who reside in the atmosphere. They are responsible for all movements of air, from the slightest breeze to the mightiest hurricane. In the Occult Tradition, air is traditionally associated with the mental body, and air elementals (sylphs) are said to work with human beings to inspire creativity, high thoughts, and intuition.

Sylphs are the archetypal spirits of the air element and, as such, are occupied with maintaining the atmosphere of the planet. In magic, sylphs are the air elementals of one of the directions (usually the east) that are invoked in rituals. The task of the elementals is to build forms in the natural world. While some occultists view elementals as soulless entities that simply disappear at death, others view them as spirits who eventually evolve into devas (angels). Due to their association with air, the sylphs are under the rule of the archangel Raphael.

See Also: Air; Gnomes; Salamanders; Undines

Further Reading

Andrews, Ted. *Enchantment of the Faerie Realm: Communicate with Nature Spirits and Elementals*. St. Paul, MN: Llewellyn, 1993.
McCoy, Edwin. *A Witch's Guide to Faery Folk*. St. Paul, MN: Llewellyn, 1994.

T

Talismans

A talisman is an object, frequently a stone or a ring, marked with magical signs and believed to confer on its bearer supernatural powers. Talismans are often confused with amulets. The difference is that talismans transmit a power to the wearer, such as the ability to transform. An amulet is more akin to a shield, which protects the wearer from evil. Examples of talismans are magic wands, King Arthur's sword (Excalibur), and Mercury's helmet of invisibility. Precious stones are often considered talismans, each mineral having its own magical or curative powers endowed by nature.

Talismans were common in ancient Egypt (3000 B.C. to A.D. 641), where they were used to attempt to alter the forces of nature. King Solomon (974–937 B.C.) had a magic ring with a hexagram (a six-pointed star, also called the Seal of Solomon) and the name of God etched on it. According to Arabic legend, this talisman enabled him to command an army of demons.

During the Middle Ages (A.D. 476–1500), holy objects were valued as talismans for their ability to cure illness. Witches and thieves made talismans out of the severed hands of criminals, which were called hands of glory. The severed hands of murderers were preserved and then fitted with candles between the fingers. When the candles were burning, the hand of glory was supposed to have the power to render people motionless and speechless. Alchemists sought a talisman called the Philosopher's Stone that would transform base metals into gold and silver.

Grimoires gave instructions for making talismans of engravings upon stones or other objects. In addition to the powers already mentioned, there are talismans for such things as winning in gambling, preventing sudden death, improving memory, and making good speeches.

See Also: Amulet; Grimoire; Rings

Further Reading

Bletzer, June G. *The Donning International Encyclopedic Psychic Dictionary.* Norfolk, VA: Donning, 1986.

Gordon, Stuart. *The Encyclopedia of Myths and Legends.* London: Headline, 1993.

Tantra

At the broadest level, Tantra refers to a movement that swept across the South Asian subcontinent during the Indian middle ages, influencing, to a greater or lesser extent, most existing forms of Hinduism and Buddhism. In contrast to the earlier forms of these two religions, Tantrism placed an emphasis on what has been termed "magical" practices, particularly sound magic associated with certain verbal formulas (called mantras). Tantra also tended toward a more positive evaluation of the physical body and of women than earlier Hinduism and Buddhism, a reevaluation reflected in Tantrism's sexual symbolism.

Tantric yoga is one branch of the complex system of spiritual disciplines that evolved in medieval India. It may go back to practices common in Asian cultures several thousand years ago; although far from certain, such a lineage would explain Tantra's apparent connections with some Buddhist practices. Probably because of Moslem persecutions of Tantrists and the wholesale burning of religious texts, the oldest surviving Tantric texts (from the eighth century A.D.) are, in fact, Buddhist.

Tantra purposely uses five means normally forbidden to orthodox Hindus in order to break through engrained habit, raise the Kundalini energy, and achieve a higher state of consciousness. These means are known as the "five Ms," after the initial letter of each word: *madya,* "wine"; *mansa,* "flesh"; *matsya,* "fish"; *mudra,* which can indicate either a ritual hand gesture or parched grain; and *maithuna,* "sexual intercourse" (usually in the form of *coitus interruptus*). The "right-handed" Tantra uses these five means only symbolically; the "left-handed" Tantra uses them physically.

The Tantras are a set of specific Hindu scriptures, usually concerned with Shiva and his wife Parvati, or Shakti; they deal with the creation and destruction of the universe, worship of the gods, spiritual disciplines, rituals, occult powers *(siddhis),* and meditation techniques.

Tantric Paganism is not a specific tradition or organization within Western Neopaganism, but rather is a movement arising out of a perception that Wicca and Tantrism are extremely similar. It has been noted by several writers that Wicca can reasonably be called "the Tantra of the West"—and whether or not this was ever historically true, it seems to be true today.

Like Wicca, Tantra focuses on a male-female duality (Shiva-Shakti) that is believed to express the ultimate divine reality as accurately as any other theology, and it focuses on the kinds of practical work that interests Wiccans. It is not too oversimplified to say that Tantra is sex magic, and as its techniques become increasingly published, they are used more and more by Wiccans.

In addition, Wiccans are growing more interested in Hindu goddesses in general. Whereas it is questionable that there was an unbroken cult of a goddess in western Europe (except insofar as devotion to Mary represents the survival of ancient goddess worship), it is clear that India has goddess cults that do go back for thousands of years. Hence, it is not at all unusual now for a Wiccan to become a devotee of a Hindu goddess as well, especially if the

Wiccan lives in the vicinity of one of the Hindu temples that are now spreading steadily across the United States, where Hindu devotional practices can be learned firsthand.

See Also: Ordo Templi Orientis; Sex and Sex Magic
Further Reading
King, Francis, ed. *Tantra, The Way of Action: A Practical Guide to Its Teachings and Techniques*. Rochester, VT: Destiny Books, 1990.
Frost, Gavin, and Yvonne Frost. *Tantric Yoga: The Royal Path to Raising Kundalini Power*. York Beach, ME: Weiser, 1989.
Mookerjee, Ajit, and M. Khanna. *The Tantric Way: Art, Science, Ritual*. New York: Graphic, 1977.
Rawson, Philip. *Tantra: The Indian Cult of Ecstasy*. London: Thames and Hudson, 1974.

Tarot

The deck of modern Tarot cards evolved from a deck of cards used in medieval times. Tarot cards constitute the basis of a divinatory method that is especially popular among contemporary Neopagans. The deck consists of two parts: 4 suits of 14 cards each, collectively called the "Minor Arcana" (from which the modern deck evolved by combining the Knight and Page of each suit into the Jack), and 22 other cards, collectively called the "Major Arcana," which are represented in the modern deck only by the Joker (seemingly derived from the Tarot card called the Fool).

The origins of the Tarot are shrouded in mystery. In a typical Tarot reading, the cards are not used for "fortune-telling," but as a means for diagnosing a person's current situation in terms of his or her overall spiritual growth. The reading process and theory of psychic perception discussed in most current books on the Tarot serve as excellent examples of the reinterpretation and revitalization of a traditional occult system.

See Also: Divination; Fortune-Telling
Further Reading
Douglas, Alfred. *The Tarot: The Origins, Meaning, and Use of the Cards*. New York: Taplinger, 1972.
Melton, J. Gordon, Jerome Clark, and Aidan A. Kelly. *New Age Encyclopedia*. Detroit, MI: Gale Research Inc., 1990.

Tasseomancy

Tasseomancy is the practice of reading tea leaves and coffee grounds for the purpose of divination. In the seventeenth century, tea was brought from the Orient to the West and tea-leaf reading became an accepted form of prediction. A patron comes to a diviner and is given a cup of tea to drink; when only a slight amount of liquid and the steeped leaves remain, the mixture is stirred and flipped onto a saucer. The diviner looks for symbols, letters, or patterns formed and, from this, the diviner will give a prediction.

The reading of coffee grounds, on the other hand, was developed by eighteenth-century Italians. The format for coffee reading is similar to that of tea-leaf reading, except that patterns are formed with coffee grounds rather than tea leaves. The *chouihani* are gypsy Witches who are well versed in the art of this type of divination. Tasseomancy is an active practice in England, Ireland, and other areas of Europe and the Middle East.

See Also: Divination; Fortune-Telling
Further Reading
Bletzer, June G. *The Donning International Encyclopedic Psychic Dictionary*. Norfolk, VA: Donning, 1986.
Shepard, Leslie A., ed. *Encyclopedia of Occultism and Parapsychology*. Detroit, MI: Gale Research Inc., 1991.

Theology/Thealogy

The term *theology* is derived from the Greek *theos*, "God." In about 1970, the new term *thealogy* (from the Greek *thea*, "Goddess") began to be used to indicate the study of beliefs about goddesses. The term has seen a fair amount of use since then, especially in the field of women's studies and in the women's spirituality movement.

Further Reading
Lovelock, J. E. *Gaia*. New York: Oxford University Press, 1979.
Zell, Oberon. "Who on Earth Is the Goddess?" In Lewis, James R., ed., *Magical Religion and Modern Witchcraft*. Albany, NY: State University of New York Press, 1996, 25–33.

Theosophy

The name *Theosophy* originated in Alexandria, Egypt, in the third century A.D., in connection with the Greek mysteries. It refers to the divine wisdom that is claimed to underlie the teachings of all religions. The metaphysical and occult subculture that has nourished contemporary Neopaganism grew out of several different nineteenth-century movements, including Theosophy. In contemporary usage, the word *Theosophy* refers to a particular synthesis of ideas from the philosophical systems of China and India and to the works of the Gnostics, the Neoplatonists, and the Cabalists. This synthesis of ideas manifested in the Theosophical Society, founded in New York in 1875 by Helena Petrovna Blavatsky (1831–1891).

As a part of the religious phenomenon known as esotericism, Theosophy refers to a gnosis offering enlightenment to an individual through knowledge of what unites her or him to the world of the divine and to its hidden mysteries. Theosophy postulates a rather complex view of the universe within which humanity's origins, evolution, and destiny after death are delineated. According to its principles, the visible world arises from an omnipresent and immutable Source, an immaterial reality of which, as in Hindu philosophy, the universe is the manifestation and, from within this universe, the immaterial reality is worked and guided.

See Also: Gnosticism

Further Reading

Campbell, Bruce F. *Ancient Wisdom Revived: A History of the Theosophical Movement.* Berkeley, CA: University of California Press, 1980.

Cranston, Sylvia. *HPB: The Extraordinary Life and Influence of Helena Blavatsky, Founder of the Modern Theosophical Movement.* New York: Jeremy P. Tarcher/Putnam Books/G. P. Putnam's Sons, 1993.

Gomes, Michael. *The Dawning of the Theosophical Movement.* Wheaton, IL: The Theosophical Publishing House, 1987.

Ransom, Josephine, comp. *A Short History of the Theosophical Society: 1875–1937.* Adyar, Madras: The Theosophical Publishing House, 1938.

Thirteen

The number 13 has been surrounded by an aura of bad luck and superstition throughout history. With the ancients, the number 12 was important—the 12 astrological signs and the 12 tribes of Israel are examples. The number 13 was considered unlucky simply because it fell after the number 12.

In 1921, Margaret Murray, an anthropologist, published a book in which she had done a study of groups of Witches in the Middle East from 1567 to 1673. The number of Witches in each of these groups was 13: 12 Witches and 1 leader. To the general public, this study led to the conclusion that all Witches' covens numbered 13 members and, therefore, it was an evil number. This generalization was supported by the fact that covens usually met at the time of the full moon, which falls 13 times a year.

The superstition is taken so seriously by some people that many buildings do not have a thirteenth floor and the fear of the number 13 has been given a name—triskaidekaphobia. It is believed that seating 13 people at dinner is unlucky and can even lead to the untimely death of 1 person (an idea that may be founded in the events after Christ's Last Supper, attended by Christ and his 12 disciples).

See Also: Astrology; Murray, Margaret; Numerology

Further Reading

Chevalier, Jean, and Alain Gheerbrant. *The Penguin Dictionary of Symbols.* London: Penguin, 1996.

Gordon, Stuart. *The Encyclopedia of Myths and Legends.* London: Headline, 1993.

Threefold Law of Return

Neopagan Witches generally believe in the "Threefold Law of Return": Whatever magic is done will return upon the Witch three times as strongly as it affects the person at whom it is directed. The implication here is, of course, that a Witch had better work only positive and beneficial magic. This law appears to have been introduced as part of the Gardnerian Tradition. Aside from some resemblance to the concept of karma, it does not have any known connection with any type of folk-magic tradition.

See Also: Karma; Magic
Further Reading
Guiley, Rosemary. *The Encyclopedia of Witches and Witchcraft*. New York: Facts on File, 1989.

Tiferet

Tiferet is the sixth sefira of the Cabala. The term means "beauty" in Hebrew. This sefira is also called *rahanim,* "compassion"—the central sefira of the tree of life, which represents balance. It is the trunk of the seforotic body and the son of Chokhmah and Binah.

See Also: Cabala
Further Reading
Fortune, Dion. *The Mystical Qabalah*. York Beach, ME: Weiser, 1994 [1935].
Myers, Stuart. *Between the Worlds: Witchcraft and the Tree of Life—A Program of Spiritual Development*. St. Paul, MN: Llewellyn, 1995.

Tools, Witches'

Upon initiation, a Witch is bestowed with a set of magical tools to aid in the processes of ritual magic. The four primary tools, symbolizing the four main elements, are blessed with water, a candle flame, incense, and salt. They are generally personalized with inscriptions of magic symbols or runes. The tools are considered most effective if purchased new or handmade.

The four primary tools consist of the athame (a black-hilted knife or sword), the pentacle, the chalice, and the wand. The athame represents the element of fire and is predominantly made of iron or steel. However, some sects of hereditary Witches (those taught by family) in England hold the belief that metal interferes with the energy of the Earth and, therefore, they use flint for their athames. The athame is used for casting the magic circle and is generally not used for cutting—a white-hilted knife is used for this purpose.

The next tool, the chalice, is viewed as the receptacle of spiritual forces and represents the element of water. The chalice is a feminine instrument that represents such qualities as fertility, beauty, love, intuition, and the sub-

A typical Wiccan altar with several traditional tools on display. (Raymond Buckland/Fortean Picture Library)

conscious mind. When the "bowl" of the chalice faces upward, it symbolizes a receiver or an open womb; when the "bowl" is inverted, birth and cognizance are indicated. In a display of the union of male and female forces, the athame, a masculine instrument, is plunged into a (feminine) wine-filled chalice.

The pentacle represents the earth element. It is used to serve food and is in the shape of a disc or square. The pentacle is made of metal, wood, clay, or wax. It maintains an association with feminine powers and is thought to base energies.

The wand represents air and is used to invoke spirits. The wand is made of wood, usually hazel, ash, or willow.

The censer is a dish designed for burning incense, herbs, or chemicals to purify the air. If the air is purified prior to a ritual, unwanted energies are held at bay and the air offered to the goddesses or gods is considered clean. The type of material to be burned in the censer coincides with the purpose of the ritual.

Cords made of silk or other organic materials are knotted in specific patterns during the recitation of chants. Cords are bound around various sections of the human body in order to decrease circulation and promote psychic power. The scourge is similar to a cord in that it is made of a light material. The scourge is similar to a whip, but its purpose is only to stimulate the blood in an area of the body in order to direct it away from the brain, thus causing drowsiness and an altered state of consciousness. The scourge can be found primarily in Gardnerian and Alexandrian traditions. It was Gardner who believed that one could learn through suffering and by exciting the body and spirit.

See Also: Athame; Cords; Cup; Magic; Scourge; Wand
Further Reading

Bonewits, P. E. I. *Real Magic,* 3d ed. York Beach, ME: Weiser, 1988.

Frost, Yvonne, and Gavin Frost. *The Magic Power of Witchcraft.* West Nyack, NY: Parker, 1976.

K., Amber. *True Magick: A Beginner's Guide.* St. Paul, MN: Llewellyn, 1991.

Tradition

The term *tradition* is used among Neopagan Witches to mean something like what *denomination* means among Protestants. A tradition will have some sort of family tree going back to its founder, some sort of loose criteria for whether a coven still belongs to the tradition, and perhaps some specific myths about its origins. In practice, however, what defines a tradition is the contents of its Book of Shadows (liturgical manual).

A tradition is usually not "organized" in the sense that a Protestant denomination is, however. With a few rare exceptions, as among the orthodox Gardnerians, there is no central authority or traditional practice that is able to expel a coven from a tradition since Witches generally believe that every coven should be autonomous.

See Also: Book of Shadows
Further Reading

Guiley, Rosemary. *The Encyclopedia of Witches and Witchcraft.* New York: Facts on File, 1989.

RavenWolf, Silver. *To Ride a Silver Broomstick: New Generation Witchcraft.* St. Paul, MN: Llewellyn, 1996.

Tree Calendar

During the 1950s, the Gardnerian movement absorbed and built upon the mythological system developed by Robert Graves in his book *The White Goddess.* Graves himself was apparently recruited as something of a propagandist for the movement. One of Graves's inventions was the "tree calendar," adopted by the Craft movement as part of its festival system.

The basis for this calendar is the Gaelic alphabet, which consists of 13 consonants and 5 vowels (and has for at least 2,000 years). Irish and Welsh poets, successors to the Druids, devised many code alphabets in order to communicate with each other secretly; these consisted of sets of 18 trees, birds, or animals, for instance, whose names began with the 18 letters of the alphabet.

Graves proposed that the tree alphabet was also used as a calendar of 13 28-day months, plus an extra day (2 in leap years) to make up the 365 days of a year. Graves assigned the five vowels to the quarter days, with the first and last quarter days falling on the day of the winter solstice—the beginning of the year as observed at Stonehenge. Although there is no persuasive or even plausible evidence that any such calendar ever was in general use in ancient Britain, it has been adopted by the Neopagan movement; and the mythological associations of the 18 trees are used as part of the symbolic system behind the ritual dramas written for the 8 Sabbats of the year.

The sequence of dates and trees in the tree calendar is as follows.

> January 21—First day of the Rowan
> February 18—First day of the Ash
> March 18—First day of the Alder
> March 21—Day of the Furze
> April 15—First day of the Willow
> May 13—First day of the Hawthorn
> June 10—First day of the Oak
> June 22—Day of the Heather
> July 8—First day of the Holly
> August 5—First day of the Hazel
> September 2—First day of the Vine
> September 23—Day of the Aspen
> September 30—First day of the Ivy
> October 28—First day of the Reed
> November 25—First day of the Elder
> December 23—Day of the Yew and Silver Fir
> December 24—First day of the Birch

See Also: Graves, Robert; Sabbats
Further Reading
Calder, George. *Auraicept na n-Éces: The Scholars' Primer.* Edinburgh, Scotland: John Grant, 1917.

Trees

Trees, as reservoirs of incalculable energy and longevity, are universally associated with significant spiritual, religious, and magical lore. They are variously depicted as the haunts of Witches and fairies, as well as the ghosts of people who died in a tragic or violent way. Trees, which have been associated with the beginning of all life, fertility, and mystical wisdom, often symbolize the universe: Their branches can be viewed as the heavens, their trunks as the Earth, and their roots as the underworld. In some parts of the world, it is believed that trees have a soul, and that cutting a limb wounds them. It is said that the person responsible for wounding a tree will suffer the same wound.

Much of the lore concerning trees comes from Europe, where the ancient Celts, Druids, and early Germans had a strong affinity with trees. They were often sites of worship; in Scandinavian lore, Yggdrasil represents the World Tree, or immortal Tree of Life. In ancient Greece, the deities were often associated with trees. The fig tree was revered by the ancient Romans, as its roots were believed to have saved the city's founding twins, Romulus and Remus, when they floated down the Tiber River.

Trees have frequently been described as oracles that can answer questions through the whispering and rustling of their leaves. They have also played a significant role in seasonal rituals and festivals in various parts of the world, such as in Eurasia, where women wishing to conceive a child would roll on the ground beneath apple trees. A traditional fertility rite involving trees is the seasonal festival taking place throughout the British Isles and continental Europe on Beltane (May Eve) or on St. John's Eve (summer solstice) in Scandinavia. It is believed that some trees protect houses against Witches, fairies, and evil spirits, as well as against lightning and accidents that can happen during construction.

Witches are said to gather around thorn and elder trees. They are also believed to disguise themselves as elder trees, the branches of which are often used in charms, as well as to keep evil spirits out of houses. It is generally claimed that cutting anything from an elder tree means bad luck, unless permission is asked of the spirits dwelling in the tree. Elderberries are used to make a strong wine, whereas elder flowers are used by herbalists in remedies for colds. Elder wood, on the other hand, is frequently used to make magic wands or amulets warding against evil and Witchcraft.

See Also: Green Man; Wand
Further Reading
Cirlot, J. E. A *Dictionary of Symbols*. New York: Dorset Press, 1991.
Davidson, H. R. Ellis. *Myths and Symbols in Pagan Europe*. Syracuse, NY: Syracuse University Press, 1988.

U

Undines

Undines are a form of fairy, associated with the element of water. They reside in oceans and other bodies of water and are said to appear in the form of sea horses that have human faces. Larger and more developed Undines are said to form the basis for the legends of mermaids and mermen. Water is traditionally associated with emotions and sensuality, and in occult sources the Undines are said to work with human beings through their "astral body" to help develop sensitivity and emotions.

Undines are the archetypal spirits of the water element and, as such, are occupied with maintaining all of the Earth's bodies of water. In magic, the Undines are the water elementals associated with one of the directions (usually the west) invoked in rituals. The task of the elementals is to build forms in the natural world. While some writers view elementals as soulless entities who simply disappear at death, others view them as spirits who eventually evolve into devas (angels). Due to their association with water, the Undines are under the rule of the archangel Gabriel.

See Also: Gnomes; Salamanders; Sylphs; Water
Further Reading
Andrews, Ted. *Enchantment of the Faerie Realm: Communicate with Nature Spirits and Elementals*. St. Paul, MN: Llewellyn, 1993.
McCoy, Edwin. *A Witch's Guide to Faery Folk*. St. Paul, MN: Llewellyn, 1994.

Ursa Maior

Ursa Maior was one of the first all-women's circles to be founded in the San Francisco area, and it sparked a great deal of debate over whether single-sex covens were "really" covens. This circle worked together from about 1973 to 1977 and exerted a great influence on the women's spirituality movement because of its vitality and creativity, especially through the summer-solstice ritual that was worked for about 150 women at the Women's Spirituality Festival in Oregon in about 1974. Founding and key members included Barbry MyOwn, Deborah Bender, Hallie Mountain Wing, Rita A., Marge, Linda, and (perhaps) Chellis. The group worked by consensus. They were signatories of the initial covenant document that allowed creation of the Covenant of the Goddess (CoG), and were active members of CoG, both nationally and in the Northern California Local Council, for as long as they worked together.

See Also: Dianic Wicca/Goddess Religion; Women's Spirituality Movement

Further Reading

MyOwn, Barbry. "Ursa Maior: Menstrual Moon Celebration." In Rush, Anne Kent, ed., *Moon, Moon*. New York: Random House/Moon Books, 1976.

V

Vodun

Vodun (popularly called "Voodoo") is a magical religion that originated in Haiti in the late 1700s. The precursor of Vodun was the religion of the Fon people of West Africa, who were brought as slaves to Haiti. *Vodun* means "spirit" in the Fon language. In Haiti, the Fon systems of veneration of the spirits came in contact with other African religious traditions and French Catholicism to produce what is now called Vodun. It has spread via emigration to New Orleans and major cities in the United States, most notably New York City.

The central religious activity of Vodun involves possession of devotees by a number of African deities. In ceremonies led by a Priest, each possessed individual enacts a highly specific ritual performance involving dance, song, and speech appropriate to the particular possessing deity. Possession is directed toward healing, warding off evil, and bringing good or evil fortune.

Vodun recognizes a remote and almighty Supreme Being who is a personification of fate or destiny. In Vodun this god is called Bondye. Individuals are given their own destinies by Bondye. In order to fulfill these destinies with grace and power, an individual requires guidance from a variety of spirits, called *lwa*. The religion of Vodun is a system of actions undertaken to develop closer relationships with the *lwa*. Human beings and spirits interact through divination and sacrifice. Trained Priests and Priestesses consult oracles to determine the sacrificial foods and actions necessary to secure the power and presence of *lwa*. One particular *lwa* will assert itself as an individual devotee's patron. When the spirit wills it, the individual will undergo an initiation into the mysteries of his or her patron spirit. This initiation marks the member's entry into the Priesthood of Vodun and gives him or her the authority to found his or her own house and consecrate other Priests and Priestesses. The spirit will identify with the devotee's inner self and this intimate relationship will offer the devotee health, success, and wisdom.

In Vodun, the spirits are venerated through symbols. Each has its own special colors, numbers, songs, rhythms, and foods. Feasts for the spirits involve complex arrangements of these colors, numbers, songs, rhythms, and foods, which incarnate the presence of the spirit in the community. In the

Priestess Yaffa, also known as Rose, heats the tip of a spear in a candle to perform a ceremony as Voodoo Queen in New Orleans, Louisiana, 1991. (Corbis/Philip Gould)

midst of the proper combination of rhythms and songs, devotees lose individual consciousness and manifest the divine personalities of the spirits.

When Vodun first came to the United States with Haitian immigrants, the appeal of the religion was primarily to fellow immigrants who were familiar with the traditions in their homeland. The tradition had been maintained in Haiti primarily by poor, black Haitians who sustained the religion despite brutal campaigns of suppression. In the United States, devotees offered similar services for cultural survival, mutual aid, and spiritual fulfillment. Vodun houses provided natural community centers where familiar practices could be enjoyed. Priests and Priestesses who were trained as diagnosticians and herbalists offered avenues for health care in the new urban environment. Vodun houses offered ways to align the individual with the force of the spirits in order to secure a job, win a lover, or revenge an injustice. As time went on, Vodun houses also offered spiritual opportunities to people who came in contact with the traditions for the first time in the United States.

White Americans as well as black Americans have found their way to Vodun houses. While there are relatively few white initiates, it is likely that there will be more as the religion becomes better known and spreads further beyond its immigrant roots.

Although the most venerable Priests and Priestesses of Vodun are likely to be older, black, working-class people who emigrated from Haiti, the next generation of initiates is much more likely to be middle-class, educated individuals, often intellectuals, who find survival skills, cultural empowerment, and aesthetic pleasure in the movement.

Teaching within Vodun traditionally is done orally, in face-to-face initiations. The teachings have been secret and available only to those who have been chosen by elders to receive them. In the environment of North American cities, more and more charlatans pretend to have been initiated, when in truth they have not. These impostors often demand large sums of money for bogus services. One solution to this crisis may be the production of ritual texts. More and more Vodun houses are producing texts for instruction and education.

The most controversial element of Vodun in the eyes of outsiders is the slaughter of animals as part of feasts for the *lwa*. Most of the important ceremonies require a feast to be prepared for the spirits and to be enjoyed by the assembled community. In order to fix the meal to the spirit's specifications, the foods must not only be prepared and cooked according to strict recipes, but they must be properly consecrated with certain prayers and rhythms. Animals for the feast (fowl, goats, and sheep) must be slaughtered by a Priest or Priestess who has been initiated specifically for this task in the presence of the community and to the accompaniment of the correct chants. Particularly in the crowded neighborhoods of New York and Miami, animal slaughter as part of Vodun ceremonies causes problems, including storage of the animals before the ceremony and disposal of the remains afterward.

An example of a Vodun group is the Afro-American Vodun, founded by Madam Arboo. In the 1960s, Madam Arboo became active in Harlem as a leader of an American Vodun group. She describes Vodun as an Afro-Christian cult centered on Damballah, the God of wisdom, personified as a serpent. (The concept of Damballah can be equated with the Bible story in which a serpent was transformed by God for Moses in the wilderness.) As High Priestess, Madam Arboo is the messenger of Damballah. Her group has reduced the remainder of the pantheon to the position of subdeities or spirits.

Healing is a high priority of Vodun, which employs psychic and psychological counseling and dispensing of folk remedies, such as rattlesnake oil. Worship is held on the evening of the new moon and consists of ecstatic dance, accompanied by flute and drum and led by the Priest and Priestess. As they dance, members enter trances and often receive revelations and messages from the spirits. Spirituals are also sung. Vodun teaches the virtues of faith, love, and joy.

See Also: Candomblé; Macumba; Orishas; Santeria

Further Reading

Hinnells, John R., ed. *A New Dictionary of Religions*. Cambridge, MA: Blackwell, 1995.

Miller, Timothy, ed. *America's Alternative Religions*. Albany, NY: State University of New York Press, 1995.

Rigaud, Milo. *Secrets of Voodoo*. San Francisco, CA: City Lights Books, 1985 [1953].

W

Wand

The wand is one of the basic magical working tools of Neopagan Witches. It is used, among other purposes, for invoking spirits. It represents the element of fire. The wand is a pointer and director of magical energy. Witches' wands may be wooden or made from bone, ivory, or amber. The rods may be straight or crooked, crystal tipped, decorated with ribbons, or set with magic stones. They vary in size. The wand is one version of the magical rod of power. Other forms include the royal scepter, a marshal's baton, a mayor's staff, a bishop's crosier, and a dowsing rod. The wand is a tool of transformation—it invokes the power of the Mother Spirit, the Goddess, who constantly transforms everything in the universe into something else. In Tarot the suit of wands represents the element of fire.

See Also: Fire; Tools, Witches'; Trees
Further Reading
Chevalier, Jean, and Alain Gheerbrant. *The Penguin Dictionary of Symbols*. London: Penguin, 1996.
Cirlot, J. E. A *Dictionary of Symbols*. New York: Dorset Press, 1991.

Watchtowers

The Lords of the Watchtowers are also called the Mighty Ones, the Guardians of the four quarters (north, east, south, and west). The term *watchtowers* is used in some documents in the Gardnerian Book of Shadows. It is not clear where the term originated, but it is in general use in the Craft.

See Also: Book of Shadows; Quarters
Further Reading
RavenWolf, Silver. *To Ride a Silver Broomstick: New Generation Witchcraft*. St. Paul, MN: Llewellyn, 1996.

Water

Water is one of the four classical elements. Some items and characteristics associated with water are the direction west, fecundity, bodily fluids, emotions, sensitivity, receptivity, instability, indifference, the color blue, the metal silver, the cup (the Witches' tool), and the Tarot suit cup. Water is considered to be a female element. Many water deities are female. The tides of the oceans are linked to the moon, a female force.

In the Middle Ages, suspected Witches were tied up and thrown into water. If they floated, they were considered to be Witches. Witches were believed to be unable to cross a running stream. If pursued by a Witch, the solution would be to cross a stream, where the Witch could not follow. Holy water was another protection against Witches and their spells. It was sprinkled in houses and drunk by sick people and animals. In the book and the film version of *The Wizard of Oz*, the Wicked Witch of the West melted away to nothing when Dorothy inadvertently threw ordinary water on her.

See Also: Cup; Undines
Further Reading
Cirlot, J. E. *A Dictionary of Symbols*. New York: Dorset Press, 1991.
Heisler, Roger. *Path to Power*. York Beach, ME: Weiser, 1990.

Wheel of the Year
The Wheel of the Year is another name for the cycle of eight Sabbats during the course of each year:

Brigid or Imbolc	February 1
Eostar	March 22 (spring equinox)
Beltane	May 1
Litha	June 22 (summer solstice)
Lughnasad	August 1
Mabon	September 22 (fall equinox)
Samhain	November 1
Yule	December 22 (winter solstice)

The dates for the solstices and equinoxes can vary on the calendar by a day either way for astronomical reasons.

It is part of the overall Wiccan foundation myth that the Wheel of the Year is a system of holidays observed by Witches from ancient times. In fact, according to members of Gardner's London coven, the Wheel of the Year is something invented by the Witches of that coven in the mid-1950s.

Though it may not be ancient, the Wheel of the Year has become a national system of Pagan holidays in the United States, Canada, the United Kingdom, and elsewhere, with national and local Sabbats and festivals being held to celebrate them. The writing of Sabbat rituals has become a popular outlet for creativity among Neopagans, and a great many recent works by Neopagans deal with the issues of how to create a magically and aesthetically effective ritual.

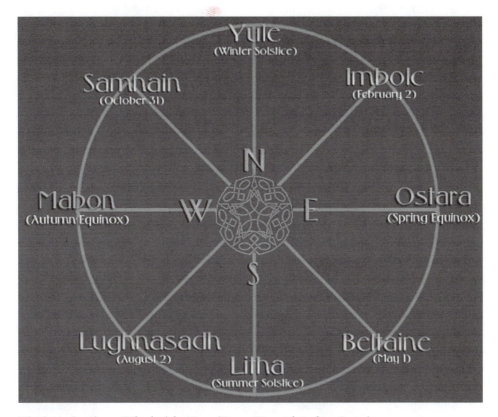

The festival cycle, or Wheel of the Year. (Dover Pictorial Archive Series)

See Also: Sabbats
Further Reading
Farrar, Stewart, and Janet Farrar. With notes by Doreen Valiente. *Eight Sabbats for Witches*. London: Robert Hale, 1981.
Fitch, Ed, and Janine Renee. *Magical Rites from the Crystal Well*. St. Paul, MN: Llewellyn, 1984.
Green, Marian. *A Harvest of Festivals*. London: Longman, 1980.
Magliocco, Sabina. "Ritual Is My Chosen Art Form: The Creation of Ritual as Folk Art among Contemporary Pagans." In Lewis, James R., ed., *Magical Religion and Modern Witchcraft*. Albany, NY: State University of New York Press, 1996, 93–120.

Wicca

The word *Wicca* was originally the Saxon term for a male Witch and was pronounced "witch-ah"; the female *wicce* was pronounced "witch-ay." The term *Wicca* was adopted by Gerald Gardner as a general name for the Witchcraft religion he had helped to found and/or revive in the 1930s. It is now used mainly in that sense and is pronounced "wick-ah." A member of the religion

An imaginative portrait of Gerald Gardner, founder of modern Wicca. (Fortean Picture Library)

is therefore a Wiccan, pronounced "wick-un." The Witchcraft religion is also referred to as the Craft; Gardner began using this term, originally a Masonic word for Freemasonry, as a name for the Witchcraft movement in the late 1950s.

See Also: Craft, The; Freemasonry

Further Reading

Lewis, James R. *The Encyclopedia of Cults, Sects and New Religions.* Amherst, NY: Prometheus, 1998.

Melton, J. Gordon. *Encyclopedia of American Religion*, 5th ed. Detroit, MI: Gale Research, 1996.

Wiccan Rede

The Wiccan Rede (old English for "advice" or "counsel") is the rule that says "An [if] it harm none, do as you will." It is an ethic of harmlessness, parallel to the Hindu concept of *ahimsa*.

Many have viewed the Wiccan Rede as a parallel to Aleister Crowley's dictum "Do as thou wilt shall be the whole of the law. Love is the law, love under will." However, the element of harmlessness is not evident here, certainly not in his first sentence. Attempts to explain that Crowley's second sentence modifies the concept of "law" in the first sentence (enough to call it an ethic of harmlessness) are not convincing to many.

There also is a genuine parallel with St. Augustine's dictum "Love—then do as you like." That is, he said that one may do whatever one wants as long as he or she is acting out of genuine love. The parallel to the Rede is real, because Augustine explained in his writings that love, as he understood it, could not cause, allow, or condone harm to anyone.

Some feel that this is too slender a "rede" on which to base an ethic adequate for a religious movement as large as Neopaganism. There are others who feel that the kind of libertarian ethic implied by the Wiccan Rede is precisely what is needed not only by the Craft, but by modern society in general.

Further Reading

Clifton, Charles S. "What Has Alexandria to Do with Boston? Some Sources of Modern Pagan Ethics." In Lewis, James R., ed., *Magical Religion and Modern Witchcraft*. Albany, NY: State University of New York Press, 1996, 269–276.

Wild Hunt

The Wild Hunt is rooted in Celtic and Germanic folklore. It consists of an assemblage of ghosts of the dead who ride through the night on phantasmal steeds accompanied by packs of howling dogs. This hunt is led by the Pagan

Goddesses Diana, Holda, Herodias, Hecate, and Berchta who, with the advent of Christianity, were denounced as devils. Sometimes Herne the Hunter, a huntsman of old English myth, is the leader of the hunt, or sometimes Holda, the Germanic Goddess of the Sky, leads the souls of the unbaptized dead. The members of the Wild Hunt are reputed to wreak havoc unless appeased by offerings from humans. In medieval depictions of the Wild Hunt, the spirits of the dead were joined by Witches. The last Wild Hunt rumored to have taken place was in the English countryside in the 1940s, falling on Hallowe'en.

See Also: Cernunnos; Diana; Hecate; Herne the Hunter; Horned God
Further Reading
Gordon, Stuart. *The Encyclopedia of Myths and Legends.* London: Headline, 1993.
Leach, Maria. *Standard Dictionary of Folklore, Mythology, and Legend.* San Francisco, CA: HarperSan Francisco, 1984 [1949].

Wiccaning

Wiccaning is a Craft ritual that is intended to be somewhat similar to a christening, or infant baptism, although the theology of Wiccaning is quite different. It is largely intended as an occasion on which a new baby can be introduced to the Craft community.

There is no standard ritual for this occasion. Rather, it is one of the "rites of passage" for which much creativity is exhibited in the Craft. For example, in the New Reformed Orthodox Order of the Golden Dawn, there is a Wiccaning ritual called the 13 Wishes, in which 13 Witches each make a wish for the baby and light a candle. After the last wish is made, all blow out their candles so that the wishes will come true. These 13 Witches are then regarded as the Fairy Godparents of the baby. This is modeled directly on the story of Sleeping Beauty—except that all 13 Witches are invited.

See Also: Initiation
Further Reading
Guiley, Rosemary. *The Encyclopedia of Witches and Witchcraft.* New York: Facts on File, 1989.

Withershins

The term *withershins,* or *widdershins*—from the Anglo-Saxon *with sith,* "to walk against"—refers to a counterclockwise circular movement used to banish spells, curses, and undesirable situations. Withershins is also used during the casting of some magic circles and in certain necromantic rituals. Withershins is thought of as walking against the sun, and thus it represents what is unnatural and negative. The opposite of withershins is deosil, meaning "to move clockwise." In some Neopagan rituals, after a magic circle is cast deosil, participants may open a small section with a withershins motion using a sword or athame and then reclose it with a deosil motion.

See Also: Cast; Circle, Magic; Deosil
Further Reading
Farrar, Stewart. *What Witches Do: The Modern Coven Revealed.* New York: Coward McCann, 1971.
Frost, Yvonne, and Gavin Frost. *The Magic Power of Witchcraft.* West Nyack, NY: Parker, 1976.

Women's Spirituality Movement

The highly varied, grassroots women's spirituality movement stems from many sources, but is primarily an artifact of the women's movement of the 1970s. It draws on many religious traditions, both old and new, to form an eclectic blend of beliefs and practices, all thought to be especially suited to the empowerment of women and the enhancement of feminist values.

The women's spirituality movement initially came together at the confluence of several streams of religious and social activity, including Jewish and Christian feminism, the secular feminist movement, and the Neopagan revival. Some Jewish and Christian feminists, increasingly frustrated by the lack of possibilities for change in their own traditions, began to explore nontraditional forms of religious practice that occurred outside established religions. Some secular feminists become so identified with their political activities and the communities that were built up around them that they came to see spiritual depths in their feminism itself. These two forces linked together and met with Neopaganism, which these feminists found attractive for its worship of goddesses (or a single Goddess), the prominent roles it accorded women (frequently as Priestesses), the opportunity to be creative in ritual, and a purported linkage of Neopaganism to religions from pre-Christian times (thus avoiding the taint of the so-called patriarchal religions against which they were rebelling).

Pioneers in women's spirituality were those women who already had some commitment to Neopaganism or Witchcraft before they took it in a more feminist direction. Two women were especially influential in the early days of feminist spirituality (and continue to be influential today): Zsusanna Budapest and Starhawk (Miriam Simos). Both were exposed to Witchcraft before the women's movement was in full swing: Budapest through folk religious practices she experienced during her childhood in Hungary, and Starhawk through the growing Neopagan movement in 1960s California. Both became committed feminists and saw in their preexisting religious interests an opportunity to provide spiritual resources to individual women and to the feminist movement as a whole.

Although experiments in women-only or feminist rituals undoubtedly occurred before then, the movement is most easily dated to 1971, when Budapest and a small number of friends held a winter solstice ritual limited to female participants and devoted to feminist personal and political aims. They dubbed their fledgling group the Susan B. Anthony Coven No. 1 and issued a manifesto claiming Witchcraft as "wimmin's religion." The group quickly drew attention throughout the women's community in Los Angeles, to the point that open rituals sometimes included over 100 participants. Similar groups sprang up elsewhere around the United States, building on the Susan B. Anthony Coven model. With no official organization or corporate linkage between the groups, a great deal of variety among the groups emerged in a very short period of time. The original focus on Witchcraft quickly expanded to include experimentation with all the religious elements of the recent counterculture and the emerging New Age movement. Women sought feminist or uniquely female interpretations of Tarot, the *I Ching*, yoga, Buddhism, past-life regressions, Native American spirituality, and so on. This experimentation had a slingshot effect on feminist initiatives in traditional religions, so that Jewish and Christian feminists were encouraged to expand in directions more "radical" than those they had previously considered.

Because of the enormous variety found in the women's spirituality movement, there are perhaps no religious elements that are held in common among all practitioners. In spite of this, there is a core set of beliefs and practices that characterize the movement, if not the spirituality of all of its individual members.

Foremost among these is a belief in, or invocation of, a female deity or deities. Women's spirituality describes itself as polytheistic, and yet reference is often made to "the great Goddess"; individual goddesses—when discussed or invoked—are usually described as manifestations or aspects of the one Goddess. Some practitioners regard the Goddess as a convenient term of pantheism; others resist all theological language and/or belief in deity. Whether plural or singular, the Goddess is understood to be an immanent deity, one that is experienced through self, others, and nature. The latter is particularly important to the women's spirituality movement: Showing strong links to ecofeminism, women's spirituality regards nature as sacred, as "the body of the Goddess."

The women's spirituality movement, with rare exception, relies on a strong notion of gender difference, viewing at least most human traits, if not all human individuals, as masculine or feminine. This "difference feminism" means that the movement is built upon a foundation of female uniqueness: There is something women have to offer, spiritually and politically, that the movement is designed to celebrate and promote. Through analogy to menstruation and childbirth, in particular, women are believed to be especially sensitive to cycles, to nature, and to relationships between people and between humans and the cosmos.

This emphasis on female uniqueness frequently finds its way into the rituals of the women's spirituality movement. Female life-cycle events, including menarche, menstruation, menopause, and childbirth, are often marked ritually. Following Neopaganism, many rituals are scheduled to coincide with solstices, equinoxes, and new and full moons, but, just as frequently, rituals are scheduled as a matter of convenience on a weekly or monthly basis or as part of workshops or retreats. Magic and divination are generally practiced alone or through one-on-one transactions between women, with one woman usually taking the role of expert (a role for which she is typically financially compensated). Apart from an emphasis on the femaleness of the participants, the ritual, magic, and divination of the women's spirituality movement bear strong resemblance to similar practices throughout the New Age movement and the alternative religious subculture.

One of the more distinctive religious contributions of the women's spirituality movement is its version of Western (or world) history, according to which all of prehistory was characterized by Goddess worship and greater social power for women. This era came to an end, the movement teaches, with "the patriarchal revolution," variously explained as a male rebellion against female rule, an incursion of foreign patriarchal tribes into Goddess-worshipping lands, or a social development resulting from the discovery of the paternal role in human reproduction. The past 3,000 to 8,000 years have been almost universally patriarchal, but this system is soon to collapse, the movement claims, either through massive devastation of the planet and its peoples or through a turning toward the "female" values advocated by the movement and embodied in the Goddess.

It would be truer to the women's spirituality movement to speak of a *lack* of organization than of an organization. Numerous attempts have been made to provide an organizational framework for women's spirituality, but all have failed to secure any real cohesion among the movement's many adherents and small-scale groupings. Nor is any such organization likely to develop, for reasons inherent in the movement's sense of itself. Women's spirituality claims that all women are leaders and that each woman needs to find her own spiritual path. Mentor-student or guru-seeker relationships are rare and, where they do exist, are likely to be carried out only in the temporary setting of a class or workshop. A further block to organization of the movement is the deep desire on the part of participants to avoid schism. There are key areas of tension and controversy within the movement, but so long as there is no effort made to organize or codify the developing religion, women holding opposing views can quite happily coexist under the large umbrella of women's spirituality.

In spite of its lack of organization, the vitality of the women's spirituality movement can be seen in the many study groups, spiritual circles, retreats, "training" schools, and so forth that form the communal expression of women's spirituality. Furthermore, the development of a relatively large literature—including books, journals, newsletters, and now audiotapes and videotapes as well—has exposed vast numbers of women to the central ideas of the women's spirituality movement. Without an efficient religious organization, this literature has become the religion's main tool of evangelism to the uninitiated and source of networking among the already committed. It allows women who cannot find or start women's spirituality groups to feel themselves part of the movement and to authenticate their solo practice.

Because women's spirituality is among the more nondogmatic of religions, most areas of tension between adherents dissipate rapidly into a "live and let live" policy. Women differ as to whether the Goddess is one or many, whether ancient matriarchies actually existed or are only a convenient myth, and so on, but debate is rarely heated. However, there are several areas of more intense controversy that will play an important role in determining the directions the women's spirituality movement will take in the future.

First, some spiritual feminists feel it is disrespectful to other cultures to borrow religious elements from them (such as goddess names and myths or divinatory methods) without their permission. Others do not find this "borrowing" problematic, regarding it rather as a splendid example of multiculturalism in action, or they justify their borrowing by citing the greater good of empowering women. Second is controversy over the similarities between the women's spirituality movement and the New Age movement. Some women feel the two movements are antithetical to one another and that the true interests of women and feminism can never be served as long as the two movements overlap. Other women believe that there are important spiritual resources being uncovered in the New Age movement and that there is no reason women cannot work within New Age religions to serve the goals of the women's spirituality movement. Related to this disagreement over the New Age is a third, and probably more divisive, controversy: that of whether and how men can be included in women's spirituality. Here debate becomes quite fiery between those who want to share their new religion with the men in their lives and those who believe that any inclusion of men would seal the doom of women's spirituality.

The trend over the past five to ten years in the women's spirituality movement has been toward greater unity of purpose and practice with other Neopagan and New Age religions, including a greater openness toward working with men. Probably the majority of practitioners of women's spirituality are in favor of cultural and religious borrowing, sharing space and resources with the New Age movement, and the judicious inclusion of men. However, it is the most committed and active adherents of women's spirituality who are also the most adamantly opposed to alliances with the New Age movement—or worse, with men—who, to a lesser extent, oppose extensive cultural and religious borrowing. Factoring this more intense commitment into the equation leaves all these controversies at a standoff for the time being.

—*Cynthia Eller*

See Also: Dianic Wicca/Goddess Religion; Susan B. Anthony Coven
Further Reading
Spretnak, Charlene, ed. *The Politics of Women's Spirituality: Essays on the Rise of Spiritual Power within the Feminist Movement.* New York: Doubleday, 1982.

Starhawk [Miriam Simos]. *Truth or Dare: Encounters with Truth, Authority, and Mystery.* San Francisco: HarperSan Francisco, 1987.

Work, Working

Work, as a technical term in Neopagan Witchcraft, is derived from its usage in Freemasonry. A Witch "works" a ritual, an initiation, a spell, or magic in general, just as Masons speak of working in the First Degree, the Second Degree, and so on. Use of the term *perform* in these circumstances is avoided, since it implies that a ritual is mere theatrics.

See Also: Freemasonry; Magic; Rite, Ritual

Further Reading

Farrar, Stewart, and Janet Farrar. *Spells and How They Work.* Custer, WA: Phoenix, 1990.

Y

Yesod

The ninth sephira of the Cabala is Yesod, foundation. It represents the phallus, the procreative life force of the universe. It is the final state of force before form. Yesod filters and protects the other energies before they are made manifest. It is the *axis mundi*, the cosmic pillar.

See Also: Cabala
Further Reading
Fortune, Dion. *The Mystical Qabalah.* York Beach, ME: Weiser, 1994 [1935].
Myers, Stuart. *Between the Worlds: Witchcraft and the Tree of Life—A Program of Spiritual Development.* St. Paul, MN: Llewellyn, 1995.

Yule

Yule is still used as an alternative name for Christmas, but it was originally the Saxon name for their winter solstice festival, and it has been adopted by Neopagan Witches as the name for their Sabbat on that date. Yule is one of the Lesser Sabbats, comprising the English quarter days, which fall approximately on the solstices and equinoxes. The other three Lesser Sabbats are Eostar (spring equinox, about March 22), Litha (summer solstice, about June 22), and Mabon (fall equinox, about September 22). The Yule Sabbat ritual usually focuses on the themes of the return of light, of the birth of the new king, and of the giving of presents, which was a Pagan custom long before Christianity.

The great festival of Saturn was celebrated by the Romans in late December, during just about the same period now observed as the "Christmas season" in the United States. The festival was marked by "reversals": cross-dressing, Lords of Misrule, the rich serving the poor, and so on, as are still practiced to some extent in the German Fasching traditions. Many critics have remarked that Christmas in the United States seems to have far more in common with the parties, fooleries, and satire of the Saturnalia than with any Christian traditions. In any event, many Neopagans celebrate a revived Saturnalia as their Yule festival, and it is usually a well-attended social event.

YULE

See Also: Sabbats; Wheel of the Year

Further Reading

Campanelli, Pauline. *Wheel of the Year: Living the Magical Life*. St. Paul, MN: Llewellyn, 1989.

Kelly, Aidan A. *Religious Holidays and Calendars: An Encyclopedic Handbook*. Detroit, MI: Omnigraphics, 1991.

Resources

Print Resources

Adefunmi, Baba Oseijeman. *Ancestors of the Afro-Americans*. Long Island City, NY: Aims of Modzawe, 1973.

Adefunmi I, Oba Efuntola Oseijeman Adelabu. *Olorisha, A Guidebook into Yoruba Religion*. Sheldon, SC: n.p., 1982.

Adler, Margot. *Drawing down the Moon: Witches, Pagans, Druids, and Other Goddess-Worshippers in America Today*, 2d ed. Boston, MA: Beacon Press, 1986.

Alfred, Randall H. "The Church of Satan." In Glock, Charles Y., and Robert N. Bellah, eds., *The New Religious Consciousness*. Berkeley: University of California Press, 1976, pp. 180–202. An excellent example of participant observation of an NRM.

Anderson, Cora. *Fifty Years in the Feri Tradition*. San Leandro, CA: n.p., 1995.

Anderson, Victor. "Faerie Shaman: An Interview with Victor Anderson." By Francesca Dubie. *Green Egg* 111 (winter 1995): 14–15.

———. *Thorns of the Blood Rose*. Thomas O. DeLong, ed. San Leandro, CA: n.p., 1970.

Andrews, Ted. *Enchantment of the Faerie Realm: Communicate with Nature Spirits and Elementals*. St. Paul, MN: Llewellyn, 1993.

Artemidorus. *The Interpretation of Dreams (Oneirocritica)*, 2d ed. Translated by Robert J. White. Torrance, CA: Original Books, 1990 [1975].

Ashcroft-Nowicki, Dolores. *Highways of the Mind: The Art and History of Pathworking*. Wellingborough, Northampshire, U.K.: Aquarian Press, 1987.

Bagnall, Oscar. *The Properties of the Human Aura*. New York: University Books, 1970 [1937].

Baker, James W. "White Witches: Historic Fact and Romantic Fantasy." In Lewis, James R., ed., *Magical Religion and Modern Witchcraft*. Albany, NY: State University of New York Press, 1996, pp. 171–190.

Barker, Eileen. *New Religious Movements: A Practical Introduction*. London: HMSO, 1989.

Barnouw, Victor. "Siberian Shamanism and Western Spiritualism." *Journal of the Society of Psychical Research* 36 (1942):140–168.

Barrett, Clive. *Egyptian Gods and Goddesses: The Mythology and Beliefs of Ancient Egypt*. Wellingborough, Northampshire, U.K.: Aquarian Press, 1991.

Barrett, Francis. *The Magus*. London: Lackington, Allen, and Co., 1801.

Becker, Robert O., M.D., and Gary Selden. *The Body Electric: Electromagnetism and the Foundation of Life*. New York: William Morrow, 1985.

Bell, Jessie W. *The Grimoire of Lady Sheba*. St. Paul, MN: Llewellyn, 1972. This book incorporates her earlier *Lady Sheba's Book of Shadows*, which was the second publication of the Craft Laws.

Bletzer, June G. *The Donning International Encyclopedic Psychic Dictionary*. Norfolk, VA: Donning, 1986.

Bolen, Jean Shinoda. *Goddesses in Everywoman: A New Psychology of Women*. New York: Harper and Row, 1984.

Bonewits, P. E. Isaac. *Real Magic*, 3d ed. York Beach, ME: Weiser, 1989.

Bourne, Lois. *Witch amongst Us*. New York: St. Martin's Press, 1985.

Bowman, Marion. "Cardiac Celts: Images of the Celts in Paganism." In Harvey, Graham, and Charlotte Hardman, eds., *Paganism Today: Wiccans, Druids, the Goddess, and Ancient Earth Traditions for the Twenty-First Century*. London and San Francisco: Thorsons, 1996, pp. 242–251.

Bracelin, Jack. *Gerald Gardner: Witch*. London: Octagon House, 1960. More than one source has indicated that Jack Bracelin is a pseudonym for Idries Shah.

Briggs, Katharine. *An Encyclopedia of Fairies*. New York: Pantheon, 1976.

Buckland, Raymond. *Anatomy of the Occult*. York Beach, ME: Weiser, 1977.

———. *Buckland's Complete Book of Witchcraft*. St. Paul, MN: Llewellyn, 1986.

———. *The Tree: The Complete Book of Saxon Witchcraft*. York Beach, ME: Weiser, 1974. A Book of Shadows for a tradition with democratic governance of covens.

———. *Witchcraft from the Inside*, 3d ed. St. Paul, MN: Llewellyn, 1996 [1971].

Budapest, Z. [Zsusanna]. *Grandmother Moon: Lunar Magic in Our Lives—Spells, Rituals, Goddesses, Legends, and Emotions under the Moon*. San Francisco, CA: HarperSan Francisco, 1991.

———. *The Grandmother of Time*. San Francisco, CA: HarperSan Francisco, 1989.

———. *The Holy Book of Women's Mysteries*, 2d ed. 2 vols. Oakland, CA: Thesmophoria, 1986.

Budge, E. A. Wallis. *Amulets and Superstitions*. New York: Dover, 1978 [1930].

Cabot, Laurie, with Tom Cowan. *Power of the Witch: The Earth, the Moon, and the Magical Path to Enlightenment*. New York: Delacorte, 1989.

Cahill, Robert Ellis. *The Horrors of Salem's Witch Dungeon*. Peabody, MA: Chandler-Smith, 1986.

Calder, George. *Auraicept na n-Éces: The Scholars' Primer*. Edinburgh, Scotland: John Grant, 1917.

Campanelli, Pauline. *Wheel of the Year: Living the Magical Life*. St. Paul, MN: Llewellyn, 1989.

Campbell, Bruce F. *Ancient Wisdom Revived: A History of the Theosophical Movement*. Berkeley, CA: University of California Press, 1980.

Campbell, Edward D. *The Encyclopedia of Palmistry*. New York: Perigee, 1996.

Carpenter, Dennis. "Emergent Nature Spirituality: An Examination of the Major Spiritual Contours of the Contemporary Pagan Worldview." In Lewis, James R., ed., *Magical Religion and Modern Witchcraft*. Albany, NY: State University of New York Press, 1996, pp. 35–72.

———. "Practitioners of Paganism and Wiccan Spirituality in Contemporary Society: A Review of the Literature." In Lewis, James R., ed., *The Astrology Encyclopedia*. Detroit, MI: Visible Ink Press, 1994, pp. 373–406.

Carr-Gomm, Philip. *The Druid Way*. Shaftesbury, England: Element Books, 1993.

———. *Elements of the Druid Tradition*. Shaftesbury, England: Element Books, 1991.

Cavendish, Richard. *The Black Arts*. New York: G. P. Putnam's Sons, 1967.

———. *A History of Magic*. London: Weidenfeld and Nicolson, 1977.

Cavendish, Richard, ed. *Encyclopedia of the Unexplained. Magic, Occultism, and Parapsychology*. London: Arkana Penguin Books, 1989.

Chevalier, Jean, and Alain Gheerbrant. *The Penguin Dictionary of Symbols*. London: Penguin, 1996.

Cirlot, J. E. *A Dictionary of Symbols*. New York: Dorset Press, 1991.

Clifton, Charles S. "What Has Alexandria to Do with Boston? Some Sources of Modern Pagan Ethics." In Lewis, James R., ed., *Magical Religion and Modern Witchcraft*. Albany, NY: State University of New York Press, 1996, pp. 269–276.

Clifton, Charles S., ed. *Witchcraft Today, Book One: The Modern Craft Movement*. St. Paul, MN: Llewellyn, 1992.

———. *Witchcraft Today, Book Two: Modern Rites of Passage*. St. Paul, MN: Llewellyn, 1993.

———. *Witchcraft Today, Book Three: Witchcraft and Shamanism*. St. Paul, MN: Llewellyn, 1994.

Clifton, Charles S., and Mary Currier-Clifton, eds. *Iron Mountain: A Journal of Magical Religion*. Artemisia Press.

Colquhoun, Ithell. *Sword of Wisdom: MacGregor Mathers and the "Golden Dawn."* New York: Putnam's, 1975.

Cook, Arthur Bernard. *Zeus: A Study of Ancient Religion*. Cambridge, England: Cambridge University Press, 1914.

Cooper, J. C. *An Illustrated Encyclopedia of Traditional Symbols*. London: Thames and Hudson, 1992 [1978].

Corby, Dana. *What Is Wicca: An Overview*. Seattle, WA: Rantin' Raven Pamphleteers, 1998 [1992].

Crabtree, Adam. *Multiple Man: Explorations in Possession and Multiple Personality*. New York: Praeger, 1985.

Cranston, Sylvia. *HPB: The Extraordinary Life and Influence of Helena Blavatsky, Founder of the Modern Theosophical Movement*. New York: Jeremy P. Tarcher/Putnam Books/G. P. Putnam's Sons, 1993.

Crowley, Aleister. *Magick in Theory and Practice*. New York: Castle, n.d. [ca. 1929].

Crowley, Vivianne. *Phoenix from the Flame: Pagan Spirituality in the Western World*. Wellingborough, Northamptonshire, U.K.: Aquarian Press, 1994.

———. "Wicca as a Modern-Day Mystery Religion." In Harvey, Graham, and Charlotte Hardman, eds., *Paganism Today: Wiccans, Druids, the Goddess, and Ancient Earth Traditions for the Twenty-First Century*. London and San Francisco: Thorsons, 1996, pp. 81–93.

———. *Wicca: The Old Religion in the New Age*. Wellingborough, Northamptonshire, U.K.: Aquarian Press, 1989.

Crowther, Arnold, and Patricia Crowther. *The Secrets of Ancient Witchcraft, with the Witches' Tarot*. Secaucus, NJ: University Books, 1974.

———. *The Witches Speak*. Douglas, Isle of Man: Athol Publications, 1965. Now a rare book.

Crowther, Patricia. *Lid off the Cauldron: A Wicca Handbook*. York Beach, ME: Weiser, 1981.

———. *Witch Blood!* New York: House of Collectibles, 1974.

Culpepper, Emily. "The Spiritual Movement of Radical Feminist Consciousness." In Needleman, Jacob, and George Baker, eds., *Understanding the New Religions*. Seabury, 1978, pp. 220–234.

Cumont, Franz. *Pagan Religions in the Roman World*. New York: Dover 1971 [1915].

Daniels, Estelle. *Astrologickal Magick*. York Beach, ME: Weiser, 1995.

Davidson, Gustav. *A Dictionary of Angels: Including the Fallen Angels*. New York: Free Press, 1971 [1967].

Davidson, H. R. Ellis. *Myths and Symbols in Pagan Europe*. Syracuse, NY: Syracuse University Press, 1988.

de Regula, Traci. *The Mysteries of Isis*. St. Paul, MN: Llewellyn, 1996.

Demos, John Putnam. *Entertaining Satan*. New York: Oxford University Press, 1982.

Denning, Melita, and Osborne Phillips. *The Magical Philosophy*. 5 vols. St. Paul, MN: Llewellyn, 1974–1981.

———. *Planetary Magick: The Heart of Western Magick*. St. Paul, MN: Llewellyn, 1989.

Dewar, James. "Masonic Ceremony." In Tiryakian, Edward A., ed., *On the Margin of the Visible: Sociology, the Esoteric, and the Occult*. New York: Wiley, 1974, pp. 101–109.

Douglas, Alfred. *The Tarot: The Origins, Meaning, and Use of the Cards*. New York: Taplinger, 1972.

Downing, Christine. *The Goddess: Mythological Images of the Feminine*. New York: Continuum, 1996.

Doyle, Sir Arthur Conan. *The History of Spiritualism*. New York: Arno Press, 1975 [1926].

Dubie, Francesca, and Victor Anderson. Interview by Ellen Evert Hopman and Lawrence Bond. In Hopman, Ellen Evert, and Lawrence Bond, eds., *People of the Earth: The New Pagans Speak Out*. Rochester, VT: Destiny Books, 1996.

Dumezil, Georges. *Camillus*. University of California Press.

Ebon, Martin. *The Devil's Bride, Exorcism: Past and Present*. New York: Harper and Row, 1974.

Edwards, Leila Dudley. "Tradition and Ritual: Hallowe'en and Contemporary Paganism." In Harvey, Graham, and Charlotte Hardman, eds., *Paganism Today: Wiccans, Druids, the Goddess, and Ancient Earth Traditions for the Twenty-First Century*. London and San Francisco: Thorsons, 1996, pp. 224–241.

Eliade, Mircea. *Shamanism: Archaic Techniques of Ecstasy*. Translated by W. Trask. Princeton, NJ: Princeton University Press, 1964.

———. "Some Observations on European Witchcraft." *History of Religions* 14, no. 3 (February 1975): 149–172.

———. *Yoga: Immortality and Freedom*, 2d ed. Translated by W. Trask. Princeton, NJ: Princeton University Press, 1969 [1954].

Eliade, Mircea, ed. *The Encyclopedia of Religion*. 16 vols. New York: Macmillan, 1987.

Elie. Interview by Ellen Evert Hopman and Lawrence Bond. In Hopman, Ellen Evert, and Lawrence Bond, eds., *People of the Earth: The New Pagans Speak Out*. Rochester, VT: Destiny Books, 1996.

Ellis, Peter Berresford. *Dictionary of Celtic Mythology*. Santa Barbara, CA: ABC-CLIO, 1992.

Ellwood, Robert S., Jr. *Alternative Altars: Unconventional and Eastern Spirituality in America*. Chicago, IL: University of Chicago Press, 1979.

———. *Religious and Spiritual Groups in Modern America*. Englewood Cliffs, NJ: Prentice-Hall, 1973.

Farrar, Janet, and Stewart Farrar. *The Witches' Goddess: The Feminine Principle of Divinity*. Custer, WA: Phoenix Publishing, 1988; London: Robert Hale, 1987.

Farrar, Stewart. *What Witches Do: The Modern Coven Revealed*. New York: Coward McCann, 1971.

Farrar, Stewart, and Janet Farrar. With notes by Doreen Valiente. *Eight Sabbats for Witches*. London: Robert Hale, 1981.

———. *The Life and Times of a Modern Witch*. Custer, WA: Phoenix Publishing, 1987.

———. *Spells and How They Work*. Custer, WA: Phoenix Publishing, 1990.

———. *The Witches' Way: Principles, Rituals, and Beliefs of Modern Witchcraft*. With notes and appendix by Doreen Valiente. London: Robert Hale, 1985.

Farren, David. *Living with Magic*. New York: Simon and Schuster, 1975.

———. *The Return of Magic*. New York: Harper and Row, 1973.

———. *Sex and Magic*. New York: Simon and Schuster, 1975.

Feuerstein, Georg. *Encyclopedic Dictionary of Yoga*. New York: Paragon House, 1990.

Fitch, Ed. *The Rites of Odin*. St. Paul, MN: Llewellyn, 1993.

Fitch, Ed, and Janine Renee. *Magical Rites from the Crystal Well*. St. Paul, MN: Llewellyn, 1984.

Fodor, Nandor. *An Encyclopaedia of Psychic Science*. Secaucus, NJ: The Citadel Press, 1966 [1933].

Fortune, Dion [Violet Mary Firth]. *The Mystical Qabalah*. York Beach, ME: Weiser, 1994 [1935].

Fox, Selena, and Dennis Carpenter. Interview by Ellen Evert Hopman and Lawrence Bond. In Hopman, Ellen Evert, and Lawrence Bond, eds., *People of the Earth: The New Pagans Speak Out*. Rochester, VT: Destiny Books, 1996.

Fox, Stephanie, and Stephen Posch. "Funny, You Don't Look Jewitch: An Interview with Stephanie Fox and Stephen Posch." By Stephen Wise. *Green Egg* 99 (winter 1992–1993): 18–19.

Frazer, James. *The Golden Bough*, 3d ed. 13 vols. New York: Macmillan, 1912.

Frost, Gavin, and Yvonne Frost. *Tantric Yoga: The Royal Path to Raising Kundalini Power*. York Beach, ME: Weiser, 1989.

Frost, Yvonne, and Gavin Frost. Interview by Ellen Evert Hopman and Lawrence Bond. In Hopman, Ellen Evert, and Lawrence Bond, eds., *People of the Earth: The New Pagans Speak Out*. Rochester, VT: Destiny Books, 1996.

———. *The Magic Power of Witchcraft*. West Nyack, NY: Parker, 1976.

———. *Who Speaks for the Witch? The Wiccan Holocaust*. New Bern, NC: Godolphin House, 1991.

Galbreath, Robert. "The History of Modern Occultism: A Bibliographical Survey." *Journal of Popular Culture*, vol. 5, no. 3 (winter 1971): 98–126.

Gardner, Gerald B. *High Magic's Aid*. New York: Michael Houghton, 1949.

———. *The Meaning of Witchcraft*. Wellingborough, Northampshire, U.K.: Aquarian Press, 1959.

———. *Witchcraft Today*. London: Jarrolds, 1954.

———. "Ye Bok of ye Art Magical." Unpublished manuscript, written between about 1945 (or earlier) and 1953, formerly owned by Ripley's International, Ltd., now owned by the Wiccan Church of Canada in Toronto.

Glanvil, Joseph, and Henry More. *Saducismus Triumphatus: or, Full and Plain Evidence Concerning Witches and Apparitions*, 3d ed. London: Lowndes, 1689. Scholar's Facsimiles, 1966. One of Margaret Murray's major sources of information.

Glass, Justine. *Witchcraft, the Sixth Sense—and Us*. London: Spearman, 1965.

Glassé, Cyril. *The Concise Encyclopedia of Islam*. San Francisco, CA: HarperSan Francisco, 1989.

Glock, Charles Y., and Robert N. Bellah, eds. *The New Religious Consciousness*. Berkeley: University of California Press, 1976.

Gomes, Michael. *The Dawning of the Theosophical Movement*. Wheaton, IL: The Theosophical Publishing House, 1987.

Gordon, Stuart. *The Encyclopedia of Myths and Legends*. London: Headline, 1993.

Grant, Michael, and John Hazel. *Who's Who: Classical Mythology*. New York: Oxford University Press, 1993.

Grant, R. M. *Gnosticism and Early Christianity*. New York: Columbia University Press, 1959.

Graves, Robert. *The Greek Myths*, rev. ed. 2 vols. New York: Penguin, 1960 [1955].

———. *The White Goddess: A Historical Grammar of Poetic Myth*, 3d ed. London: Farrar, Straus, and Giroux, 1966 [2d ed., 1956; 1st ed., 1948].

———. "Witches in 1964." *Virginia Quarterly Review* XL (1964): 550–559.

Greeley, Andrew. "Implications for the Sociology of Religions of Occult Behavior in the Youth Culture." In Tiryakian, Edward A., ed., *On the Margin of the Visible: Sociology, the Esoteric, and the Occult*. New York: Wiley, 1974, pp. 295–302.

Green, Marian. *The Elements of Ritual Magic*. Longmead, Shaftesbury, Dorset, U.K.: Element, 1990.

———. *Experiments in Aquarian Magic*. Wellingborough, Northamptonshire, U.K: Aquarian Press, 1985.

———. *A Harvest of Festivals*. London: Longman, 1980.

———. *Magic for the Aquarian Age*. Wellingborough, Northamptonshire, U.K: Aquarian Press, 1983.

Green, Miranda J. *Dictionary of Celtic Myth and Legend*. London: Thames and Hudson, 1992.

Greenwood, Susan. "The British Occult Subculture: Beyond Good and Evil?" In Lewis, James R., ed., *Magical Religion and Modern Witchcraft*. Albany, NY: State University of New York Press, 1996, pp. 277–296.

———. "The Magical Will, Gender, and Power in Magical Practices." In Harvey, Graham, and Charlotte Hardman, eds., *Paganism Today: Wiccans, Druids, the Goddess, and Ancient Earth Traditions for the Twenty-First Century*. London and San Francisco: Thorsons, 1996, pp. 191–203.

Grim, John A. *The Shaman: Patterns of Siberian and Ojibway Healing*. Norman, OK: University of Oklahoma Press, 1983.

Grimassi, Raven. *The Teachings of the Holy Strega*, 2d ed. Escondido, CA: Moon Dragon Publications, 1991.

———. *Whispers: Teachings of the Old Religion of Italy; An Introduction to the Aradian Tradition*, 2d ed. Escondido, CA: Moon Dragon Publications, 1991.

Grossman, Richard. *The Other Medicines*. Garden City, NJ: Doubleday, 1985.

Guiley, Rosemary Ellen. *The Encyclopedia of Ghost and Spirits*. New York: Facts on File, 1992.

———. *The Encyclopedia of Witches and Witchcraft*. New York: Facts on File, 1989.

———. *Harper's Encyclopedia of Mystical and Paranormal Experience*. San Francisco, CA: HarperSan Francisco, 1991.

Harris, Adrian. "Sacred Ecology." In Harvey, Graham, and Charlotte Hardman, eds., *Paganism Today: Wiccans, Druids, the Goddess, and Ancient Earth Traditions for the Twenty-First Century*. London and San Francisco: Thorsons, 1996, pp. 149–156.

Harrow, Judy. "The Contemporary Neo-Pagan Revival." In Lewis, James R., ed., *Magical Religion and Modern Witchcraft*. Albany, NY: State University of New York Press, 1996, pp. 9–24.

Harrow, Judy, Phyllis Curott, Rowan Fairgrove, and Russell Williams. Interview by Ellen Evert Hopman and Lawrence Bond. In Hopman, Ellen Evert, and Lawrence Bond, eds., *People of the Earth: The New Pagans Speak Out*. Rochester, VT: Destiny Books, 1996.

Harvey, Graham. *Contemporary Paganism: Listening People, Speaking Earth.* New York: New York University Press, 1997.

———. "Heathenism: A North European Pagan Tradition." In Harvey, Graham, and Charlotte Hardman, eds., *Paganism Today: Wiccans, Druids, the Goddess, and Ancient Earth Traditions for the Twenty-First Century.* London and San Francisco: Thorsons, 1996, pp. 49–64.

Harvey, Graham, and Charlotte Hardman, eds. *Paganism Today: Wiccans, Druids, the Goddess, and Ancient Earth Traditions for the Twenty-First Century.* London and San Francisco: Thorsons, 1996.

Hawkins, Gerald S. *Stonehenge Decoded.* New York: Dorset Press, 1965.

Head, Joseph, and S. L. Cranston, eds. *Reincarnation in World Thought.* New York: Julian Press, 1967.

Heisler, Roger. *Path to Power.* York Beach, ME: Weiser, 1990.

Hess, David J. *Samba in the Night: Spiritism in Brazil.* New York: Columbia University Press, 1994.

Hinnells, John R., ed. *A New Dictionary of Religions.* Cambridge, MA: Blackwell, 1995.

Hohman, John George. *Pow-wows or Long Lost Friend.* Brooklyn, NY: Fulton Religious Supply Co., n.d. (first published 1820).

Holzer, Hans. *The New Pagans.*

———. *The Truth about Witchcraft.* Garden City, NJ: Doubleday, 1969.

———. *The Witchcraft Report.* New York: Ace Books, 1973.

Hopman, Ellen Evert, and Lawrence Bond, eds., *People of the Earth: The New Pagans Speak Out.* Rochester, VT: Destiny Books, 1996.

Houston, Jean. *The Search for the Beloved: Journeys in Mythology and Sacred Psychology.* Los Angeles, CA: Jeremy P. Tarcher, 1987.

Howard, Michael. *The Occult Conspiracy: Secret Societies—Their Influence and Power in World History.* Rochester, VT: Destiny Books, 1989.

Hultkrantz, Ake. "A Definition of Shamanism." *Temenos* 9 (1973): 25–37.

Hundingsbani, Heigi. *The Religion of Odin: A Handbook.* Red Wing, MN: Viking House, 1978.

Hunt, Carl M. *Oyotunji Village.* Washington, D.C.: University Press of America, 1979.

Hutton, Ronald. *The Pagan Religions of the Ancient British Isles: Their Nature and Legacy.* Cambridge, MA: Blackwell, 1991.

———. "The Roots of Modern Paganism." In Harvey, Graham, and Charlotte Hardman, eds., *Paganism Today: Wiccans, Druids, the Goddess, and Ancient Earth Traditions for the Twenty-First Century.* London and San Francisco: Thorsons, 1996, pp. 3–15.

Hymenaeus Beta, ed. *Equinox* III, no. 10. York Beach, ME: Weiser, 1991.

Iglehart, Hallie Austen. *WomanSpirit.* Harper and Row, 1983.

Ivakhiv, Adrian. "The Resurgence of Magical Religion as a Response to the Crisis of Modernity: A Postmodern Depth Psychological Perspective." In Lewis, James R., ed., *Magical Religion and Modern Witchcraft.* Albany, NY: State University of New York Press, 1996, pp. 237–265.

James, Scott. "New York's Witches Fight City Hall . . . and Win." *Liberty* (July/August 1985).

Jeanne. *Numerology: Spiritual Light Vibrations.* Salem, OR: Your Center for Truth Press, 1987.

Johns, June. *King of the Witches: The World of Alex Sanders.* New York: Coward McCann, 1969.

Jonas, Hans. *The Gnostic Religion: The Message of the Alien God and the Beginnings of Christianity*, 2d ed. Boston, MA: Beacon Press, 1963.

Jones, Evan John, with Doreen Valiente, eds. *Witchcraft: A Tradition Renewed*. London: Robert Hale; Custer, WA: Phoenix Publishing, 1990.

Jones, Prudence. "Pagan Theologies." In Harvey, Graham, and Charlotte Hardman, eds., *Paganism Today: Wiccans, Druids, the Goddess, and Ancient Earth Traditions for the Twenty-First Century*. London and San Francisco: Thorsons, 1996, pp. 32–46.

Jones, Prudence, and Caitlín Matthews, eds. *Voices from the Circle*. Wellingborough, Northamptonshire, U.K.: Aquarian Press, 1990.

Jones, Prudence, and Nigel Pennick. *A History of Pagan Europe*. New York: Routledge and Kegan Paul, 1995.

Judith, Anodea. "CAW: Who Are We? Where Are We Going? And How Will We Get There?" *Green Egg* 81 (May 1988): 15.

————. *Wheels of Life*. St. Paul, MN: Llewellyn, 1987.

K., Amber. *True Magick: A Beginner's Guide*. St. Paul, MN: Llewellyn, 1991.

Kaplan, Jeffrey. "The Reconstruction of the Asatru and Odinist Traditions." In Lewis, James R., ed., *Magical Religion and Modern Witchcraft*. Albany, NY: State University of New York Press, 1996, pp. 193–236.

Keizer, Lewis S. *Initiation: Ancient and Modern*. San Francisco, CA: St. Thomas Press, 1981.

Kelly, Aidan A. *Crafting the Art of Magic, Book I: A History of Modern Witchcraft, 1939–1964*. St. Paul, MN: Llewellyn, 1991.

————. *Hippie Commie Beatnik Witches: An Historical Memoir on Witchcraft in California, 1967–1977, with the NROOGD Book of Shadows*, 2d ed. Los Angeles, CA: Art Magickal Publications, 1996.

————. "How It Happened That We Got the NROOGD Together." *The Witches Trine* 3, no. 4 (August 1974): 9–12, and no. 5 (November 1974): 18–22.

————. *Inventing Witchcraft: A Case Study in the Creation of a New Religion*. Los Angeles, CA: Art Magickal Publications, 1996.

————. "The Invention of Witchcraft: Uses of Documentary and Oral-Historical Materials in Reconstructing the History of the Gardnerian Movement." *Zetetic Scholar* 10 (1981).

————. *Religious Holidays and Calendars: An Encyclopedic Handbook*. Detroit, MI: Omnigraphics, 1991.

Kelly, Aidan A., ed. *Neo-Pagan Witchcraft*. In Melton, J. Gordon, ed. *Cults and New Religions*, vols. 23 and 24 (Garland series). New York: Garland, 1990.

Kilner, Walter J. *The Human Aura*. New Hyde Park, NY: University Books, 1964 [1920].

King, Francis. *Ritual Magic in England, 1887 to the Present*. London: Spearman, 1970.

————. *Sexuality, Magic, and Perversion*. London: New English Library, 1971.

King, Francis, ed. *Astral Projection, Ritual Magic, and Alchemy*, 2d ed. Wellingborough, Northamptonshire, U.K.: Aquarian Press, 1987 [1971].

————. *Crowley on Christ*, 2d ed. London: C. W. Daniel, 1974 [1953].

————. *Magic: The Western Tradition*. London: Thames and Hudson, 1975.

————. *Tantra, The Way of Action: A Practical Guide to Its Teachings and Techniques*. Rochester, VT: Destiny Books, 1990.

Knight, Gareth. *A History of White Magic*. York Beach, ME: Weiser, 1979; London: Mowbray, 1978.

————. *A Practical Guide to Qabalistic Symbolism*. York Beach, ME: Weiser, 1978.

Kondratiev, Alexei, Ph.D. Interview by Ellen Evert Hopman and Lawrence Bond. In Hopman, Ellen Evert, and Lawrence Bond, eds., *People of the Earth: The New Pagans Speak Out*. Rochester, VT: Destiny Books, 1996.

Lady Sheba. *Book of Shadows*. St. Paul, MN: Llewellyn, 1971.

Lea, Henry Charles. *A History of the Inquisition of the Middle Ages*. 3 vols. New York: Harper and Bros., 1888. On the Cathars, see vol. I, chapters 3 and 4, especially pp. 91–107.

Leach, Maria. *Standard Dictionary of Folklore, Mythology, and Legend*. San Francisco, CA: HarperSan Francisco, 1984 [1949].

Leek, Sybil. *The Complete Art of Witchcraft*. New York: World Publishing Company, 1971.

Leland, Charles Godfrey. *Aradia: The Gospel of the Witches of Tuscany*. York Beach, ME: Weiser, 1974 [New York: Scribner's, 1897].

Levi, Eliphas [Alphonse-Louis Constant]. *Dogma and Ritual of High Magic*.

———. *History of Magic*. York Beach, ME: Weiser, 1969.

———. *Key to the Great Mysteries*. York Beach, ME: Weiser, 1970.

———. *Transcendental Magic*. York Beach, ME: Weiser, 1970.

Lewis, James R. *Encyclopedia of Afterlife Beliefs and Phenomena*. Detroit, MI: Gale Research Inc., 1994.

———. *The Encyclopedia of Cults, Sects, and New Religions*. Amherst, NY: Prometheus Books, 1998.

Lewis, James R. *The Astrology Encyclopedia*. Detroit, MI: Visible Ink Press, 1994.

Lewis, James R., and J. Gordon Melton, eds. *Perspectives on the New Age*. Albany: State University of New York Press, 1992.

———. *Magical Religion and Modern Witchcraft*. Albany, NY: State University of New York Press, 1996.

Lockhart, J. G. *Curses, Lucks, and Talismans*. Detroit, MI: Single Tree Press, 1971 [1938].

Lovelock, J. E. *Gaia*. New York: Oxford University Press, 1979.

Luhrmann, T. M. *Persuasions of the Witch's Craft: Ritual Magic in Contemporary England*. Cambridge, MA: Harvard University Press, 1989.

MacLellan, Gordon. "Dancing on the Edge: Shamanism in Modern Britain." In Harvey, Graham, and Charlotte Hardman, eds., *Paganism Today: Wiccans, Druids, the Goddess, and Ancient Earth Traditions for the Twenty-First Century*. London and San Francisco: Thorsons, 1996, pp. 138–148.

Magliocco, Sabina. "Ritual Is My Chosen Art Form: The Creation of Ritual as Folk Art among Contemporary Pagans." In Lewis, James R., ed., *Magical Religion and Modern Witchcraft*. Albany, NY: State University of New York Press, 1996, pp. 93–120.

Marlbrough, Ray L. *Charms, Spells, and Formulas*. St. Paul, MN: Llewellyn, 1987.

Martello, Leo Louis. *Witchcraft: The Old Religion*. Secaucus, NJ: University Books, 1973.

Marty, Martin. "The Occult Establishment." *Social Research* XXXVII (summer 1970): 212–230.

Masello, Robert. *Fallen Angels and Spirits of the Dark*. New York: Perigee, 1994.

Mathers, S. L. MacGregor. *The Book of the Sacred Magic of Abra-Melin the Mage*. Wellingborough, Northamptonshire, U.K.: Aquarian Press, 1976.

Mathers, S. L. MacGregor, ed. and trans. *The Greater Key of Solomon*. Chicago: De Laurence, Scott, 1914.

Matt, Daniel C. *The Essential Cabala: The Heart of Jewish Mysticism*. San Francisco, CA: HarperCollins, 1995.

Matt, Daniel C., ed. and trans. *Zohar: The Book of Enlightenment*. New York: Paulist Press, 1983.

Matthews, Caitlín, and John Matthews. *The Western Way: A Practical Guide to the Western Mystery Tradition*. London: Arkana, 1994.

McCoy, Edwin. *A Witch's Guide to Faery Folk*. St. Paul, MN: Llewellyn, 1994.

McNallen, Stephen A. *Rituals of Asatru*. Breckenridge, TX: Asatru Free Assembly, 1985.

Melton, J. Gordon. *The Cult Experience: Responding to the New Religious Pluralism*. Pilgrim Press, 1982.

———. *Encyclopedia of American Religions*, 5th ed. Detroit, MI: Gale Research Inc., 1996.

———. "Modern Alternative Religions in the West." In Hinnells, J. R., ed., *A Handbook of Living Religions*. New York: Viking/Penguin, 1984, pp. 455–474.

Melton, J. Gordon, ed. *Magic, Witchcraft, and Paganism in America: A Bibliography*, 2d ed. New York: Garland, 1992 [1982].

Melton, J. Gordon, Jerome Clark, and Aidan A. Kelly. *New Age Encyclopedia*. Detroit, MI: Gale Research Inc., 1990.

Mickaharic, Draja. *A Century of Spells*. York Beach, ME: Weiser, 1988.

Midelfort, H. C. Erik. "Recent Witch Hunting Research, or Where Do We Go from Here?" *Papers of the Bibliographical Society of America* LXII (1968): 373–420.

Miller, David L. *The New Polytheism: Rebirth of the Gods and Goddesses*. New York: Harper and Row, 1974.

Miller, Timothy, ed. *America's Alternative Religions*. Albany, NY: State University of New York Press, 1995.

Mills, A. Rud. *The Odinist Religion: Overcoming Jewish Christianity*. Melbourne, Australia: n.p., 1930.

Mookerjee, Ajit, and M. Khanna. *The Tantric Way: Art, Science, Ritual*. New York: Graphic, 1977.

Moore, Virginia. *The Unicorn: William Butler Yeats' Search for Reality*. New York: Macmillan, 1954.

Morgan, Lynne. "Women and the Goddess Today." In Harvey, Graham, and Charlotte Hardman, eds., *Paganism Today: Wiccans, Druids, the Goddess, and Ancient Earth Traditions for the Twenty-First Century*. London and San Francisco: Thorsons, 1996, pp. 94–108.

Muldoon, Sylvan J., and Hereward Carrington. *The Phenomena of Astral Projection*. London: Rider and Company, 1969.

———. *The Projection of the Astral Body*. York Beach, ME: Weiser, 1970.

Murphy, Joseph M. "Santeria and Vodou in the United States." In Miller, Timothy, ed., *America's Alternative Religions*. Albany, NY: State University of New York Press, 1995.

Murray, Margaret A. *The God of the Witches*. New York: Doubleday Anchor, 1960; Oxford: Oxford University Press, 1934.

———. *The Witch-Cult in Western Europe*. Oxford: Oxford University Press, 1962 [1921].

Myers, Stuart. *Between the Worlds: Witchcraft and the Tree of Life—A Program of Spiritual Development*. St. Paul, MN: Llewellyn, 1995.

MyOwn, Barbry. "Ursa Maior: Menstrual Moon Celebration." In Rush, Anne Kent, ed., *Moon, Moon*. New York: Random House/Moon Books, 1976.

Needleman, Jacob, and George Baker, eds. *Understanding the New Religions*. Seabury, 1978.

Nemorensis, Rex [Charles Cardell]. *Witch*. London: n.p., 1964.

Nugent, Donald. "The Renaissance and/of Witchcraft." *Church History* XL (March 1971): 69–78.

———. "Witchcraft Studies, 1959–1971: A Bibliographic Survey." *Journal of Popular Culture* V, no. 3 (winter 1971): 82–97.

Odunfonda I, Adaramila. *Obatala, The Yoruba God of Creation*. Sheldon, SC: Great Benin Books, n.d.

Onions, C. T., ed. *The Oxford Dictionary of English Etymology*. New York: Oxford University Press, 1985 [1966].

Osborn, Arthur. *Superphysical: A Review of the Evidence for Continued Existence, Reincarnation, and Mystical States of Consciousness*. New York: Barnes and Noble, 1974.

Ostrander, Sheila, and Lynn Schroeder. *Psychic Discoveries behind the Iron Curtain*. Englewood Cliffs, NJ: Prentice-Hall, 1970.

Parisen, Maria. *Angels and Mortals: Their Co-Creative Power*. Wheaton, IL: Quest, 1990.

Paungger, Johanna. *Moon Time: The Art of Harmony with Nature and Lunar Cycles*. New York: Barnes and Noble, 1995.

Pike, Sarah M. "Forging Magical Selves: Gendered Bodies and Ritual Fires at Neo-Pagan Festivals." In Lewis, James R., ed., *Magical Religion and Modern Witchcraft*. Albany, NY: State University of New York Press, 1996, pp. 121–140.

Plaskow, Judith, and Carol P. Christ, eds. *Weaving the Visions: New Patterns in Feminist Spirituality*. San Francisco, CA: HarperSan Francisco, 1989.

———. *WomanSpirit Rising: A Feminist Reader in Religion*. San Francisco: HarperSan Francisco, 1979.

Pratt, J. Gaither. *ESP Research Today: A Study of Developments in Parapsychology since 1960*. Metuchen, NJ: The Scarecrow Press, 1973.

Price, Nancy. *Pagan's Progress: High Days and Holy Days*. London: Museum Press, 1954.

Pritchard, James B., ed. *Ancient Near Eastern Texts Relating to the Old Testament*, 3d ed. Princeton, NJ: Princeton University Press, 1969.

Rabinovitch, Shelley TSivia. "Spells of Transformation: Categorizing Modern Neo-Pagan Witches." In Lewis, James R., ed., *Magical Religion and Modern Witchcraft*. Albany, NY: State University of New York Press, 1996, pp. 75–92.

Randolph, Paschal Beverly. *Eulis: Affectional Alchemy*, 5th ed. Quakertown, PA: Beverly Hall, Confederation of Initiates, 1930.

Randolph, Vance. *Ozark Magic and Folklore*. New York: Dover, 1964 [Reprint of *Ozark Superstition*. New York: Columbia University Press, 1947].

Ransom, Josephine, comp. *A Short History of the Theosophical Society: 1875–1937*. Adyar, Madras: The Theosophical Publishing House, 1938.

RavenWolf, Silver. *To Ride a Silver Broomstick: New Generation Witchcraft*. St. Paul, MN: Llewellyn, 1996.

Rawson, Philip. *Tantra: The Indian Cult of Ecstasy*. London: Thames and Hudson, 1974.

Reed, Ellen Cannon. *Evocation of the Gods*. St. Paul, MN: Llewellyn, 1990.

———. *The Goddess and the Tree: The Witches' Qabala, Book I*, 2d ed. St. Paul, MN: Llewellyn, 1989 [1985].

Rees, Aylwin, and Brinsley Rees. *Celtic Heritage: Ancient Tradition in Ireland and Wales*. London: Thames and Hudson, 1961.

Rees, Kenneth. "The Tangled Skein: The Role of Myth in Paganism." In Harvey, Graham, and Charlotte Hardman, eds., *Paganism Today: Wiccans, Druids, the*

Goddess, and Ancient Earth Traditions for the Twenty-First Century. London and San Francisco: Thorsons, 1996, pp. 16–31.

Regardie, Israel. *The Golden Dawn: An Account of the Teachings, Rites, and Ceremonies of the Order of the Golden Dawn, 1937–1940,* 2d ed. Hazel Hills, 1969.

Regardie, Israel, ed. *Gems from the Equinox: Selected Writings of Aleister Crowley.* St. Paul, MN: Llewellyn, 1974.

Reid, Sian. "As I Do Will, So Mote It Be: Magic as Metaphor in Neo-Pagan Witchcraft." In Lewis, James R., ed., *Magical Religion and Modern Witchcraft.* Albany, NY: State University of New York Press, 1996, pp. 141–167.

Renfrew, Colin. "Carbon-14 and the Prehistory of Europe." *Scientific American* (October 1971): 63–72.

———. "The Origins of Indo-European Languages." *Scientific American* (October 1989): 106–114.

Richardson, Alan. *Dancers to the Gods.* St. Paul, MN: Llewellyn, 1990.

Richardson, James T., Joel Best, and David G. Bromley, eds. *The Satanism Scare.* New York: Aldine de Gruyter, 1991.

Rigaud, Milo. *Secrets of Voodoo.* San Francisco, CA: City Lights Books, 1985 [1953].

Robbins, Russell Hope. *The Encyclopedia of Witchcraft and Demonology.* New York: Crown, 1959. Lists virtually everything published about any kind of Witchcraft up to 1958.

Roberts, Susan. *Witches U.S.A.,* 2d ed. Custer, WA: Phoenix House, 1974; New York: Dell, 1971.

Robinson, James M., ed. *The Nag Hammadi Library in English,* 3d ed. San Francisco, CA: HarperSan Francisco, 1988 [1979].

Robison, John. *Proofs of a Conspiracy.* Belmont, MA: Western Islands, 1967 [1798].

Rose, Elliott. *A Razor for a Goat: A Discussion of Certain Problems in the History of Witchcraft and Diabolism.* Toronto, Alberta: University of Toronto Press, 1962.

Rush, John A. *Witchcraft and Sorcery.* Springfield, IL: Charles C. Thomas, 1974.

Russell, Jeffrey B. "Darklight Philosophy: A Ritual Praxis." In Harvey, Graham, and Charlotte Hardman, eds., *Paganism Today: Wiccans, Druids, the Goddess, and Ancient Earth Traditions for the Twenty-First Century.* London and San Francisco: Thorsons, 1996, pp. 204–223.

———. "Druidry Today." In Harvey, Graham, and Charlotte Hardman, eds., *Paganism Today: Wiccans, Druids, the Goddess, and Ancient Earth Traditions for the Twenty-First Century.* London and San Francisco: Thorsons, 1996, pp. 65–80.

———. *A History of Witchcraft: Sorcerers, Heretics, and Pagans.* London: Thames and Hudson, 1980.

Ryall, Rhiannon. *West Country Wicca: A Journal of the Old Religion.* Custer, WA: Phoenix Publishing, 1989.

Schueler, Gerald J. *Enochian Magick: A Practical Manual.* St. Paul, MN: Llewellyn, 1987.

Seth, Ronald, ed. *In the Name of the Devil: Great Witchcraft Cases.* London: Jarrolds, 1969.

Shah, Sayed Idries. *The Secret Lore of Magic: Books of the Sorcerers.* New York: Citadel 1970 [1957].

Shalcrass, Philip, ed. *A Druid Directory.* St. Leonards–on–Sea, England: British Druid Order, 1995.

Shan, Jayran. *Circlework: A DIY Handbook of Ritual, Psychology, and Magic.* London: House of the Goddess, 1994.

———. *Pagan Index.* London: House of the Goddess, 1994.

Shepard, Leslie A., ed. *Encyclopedia of Occultism and Parapsychology*. Detroit, MI: Gale Research Inc., 1991.

Simes, Amy. "Mercian Movements: Group Transformation and Individual Choices amongst East Midlands Pagans." In Harvey, Graham, and Charlotte Hardman, eds., *Paganism Today: Wiccans, Druids, the Goddess, and Ancient Earth Traditions for the Twenty-First Century*. London and San Francisco: Thorsons, 1996, pp. 169–190.

Smith, Bradford. *Meditation*. Philadelphia, PA: J. B. Lippincott, 1963.

Spence, Lewis. *The Fairy Tradition in Britain*. London: Rider and Company, 1948.

Spretnak, Charlene, ed. *The Politics of Women's Spirituality: Essays on the Rise of Spiritual Power within the Feminist Movement*. New York: Doubleday, 1982.

Starhawk [Miriam Simos]. *Dreaming the Dark: Magic, Sex, and Politics*. Boston, MA: Beacon Press, 1982.

———. Interview by Ellen Evert Hopman and Lawrence Bond. In Hopman, Ellen Evert, and Lawrence Bond, eds., *People of the Earth: The New Pagans Speak Out*. Rochester, VT: Destiny Books, 1996.

———. *The Spiral Dance: A Rebirth of the Ancient Religion of the Great Goddess*, 2d ed. San Francisco, CA: HarperSan Francisco, 1989 [1979].

———. *Truth or Dare: Encounters with Power, Authority, and Mystery*. Boston, MA: Beacon Press, 1987.

Stewart, R. J. *Advanced Magical Arts*. Longmead, Shaftesbury, Dorset, U.K.: Element, 1988.

Suster, Gerald, ed. *John Dee: Essential Readings*. Wellingborough, Northamptonshire, U.K.: Crucible, 1986.

Sutcliffe, Richard. "Left-Hand Path Ritual Magick: An Historical and Philosophical Overview." In Harvey, Graham, and Charlotte Hardman, eds., *Paganism Today: Wiccans, Druids, the Goddess, and Ancient Earth Traditions for the Twenty-First Century*. London and San Francisco: Thorsons, 1996, pp. 109–137.

Sykes, Egerton. *Who's Who: Non-Classical Mythology*. New York: Oxford University Press, 1993.

Tiryakian, Edward A., ed. *On the Margin of the Visible: Sociology, the Esoteric, and the Occult*. New York: Wiley, 1974.

Tolkien, J. R. R. *The Silmarillion*. New York: Houghton Mifflin, 1977.

Truzzi, Marcello. "The Occult Revival as Popular Culture: Some Random Observations on the Old and the Nouveau Witch." Paper presented to the Ohio Valley Sociological Society, Akron, OH, May 1, 1970. *Sociology Quarterly* 13 (winter 1972): 16–36. Excerpted in Tiryakian, Edward A., ed. *On the Margin of the Visible: Sociology, the Esoteric, and the Occult*. New York: Wiley, 1974, pp. 215–222.

———. "Towards a Sociology of the Occult: Notes on Modern Witchcraft." In Zaretsky and Leone, 1974.

Turner, Alice K. *The History of Hell*. New York: Harcourt Brace and Co., 1993.

Valiente, Doreen. *An ABC of Witchcraft: Past and Present*. New York: St. Martin's Press; Custer, WA: Phoenix, 1973.

———. Letter to the Editors. *Iron Mountain* 1, no. 3 (fall 1985): 3–6.

———. *The Rebirth of Witchcraft*. London: Robert Hale; Custer, WA: Phoenix, 1989.

———. *Where Witchcraft Lives*. Wellingborough, Northampshire, U.K.: Aquarian Press, 1962.

———. *Witchcraft for Tomorrow*. New York: St. Martin's Press, 1978.

Van de Castle, Robert L. *Our Dreaming Mind*. New York: Ballantine, 1994.

Von Karman, Theodore, with Lee Edson. *The Wind and Beyond: Theodore Von Karman, Pioneer in Aviation and Pathfinder in Space*. Boston, MA: Little, Brown and Co., 1967.

Waite, Arthur Edward. *A New Encyclopedia of Freemasonry*. New York: Weathervane Books, 1970 [1921].

Walker, Benjamin. *Encyclopedia of Metaphysical Medicine*. London: Routledge and Kegan Paul, 1978.

Ward, Gary L., ed. *Spiritualism I: Spiritualist Thought*. New York: Garland, 1990.

Webb, James. *The Occult Establishment*. La Salle, IL: Open Court, 1976.

———. *The Occult Underground*. La Salle, IL: Open Court, 1974.

Wickland, Carl A. *Thirty Years among the Dead*. North Hollywood, CA: Newcastle Publishing Co., 1974 [1924].

Wilson, Robert Anton. *Cosmic Trigger: The Final Secret of the Illuminati*. Berkeley, CA: And/Or Press, 1977.

———. *The Illuminati Papers*. Berkeley, CA: And/Or Press, 1980.

———. *Masks of the Illuminati*. New York: Pocket Books, 1981.

Wilson, Robert Anton, and Robert Shea. *The Illuminatus Trilogy*. New York: Pocket Books, 1973.

York, Michael. *The Emerging Network: A Sociology of the New Age and Neo-Pagan Movement*. Plainfield, NJ: Rowman and Littlefield, 1995.

———. "New Age and Paganism." In Harvey, Graham, and Charlotte Hardman, eds., *Paganism Today: Wiccans, Druids, the Goddess, and Ancient Earth Traditions for the Twenty-First Century*. London and San Francisco: Thorsons, 1996, pp. 157–165.

Zaretsky, I. J., and M. P. Leone, eds. *Religious Movements in Contemporary America*. Princeton, NJ: Princeton University Press, 1974.

Zell, Oberon. "Who on Earth Is the Goddess?" In Lewis, James R., ed., *Magical Religion and Modern Witchcraft*. Albany, NY: State University of New York Press, 1996, pp. 29–33.

Zell, Oberon, and Anodea Judith. Interview by Ellen Evert Hopman and Lawrence Bond. In Hopman, Ellen Evert, and Lawrence Bond, eds., *People of the Earth: The New Pagans Speak Out*. Rochester, VT: Destiny Books, 1996.

Zimmer, Heinrich. *Philosophies of India*. New York: Bollingen, 1951.

Zolar's Book of the Spirit. New York: Prentice Hall Press, 1987.

Nonprint Resources

With respect to nonprint resources, most of the films that have been made about Witches are quite poor. On the other hand, modern Wiccans are notorious for their addiction to the Internet and the World Wide Web.

I have included a selection of web sites, with the caveat that this medium is in constant flux. By the time this book goes to press, many of the following sites may have already disappeared. Nevertheless, it is possible to find Wiccan networks using any good Internet search engine.

Neopagan Witchcraft

Anders Magick Page

http://www.student.nada.kth.se/~nv91-asa/magick.html

Resources on occult and magical subjects. Includes a listing of less well-known resources and sites.

B. Occult and Related
The Alternative Spiritualities Club Home Page Arts-Esoterica-Hermetica
http://yoyo.cc.monash.edu.au/groups/eas/
Australia-based web site with an index of occult and Wiccan groups.

Brenna's Page
http://www.argyll.demon.co.uk/
Good graphics and good links to other sites by a Neopagan.

Dark Side of the Net
http://www.gothic.net/darksite/
A monumental collection of data on occult-related web sites.

The Golden Dawn FAQ
http://www.bartol.udel.edu/~cranmer/cranmer_gdfaq.html
Comprehensive web site on the Hermetic Order of the Golden Dawn.

Joan's Witch Directory
http://www.rci.rutgers.edu/~jup/witches
Historical Witchcraft, including information on persecution and the *Malleus Malificarum*, a Witch-hunting manual from the 1400s.

Loki Cult Web Page
http://www.memoria.com/loki/
A site for those who worship Loki, the Norse trickster god.

Pagan Pages
http://www.eor.com/pages
Free listings of events, ads, and other announcements for Neopagans and Neopagan businesses.

Satanism and the History of Wicca
http://ourworld.compuserve.com/homepages/hpaulis/swc.htm
Text article examining links between modern Witchcraft and the "literary Satanism" of the nineteenth century.

White Mountain Education—A Source for the Ageless Wisdom
http://www.wmea-world.org
Esoteric psychology and astrology. Online monthly magazine: *Meditation Monthly International.*

Witches League for Public Awareness
http://www.celiccrow.com/
Sort of a Neopagan anti-defamation league, the Witches League for Public Awareness web site examines the portrayal of Witches in the media. Also, this site contains many links to other useful web sites.

The Witches' Voice

http://www.witchvox.com/

An educational web site devoted to dispelling misperceptions about Witches and Witchcraft. Features an annotated listing of over 800 Pagan web sites.

The Witches' Web Home Page

http://www.witchesweb.com/home.html

Good basic site with professional graphics and a wide variety of features, such as a calendar of Wiccan festivals, a forum for discussion, information on historical and current beliefs and practices, and even a recipe section.

Appendix A: Chronology

The Neopagan movement proper, while clearly distinct from other occult groups, has nevertheless been heavily dependent upon these traditions. The following chronology thus begins with earlier manifestations of the Western occult tradition, particularly those that provide a background for the creation of modern Witchcraft in the mid–twentieth century. The chronology also takes note of certain developments in the larger occult subculture after the emergence of Neopaganism as an independent religious movement in the latter half of the century.

1608   Astrologer John Dee (1527–1608) is born in London. Dee is best known for his Enochian Magic, a system of magic teaching communication with angels and spirits.

1692   Salem Witch craze gets under way in Salem—now Danvers—Massachusetts. During the course of the Witchcraft trials, 141 people were arrested as suspects, 19 were hanged, and 1 was pressed to death.

1717   Formal beginning of Freemasonry, when four lodges met in London and established the Grand Lodge in order to "restore" Masonry. Freemasonry influenced the rituals of both Ceremonial Magic and Neopagan Witchcraft.

1781   The Ancient Order of Druids is founded by Henry Hurle, a carpenter, as a Masonic offshoot and charitable organization.

1801   Francis Barrett publishes *The Magus*, the first modern book that attempted to make the arcana of magic accessible to the middle class.

1848   The events that are generally regarded as constituting the origin of modern Spiritualism take place when the sisters Maggie and Katie Fox begin to communicate with spirits through knockings in their house in Hydesville, New York.

1858   The Fraternitas Rosae Crucis is founded by physician P. B. Randolph (1825–1875). It is generally considered the oldest Rosicrucian body.

1861   *The Dogma and Ritual of High Magic*, the most popular book by French occultist Eliphas Levi (Alphonse-Louis Constant) is published. A major link in the chain that led to modern magical practices, Levi's system was adopted and improved by the Hermetic Order of the Golden Dawn and so became the source of all modern systems of magic.

1865   The Societas Rosicruciana in Anglia is founded by Robert Wentworth Little.

1875   The Theosophical Society is founded in New York City.

1884   Gerald Brosseau Gardner, the founder of modern Witchcraft, is born at Great Crosby, near Blundell Sands in Lancashire, England.

1888   The Hermetic Order of the Golden Dawn is founded in London with Dr. William Wynn Westcott, Samuel Liddell MacGregor Mathers, and W. R. Woodman as its ruling triumvirate.

1889   Olney H. Richmond founds the Order of the Magi in Chicago, Illinois, one of the new astrological religions (like Thomas Burgoyne's Brotherhood of Light and Hiram Butler's Esoteric Fraternity) founded in America in the nineteenth century. The Order of the Magi was the "Outer Court" (as it would now be called) for a coven of Witches.

The term *parapsychology* is coined by the German psychologist Max Dessoir to refer to the scientific study of paranormal and mediumistic phenomena.

1897   Publication of *Aradia: The Gospel of the Witches of Tuscany*, one of the sources of modern Witchcraft. This "Witches' Gospel" was said to have been given to Charles Godfrey Leland in Italy by a Witch named Maddelena.

Aurum Solis, originally a school of high Cabalistic magic, is founded in England by Charles Kingold and George Stanton.

1904   Aleister Crowley writes *The Book of the Law* (said to have been dictated to Crowley by a disembodied spirit), one of the most important of modern magical treatises and the basis of all Thelemic magic.

1907   Aleister Crowley founds his own organization, the Astrum Argentinum ("Silver Star").

The Rosicrucian Fellowship is established by the well-known astrological author Max Heindel.

1909   Aleister Crowley begins publication of *The Equinox* (semiannually until 1913) in order to spread his ideas.

1915   Ancient and Mystical Order of the Rosae Crucis (AMORC), an esoteric fraternal movement, is founded in New York by occultist H. Spencer Lewis.

1922   Margaret Murray's *The Witch-Cult in Western Europe* is published by Oxford University Press. Murray's thesis, that transcripts of the Witch trials provide evidence of the survival of a Pagan religion that the religious establishment was attempting to exterminate, becomes one of the founding ideas of modern Witchcraft.

Builders of the Adytum (BOTA), a mystery school based on the Cabala, is established by Paul Foster Case.

Dion Fortune (Violet Mary Firth) organizes the Community of the Inner Light, later the Fraternity of the Inner Light, one of the organizations with a direct influence on Gerald Gardner.

1923   Marc Edmund Jones founds the Sabian Assembly, a group that began with Jones's initial astrological interests and then sought to apply occult teachings to their daily lives.

1927   The Institute of Mentalphysics is founded in New York City by Edwin John Dingle.

1933   Margaret Murray's *The God of the Witches* appears and inspires several attempts to re-create the ancient Pagan religion Murray purports to describe.

1939   In England, Gerald Gardner establishes the kernel of what will become the modern Neopagan movement.

        The Church of Aphrodite, Goddess of Love, is founded by Gleb Botkin, a Russian immigrant, in Long Island, New York.

1948   Publication of the first edition of Robert Graves's *The White Goddess*, a source of current enthusiasm about an ancient matriarchal period in history. His ideas are adopted by the Neopagan movement.

        Our Lady of Endor Coven, known also as the Ophite Cultus Satanas, is founded by Herbert Arthur Sloane of Toledo, Ohio.

1949   Publication of Gerald Gardner's novel *High Magic's Aid*, a fanciful and rather detailed description of the beliefs and practices of an English Witch cult in about the fifteenth century.

1951   The very last British anti-Witchcraft law—enacted in 1736—is repealed due to lobbying by the Spiritualist churches. This repeal, Witches like Gerald Gardner later implied, made it possible to openly admit the existence of the religion.

        Old Dorothy Clutterbuck Fordham, the woman Gerald Gardner claimed had initiated him into one of the very last Wiccan covens, dies.

1952   The Gnostic Association of Cultural and Anthropological Studies is founded by esotericist Samuel Aun Weor. His teachings emphasize the importance of other planes of consciousness, and draw upon a basic theosophical framework.

1953   Doreen Valiente is initiated into Gardnerian Witchcraft by Gerald Gardner and "Dafo." She rewrote most of Gardner's earlier drafts for the Book of Shadows, thus creating some of the most important statements of the Craft's theology, as in her "Charge of the Goddess."

1954   *Witchcraft Today* is published. In it, Gardner claims that the speculative scholarship of Margaret Murray is correct: The "Witchcraft" of the Middle Ages is a surviving Pagan religion.

1955   Walter Eugene King founds the Order of Damballah Hwedo Ancestor Priests, which successively changed its name to the Order of the Damballah and became the Shango Temple and, later, the Yoruba Temple.

1956   The Universal Spiritualist Association is founded after Camp Chesterfield. This popular Spiritualist camp in Indiana severs ties with the Spiritualist Episcopal Church.

1957   Frederick Adams founds Feraferia, a Nature Goddess religion, as a utopian response to a planet in crisis. It is incorporated in 1967. The scripts Adams wrote for the eight Sabbats of the year have been influential in the Neopagan movement.

The Discordian Society, also known as the Parathea-anametamystikhood of Eris Esoteric (POEE), is founded in a bowling alley in Hawthorne, California, by Gregory Hill and Kerry Thornley.

1960   Carl Weschcke purchases Llewellyn Publishing Co., a small mail-order house that Weschcke develops into the largest publisher of occult and Neopagan titles in the world.

1962   The Church and School of Wicca is founded by Gavin and Yvonne Frost.

Raymond and Rosemary Buckland move to the United States from Great Britain. The next year they meet with Gerald Gardner in Scotland, where they undergo a brief, intense training and are initiated. Returning to the United States, they found the New York Coven in Bay Shore, Long Island, which becomes the center of the Gardnerian movement and, to a lesser extent, the center of the Neopagan movement in the United States for the next 20 years.

The Church of Tzaddi (named after the eighteenth letter of the Hebrew alphabet, identified in the Church of Tzaddi's metaphysical system with the Age of Aquarius) is founded by Amy Merritt Kees in Orange, California.

1963   Alexander Sanders, founder of the Alexandrian Tradition, is initiated into Gardnerian Witchcraft. Although in terms of ritual, Alexandrian Witchcraft is a minor variant of Gardnerian Witchcraft, its adherents far outnumber traditionalist Gardnerians as of the time of this publication.

The Reformed Druids of North America begin as a satire in protest of a requirement at Carleton College, in Northfield, Minnesota, that students attend religious services.

The Process Church of the Final Judgment is established by a group that gathers around the charismatic Robert de Grimston, a resident of London.

1964   Gerald Gardner, founder of modern Witchcraft, dies.

Gerard Noel starts publishing *Pentagram* in the United Kingdom. Though short-lived, it is the world's first Neopagan periodical.

Joseph B. Wilson founds *The Waxing Moon*—apparently the very first Neopagan periodical to be published in America—in Topeka, Kansas.

1965   *Pentagram* sponsors a dinner that subsequently is viewed as a turning point in the history of the Craft. It begins the process of creating regional and national networking organizations for Witches in the United Kingdom and establishes a network of friendships among coven and Craft leaders who did not know each other very well beforehand.

1966   Anton LaVey announces the formation of the Church of Satan. Highly theatrical, but not actually dangerous, the existence of the Church of Satan provides a concrete target of attack for conservative Christians with vague fears about the machinations of the Prince of Darkness.

1967   The New Reformed Orthodox Order of the Golden Dawn (NROOGD) Tradition begins as a project for a graduate class in the study of ritual at San Francisco State University. The group of friends who work on the project (including Sarah T., Aidan A. Kelly, Glenn Turner, and Judy G.) proceed to transform themselves into an occult study group during the next year.

The Hollywood Coven is founded by E. Tanssan of Hollywood, Florida.

The Association of Cymry Wicca, also known as the Church of Y Tylwyth Teg, is founded in Washington, D.C., by William Wheeler (Rhuddlwm Gawr).

1968   The Church of All Worlds, organized by Oberon Zell, is incorporated and, in 1971, becomes the first Neopagan group to win federal tax-exempt status— the state ruling against it was overturned as unconstitutional.

1969   Founding of the (now-defunct) Psychedelic Venus Church, a counterculture-oriented group.

Anton LaVey publishes the first of three books, *The Satanic Bible*, containing the perspective of the Church of Satan. It is followed by *The Compleat Witch* (1970) and *The Satanic Rituals* (1972).

1970   The Church of the Eternal Source, a revival of ancient Egyptian religions, is founded by Donald Harrison, Elaine Amiro, and Harold Moss.

Nemeton is founded in Oakland, California, by Thomas DeLong (Gwydion Pendderwen) and Alison Harlow, a fellow initiate of the Fairy Tradition and a fellow member of the Society for Creative Anachronism.

The Witches International Craft Associates (WICA) is founded by Leo Martello as one of the very first networking organizations for Neopagan Witches in the United States. Its newsletters are instrumental in tying together the Witches scattered across the United States before the rise to prominence of the periodical *Green Egg* in about 1972.

The Tayu Fellowship is established by Daniel Inesse, a group open to homosexuals wishing to follow the Path of Truth, based upon the wisdom of the ancient Greeks.

The Pagan Way emerges in the United States in anticipation of a flood of inquiries set off by the publication of Susan Roberts's *Witches U.S.A.* The Pagan Way is a nature-oriented system that emphasizes celebration of nature over magic and has no formal initiation or membership requirements.

The Pagan movement begins as the United Kingdom wing of the Pagan Way movement, headed by Joseph B. Wilson.

1971   John Score breaks away from the United Kingdom Pagan Way movement to form the Pagan Front, later called the Pagan Federation.

Gavin and Yvonne Frost's *The Witch's Bible*, based on the correspondence courses they taught, is published, causing much controversy among Neopagan Witches.

The *Green Egg*, originally a newsletter for the Church of All Worlds, emerges as the major national communication channel for the Neopagan movement and remains so for the next five years.

A talk given by Morning Glory (Julia Carter) Zell to a women's group at the Worldcon (science-fiction world convention) in Los Angeles, California, becomes a key event in the transmission of Neopagan spirituality to the women's movement.

Zsusanna Budapest collects six friends and begins to hold Sabbats (for women only) in Los Angeles. The Susan B. Anthony Coven is born on the winter solstice, named after the leader of the women's suffrage movement.

Carl Weschcke holds the first of several annual festivals, which becomes one of the models for later Craft festivals.

The American Tradition is created by founders of the Pagan Way to serve as a form of Wicca that is not as restricted by oaths of secrecy.

Publication of *What Witches Do*, the first in a steady stream of books by the Alexandrian Witches Janet and Stewart Farrar, is influential worldwide in defining the self-concept of the Craft as a religion.

1972   The Church and School of Wicca's first Samhain Seminar is held. It becomes one of the models on which the current system of festivals is based.

Elders of several traditions in Maryland form KAM, Keepers of the Ancient Mysteries.

The Viking Brotherhood, the first American Asatru organization, is founded by Stephen A. McNallen.

1973   The Council of American Witches is founded at Carl Weschcke's annual festival. Although short-lived, the meeting establishes the Council as a forum for an unprecedented intertradition discussion, constituting a model for future cooperative endeavors.

The Calumet Pagan Temple is incorporated in Indiana by Richard Clarke as an offshoot of the Temple of the Pagan Way in Chicago, Illinois.

Ursa Maior, one of the first all-women's circles, is founded in the San Francisco area. It is said that this group exerted a great influence on the women's spirituality movement.

The Temple of Truth (TOT) is begun by Nelson H. White, a former member of the Ordo Templi Astarte, and his wife, Anne White (Soror Veritas).

The First Church of Voodoo is established in Tennessee in 1973 by Robert W. Pelton.

The New Wiccan Church is founded as the Neo-Celtic Church.

1974   The Circle Sanctuary is founded by Selena Fox and Jim Alan. The Church of Circle Wicca is incorporated in 1978. Circle's *Circle Network News*, which begins in 1979, is a major networking periodical within the larger Neopagan community.

In his role as chair of the Council of American Witches, Carl Weschcke proposes a general set of 13 principles that are as close as anyone has come yet to a universal creed for Witches. Incorporated in the U.S. Defense Department's *Chaplains' Handbook*, they form the basis for the rights of Wiccans serving in the American Armed Forces and, therefore, have legal standing in American law.

The Thee Satanic Church is formed by Dr. Evelyn Paglini when the Thee Satanic Church of the Nethilum Rite divides.

The first meeting of the Pagan Ecumenical Council is held, out of which arises the Covenant of the Goddess.

1975   The Covenant of the Goddess (CoG) is established as a nonprofit California corporation on Hallowe'en with the intention to serve the Neopagan movement nationally as a legal church. It is the largest organization serving this purpose.

Isaac Bonewits founds the Aquarian Anti-Defamation League as a civil liberties organization for members of all minority religions. An idea ahead of its time, the organization dissolves the next year. At the same time, it becomes a model for subsequent efforts.

The Venusian Church is created by Seattle businessman Ron Peterson.

The Southern California Local Council of the Covenant of the Goddess is founded.

Michael A. Aquino, formerly a member of the Church of Satan, founds the Temple of Set.

1976   The Fellowship of Isis is founded by the Rt. Hon. Lawrence Durdin-Robertson, twenty-first Baron Robertson of Strathloch (1920–1994); his wife, the Lady Pamela; and his sister, the Hon. Olivia Durdin-Robertson.

The Midwest Pagan Council is formed in the Chicago, Illinois, area, with ten groups as members. The Council sponsors the first Pan Pagan Festival at Lake Holiday on July 14–16, 1976—one of the very first genuinely open, national festivals to be established.

The Pagan/Occult/Witchcraft Special Interest Group of Mensa is founded.

1977   The Church of Seven Arrows establishes itself in Wheat Ridge, Colorado, a suburb of Denver, and begins publishing a monthly periodical, *Thunderbow.*

1978   Our Lady of Enchantment, Church of the Old Religion, is founded in California by Lady Sabrina.

1979   Publication of first edition of Starhawk's *The Spiral Dance* and Margo Adler's *Drawing down the Moon*, books that simultaneously document and stimulate the expansion of the Neopagan movement, occurs this year.

The Wiccan Church of Canada (WCC) is cofounded by Richard and Tamara James.

The Aquarian Tabernacle Church is founded by Pete Davis and other Pagans in the Seattle, Washington, area. It is later incorporated in 1983 and, in 1991, receives tax-exempt status from the Internal Revenue Service of the United States.

The Maidenhill Coven is founded by Deirdre and Edward, who were initiated into a coven in New York in 1978 and were trained by mentors in the Welsh and Alexandrian Traditions.

1980   Raymond Buckland founds the School of Seax-Wica, marking his formal departure from the traditionalist Gardnerian Witchcraft that he and his first wife brought to the United States in 1963.

A new concern about the possible presence of Satanism in the United States centering upon the sexual abuse of children in Satanic rituals is initiated by the publication of *Michelle Remembers*.

The Council of the Magical Arts is founded by Flamekeepers (Isian trad) and Our Lady of the Sacred Flame to serve as a Neopagan networking organization for the Houston, Texas, area.

1981   Oxford Golden Dawn Occult Society (OGDOS) is founded by Frater Katon Shu'al, a member of the Typhonian branch of the Ordo Templi Orientis.

1982   Prominent Neopagan Gwydion Pendderwen (Thomas DeLong), cofounder of the influential Fairy Tradition of Witchcraft, dies in an automobile accident.

Sybil Leek, prominent proponent of Witchcraft in the 1960s and 1970s, dies on the same day that Gwydion Pendderwen passes over.

The Earth Song Community is founded as a local Pagan networking and Sabbat-management organization.

The Ordo Lux Kethri is formed by April Schadler Bishop and Michael Albion MacDonald of the Builders of the Adytum.

1983   Anodea Judith founds Lifeways, a school for the study of consciousness and healing arts, now a subsidiary and teaching arm of the Church of All Worlds.

Ar nDraiocht Fein (ADF), "Our Own Druidism," is founded by P. E. I. (Isaac) Bonewits and Shenain Bell.

Brothers of the Earth, a male-oriented Neopagan fellowship, is founded by Gary Lingen.

The Reformed Congregation of the Goddess (RCG) is founded by Lynnie Levy and Jade Goldenfire. The RCG is the only legally incorporated, tax-exempt, Pagan women's religion in the United States.

Founding of Judy Harrow's Protean Gardnerian Lineage and Protean Lineage takes place.

1984   The Pallas Society, later renamed the Educational Society for Pagans, is formed by individuals who resign from the Southern California Local Council of the Covenant of the Goddess.

1985   The Covenant of Unitarian Universalist Pagans is founded by Leslie Philips.

The American Gnostic Church is established by the Reverend James M. Martin.

1986   Publication of Anodea Judith's *Wheels of Life: A User's Guide to the Chakra System*, widely regarded as one of the best books ever written on the chakras, incorporates a Neopagan approach to the chakra system.

Witches and other Neopagans in the Kansas City area create the Council of the Southwinds to serve as a local networking organization, later renamed and reorganized into the not-for-profit Heartland Spiritual Alliance.

DAWN (Denver Area Wiccan Network) is founded in Denver by a consortium of Witches and other Neopagans to serve as a local networking and coordinating organization.

The Church of the Most High Goddess is founded by Wilbur and Mary Ellen Tracy.

1987 Wicca gains legal recognition as a religion for the first time in Canada as the result of a lengthy and highly publicized case fought in court by Charles Arnold over his right to be granted paid leave to observe two Neopagan holidays, Beltane and Samhain.

The Ring of Troth is formed by Edred Thorsson almost contemporaneously with the Asatru Alliance.

The founding of the Guardians of the Fourth Face, a group of "Pagan warriors" who serve as a volunteer security force at festivals and other large public gatherings of Neopagans, takes place.

The city of Hialeah, Florida, enacts a ban against "animal sacrifice," directly aimed at the growing Santeria community of the city. One Santeria house challenges the ban and, in 1993, the Supreme Court unanimously declares the Hialeah ordinance unconstitutional in *Church of Lukumi Bablu Aye* v. *City of Hialeah*.

South Bay Circles begins meeting formally in order to organize and sponsor semiopen Sabbats in the South Bay (the area between San Mateo and San Jose in Northern California).

The Temple of Astarte is established in the resort area of the central coast of Oregon, with members residing throughout the Pacific Northwest.

1988 Oberon Zell revives the *Green Egg*, whose niche in the Neopagan scene was never filled by any other periodicals that came and went during the intervening years.

The Tucson Area Wiccan Network (TAWN) is formed as a networking group.

The Pagan Community Council of Ohio (PCCO), a not-for-profit corporation sponsoring social, educational, and religious activities for the Pagan residents of Ohio, is founded.

1989 Bodies are discovered on the grounds of a ranch near Matamoros, Mexico, not far from the Texas border, and make headlines. The murders, associated with a drug-smuggling operation, are immediately linked to Satanic worship.

The Northwest Web serves as a clearinghouse of information for Neopagans of all paths. It is a nonprofit organization operated for the public benefit by the members of the Temple of Astarte.

1990 The Fellowship of Earth Religions, Awakenings, and Lore (FERAL) is founded as a successful local Neopagan networking organization in Los Angeles, California, by Stasia Spade and Calvin Ogawa.

1992 The United Federation of Pagans is founded at its initial meeting at the Gathering of the Tribes Festival sponsored by the Church of Tylwyth Teg near Gainesville, Georgia.

The United We Circle, a Los Angeles–area networking organization, arises as part of the Craft community's response to the 1992 riots there, coordinating Wiccan participation in the "Hands Across L.A." event.

Members of the Covenant of the Goddess in the San Diego, California, area form their own local council, separate from the Southern California Council, and hive off as the Califia Council.

1993 The significant Neopagan presence at the Second World Parliament of Religions in Chicago, Illinois, brings the Neopagan movement into contact and dialog with representatives of other world religions.

The Alpha Community is founded. The community is a "church without walls" focused on the "old religion" of Europe. The church celebrates the Sabbats and moons usually observed by Neopagan Witches.

The Life Temple of Anderson, South Carolina, a Wiccan church that is open to public attendance, is chartered, receiving its Internal Revenue Service tax-exempt status the next year.

1994 The first academic conference focusing on Neopaganism is held at Newcastle-on-Tyne in the United Kingdom.

1995 Publication of Michael York's *The Emerging Network: A Sociology of the New Age and Neo-Pagan Movement* occurs this year.

1996 "Nature Religions Today," the world's first international and interdisciplinary conference on Pagan studies, takes place at Charlotte Mason College near Manchester, England. It is inspired by previous conferences at Bath in 1993 and at Newcastle-on-Tyne in 1994—out of which came the anthology *Paganism Today*.

The first scholarly anthologies featuring articles by Craft insiders appear, marking a threshold in the maturation of the Neopagan movement. These collections are: Graham Harvey and Charlotte Hardman, eds., *Paganism Today: Wiccans, Druids, the Goddess, and Ancient Earth Traditions for the Twenty-First Century*, and James R. Lewis, ed., *Magical Religion and Modern Witchcraft*.

1997 Neopagan academic activity intensifies, as indicated by the emergence of a Nature Religious group of scholars within the American Academy of Religion; the appearance of *Pomegranate*, the first Neopagan academic journal; and the publication of Graham Harvey's *Contemporary Paganism: Listening People, Speaking Earth*.

Appendix B: Documents

Charge of the Goddess

The "Charge of the Goddess" is a central document in the Gardnerian Book of Shadows. The term *charge* here is borrowed from the Masonic vocabulary: In a Masonic initiation a charge is a speech or set of instructions read to a candidate standing in the temple.

Gardner's first draft of the "Charge of the Goddess" was a hodgepodge of quotes from Aleister Crowley's *Gnostic Mass* and Charles Godfrey Leland's *Aradia*. It was intended to be a theological statement justifying the ensuing sequence of initiations, which included what would now be considered the three Degrees. Gardner's text (and spelling) for this read as follows.

List to the words of the Great Mother who of old was also called among men Artimis: Astarte: Dione: Melusine: Aphrodite and by meny other names.

At mine Altars the youth of Lacedmonia and Spala made due sacrifice.

Whenever ye have need of anything, once in the month, and better it be when the moon is full. They ye shall assemble in some secret place and adore the spirit of me who am Queen of all Witcheries.

There ye shall assemble, ye who are fain to learn all Sorcery, yet have not won to its deepest secrets, to those will I teach things that are yet unknown.

And ye shall be free from slavery, And as a sign that ye be realy free, ye shall be naked in your rites, both men and wemen, And ye shall dance, sing, feast make music, and love, all in my praise.

For ecstasy is mine, and joy on earth.

For love is my law. "Keep pure your highest ideal: strive ever toward it. Let naught stop you or turn you aside."

There is a Secret Door that I have made to establish the way to taste even on earth the elixir of immortality. Say "Let exstacy be mine, and joy on earth even to me, To Me" For I am a gracsous Goddess. I give unimaginable joys, on earth certainty, not faith while in life! And upon death, peace unutterable, rest, and ecstacy, nor do I demand aught in sacrifice.

Hear ye the words of the Star Goddess.

I love you: I yearn for you: page or purple, veiled or volupluous.

Let it be your inmost devine self who art lost in the constant rapture of infinite joy.

Let the rituals be rightly preformed with joy and beauty. Rember that all acts of love and pleasure are my rituals. So let there be beauty and strength, leaping laughter, force and fire be within you.

And if thou sayest, I have journied unto thee, and it availed me not, Rather shalt thou say, I called upon thee, and I waited patiently, and Low, Thou wast with me from the begining For they that ever desired me, shall ever attain me, even to the end of all desire.

Doreen Valiente felt that the influence of Crowley here was simply too obvious, and Crowley's reputation was not one with which she wanted the Craft to be saddled. Gardner invited her to try to rewrite the Charge, and she proceeded to do so: first into verse and then into the following prose form, which is considered perhaps the most important theological document in the Craft.

[Magus]: Listen to the words of the Great mother, who was of old also called among men Artimis, Astarte, Dione, Melusine, Aphrodite, Cerridwen, Diana, Arianrhod, Bride, and by many other names.

[High Priestess]: At mine Altars the youth of Lacedaemon in Sparta made due sacrifice.

Whenever ye have need of anything, once in the month, and better it be when the moon is full, then ye shall assemble in some secret place and adore the spirit of Me who am Queen of all Witcheries. There ye shall assemble, ye who are fain to learn all sorcery, yet who have not won its deepest secrets. To these will I teach things that are yet unknown.

And ye shall be free from slavery, and as a sign that ye be really free, ye shall be naked in your rites, and ye shall dance, sing, feast, make music, and love, all in my praise.

For mine is the ecstasy of the Spirit, and mine is also joy on earth, For my Law is Love unto all beings.

Keep pure your highest ideals. Strive ever towards it. Let naught stop you or turn you aside.

For mine is the secret which opens upon the door of youth; and mine is the cup of the Wine of Life: and the Cauldron of Cerridwen; which is the Holy Grail of Immortality.

I am the Gracious Goddess who gives the gift of Joy unto the heart of Man.

Upon Earth I give the knowledge of the Spirit Eternal; and beyond death I give peace and freedom; and reunion with those who have gone before; nor do I demand aught in sacrifice; for behold, I am the Mother of all things; and my love is poured out upon earth.

[Magus]: Hear ye the words of the Star Goddess, She in the dust of whose feet are the hosts of Heaven; whose body encircleth the Universe.

[High Priestess]: "I who am the beauty of the green earth; and the White Moon amongst the Stars; and the mystery of the Waters; and the desire of the heart of man; I call unto thy soul; arise and come unto me."

For I am the Soul of nature who giveth life to the Universe; "From me all things proceed; and unto me, all things must return"; Beloved of the Gods and men; thine inmost divine self shall be enfolded in the raptures of the infinite.

Let my worship be within the heart that rejoiceth; for behold, all acts of Love and Pleasure are my rituals; and therefore let there be Beauty and Strength; Power and compassion; Honour and Humility; Mirth and Reverence within you.

And thou who thinkest to seek me; Know that thy seeking and yearning shall avail thee not unless thou know the mystery, that if that which thou seekest thou findest not within thee, thou wilt never find it without thee. For behold: I have been with thee from the beginning, and I am that which is attained at the end of desire.

Note that this form of the Charge lacks a context—it is meant to be read immediately before an initiation, as is true for Charges in Masonic ritual.

Initiation

Initiation is an integral part of every secret society and of every religion, if one defines *initiation* as what a person must do or experience in order to become a member of that religion. To become a Christian, one must be baptized; to become a Moslem, the adherent must submit to the will of God; and to become a Witch, one must be initiated (although Witches do recognize that they all have the right to do a self-initiation in order to become a member of the Wiccan religion).

Almost all Wiccan initiations are modeled on or are simply borrowed from the Gardnerian initiations. The earliest form of the Gardnerian initiation rituals, that in *Ye Bok of ye Art Magickal,* which is now owned by the Wiccan Church of Canada, is as follows (though some data from *High Magic's Aid* have been added). Gardner's spelling and punctuation have been left almost unchanged here.

Magus leaves circle by the doorway, goes to Postulant, and says, "Since there is no other brother here, I must be thy sponsor, as well as Priest. I am about to give you a warning. If you are still of the same mind, answer it with these words: 'Perfect Love and Perfect Trust.'"

Placing the point of the sword to the Postulant's breast, he says, "O thou who standeth on the threshold between the pleasant world of men and the domains of the Dread Lords of the Outer Spaces, hast thou the courage to make the Assay? For I tell thee verily, it were better to rush on my weapon and perish miserably than to make the attempt with fear in thy heart."

Postulant: "I have two Passwords: Perfect Love and Perfect Trust."

Magus drops the sword point, saying, "All who approach with perfect love and perfect trust are doubly welcome."

Going around behind her, he blindfolds her, then, putting his left arm around her waist and his right arm around her neck, he pulls her head back, says, "I give you the third password, a Kiss to pass through this dread Door," and pushes her forward with his body, through the doorway and into the circle. Once inside, he releases her saying, "This is the way all are first brought into the circle."

Magus closes the doorway by drawing the point of the sword across it three times, joining all three circles, saying "Agla, Azoth, Adonai," then drawing three pentacles to seal it.

Magus guides Postulant to south of altar, and whispers, "Now there is the Ordeal." Taking a short piece of cord from the altar, he ties it around her right ankle, saying, "Feet neither bound nor free." Taking a longer cord, he ties her hands together behind her back, then pulls them up, so that the arms form a triangle, and ties the cord around her neck, leaving the end dangling down in front as a Cable Tow.

With the Cable Tow in his left hand and the sword in his right hand, the Magus leads her sunwise around the circle to the east, where he salutes with the sword and proclaims, "Take heed, O Lords of the Watchtowers of the East, [name], properly prepared, will be made a Priestess and a Witch."

Magus leads her similarly to the south, west, and north, making the proclamation at each quarter.

Next, clasping Postulant around the waist with his left arm, and holding the sword erect in his right hand, he makes her circumambulate three times around the circle with a half-running, half-dancing step.

He halts her at the south of the altar, and strikes 11 knells on the bell. He then kneels at her feet, saying, "In other religions the Postulant kneels, as the Priests claim supreme power, but in the Art Magical, we are taught to be humble, so we kneel to welcome them and say:

"'Blessed be thy feet that have brought thee in these ways.' (He kisses her feet.)

"'Blessed be thy knees that shall kneel at the sacred altar.' (He kisses her knees.)

"'Blessed be thy womb, without which we would not be.' (He kisses her Organ of Generation.)

"'Blessed be thy breasts, formed in beauty and in strength.' (He kisses her breasts.)

"'Blessed be thy lips, which shall utter the sacred names.'" (He kisses her lips.)

Take measure thus: height, around forehead, across the heart, and across the genitals.

Magus says, "Be pleased to kneel," and helps her kneel before the altar. He ties the end of the Cable Tow to a ring in the altar, so that the Postulant is bent sharply forward, with her head almost touching the floor. He also ties her feet together with the short cord.

Magus strikes three knells on the bell and says, "Art ready to swear that thou wilt always be true to the Art?"

Witch: "I am."

Magus strikes seven knells on the bell and says, "Before ye are sworn, art willing to pass the ordeal and be purified?"

Witch: "I am."

Magus strikes 11 knells on the bell, takes the scourge from the altar, and gives a series of 3, 7, 9, and 21 strokes with the scourge across the Postulant's buttocks.

Magus says, "Ye have bravely passed the test. Art always ready to help, protect, and defend thy Brothers and Sisters of the Art?"

Witch: "I am."

Magus: "Art armed?"

Witch: "With a knife in my hair."

Magus: "Then on that knife wilt thou swear absolute secrecy?"

Witch: "I will."

Magus: "Then say after me. 'I, [name], in the presence of the Mighty Ones, do of my own will and accord, most solemnly swear that I will ever keep secret and never reveal the secrets of the Art, except it be to a proper person, properly prepared, within a circle such as I am now in. All this I swear by my hopes of a future life, mindful that my measure has been taken, and may my weapons turn against me if I break this my solemn oath.'"

Magus now unbinds her feet, unties the Cable Tow from the altar, removes the blindfold, and helps her up to her feet.

Magus says, "I hereby sign thee with the triple sign."

"I consecrate thee with oil." (He anoints her with oil on the womb, the right breast, the left breast, and the womb again.)

"I consecrate thee with wine." (He anoints her with wine in the same pattern.)

"I consecrate thee with my lips" (he kisses her in the same pattern), "Priestess and Witch."

Magus now unbinds her hands and removes the last cord, saying, "Now I Present to thee the Working Tools of a Witch."

"First the Magic Sword. With this, as with the Athame, thou canst form all Magic Circles, dominate, subdue, and punish all rebellious Spirits and Demons, and even persuade the Angels and Geniuses. With this in your hand you are the ruler of the Circle."

[Here "kiss" means that the initiate kisses the tool and the Magus then kisses the Witch being initiated.] "Next I present the Athame. This is the true Witch's weapon and has all the powers of the Magic Sword [kiss]."

"Next I present the White-Handled Knife. Its use is to form all instruments used in the Art. It can only be properly used within a Magic Circle [kiss]."

"Next I present the Wand. Its use is to call up and control certain Angels and geniuses, to whom it would not be mete to use the Magic Sword [kiss]."

"Next I present the pentacles. These are for the purpose of calling up appropriate Spirits [kiss]."

"Next I present the Censer of Incense. This is used to encourage and welcome Good Spirits and to banish Evil Spirits [kiss]."

"Next I present the scourge. This is a sign of power and domination. It is also to cause suffering and purification, for it is written, to learn you must suffer and be purified. Art willing to suffer to learn?"

Witch: "I am." [kiss]

Magus: "Next, and lastly I present the Cords. They are of use to bind the sigils in the Art, the material basis, and to enforce thy will. Also they are necessary in the oath. I Salute thee in the name of Aradia and Cernunnos, Newly made Priestess and Witch."

Magus strikes seven knells on the bell and kisses Witch again, then circumambulates with her, proclaiming to the four quarters, "Hear, ye Mighty Ones, [name] hath been consecrated Priestess and Witch of the Gods."

Note, if ceremony ends here, close circle with "I thank ye for attending, and I dismiss ye to your pleasant abodes. Hail and farewell." If not, go to next Degree.

Magus binds Witch as before, but does not blindfold her, and circumambulates with her, proclaims to the four quarters, "Hear, ye Mighty Ones, [name], a duly consecrated Priestess and Witch, is now properly prepared to be made a High Priestess and Witch Queen."

Magus now leads her thrice around the circle with the half-running, half-dancing step, halts south of the altar, has the Witch kneel, and ties her down to the altar as before.

Magus: "To attain this sublime Degree, it is necessary to suffer and be purified. Art ready to suffer to Learn?"

Priestess Witch: "I am."

Magus: "I prepare thee to take the great oath."

He strikes 3 knells on the bell, and again gives the series of 3, 7, 9, and 21 strokes with the scourge as before.

Magus: "I now give thee a new name: [name]. [kiss]

Magus: "Repeat thy new name after me, [saying] 'I, [name], swear upon my mother's womb and by mine Honor among men and among my brothers and sisters of the Art, that I will never reveal to any at all any of the secrets of the Art, except it be to a worthy person, properly prepared, in the center of a Magic Circle, such as I am now in. This I swear by my hopes of Salvation, my past lives, and my hopes of future ones to come, and I devote myself to utter destruction if I break this my solemn oath.'"

Magus kneels, placing left hand under her knees and right hand on her head, thus forming magic link.

Magus: "I hereby will all my power into you." Wills.

Magus now unties her feet, unties the Cable Tow from the altar, and helps the Witch to her feet.

Magus: "I hereby sign and consecrate you with the great Magic Sign. Remember how it is formed and you will always recognize it.

"I consecrate thee with oil. (He anoints her with oil on her womb, right breast, left hip, right hip, left breast, and womb again, thus tracing a point-down pentacle.)

"I consecrate thee with wine. (He anoints her with wine in the same pattern.)

"I consecrate thee with my lips" (he kisses her in the same pattern), "High Priestess and Witch Queen."

Magus now unbinds Witch's hands and removes the cord, saying, "Newly made High Priestess and Witch Queen" [kiss] "you will now use the working tools in turn. First, the Magic Sword; with it you will scribe the Magic Circle. [kiss]

"Secondly, the Athame. (Form Circle) [kiss]

"Thirdly, the White Handled Knife. (use) [kiss]

"Fourthly, the Wand. (Wave to four Quarters) [kiss]

"Fifthly, the Pentacle. (Show to four Quarters) [kiss]

"Sixthly, the Censer of Incense. (Circle, cense) [kiss]

"Seventhly, the cords; bind me as I bound you."

Witch binds Magus and ties him to Altar.

Magus: "Learn, in Witchcraft, thou must ever return triple. As I scourged thee, so thou must scourge me, but triple. So where you received 3, return 9; where you received 7, return 21; where you received 9, return 27; where you received 21, return 63."

Witch scourges Magus as instructed, 120 strokes total.

Magus: "Thou hast obeyed the Law. But mark well, when thou receivest good, so equally art bound to return good threefold."

Witch now unbinds Magus and helps him to his feet.

Magus, taking the new Initiate by the hand and holding the Athame in the other, passes once round the Circle, proclaiming at the Four Quarters, "Hear, Ye Mighty Ones, [name] hath been duly consecrated High Priestess and Witch Queen."

Note, if ceremony ends here, close circle with "Hail and farewell." If not go to next Degree.

Magus: "Ere we proceed with this sublime degree, I must beg purification at thy hands."

High Priestess binds Magus and ties him down to the altar. She circumambulates three times, and scourges Magus with 3, 7, 9, and 21 strokes. She then unbinds him and helps him to his feet.

Magus now binds the High Priestess and ties her down to the altar. He circumambulates, proclaiming to the four quarters, "Hear, ye mighty Ones, the twice consecrated and Holy [name], High Priestess and Witch Queen, is properly prepared and will now proceed to erect the Sacred Altar."

Magus scourges High Priestess with 3, 7, 9, and 21 strokes.

Cakes and wine may now be taken.

Magus: "Now I must reveal to you a great Mystery." [kiss]

Note: If High Priestess has performed this rite before, omit these words.

High Priestess assumes Osiris position.

Magus: "Assist me to erect the Ancient Altar, at which in days past all worshipped, the Great Altar of all things. For in the old times a woman was the Altar. Thus was the altar made and so placed, and the sacred place was the point within the center of the circle, as we of old times have been taught, that the point within the center is the origin of all things. Therefore should we adore it. [kiss]

"Therefore, whom we adore, we also invoke, by the power of the lifted lance." Invokes.

"O circle of stars [kiss], whereof our Father is but the younger brother [kiss],

"Marvel beyond imagination, soul of infinite space, before whom time is ashamed, the mind bewildered, and understanding dark, not unto thee may we attain unless thine image be of love [kiss].

"Therefore, by seed and root, and stem and bud and leaf and flower and fruit do we invoke thee, O, Queen of space, O dew of light, O continuous one of the Heavens [kiss].

"Let it be ever thus, that men speak not of Thee as one, but as none, and let them not speak of thee at all, since thou art continuous, for thou art the point within the circle [kiss], which we adore [kiss], the fount of life without which we would not be [kiss].

"And in this way truly are erected the Holy Twin Pillars Boaz and Jachin [kisses breasts]. In beauty and strength were they erected, to the wonder and glory of all men."

(Eightfold Kiss: three points, Lips, two Breasts and back to lips; five points)

"O Secrets of secrets that art hidden in the being of all lives. Not thee do we adore, for that which adoreth is also thou. Thou art that and That am I [kiss].

"I am the flame that burns in every man, and in the core of every star [kiss].

"I am Life and the giver of Life, yet therefore is the knowledge of me the Knowledge of Death [kiss].

"I am alone, the Lord within ourselves whose name is Mystery of Mysteries [kiss].

"Make open the path of intelligence between us. For these truly are the five points of fellowship [on the right appears an illuminated diagram of the point-up triangle above the pentacle, the symbol for the third Degree], feet to feet, knee to knee, groin to groin, breast to breast, arms around back, lips to lips, by the Great and Holy Names Abracadabra, Aradia, and Cernunnos."

Magus and High Priestess: "Encourage our hearts, Let thy Light crystallize itself in our blood, fulfilling us of Resurrection, for there is no part of us that is not of the Gods." (Exchange Names.)

We may note that in this early text, all of this is conceived of as a long, single ritual, not three separate rituals. An analysis of what the significance is of all these words and actions would be far too long to be included here.

Craft Laws

When Doreen Valiente hived off a new coven from Gerald Gardner's London Coven in February 1957, the hiving off began as a peaceful process, and the two covens continued to cooperate with one another and to meet jointly on occasion. However, because of Gardner's publicity-seeking tendencies, tensions rose between the two groups. As a consequence, Ned, Valiente's High Priest, drew up a set of proposals entitled "Proposed Rules for the Craft," hoping that Gardner would agree to abide by them. Valiente typed them up and sent them to Gardner in about June 1957. The text of these rules, a copy of which is among the papers in Toronto now owned by the Wiccan Church of Canada, reads as follows.

1. No member of the Craft will initiate any person unless that person has been interviewed by at least two Elders and accepted as suitable.
2. No affairs of the Craft will be discussed by members in the presence of uninitiated persons or in places where conversation is likely to be overheard.
3. No copies of any papers relating to the Craft will be made or retained without the Elders' permission. Such papers as are permissible will be kept in a secure place.
4. As it is essential for the successful working of ritual by a group that there should be unity of purpose and an harmonious psychic atmosphere, members who create dissension and discord within the Craft will be asked to resign. Should they fail or refuse to do so they will be informed in writing by the Elders that they have been expelled.
5. No member of the Craft will give any information or interview about the Craft to any journalist or writer or cause any such information to be published in any way, without the approval of the Elders, nor will any of the Elders do so without the approval of the rest of the Elders.
6. If any member of the Craft feels that he or she has reason to complain of the conduct of any other member in matters affecting the Craft, or of any misdemeanour towards any member whilst on Craft premises, he or she will bring the said complaint to the notice of the Elders as soon as possible. The Elders, after considering all available evidence, will, if they find the complaint justified, take appropriate action.
7. No member will be present at any meeting where the working is that of a higher Grade than he or she has attained, except by invitation of the Elders. These invitations will only be extended on very rare occasions where special circumstances exist.
8. No member will disclose the name and address or telephone number of any other member to any person whatsoever, without the said other member's previous permission.
9. Members will meet upon the traditional occasions, or as near to them as possible, and such meetings will be arranged by the Elders, or such Officers as the Elders authorise to do so. If the Elders be not present at such meetings, they will receive a report of them. Members may arrange other meetings for their private working if they so desire, but if more than two members be present at such a meeting the Elders will receive a report of it. This report will take the form of a short letter to the Elders giving place and date of the meeting, names of members attending, and details of ceremonies carried out. Where convenient, verbal reports will be accepted.
10. Members will endeavour to acquaint themselves with the traditions of the Craft and will not introduce innovations into the workings without the Elders' approval. Nor will the Elders give approval to any important innovation without first asking the approval of the rest of the Craft.
11. In the event of any member resigning from the Craft, he or she will honourably observe the Oath of Secrecy taken at initiation and will also return to the Elders any written matter relating to the Craft which may be in his or her possession.

12. All members will receive a copy of these rules and all new members will be given a copy of these rules upon initiation. New members, prior to initiation, will read these rules and declare upon their honour that they will abide by them in letter and in spirit. This declaration will be made to the Elders in writing and signed.

13. It will be understood by all members that these rules are equally binding upon all Grades of the Craft, including the Elders, and that serious and/or persistent breach of these rules will be grounds for expulsion.

Notice that here the term *Craft* must actually mean something like "coven" (in rules 4, 6, 10, and, by implication, 9); that is, it is the affairs of a group not much larger than a single coven that are dealt with here, not the affairs of a large movement. In 1957, there was, for the first time, not a single small group, which could run by unwritten rules, but an organization—the "Craft"—with at least two covens, which therefore needed written rules about which all could agree. Obviously, there were not so many members in the group: Consultations required by rules 5 and 10 would have been clumsy to carry out.

Probably some (if not all) of the things forbidden by these new rules had happened; otherwise why create a rule against them? The intended audience of these rules was most likely Gardner himself. In these circumstances, the Elders felt they had to insist on their authority to maintain order in the organization.

Although Gardner did not like the Proposed Rules as such, the idea of having some sort of rules in the Book of Shadows apparently appealed to him, and he began to work on the project. Certainly he would have felt that the new document had to be in the sort of formal, archaic-sounding language in which most of the other documents had been written. He would also have wanted the Proposed Rules to look and sound traditional. Furthermore, he would have wanted them to have some theological content—to be concerned with how a coven is to work magic—not to be just a set of organizational rules. Gardner combed through his earlier writings, both the published books and various Book of Shadows documents, gathered passages that had some connection with the concept of a traditional collection of laws that defined and governed the Craft, and rewrote them.

Valiente wrote that, after Gardner received the Proposed Rules, he delayed responding to them. Then Gardner astonished Ned and Valiente: From Gardner's museum on the Isle of Man he sent them a long document, with a message saying that there was no need for the Proposed Rules, because these "Laws of the Craft" already existed. His document, Valiente said, "was couched in mock-archaic language and ornamented with awesome threats of 'So be it ardane' [meaning 'ordained'] and invocations of 'the Curse of the Goddess' upon anyone who dared to transgress them."

Valiente further said that, apparently, they were supposed to be in awe of his document. Their actual reaction was extremely skeptical. None of them had ever set eyes on these alleged "Laws" before, though they noticed that the laws incorporated the "Warning" that appeared at the beginning of the Book of Shadows, and which had always been a complete document in its own right. Ned and Valiente asked why, if these laws were so ancient and authoritative, Gardner had never mentioned them before. The issue became one of waning confidence in Gardner, and the more they examined the alleged "Laws," the less confidence they felt. Valiente specifically rejected the passages (about "a man loveth a woman by mastering her" and passages about retiring in favor of a younger woman) that she believed were sexist. She believed that Ned wrote back to Gardner and told him that the alleged "Laws" were regarded as "an *ad hoc* invention of your own." Valiente did not realize that there was any direct connection between the "Proposed Rules" and the "Craft Laws." It was not until about 1991 that she grasped the fact that Gardner had followed her (and Ned's) proposal and had taken the Craft Laws and rewritten it into archaic language.

A technical analysis of the Craft Laws is beyond the scope of this book. Nevertheless, these Laws are a fundamental theological document of the Craft movement, almost as important as the "Charge of the Goddess," and are continually being invoked. It is therefore important to present them here as Gardner wrote them (his spelling and punctuation have been left almost unchanged here).

[A] The Law was made and Aredan of old. The law was made for the Wicca, to advise and help in their troubles. The Wicca should give due worship to the Gods and obey their will, which they Aredan, for it was made for the good of the Wicca, As the Wicca's worship is good for the Gods, For the Gods love the Wicca. As a man loveth a woman, by mastering her, so the Wicca should love the Gods, by being mastered by them.

And it is necessary that the Circle, which is the Temple of the Gods, should be truly cast and purified, that it may be a fit place for the Gods to enter. And the Wicca should be properly prepared and purified, to enter into the presence of the Gods.

With love and worship in their hearts they shall raise power from their bodies to give power to the Gods, as has been toughed us of old, For in this way only may man have communion with the Gods, for the Gods cannot help man without the help of men.

[B] And the High Priestess shall rule her Coven as representative of the Goddess, and the High Priest shall support her as the representative of the God, And the High Priestess shall choose whom she will, if he have sufficient rank, to be her High Priest.

For the God himself, kissed her feet in the fivefold salute, laying his power at the feet of the Goddess, because of her youth and beauty, her sweetness and kindness, her wisdom and Justice, her humility and generosity. So he resigned his lordship to her.

But the Priestess should ever mind that all power comes from him. It is only lent when it is used wisely and justly. And the greatest virtue of a High Priestess is that she recognizes that youth is necessary to the representative of the Goddess, so that she will retire gracefully in favour of a younger woman, Should the Coven so decide in Council, For the true High Priestess realizes that gracefully surrendering pride of place is one of the greatest of virtues, and that thereby she will return to that pride of place in another life, with greater power and beauty.

[C] In the days when Witchdom extended far, we were free and worshipped in Alther Greatest Temples, but in these unhappy times we must hold our sacred mysteries in secret. So it be Aredan, that none but the Wicca may see our mysteries, for our enemies are many, And torture looseth the tongues of many. It be aredan that each Coven shall not know where the next Coven bide, or who its members are, save the Priest and Priestess, That there shall be no communication between them, save by the Messenger of the Gods, or the Summoner. Only if it be safe, may the Covens meet, in some safe place, for the great festivals.

And while there, none shall say whence they come, or give their true names, to the end that, if any are tortured, in their agony, they cannot tell if they know not. So it be Aredan that no one may tell any not of the Craft who be of the Wicca, nor give any names, or where they bide, or in any way tell anything which can betray any to our foes, nor may they tell where the Covenstead be, or where is the Covendom, or where be the meetings or that there have been meetings.

And if any break these laws, even under torture, The Curse of the Goddess shall be upon them, so they never reborn on earth, And may they remain where they belong, in the Hell of the Christians.

[D] Let each High Priestess govern her Coven with Justice and love, with the help of the advice of the elders, always heeding the advice of the Messenger of the Gods, if he cometh. She will heed all complaints of brothers, and strive to settle all differences among them, but it must be recognized that there be people who will ever strive to force others to do as they will. They are not necessarily evil, and they often do have good ideas, and such ideas should be talked over in council. And if they will not agree with their brothers, or if they say, "I will not work under this High Priestess," it hath always been the old law to be convenient for the brethren, and to void disputes, any of the Third may claim to found a new Coven because they live over a league from the Covenstead, or are about to do so. Anyone living within the Covendom wishing to form a new Coven, to avoid strife, shall tell the Elders of his intention and on the instant void his dwelling and remove to the new Covendom.

Members of the old Coven may join the New one when it be formed, but if they do, must utterly void the old Coven. The Elders of the New and the Old Covens should meet in peace and brotherly love, to decide the new boundaries. Those of the Craft who dwell outside both Covendoms may join either indifferent, but not both, though all may, if the Elders agree, meet for the Great Festivals, if it be truly in peace and brotherly love. But splitting the coven oft means strife, so for this reason these laws were made of old, And may the curse of the Goddess be on any who disregard them. So be it aredan.

[E] If you would Keep a book let it be in your own hand of write. Let brothers and sisters copy what they will, but never let the book out of your hands, and never keep the writings of another, for if it be found in their hand of write, they well may be taken and Engined. Each should guard his own writings and destroy it whenever danger threatens. Learn as much as you may by heart, and when danger is past, rewrite your book an it be safe. For this reason, if any die, destroy their book if they have not been able to, for an it be found, "'tis clear proof against them," And our oppressors well know, "Ye may not be a witch alone." So all their kin and friends be in danger of torture. So ever destroy anything not necessary.

If your book be found on you. 'tis clear proof against you alone. You may be engined. Keep all thoughts of the Craft from your mind. Say you had bad dreams; a devil caused you to write it without your knowledge. Think to yourself, "I know nothing. I remember nothing. I have forgotten everything." Drive this into your mind. If the torture be too great to bear, say, "I will confess. I cannot bear this torture. What do you want me to say? Tell me and I will say it." If they try to make you speak of the brotherhood, Do NOT, but if they try to make you speak of impossibilities, such as flying through the air, consorting with the Christian Devil, or sacrificing children, or eating men's flesh, to obtain relief from torture, say, "I had an evil dream. I was not myself. I was crazed."

Not all Magistrates are bad. If there be an excuse they may show mercy. If you have confessed aught, deny it afterwards; say you babbled under torture, you knew not what you did or said. If you are condemned, fear not. The Brotherhood is powerful. They may help you to escape, if you stand steadfast, but if you betray aught, there is no hope for you, in this life, or in that which is to come. Be sure, if steadfast you go to the pyre, Dwale will reach you. You will feel naught. You go but to Death and what lies beyond, the ecstasy of the Goddess.

[F] 'Tis probable that before you are engined, Dwale will reach you. Always remember that Christians fear much that any die under torture. At the first sign of swoon, they cause it to be stopped, and blame the tormentors. For that reason, the tormentors themselves are apt to feign to torment, but do not, so it is best not to die at first. If Dwale reaches you, 'tis a sign that you have a friend somewhere. You may be helped to escape, so despair not. If the worst comes, and you go to the pyre, wait till the flames and smoke spring up, bend your head over, and breath in with long breaths. You choke and die swiftly, and wake in the arms of the Goddess.

[G] To void discovery, let the working tools be as ordinary things that any may have in their houses. Let the Pentacles be of wax, so they may be broken at once. Have no sword unless your rank allows you one. Have no names or signs on anything. Write the names and signs on them in ink before consecrating them and wash it off immediately after. Do not Bigrave them, lest they cause discovery. Let the colour of the hilts tell which is which.

[H] Ever remember, ye are the Hidden Children of the Gods. So never do anything to disgrace them. Never boast, Never threaten, Never say you would wish ill to anyone. If you or any not in the Circle speak of the Craft, say, "Speak not to me of such. It frightens me. 'Tis evil luck to speak of it."

For this reason: the Christians have spies everywhere. These speak as if they were well affected, as if they would come to Meetings, saying, "My mother used to go to worship the Old Ones. I would that I could go myself." To these ever deny all knowledge.

But to others ever say, "'Tis foolish men talk of witches flying through the air; to do so they must be light as thistledown," and "Men say that witches all be blearedeyed old crones, so what pleasure can there be in witch meetings such as folk talk on?" Say, "Many wise men now say there be no such creatures." Ever make it a jest, and in some future time, perhaps the persecution will die, and we may worship safely again. Let us all pray for that happy day.

[I] May the blessings of the Goddess and the God be on all who keep these laws which are Aredan.

[J] If the Craft hath any Appanage, let all brothers guard it, and help to keep it clear and good for the Craft, and let all justly guard all monies of the Craft.

But if some brothers truly wrought it, 'tis right that they have their pay, an it be just, an this be not taking money for the use of the Art, but for good and honest work. And even the Christians say, "A labourer is worthy of his hire." But if any brothers work willingly for the good of the craft without pay, 'tis but to their greater honour. So it be Aredan.

[K] If there be any disputes or quarrels among the brethren, the High Priestess shall straight convene the Elders and enquire into the matter, and they shall hear both sides, first alone, then together, and they shall decide justly, not favouring the one side or the other, ever recognizing that there be people who can never agree to work under others, but at the same time there be some people who cannot rule justly. To those who ever must be chief, there is one answer, "Void the Coven and seek another, or make a Coven of your own, taking with you those who will to go." To those who cannot rule justly, the answer be, "Those who cannot bear your rule will leave you," for none may come to meetings with those with whom they are at variance; so, an either cannot agree, get hence, for the Craft must ever survive. So it be Aredan.

[L] In the olden days when we had power, we could use our Arts against any who ill-treated any of the Brotherhood, but in these evil times, we may not do so, for our enemies have devised a burning pit of everlasting fire, into which they say their God casteth all the people who worship him, except it be the very few who are released by their priests' spells and Masses, and this be chiefly by giving money and rich gifts to receive his favour, for their Alther Greatest God [Greatest God of all] is ever in need of Money. But as our Gods need our aid to make fertility for men and crops, So the God of the Christians is ever in need of man's help to search out and destroy us.

Their priests tell them that any who get our help or our cures are damned to the Hell forever, so men be mad for the terror of it. But they make men believe that they may scape this hell if they give victims to the tormentors. So for this reason all be forever spying, thinking, "An I can but catch one of the Wicca I will scape this fiery pit." But we have our hidels, and men searching long and not finding say, "there be none, or if they be, they be in a far country."

But when one of our oppressors die, or even be sick, ever is the cry, "This be Witches Malice," and the hunt is up again. And though they slay ten of their people to one of ours, still they care not; they have many thousands, while we are few indeed. So it is Aredan that none shall use the Art in any way to do ill to any, howevermuch they have injured us. And for long we have obeyed this law, "Harm none" and nowtimes many believe we exist not. So it be Aredan that this law shall still continue to help us in our plight. No one, however great an injury or injustice they receive, may use the Art in any to do ill or harm any. But they may, after great consultations with all, use the Art to prevent or restrain Christians from harming us and others, but only to let or constrain them and never to punish, to this end. Men say, "Such an one is a mighty searcher out and persecutor of Old Women whom he deemeth to be Witches, and none hath done him Skith [harm], so this be proof they cannot, or more truly, that there be none," For all know full well that so many folk have died because someone had a grudge against them, or were persecuted because they had money or goods to seize, or because they had none to bribe the searchers. And many have died because they were scolding old women, so much so that men now say that only old women are witches, and this be to our advantage, and turns suspicion away from us.

In England 'tis now many a year since a witch hath died the death, but any misuse of the power might raise the Persecution again; so never break this law, however much you are tempted, and never consent to its being broken. If you know it is being broken in the least, you must work strongly against it, and any High Priestess or High Priest who consents to it must be immediately deposed, for 'tis the blood of the Brethren they endanger. Do good, an it be safe, and only if it be safe, for any talk may endanger us.

[M] And strictly keep to the Old Law, never accept money for the use of the art. It is Christian priests and sorcerers who accept money for the use of their Arts, and they sell Dwale and evil love spells and pardons to let men scape from their sins. Be not as these. *Be not as these.* If you accept not money, you will be free of temptation to use the Art for evil causes.

[N] You may use the Art for your own advantage, or for the advantage of the Craft, only if you be sure you harm none. But ever let the Coven debate the matter at length. Only if all are satisfied that none may be harmed may the Art be used. If it is not possible to achieve your ends one way without harming any, perchance the aim may be achieved by acting in a different way, so as to harm none. May the Curse of the Goddess be on any who breach this law. So it be aredan.

[O] 'Tis adjudged lawful an anyone need a house or land, an none will sell, to incline the owner's mind to be willing to sell, provided it harmeth him not in any way, and that the full worth is paid, without haggling. Never bargain or cheapen anything which you buy by the Art. So it be Aredan.

[P] It is the Old Law and the most important of all Laws that no one may do or say anything which will endanger any of the Craft, or bring them in contact with the law of the land, or the Law of the Church or any of our persecutors. In any disputes between the brethren, no one may invoke any laws but those of the Craft, or any Tribunal but that of the Priestess and the Priest and the Elders. And may the Curse of the Goddess be on any who so do. So it be Aredan.

[Q] It is not forbidden to say as Christians do, "There be Witchcraft in the Land," because our oppressors of old made it Heresy not to believe in Witchcraft, and so a crime to deny it, which thereby put you under suspicion. But ever say "I know not of it here, perchance they may be, but afar off. I know not where." But ever speak so you cause others to doubt they be as they are. Always speak of them as old crones, consorting with the Devil and riding through the air. But ever say, "But how may men ride through the air an they be not as light as thistledown?" But the curse of the Goddess be on any who cast any suspicion on any of the Brotherhood, or speaks of any real meeting place, or where any bide. So it be Aredan.

[R] Let the Craft keep books with the names of all Herbs which are good for man, and all cures, that all may learn. But keep another book with all the Banes [poisons] and Apies and let only the elders and trustworthy people have this knowledge. So it be Aredan.

[S] And may the Blessings of the Gods be on all who keep these Laws and the Curses of both God and Goddess be on all who break them So it be Aredan.

[T] Remember the Art is the secret of the Gods and may only be used in earnest and never for show or vainglory. Magicians and Christians may taunt us, saying, "You have no power. Do magic before our eyes. Then only will we believe," seeking to cause us to betray our Art before them. Heed them not, for the Art is holy, and may only be used in need. And the curse of the Gods be on any who break this law.

[U] It ever be the way with women, and with men also, that they ever seek new love, nor should we reprove them for this, but it may be found to disadvantage the Craft, as so many a time it has happened that a High Priest or High Priestess, impelled by love, hath departed with their love; that is, they have left the coven. Now, if a High Priestess wishes to resign, she may do so in full Coven, and this resignation is valid. But if they should run off without resigning, who may know if they may not return within a few months? So the law is, if a High Priestess leaves her coven, but returns within the space of a year and a day, then she shall be taken back, and all shall be as before. Meanwhile, if she has a deputy, that deputy shall act as High Priestess for as long as the High Priestess is away. If she returns not at the end of a year and a day, then shall the coven elect a new High Priestess. Unless there be a good reason to the contrary. The person who has done the work should reap the benefit of the reward, Maiden and deputy of the High Priestess.

[Above versions of the Craft Laws courtesy Aidan A. Kelly]

Index